REASON AND PERSUASION
THREE DIALOGUES BY PLATO
4TH EDITION

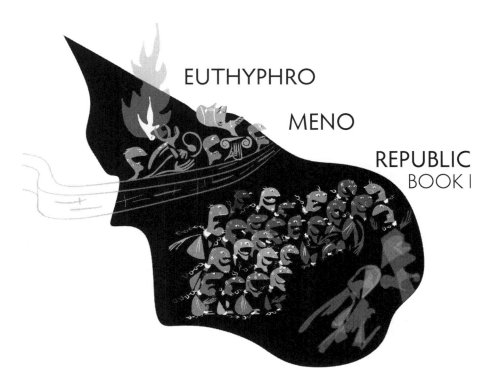

EUTHYPHRO

MENO

REPUBLIC
BOOK I

COMMENTARY & ILLUSTRATIONS BY JOHN HOLBO
TRANSLATIONS BY BELLE WARING

4th Edition

Reason and Persuasion
Three Dialogues By Plato: Euthyphro, Meno, Republic Book I

Translations copyright © 2015 by Belle Waring. Commentary and illustrations copyright © 2015 by John Holbo. All rights reserved.

This print edition is self-published by John Holbo and Belle Waring, using Amazon CreateSpace.

3rd edition © 2010, published by Prentice Hall (Pearson); the 1st and 2nd editions were made available to students on an informal basis from 2004-2010.

Non-cartoon illustrations are from H. Schliemann, **Mycenae, A Narrative of Researches and Discoveries at Mycenae and Tiryns** (Scribner, 1878).

All quotations in the text from copyrighted material are fair use and remain the property of their respective owners.

Book designed by John Holbo.

ISBN-13: 978-1522907527

ISBN-10: 1522907521

The text of this print edition is set in Hypatia Sans Pro.

About the Book

This book contains three Plato dialogues: **Euthyphro, Meno, Republic**, Book 1. The translations are by Belle Waring.

If you are new to Plato you may be puzzled by the number/letter combinations you see in the dialogue sidebar margins — 6b, 71c, so forth. These are so-called Stephanus page numbers. In 1578, Henricus Stephanus published a complete Plato. It became the basis for a standardized reference system. You can cite passages, across editions and translations, by Stephanus page, as in the commentary chapters in this book, which were written by me, John Holbo.

Speaking of commentary: there are more books about Plato than you could read in a lifetime. What is worse, quite a few are good. For an author of commentary this poses a challenge. One needs to say something new, or something old in a new way. This book is intended for beginners but I do hope more advanced students will get something out of it. The writing straddles this divide in ways that may (we apologize for the inconvenience) get uncomfortable. The chapters start short and sweet but get longer and longer. The goal is always to find odd angles that are fresh angles (for advanced students) yet basic angles (for beginners.) It's tough being a writer, not so easy to be a reader. All the commentary chapters precede the dialogues they discuss. These chapters have been written to be basically understandable by a thoughtful person who hasn't yet read the dialogue. But maybe you should read the dialogue first?

What do I know about what you know, hence need to know?

Figure out what works for you. I designed the book carefully. Feel free to ignore all that.

The cartooning? That started as a theatrical adaptation to large-class teaching and ended as a hobby or minor compulsion. I hope the cartoons are true to Plato's better nature as comic, cosmic puppeteer. I hope they are iconic without being dogmatic. By which I mean: textbooks these days! Full of pull boxes with bullet points! Socrates would have hated it. He didn't want you to extract some simple thing to memorize! I hope my cartoons point you in the direction of the point without looking like short-cuts or the thing itself.

If this Plato journey is worth taking, it's worth taking the long way around.

I suppose the cartoons do say a lot about what Plato means to me. Nietzsche writes:

> Nothing I know has given me better dreams of Plato's secretive and Sphinx-like nature than one happily preserved small fact: under the pillow of his deathbed they found no "Bible", nothing Egyptian, Pythagorean, or Platonic — but instead, Aristophanes. How could even a Plato have endured life — a Greek life he said 'no' to — without an Aristophanes![1]

I think I would find Plato pretty unendurable if he didn't seem to me Aristophanic in his way. (Aristophanes was a comic playwright. You'll hear about him. But Nietzsche's 'small fact', just so you know, is just a rumor. Who knows what was under Plato's head while he slept? Hard enough to figure what was in it while he was awake.)

This is the 4th edition of the book. It is substantially revised. We secured the rights back from the publisher of the 3rd edition after it went out of print, intending to make it newly available in a variety of formats and versions. Check online; see what we've done with it.

www.reasonandpersuasion.com

I re-dedicate this new edition to my teachers: Hans Sluga, who let me make jokes in my dissertation; Bert Dreyfus, who taught me Aeschylus' **Oresteia**.

John Holbo (December, 2015)

About the Authors

John Holbo is Associate Professor of Philosophy at the National University of Singapore.

Belle Waring received an MA in Classics from the University of California at Berkeley.

They live in Singapore with their two daughters.

---

1   Friedrich Nietzsche, **Jenseits von Gut und Böse** (1886), §28. trans. John Holbo

Contents

Chapter 1   How To Read This Book, Part I:
Masks

1

THE MAIN READINGS in this book are three philosophical dialogues. What's that? Maybe a cross between a play and a problem set? Doesn't help much. Let's try to do better.

The author of these texts is Plato, an ancient Greek philosopher (429-347 BCE). All of Western philosophy is footnotes to Plato. So they say.

And yet: these texts do not tell us what Plato thinks — not obviously. Rather, they narrate encounters between another philosopher, Socrates, and various further figures, who tend to lend their names to the dialogues.

In **Euthyphro**, Socrates debates holiness with a priest named Euthyphro.

In **Meno**, he argues with Meno about the nature of virtue.

Republic is not about anyone named 'Republic'. It's about justice. Socrates debates three different characters with different views about that.

Not only is Plato himself nowhere to be seen. The conclusions of these debates he stage-manages tend to be inconclusive. The problem set has no answer key. We don't get answers from Plato, Socrates or anyone. So it would seem.

So what's he playing at, this Plato?

2

The main character in the dialogues is Socrates. He was a real, historical figure. We know roughly when he was born (470's BCE) and exactly when he died (399) because that was the year he was convicted, sentenced to death and executed. For what? For doing the sorts of things he is described as doing in these dialogues.

Socrates was Plato's teacher. Unlike Plato, whose complete works make a thick book, Socrates never wrote a word. He **talked**. To his fellow Athenians, to anyone he met. Unlike Plato, who founded a famous Academy, Socrates never taught, in any formal sense. Still, he had followers — admirers, imitators, spectators. Plato was one of these.

Plausibly, then, the purpose of these philosophical dialogues is to preserve, for posterity, a portrait of a man Plato admired. Since what was so distinctive about Socrates was, apparently, the way he asked questions and interacted with others, the portrait is a dramatic one, as opposed to being a book of wise sayings or a body of doctrine or theory. Not that these dialogues can be anything like transcriptions! Socrates' followers, including Plato, did not follow him around, taking verbatim notes. The dialogues cannot be attempts to reconstruct specific exchanges from memory, at least they can't **all** be. Plato could have been with Socrates around the time of his trial. So it is not impossible that he might have witnessed an encounter with a man named Euthyphro. But dramatic events in **Republic** are set much earlier, when Plato was just a child.

If **Republic** is fiction it seems reasonable to suspect **Euthyphro** is, too. Still, it could be that Plato is trying to write realistic fiction. Plato's Socrates is being made to ask the sorts of questions, say the sorts of things, that the real Socrates did. Plato fictionalizes unrecoverable detail in the service of overall historical, biographical, intellectual fidelity.

On this view Plato, the author, is a bit like one of those Russian dolls. We crack the Plato case to get to an authentic, Socratic core.

3

What's the alternative? Maybe we need to keep cracking. "All that is profound wears a mask." So says Friedrich Nietzsche (who had the moustache to prove it.)

Maybe what looks like Socrates is really Plato, wearing a Socrates mask. Plato puts ideas into the mouth of his martyred teacher. Perhaps the historical Socrates didn't say at least some of these kinds of things at all.

Why would Plato misrepresent his dead teacher's philosophy? For any number of reasons. Let's start with simple ones.

Socrates was executed. Plato might not want to risk that himself. Speaking through a mask affords deniability. Or perhaps using Socrates as a mouthpiece is an attempt to borrow authority, or is a sincere gesture of filial piety. Obviously it can be hard for students to know at what point, exactly, they come into their own.

Where does teacher stop and student begin?

Here is an interesting fact. Plato was not the only one writing 'dialogues with Socrates'. Several followers of Socrates did so in the generation following his death. Aristotle (Plato's most famous pupil) apparently thought Alexamenos of Teos was the first; sadly, that's all we know about Alexamenos. Mostly these early works are lost, except for scraps and half-forgotten author names: Aeschines, Antisthenes, Phaedo, Eucleides. But some of these writers were, apparently, prolific.

Plato had the foresight to start a school in which his writings were preserved and passed down. He towers over these others — no doubt in part due to the fact that he was a tremendous writer and thinker. But even if his reputation as a uniquely great thinker is deserved, the loss of these other writings gives us a skewed perspective on the Athenian intellectual scene. Plato was one of Socrates' younger followers. A little late to this literary party, Socratic dialogue writing, Plato's Socrates presumably had to distinguish himself somehow.

We do see distinctions. We have intact dialogues by only one other author, Xenophon. His Socrates is, in many ways, a different character. Xenophon's Socrates is practical, down-to-earth, less ironic and paradoxical, more conventional in his opinions and attitudes.

Suppose — just suppose! — all those other socratic dialogues hadn't been lost. Suppose scholars today simply refused to consult them, insisting Plato's powerful intelligence gives us reason to place our trust in him alone. Obviously this would be an unscholarly attitude. We aren't being irresponsible like that, since we don't have the option. But the fact that our approach would be grossly irresponsible, under ideal conditions, reminds us how far from ideal our condition is. Just because we are doing our very best doesn't mean we have a reasonable expectation our best will be very good. Hypothesizing Plato's Socrates as the real Socrates is a historical stretch. We **want** to know who Socrates really was. But it's hard.[1]

And another thing. As readers we tend to think of Plato as contemporary with these characters who inhabit his works. We are drawn into this milieu and may think of it as Plato's intellectual scene. He is bemused by Euthyphro, messes with Meno's head, thrashes Thrasymachus. But Thrasymachus was dead before Plato put pen to papyrus to write his first dialogue, never mind his mature masterpiece, **Republic**. Plato is re-fighting the last generation's intellectual fights, while he himself is surely fighting his own battles **by** re-litigating these past ones. The picture has holes in it, but the mind insists on seeing definite faces. Try to keep that in mind.

4

On the Russian doll model we assume Plato gives us more or less the real Socrates. On the mask view we are basically talking to Plato himself. For a variety of reasons — some common sense, some having to do with features of texts and independently known facts — neither of these extremes is quite believable.

[1]   For a longer discussion of some points made in this section, see Charles H. Kahn, **Plato and the Socratic Dialogue: The Philosophical Use of a Literary Form** (Cambridge University Press, 1998), Chapter 1.

The truth probably lies somewhere in between.

What do scholars think? They disagree and debate. (What did you expect?) An intermediate, fairly standard position is that it is possible to establish a rough chronology, an approximate order in which the dialogues must have been composed.

A path of intellectual development for Plato corresponds to this chronology — several, in fact. There is more consensus about chronology than interpretation. Many an interesting argument begins in the space between. But, broadly, no one will look at you as if you are crazy if you say this: there are early, middle and late dialogues. We think we can mostly tell which are which.

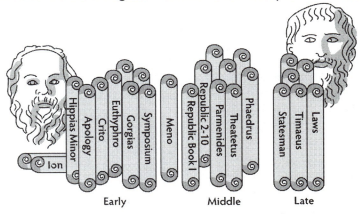

Early   Middle   Late

In early dialogues we may find something closer to an accurate portrait of the historical Socrates. Middle Plato is coming into his own as a thinker, so in middle dialogues we may meet a hybrid Socrates. Late Plato may have left his teacher behind. It fits with this view that, in one late dialogue, **Laws**, Socrates does not appear at all. In a few others Socrates is a minor character.

In saying this view is 'standard' I don't insist it is correct. Some scholars seriously doubt it. But everyone familiar with these debates will be familiar with this view. It provides the basis for many discussions.

There isn't any competing overall view of the whole body of Plato's writings that is comparably influential. The standard view is plausible and seems to explain a lot. It provides a coherent picture. But think about how, if you interpret a given dialogue on the assumption that it is early, you have to be extra careful not to double-count your interpretation as independent **evidence** that the dialogue really is early, or that the early-middle-late scheme is right. Coherence is not truth. Think of the standard view as a nice, negotiable starting-point.

Assuming these 'early', 'middle', and 'late' labels make at least some sense: our first dialogue, **Euthyphro**, is early. **Meno** is early-middle. The third, **Republic**, is middle. But Book 1 may have been written earlier. Call it, like **Meno**, early-middle.[2]

Have I answered my question: how to read this book?

Maybe I've just said who you'll meet, which isn't the same. I didn't even give you a straight answer about that! Fortunately, I'll get another crack at the case in Chapter 4. In the meantime, the next two chapters will pursue the crucial **who are we dealing with?** questions in greater depth.

Who was Socrates?

Who was Plato?

What did they say?

What did they mean by saying it?

What did they think?

2   The standard view is most associated with the writings of an influential philosopher and classical scholar, Gregory Vlastos. For an authoritative expression of doubt about the standard view, see the Introduction to John M. Cooper (ed.) **Plato: Complete Works** (Hackett, 1997).

Chapter 2   Socrates: The Gadfly of Athens

1

IN THIS CHAPTER I present a view of what the real, historical Socrates may have been like — a view the reader now knows to take with a grain of salt. I do so by means of a generous excerpt from Plato's **Apology**, an early dialogue. But first, let me introduce the excerpt itself. Socrates is thought to have practiced a so-called 'negative method'. Meaning: he asked, he didn't answer. What he asked were ethical questions. **How should I live?** Not broad, metaphysical questions about the nature of the universe. **Apology** gives us a description of this negative procedure and purports to provide, as well, a justification for such a practice.

Apology is not about anyone named 'Apology', nor does it mean **I'm sorry**. **Apologia** means **defense**. The dialogue purports to contain speeches Socrates delivered at the trial at which he was convicted and sentenced to death.

What was the charge? According to Socrates in **Apology**, "it runs somewhat as follows: Socrates is guilty of wrongdoing in that he occupies himself studying things in the sky and below the earth; he makes the weaker into the stronger argument, and these things he also teaches to others" (18b).

We hear about the case again in **Euthyphro**, where the charge is formulated in slightly different terms. Socrates explains that a young man, Meletus, is seeking to make his mark in politics by prosecuting him for "corrupting the youth." "It sounds like an outlandish business, my friend, when you first hear it. He says I fabricate gods. He indicts me, so he says, on behalf of the old gods, whom I don't believe in, since I'm busy making new ones" (3b).

Euthyphro suggests this accusation must be due to "the divine sign" Socrates says comes to him.

Divine sign?

Socrates says he has a **daimonion** — spirit voice he hears — that only ever says 'no' when he is about to do wrong. In **Apology** Socrates confirms this is, indeed, an item in Meletus' list of charges. But this is not the root of the bad feeling towards him. I'll let (Plato's) Socrates speak for himself. Here he is, pleading innocent as charged, addressing the citizen jurymen at his trial:

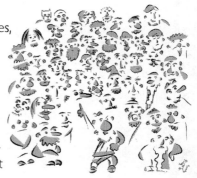

One of you may well respond: But Socrates, what's the matter with you? Where did all these false accusations against you come from? Obviously all this gossip and talk about you haven't materialized because you were doing nothing more noteworthy than other people — you must have been doing something quite different from most everyone else. So tell us what it was, if you don't want us to make something up ourselves.

This seems like a perfectly fair objection, so I will try to show you what it was that I did to earn this notoriety and disrepute. Listen then — and it may seem to some of you that I'm joking, but be assured that I'm going to tell you the complete truth.

I have gained this reputation, men of Athens, on account of nothing other than a sort of wisdom. What kind of wisdom? It is, perhaps, just human wisdom — for I probably really am wise in this limited respect. The men I was talking about just now may be wise with respect to some greater-than-human wisdom. I don't know how to explain it. I certainly don't understand it, and anyone who says I do is lying and willfully slandering me. And, men of Athens, don't shout and interrupt me, even if you think I'm saying extravagant things; for the words I'm about to speak are not my own, rather, I will refer you to a trustworthy authority. I will offer you the god of Delphi as a witness to my wisdom — such as it is — and its nature. (20c-e)

2

Who are these men Socrates says may have greater-than-human wisdom? They are the **sophists** — wise ones, wise guys — who charge stiff fees to educate aristocratic Athenian youths. One of these — Gorgias — we hear about from Meno, his student. Thrasymachus is another, in **Republic**, Book 1. Socrates says it is hard for him to separate his reputation from theirs. So they say, Socrates is a sophist, a student of all things in the sky and below the earth, who makes the worse argument the stronger. It isn't true, so he says, but 'they' are hard to argue with. He says the only accuser he can name, besides his prosecutors, is an "author of comedies." Aristophanes was the premier comic playwright of the age. He wrote **The Clouds** (423 BCE), in which Socrates appears as a character, floating above the action in a basket. (Head in the clouds — obvious metaphor.) Socrates is portrayed as master of a school, the Thinketeria. The action revolves around a pair of fools — father and son. Father makes son enroll in Socrates' school because he has heard they have "two arguments: right and wrong." The son, who has run up too many debts, is ordered to study **wrong**, the one that wins at court, so you don't have to pay your debts. The son dutifully goes off to learn the 'wrong' lesson. Turns out, it is fine to beat elderly parents, because it is fine to beat children, to discipline them. And elderly parents are in their second childhood. QED.

There are plot twists involving the father's own brief, unhappy period of study. But we skip to the happy ending. The father leads a mob to burn down the school, with the philosophers inside. So the story goes, Socrates was present on opening night and took a bow, so everyone could see what he really looked like.

3

The point is not just that Socrates has a bad reputation because he was publicly roasted by a famous comedian. The point is: in his defense speech, he denies he is, or has ever claimed to be, 'above' his fellow humans. No basket in the clouds for him! He does not have special, superior wisdom. And yet, reading on in **Apology**:

> You know Chaerephon, I imagine. He was a friend of mine from childhood, and a friend to your democratic party; he went into exile with you and returned with you as well. You know what Chaerephon was like, and how impetuous he was when he had decided to do something. One day he went to Delphi, and was bold enough to ask the oracle this question — and, gentlemen, don't shout and interrupt what I'm saying — he asked whether anyone was wiser than me. The Pythia replied that there was no one wiser than me. And his brother here will offer testimony to this effect, since Chaerephon himself is dead.

In 404, the Peloponnesian War ended with the defeat of democratic Athens by Sparta. The Spartans imposed an oligarchy: rule by a group of wealthy Athenians sympathetic to Sparta's aristocracy, willing to collaborate in exchange for power. These were the Thirty Tyrants, including Plato's uncle, Critias. Their rule lasted nine months. Democracy was restored in 403 BCE. The exile Socrates mentions was suffered by democrats while the Thirty held power. Socrates is emphasizing his friendship with a democrat while at the same time acknowledging a certain distance. He was critical of democracy and disrespectful to prominent democrats when they were in power. Later he emphasizes how he was also a thorn in the side of the Thirty, refusing an unjust order at the risk of his own life. Still, it may be Socrates was suspected of being a Spartan sympathizer. But, because of an post-restoration amnesty, no charge could be made in such terms. Perhaps the rather vague charge of "corruption of youth and belief in gods other than those of the city" was, to some degree, an attempt to lodge a political charge without saying anything about politics. Reading on:

> But consider **why** I am saying these things, for I'm going to tell you where this prejudice against me has come from. Because, when I heard this, I thought to myself, what on earth can the god mean, and what is he hinting at with this riddle? I know perfectly well that I am not very wise — not even a little wise! Then what does he mean by saying I am the wisest? Obviously the god isn't lying; that wouldn't be right for him.
>
> And for a long time I was at a loss as to what he meant, and then I set about — very reluctantly — to investigate him somewhat in the following way.
>
> I went to someone with a reputation for wisdom, thinking that there, if anywhere, I could disprove the divination and show the oracle: Here is one wiser than me, but you said I was the wisest.
>
> Well, I examined the man — I don't need to tell you his name, but it was one of our politicians I was assessing when I had this experience, gentlemen of Athens — and in my discussion with him it struck me that although this man was regarded as wise by many other men, and rated particularly high in his own opinion, he was not, in fact, wise. Then I tried to show him that, though he thought he was wise, he wasn't. But at that point he got mad, and so did a lot of the other people there.
>
> And as I was leaving I thought to myself, well, I **am** actually wiser than that fellow. Probably neither of us knows anything all that wonderful, but he **thinks** he knows something he doesn't know. I, on the other hand, don't think that I know — because I don't. So it seems I **really am** wiser than he is, just to this small extent: I don't think I know the things I don't know.

After this I went on to another man thought to be even wiser, and it was the same story all over again, and at that point people started hating me — both the man in question and many others, too.

From there I went on from one man to the next, realizing that I was widely detested, and upset and fearful about it. Nevertheless I thought I was obligated to consider the god's interests first and foremost. Since I was investigating the oracle's meaning, I had to go around to all those people who were alleged to know something. And, by the Dog, gentlemen of Athens — for I have to tell you the truth — what I experienced was this: those who had the most favorable reputations seemed to me, as I went about my investigations as the god directed, pretty much to be those most lacking in good sense, while many others who were supposed to be much inferior were in fact much more capable men in this regard.

So I must point out to you that my wanderings amounted to a Herculean labor I was performing in an attempt to demonstrate the oracle's infallibility. After the politicians I went to the poets — the tragedians, the lyric poets, and all the rest — thinking that there, at least, I would catch myself red-handed, right in the act of being much less learned than they were. I used to pick up those of their poems that I thought they had elaborated with particular care, and ask them what they meant, so that I could learn something from them at the same time. I'm ashamed to tell you the truth, gentlemen, but it must be told: practically any random bystander could talk more sense about the poems than the authors themselves.

And so, again, I soon came to a realization about the poets, that it wasn't through wisdom that they wrote what they did, but through some natural faculty, and that they were divinely inspired, just as prophets and oracles are; for they say many beautiful things, but have no idea what they're talking about. It seemed clear to me that the poets had much the same experience, and at the same time I saw they thought that **because** they were poets they were the wisest of men with regard to **every** topic — of which they were ignorant. And I left the poets with the same sense of superiority I had acquired from the politicians.

Finally I went to the skilled craftsmen. I was quite conscious of the fact that I am practically without any technical knowledge, and I thought that I would find they knew all sorts of wonderful things. And here I wasn't disappointed. They did indeed know things I didn't, and in this respect they were wiser than I. But, gentlemen of Athens, I thought the skilled craftsmen were making the same error that the poets did — each of them thought that because he knew his own technical subject matter so well that he

was as wise as possible on every other subject too, even the most crucial ones — and this fault seemed to me to outweigh their wisdom. And so I asked myself on behalf of the oracle whether I would rather remain as I was, neither wise with their wisdom, nor ignorant with their ignorance, or, like them, have both at once. My answer to myself and to the oracle was that I was better off as I was. (21b-22e)

4

I present this stretch of text in full because you, the reader, should decide what **you** make of it. Socrates anticipates the jurors will think he's joking, but he assures them he is not. But maybe that assurance is just part of the joke?

What is the relationship between so-called Socratic irony and the so-called Socratic method? There is something **ironic** about that speech, make no mistake.

Who is the Socrates behind this Socrates mask?

Socrates not only swears to the god but comes close to swearing the god in as witness. That is faintly ridiculous. Then the god's message turns out to be almost a parody of what we expect from a divine inspiration. How so?

Imagine a wide-eyed, enthusiastic proselytizer, bursting with inspiration, urgently pressing leaflets and tracts into the hands of passers-by. 'Listen to me! Here is the word from the god! I have been chosen to give you a message!' What does it say? Upon examination, the pages are blank, except for a single sentence:

The god told me to give you the special message that I have no special message to give you!

This is witty enough fortune cookie fodder/performance art that we may declare it wise. Then again, maybe we should not allow ourselves to be won over by the cleverness of the comedy.

Let's try this. Socrates' negative questioning method is called **elenchus**, which just means **refutation**. (As with 'irony', Socrates' performances were so distinctive he made these generics his intellectual property.) Refutation seems straightforward. Ask a question. Get an answer. Repeat. Eventually you have the makings of a contradiction and you hang your debating partner from that hook. His friends laugh at him, perhaps, and you have taken one more step towards unpopularity.

For example, in **Euthyphro** the priest wants to maintain the following:

1) **What the gods love is holy. What they hate is unholy.**
2) **Different gods love and hate different things.**
3) **Nothing is both holy and unholy.**

Lay them out like that and it's obvious: they don't fit. The truth of 1 plus 2 implies the falsehood of 3. (Zeus loves what you are doing, so it is holy. Kronos hates it, so it is unholy. So it is holy **and** unholy.) Logicians say 1-3 is an inconsistent set. But how does the discovery that your beliefs are inconsistent help you become wiser?

You wise up by clearing up the contradiction.

But how do you do **that**?

Euthyphro modifies 1 (see 9e); he seems potentially willing to let go of 3 (see 9d). But he might fiddle with 2 instead (8b). In general, how can you know you haven't dropped the **true** and kept the **false**? It is easy to form a consistent set of false propositions. No contradiction is implied. The pieces fit, but the picture they show isn't **true**. It seems the only way to use **elenchus** as a method for becoming wise — for attaining knowledge of anything — is by having at least some knowledge to begin with; some touchstone of truth. You need a secure point you can build out from, testing other beliefs as you go.

Let's consider the matter practically, in terms of what has come to be known as the Socratic method: **teaching by questioning**. Teachers who employ this method do not lecture but ask questions which students answer. Sometimes it is suggested this works for questions to which there is no one 'right' answer. But that can't be quite right. No one bothers to apply the Socratic method to answers to 'what is your favorite color?'-type 'no right answer' questions. There may be something to the notion that the Socratic method is suited to The Big Questions, to which there are no final, right answers. But this much seems right: there must be better and worse answers, in some solid sense, or the method has no point. Pedagogically, the idea is that students won't understand how and why better answers **are** better except by seeing what was worse about what they were at first inclined to say.

This approach corresponds, roughly, to Socrates' method of roughing up his fellow citizens, when they get puffed up with a sense of wisdom. But there is a difference, apparently. A teacher who conducts her class this way had better know better than her students. Teachers who set questions like traps along wrong paths, or trail them like bread crumbs along more promising ones, had better know which is which. You don't teach by asking questions at random. For their part, the students need to have some notion of what the subject is about, as opposed to having no notion whatsoever. They need to have ideas bad enough that they stand in need of knowing better, not **so** bad that they are unteachable in this way. You can't pull anything out of an empty head. The students' beliefs need to touch down on the truth, need to be half-right to start with. The teacher must see and seize on this point of contact; firm it up, expand it.

A Socratic teaching style must straddle right and wrong (better and worse) ways of thinking in specific and often delicate ways. It isn't **easy** to teach this way.

So who does Socrates — this man of no special wisdom — think he is, employing such a delicate method? Here is another famous passage from **Apology**:

> I was attached to this city by the god — though it seems a ridiculous thing to say — as upon a great and noble horse which was somewhat sluggish because of its bulk and needed to be roused up by a kind of gadfly. It is to fulfill such a purpose that I believe the god has placed me in the city. I never leave off rousing each and every one of you, persuading and reproaching you all day long and everywhere I find myself in your company. (30e)

Gadfly stings **hurt**. In **Meno**, Anytus says as much about Socrates' signature provocations: "it is probably easier to do people harm than good" (94e). How can Socrates be so sure he is improving his fellow citizens by stinging them all day, unless he has superior — if not divine — knowledge of the very things he denies knowing: namely, the answers to his questions? If he doesn't have answers, how can he be sure this pattern of stings isn't making his fellow citizens worse. Pain, no gain? (Perhaps he is 'corrupting youth'? Well, he could be, for all **he** claims to know to the contrary.) On the other hand, if he **does** have answers, why not tell us? It may sound fine to say we have to figure out for ourselves what is so wrong with our dumb ideas; but couldn't he at least provide clearer, more positive hints?

5

Let's start over. The suggestion that the historical Socrates' method was purely negative may simply be wrong. We should not assume, just because we can't really know much about the historical Socrates' philosophy, that there can't have been much to know. (Absence of evidence not evidence of absence!) Some scholars argue that we can be confident about a good deal more.[1] What would be the basis? Basically, you trust the standard picture (sketched in chapter 1) according to which Plato's portrait of his teacher is fairly accurate, at least in what we are sure are the early dialogues. Suppose we decide to be trusting. What further features of Socrates' philosophy emerge? The most significant is, perhaps, the following: Socrates seeks definitions. He does not try to trip up his debating partners just any which way. He tangles them up, again and again, with **What is X?** (or **the X.**)

What IS
the X?

He does so because he believes virtue — ethical excellence — to be a matter of intellectual knowledge of essences. Being a good person is more a matter of **knowing that** than **know-how**. It's intellectual, not a practical knack. Furthermore, from the fact that there **is** something latently "great and noble" in his fellow citizens (so he says!) it seems to follow that Socrates thinks this **knowledge** is latent in them. We know it, but we don't **know** we know it.

But then Socrates must think he and his fellow humans know a great deal, after all, notwithstanding that know-nothing line he takes with the jury. He thinks he knows that, by nudging fellow citizens to regard ethics as a known unknown, as it were, he can activate it in them as a kind of . . . unknown known?

Does that make sense?

Can't we keep it simpler? Surely Socrates can know he is helping his fellow citizens somewhat. Surely proving there must be **something** wrong with his fellow citizens' beliefs is some help. Then again, unless there is some

---

1   See, for example, Gregory Vlastos, **Socrates: Ironist and Moral Philosopher** (Cornell UP, 1991), especially Chapter 1. Charles H. Kahn, **Plato and the Socratic Dialogue: The Philosophical Use of a Literary Form** (Cambridge University Press, 1998), Chapter 3, presents a more 'minimal' view.

way to take positive steps to fix the problem, is it clear this is so? Mightn't it be depressing or paralyzing, or just a way to take advantage of people?

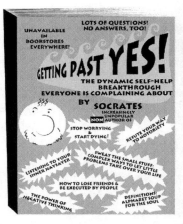

Take advantage? How?

Suppose you have the knack for spying contradictions in an opponent's positions. If you are in the persuasion business, teasing out contradictions is a handy talent. Let's say you are a lawyer. It's no accident the Socratic method is sometimes practiced in law schools. Lawyers argue tough 'what should be done?' cases. Such cases require that we balance contrary considerations. Here's a good trick. In cross-examination, demand a simple answer to some question that has no simple answer. Then, if your opponent is fool enough to play your game, draw out a contradiction or unwanted implication. The opponent whose position is exposed in this way may be opened up to ethical improvement — or you can just play it for the win! **He's down, you're up!** Your audience sees his tongue tied in your thought knot. Now say anything! You look smart, so the audience will probably buy whatever you want to sell. The Socratic method is a great way to make yourself look smart, and other people look dumb, whether you know what you are talking about or not! It's a powerful rhetorical tool.

Is it any wonder the Athenians distrust Socrates, even while they are grudgingly respectful of his logic chops? The way to get ahead in modern, up-to-the-minute ancient Athens is to be an effective speaker. The money and the power are in politics and the courts. Socrates is the master of a powerful, flexible, forensic technique. No wonder rich young Athenians follow him around, trying to pick up a trick or two.

If Socrates truly is practicing this dialectical martial art **igno-rantly** — tearing away any and all beliefs within arm's reach without any sort of higher wisdom to guide him — there seems to be no reason to assume he is doing more good than haphazard harm. And if he knows what he's doing, he's dishonest. Because he isn't saying what he thinks he knows. Why shouldn't people suspect he is just softening them up to sell them something? Why should the sluggish horse of Athens trust its Gadfly is good for its health?

That's not a rhetorical question.

6

Let me conclude this sketch of the historical Socrates by returning to my Chapter 1 question: what is the relationship between Plato and Socrates? One possible answer is that it doesn't really matter. If the ideas and arguments in these dialogues have value for us today, it can't be crucial to settle whose intellectual property they were in the first place, over 2,000 years ago.

This makes sense and certainly promises to simplify matters. It might be objected that it **over**simplifies, flattening layers of literary complexity. But you can appreciate a great novel without being sure you can quite tell author from narrator. It might be that one can appreciate the subtle drama of Plato's dialogues, as well as the abstract ideas and argument they present, without deciding whether one of the characters is really Socrates or really Plato or a bit of both.

But let me sketch one final view, according to which making a judgment about the relationship between Plato and Socrates is an important step, even if it is never going to be one we can take with a high degree of confidence.

So the story goes: a young Plato was preparing to submit a set of tragedies he had written as competition entries for the Festival of Dionysus (the god Dionysus is a great patron of the arts.) On the way Plato met Socrates. After their conversation, he returned home and burnt all his poetic works. This sounds to me like a story that can't be true because **it** sounds **too** true. Because this much is true: Plato has a love-hate relationship with the arts. In **Republic** his Socrates refers to philosophy's long-standing 'quarrel with the poets.' Philosophy aims at truth, at reality; poets, by contrast, are in the lies and illusions business.

In the ideal city sketched in **Republic**, poetry and drama will be severely censored. Plato is especially stern on the subject of comedy: low-minded foolery, ugly masks provoking violent outbursts of laughter. All this is **bad**, he suggests.

In **Laws** — a very late dialogue, the one in which Socrates does not appear — Plato considers what might happen if artists were permitted to stage puppet shows as entries in dramatic contests.

They might win.

The kids would love it!

Plato would not approve.

But isn't Plato himself a dramatist, even a comedian?

Even a puppeteer? Plato is writer, director and producer of these dialogues, which are, for the most part, dramas of human weakness. Socrates' debating partners are (not to put too fine a point on it) mostly fools. In comedies, fools are mostly for laughs. In Plato's case, we infer that there is supposed to be much more to all the banana-peel slippage of failed definitions than just a good laugh at someone's expense. But what more is there? In **Laws**, which never cracks a smile, Plato suggests we humans are like puppets in the hands of the gods, who put on a show by manipulating us.

To be a puppeteer is, then, a divine calling. How not?

But how so? Perhaps Plato is not simply speaking through Socrates. Perhaps we should imagine him hovering above, with an air of superiority, commenting on the whole scene. He is telling us something by pulling the strings just **so**. Maybe dramatizing Socrates knocking the competition with such an air of effortless superiority is Plato's way of saying Socrates must have been on the right track. Or his way of up-selling abstract truths to an audience not yet sold on anything but verbal fights.

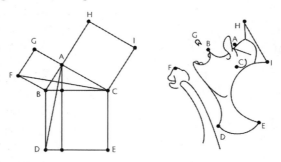

On the other hand, maybe we should regard the dialogues as dramatized anthropological investigations of how and why Socrates, although he was on the right track, was a failure. Socrates' whole 'how to lose friends and be executed by people' martial arts style of divinely-inspired self-help is insufficiently **winning**. It is rational but unpersuasive. Those who need a slap upside the head, for medicinal purposes, won't take their medicine.

Don't take it from me, however. And don't assume there has to be **one** answer to the question of what the message of this medium has to be.

By the way: how do they **play**, these dialogues? Sometimes the dramatic effect is bit wooden, which can be off-putting. Still, it is skillful and fascinating. Even the stiffness of certain movements can become an attractive feature. Superficial crudity can be a subtle affair. If artists were permitted to stage puppet shows, as entries in intellectual contests, **philosophers** might love it.

Chapter 3 Plato: Out of the Cave

1

PLATO MAY OR may not have once aspired to be a prize-winning dramatist. He was certainly born to rule. He was born into an Athenian, aristocratic family whose sons would expect — and be expected — to achieve prominence in politics and public affairs. Plato disappointed expectations except through his philosophy. It seems he acquired a **daimon** named Socrates who kept whispering **no**; who made him burn his plans for entering into politics in any manner he regarded as philosophically unjustified. He would not compromise his ideals. Political reality could not live up to them.

In **Republic**, Socrates remarks that the few who are truly appreciative of philosophy will be, in political life, like travelers huddled against a wall in a dust storm (496d). They will stand apart from those who dominate public affairs and be content if they can keep their hands clean and, in the end, depart in peace. To achieve even as much as that would be a great thing. And yet: greater would be to take a proper, active role in politics, for this is what man is born to do.

Plato negotiated these competing demands of purism and practicality, retreat and engagement, by making himself the original academic. He founded his famous Academy around 385 BCE. The word 'academy' — as in 'the groves of academe' — derives from the name for the site of Plato's school, in a suburb of Athens. It was planted with olive groves and dedicated to an ancient hero, Akademus. (Not a scholar-hero, in case you were wondering.)

Plato apparently made one serious attempt to play what he could regard as an appropriate role in politics, not in his home city but in Sicily. He was invited to be an advisor to Dion of Syracuse (a Greek city.) Dion was the son of the king. Apparently Plato traveled there two or three times, hoping to become the wise power behind the throne. But it came to nothing, beyond awkward and potentially hazardous entanglement in power struggles. Plato retreated to his Academy, where he taught and presided for decades until his death.

Most of Plato's dialogues must have been written after the time of the founding of the Academy, with perhaps only the earliest being written before. It is useful to keep in mind how much time must have passed since the events they purport to narrate. **Euthyphro** has to be set in 399 BCE, the year of Socrates' trial. The dialogue may have been written ten years later. **Meno** is set earlier and was almost certainly written still later. **Republic** may be set in 428 or 413 (good guesses as to when the festival taking place at the start of the dialogue may have really taken place.) The dialogue is thought to have been written around 375 — half a century after the fact.

2

This is a good place to say a few words about Athens. Plato's **Republic** contains, famously, a blueprint for an ideal city. Classical ancient Greek discussions of politics revolve back to the level of the city — **polis**: hence our 'politics'. This is due to the distinctive political geography of that time and place. The Greek world, meaning the Greek-speaking world, was extensive. Greeks had colonies around the Mediterranean, from Sicily to Asia Minor. This world was, by and large, divided into city-states. These were politically autonomous units, with a wide variety of government-types, typically consisting of an urban center and enough land around it to support the population. Athens was one of the largest of these and was remarkable in other ways as well.

Socrates, the Gadfly of Athens, lived through most of the Golden Age of Athens, a century-long period that began with glorious military victory and rose up and up with imperial expansion, substantial domination of the Greek world, cultural transformation, wealth, democratic self-confidence, intellectual ferment and artistic achievement. Socrates' execution squats at the end of this period, a sorry monument to defeat — militarily, at the hands of the Spartans; but also culturally. In the end, Athens no longer had the self-confidence to tolerate her Gadfly. Plato was still a young man as this period of civic flourishing was, effectively, drawing to a close. His literary preoccupations are almost as much a memorial to a time and place as to a man.

A postscript: Plato's most famous pupil, Aristotle (384-322 BCE) was briefly the tutor to Alexander the Great, who brought an end to the era of the **polis** by uniting Greece. But Plato's Academy preserved its autonomous existence past the point when Athens lost hers. The Academy survived for centuries until the Christian Emperor Justinian shut down all pagan institutions of learning in 529 CE. But the academy may not have operated continuously through this long period.

3

Shifting our attention now to Plato's philosophy, let's begin with another generous stretch of dialogue. What follows is the so-called Myth of the Cave, aka the Allegory of the Cave. It is a very famous passage from Book 7 of **Republic**. (The books are like chapters. There are ten in all.)

> Imagine men living in sort of subterranean cave, from which there is a way up to the light running along one side, but the exit is a long way up. The men have been there since childhood, necks and legs fettered so that they remain in place and can only see straight ahead. Their restraints prevent them from turning their heads. Light streams down from a fire burning far behind and above them. Between the fire and the prisoners, some distance back and somewhat higher up, a path runs across the width of the cave, in front of which stands a low wall, built like the façade of a puppet theater, as if to conceal the bodies of performers who will show their puppets along the top.
>
> — I can see it.
>
> Then see also how men are carrying along the wall — so that these things appear above it — all sorts of artifacts: statues of men, of animals, made of stone, of wood, fashioned in various ways. And, just as would be expected, some of these carriers are talking while others are silent.
>
> — This is a strange picture, and strange prisoners. (514a-b)

Let's pause to consider just **how** strange. We are about to hear tell of a prisoner who escapes, passing from darkness to light. Obviously this is allegory
of intellectual and/or spiritual enlightenment.

That is not such a strange story.

Anyone who has seen **The Matrix** gets
how such a drama can be compelling.

Do you take the red pill or the blue pill?

Plato's audience would have been familiar with their own tales of bold
trips into and out of some underworld. Specifically, Plato may be adapting
religious and mythic elements from the Orphic tradition — ancient Greek
'mystery cult', offering its initiates rites of purification and doctrines of rebirth.
'Orphic' from Orpheus, mythical poet-hero whose music was so beautiful he
could sooth the savage spirits of wild beasts. He descended into the underworld to save the woman he loved from death itself.

Plato's philosophy is likewise concerned with
self-purification, with rebirth and eternal life,
with harmonies that calm beasts and dispel
shadows. (If Plato means to compare the true
philosopher to Orpheus, it may be rather
an ironic gesture. Orpheus did manage to
charm the shades of the underworld, but
he couldn't save the girl, and he died hor-
ribly — torn to shreds by **maenads**, frenzied
followers of Dionysus. But that's another story.)

Before we get too comfortable with the notion that we — or the
Greeks — already get how this sort of story goes, we should pause to examine
the props we pass on the way. The prisoners are forced to watch a kind of
shadow-puppetry — but then again not. Shadow-puppetry — popular, traditional art form in many parts of the world — is usually set up like so.

You see?

The light is coming from the wrong side, for purposes of comparisons to Plato. He is giving us a physical set-up much more reminiscent of a modern cinema.

Imagine the various artifacts carried along the wall as individual film cells, parading past a projector's light.

It's remarkable! Plato invented the first film projector!

Then again, he invented the first **broken** film projector. A fire behind a wall, casting shadows of physical objects a long distance over the heads of an audience would lose focus completely. It would be more like a light show at a concert than a movie.

It would be **pure** spectacle, not **even** a picture of anything.

But who expects myths to be, strictly, technologically worked-out? (Where's the bathroom?) Plato is obviously imagining the projection mechanism works **somehow**. Maybe. But the point may indeed be that the images on the screen will necessarily be **so** flickering, riotous, blurry and untrue that the show is unusable as a source of information about anything. You can't get any more idea about reality by watching such a spectacle than by staring at a revolving disco ball in a dark club.

Whether we imagine the prisoners as passive zombies in a run-down movie theater or ecstatic concert-goers — ravers in chains — we are **like** these people. Or so Plato would have us believe. Let's sit back and watch the rest of the show.

4

They are like us, I said. Do you think, first of all, that such men could see any more of themselves and one another than their shadows, cast by the fire onto the wall of the cave in front of them?

— How could they, if their heads are locked into position all their lives?

And won't the same go for those objects carried along the wall?

— Quite.

If they could talk to each other, don't you think the names they attached to these shadows would be taken for names of the real things?

— Necessarily.

What if their prison had an echo which reached them off the front wall? Whenever one of the carriers spoke, while passing behind the wall, wouldn't they think it was the shadow passing in front that was doing the talking? Do you agree?

— By Zeus I do.

All in all then, I said, such men would take reality to consist of nothing above and beyond these shadows of artifacts?

— They have to believe that.

Consider then what deliverance and relief from bondage and ignorance would mean to them, if such an event ever naturally occurred among them. Whenever one was freed, had to stand up all at once, turn his head, walk, look up toward the light — doing all this would mean pain. The glare of the flame would make it impossible for the man to see those objects whose shadows were so familiar to him. What do you think he would say if told that what he saw before was just a lie, a delusion — that he had come a step closer to reality, had turned to face things that existed more fully, that he now saw more truly? If one proceeded to point out each passing object, asking him what it was, and making him answer, don't you think he would be at a loss and believe the things he saw earlier were truer than those now before him?

— Much truer.

If one forced him to gaze into the fire itself, his eyes would hurt. He would turn round and flee back toward those things which he could see, supposing they were in fact clearer than those now revealed to him.

— Quite so.

And if one were to drag him by force from that spot, up the steep and difficult path, if one refused to let him go before he entered the sunlight, wouldn't he be in physical pain and furious as he was hauled along? When he emerged into the light, when sunlight filled his eyes, he would not be able to see a single one of the things which are now said to be true.

— Not at once, certainly.

I think he would need time to adjust before he could see things in the world above. At first he would find it easiest to see shadows, then reflections of men and other things in water, then things themselves. Eventually he would see things in the sky, and the sky itself — but more easily at night: the light of the stars and moon being easier to bear than the sun and its light during the day.

— Of course.

Then, in the end, he would be able to see the sun; not just images of it in water or in some other place but the sun itself in its own proper sphere. He would be able to contemplate it.

— That must be so.

After this he would reflect that it is the sun which brings on the seasons and the years, which governs everything in the visible world, and which is also, in some sense, the cause of those other things which he used to see.

— Clearly that would be the next stage.

What then? When he thinks back to that place where he grew up, recollecting what passed for wisdom there and reminiscing about his fellow prisoners, wouldn't he think what had happened to him was fortunate indeed; wouldn't he pity the others?

— Surely.

And suppose the men below had praise and honors to bestow upon one another: a prize for the keenest eye for spying out shadows, and one for the best head for remembering which shadows usually come earlier, later, and simultaneously—thus enabling predictions of the future. Do you think our man would covet these rewards and envy those so honored, who thereby held sway over the prisoners? Or would he feel, as Homer put it, that he certainly preferred to be, "slave to another man without possessions on the earth," enduring any suffering for the sake of being spared such opinions, and such a life as these others live?

—Quite so, he said, I think he would rather suffer anything else.

Reflect on this as well, I said. If this man went back into the cave and sat down in his old seat, wouldn't his eyes be filled with darkness, leaving the sunlight so suddenly behind?

—They certainly would be.

And if he were compelled to enter once again into all those games of shadow-gazing? If—while his sight was still affected, and before his eyes readjusted—he had to contend in this way with those who had remained prisoners, wouldn't he be mocked at? Wouldn't it be said that his upward journey had wrecked his eyesight, that this showed it was not worthwhile even to try to travel upward? And as for any man who tried to free them and lead them upward: if they could lay hands on him and kill him, they would.

—They certainly would.

This whole image, my dear Glaucon, I said, must be related to what we spoke of before. The visible world should be compared to the prison dwelling, the fire inside to the power of the sun. If you interpret the upward journey and the contemplation of things above as the upward journey of the soul to the intelligible realm, you will grasp what I take to be the case, since you were keen to hear it. Whether it is true or not only the god knows, but this is how I see it. In the intelligible realm, the Form of the Good is the last to be seen, and it is seen only with difficulty. When seen it must be accounted the cause of all that is right and beautiful, the source and wellspring of light in the visible world; while in the intelligible world it itself is the cause and control of truth and reason. He who would act rationally in public or private must see it.

—I share your thought so far as I can. (514c-517d)

Plato's Cave Myth is an allegorical expression of thoughts about how to live **and** it is a presentation of thoughts about "things in the sky and below the earth." That is, it is about things the historical Socrates asked about **and** things the historical Socrates may have denied special knowledge of. So perhaps the Socrates who narrates this myth is Plato, adding a positive metaphysical vision — and a theory of knowledge — to his teacher's negative, ethical teachings? And yet: surely we are supposed to be reminded of the case of the historical Socrates when we hear tell of prisoners killing their would-be liberator. Is Plato implying that his teacher really did have "more than human knowledge?" He had been out of the Cave? Had been half-blinded by the light to the point where he seemed half a fool?

Let's take it one step at a time. The myth operates on two levels: ethics and metaphysics (how to live; what is the nature of reality.) But in fact we should immediately subdivide these. It is about ethics **and politics** and metaphysics **and epistemology**. (Epistemology: the study of the nature of knowledge.) At the same time, the myth implies these four subjects are somehow deeply unified. You can get the answers to your ethical and political questions **by** getting the answers to metaphysical and epistemological questions and **vice versa**.

In a sense, this unity is quite intuitive. A film like **The Matrix** works the same way, running together ethico-political anxiety with wild speculation about unreal worlds and the limits of knowledge. As a matter of storytelling, it is not hard to combine these themes. But argumentatively and theoretically, the fact that we are pretty clearly supposed to read the myth several ways at once only makes it trickier to process.

I may as well mention, while I'm at it: the Cave allegory is a simplification of Plato's full theory, a vivid condensation of intricate arguments and positions laid out in **Republic**, especially in books 5-7, and in other dialogues. Still, there is quite enough in the Cave itself to keep us busy.

5

The most puzzling feature of the Cave is probably the implication that there are **two** worlds, a 'visible' and an (invisible but) 'intelligible' one.

Again, a film like **The Matrix** gives us a quick clue: Plato really is saying we are stuck in a dream world — the merely visible one — and **true** reality is elsewhere. True reality is a thing we can access only by closing our eyes and opening our **real** eyes, something we have, allegedly never done before. But why would you think **that**?

Let's start from the other end, reading the allegory ethically and politically. The prisoners are the **demos** — that is, the people. ('Democracy' means **rule by the people**.) I think it's safe to add: the prisoners are, plausibly, the democratic people of Athens. Those curious characters parading their statues and artifacts are movers and shakers in politics and public affairs generally — in Athens in particular.

Plato isn't **just** talking about Athens, of course. But I think it is fair to speculate that he theorizes the general case with a constant eye on what he takes to be his hometown situation. Some of the reasons for thinking so are obvious. His dialogues are set in Athens and full of Athenians. Here is a slightly less obvious reason.

Republic opens with Socrates "going down to Piraeus" (327a). That's the port. But that **does** not just mean a set of docks. It's a long descent. Socrates is 'going down' to attend a civic festival. He is compelled by a crowd of friends to remain for a night revel that is to follow the more sober, ritual observances of the day. There will be a horseback torch-race, with riders passing burning batons — spectacle of motion, dancing light and shadow.

Turning our heads around:

above the walls, high on the Acropolis, stands visible the great bronze statue of Athena, commemorating victory at the Battle of Marathon. She casts a long shadow over the port — shadow of wealth, imperial glory, civic pride, traditional religion. So they say, sailors can see the glint off her spear, far out to sea.

In describing conditions in his Cave, Plato may be saying the democratic masses have a false, distorted picture of political reality. True, they are preoccupied with civic activities and public figures, but only insofar as they are attracted to spectacle, bright sights or loud noises. A festival with torch-races, for example.

The movers and shakers, walkers along the wall, correspond to influential figures in public life. But the people do not really even **see** what these people are up to, who they **really** are. The people see distorted **images**. Their idea of the great Pericles (greatest orator and most influential politician of the age) is more like a bust of Pericles — image for public consumption — than like the man himself. The people are taken in by advertising and propaganda, to use modern terms. They have a sense of things happening, deeds done, events unfolding. But in their eyes it just looks like a baton race.

Think about horse-race coverage of modern elections.

Who's up? Who's down?

Shrewd predictions are made. But a week from now, the burning issue of who was ahead in the polls last week will have burned out. Furthermore, even if the people had a deeper picture of political events, this would only amount to insight into things that are, in essence, hollow and artificial. Politics, as it stands, is a sorry, empty affair, because it is not truly directed at any good end.

That which moves and shakes is a whole lot of nothing. What the people see, then, is just a **shadow** of nothing.

Here is another way to put the same basic point: popular entertainment — what used to be called mass culture — is escapist nonsense. Escape from illusion into deeper illusion. The people are the power in the city, but they do not spend their days trying to achieve knowledge of what is best for the city. They amuse themselves to death. They crave action and conflict. They erupt in violent laughter at low comedy. Politics and the courts are, in their eyes, merely the highest form of puppet theater. **Look! The fool is beating that other fool!** Politically, this is bound to be disastrous. No one who actually understands what is best for the city will be able to take effective action in such an environment. The virtuous actually become useless in these circumstances.

This early expression of political-criticism-as-media-criticism provides the template for similar complaints down the centuries. In contemporary terms: infotainment, celebrity culture, sound-bite culture, media bias, propaganda — concerns about all such things, from all points on the political compass, tend to be retellings of Plato's Myth of the Cave.

Cast off your shackles, see the light! Be yourself! Fix society!

As allegory, the main defect of Plato's Cave may therefore not be that these prisoners are too strange but that they are not strange enough. Everyone always thinks everyone else is deeply confused about something — usually politics, ethics and popular culture. Maybe the first thing that happens when you take the blue pill, the one that means illusion, is you dream you took the red one? Whose Sun is real? (Speaking of which: many scholars will feel I am straining to make these links between the geography and politics of Athens itself. It's not as though I can prove Plato's Cave should be read in this way. You'll have to make up your own mind about what is plausible.)

6

What else is going in Plato's version of the Cave? More to the point, perhaps: what is supposed to be going on outside the Cave? What are we to make of the mysterious denizens of the Sun-lit surface? What is this alleged division between visible and intelligible domains? It is one thing to tell some Matrix tale as **pure** ethical, political allegory. The shadows on the Cave wall fit well with concerns we — who spend so much of our lives gazing at screens — are likely to have about media, society, culture, every informational aspect of life. It is impressive that Plato went to the trouble of inventing the first film projector, just so he could complain about how **bad** the movies are these days. But it is a step beyond all this to say the Matrix set-up is **literally true**.

Socrates says all this is "related to what we spoke of before." What's that? The so-called Theory of Forms, probably the best-known Platonic doctrine. It does not figure explicitly in any of our three dialogues — **Euthyphro, Meno, Republic**, Book 1. But it is prefigured. It seems fair to say the shadow-play comedy of these dialogues, all this bumping around in the dark, is intended, ultimately, to **direct our gaze upwards and elsewhere**, to a more satisfactory plane of conceptualization. So I'm going to do my best to tell you what I think Plato wants you to think, at the end of it all.

7

How many cows? You could answer **three** or **one**.

How many letters are in the phrase 'dancing cow'? Eight or ten, depending whether you count two 'n's and two 'c's twice or once. How many words in this book?

dancing cows

Each of these questions is ambiguous. The source of the ambiguity is the so-called type-token distinction (not a Platonic term, but it will do for getting at a Platonic idea.) When you see three dancing cows you are seeing one **type** of thing, three **tokens** of that type. The same goes for letters and words. The letter **e** is one **type** of letter. There are many individual **tokens** of the letter **e** on this page. We see the same letters, over and over. We see each letter only once, as we read it. The ambiguity in questions like **how many dancing cows? how many letters in 'dancing cow'?** is a function of uncertainty as to whether we are talking tokens or types.

Let's switch to more Platonic labels: the **type** level is the intelligible level. The **token** level is the visible level. (Well, it's true. You've never seen **the** letter **e**, only particular **tokens** of it.) The next step is the big one. Imagine there are two worlds — domains, call them what you will — corresponding to the two levels of the picture. There is an intelligible world, containing a permanent stock of re-usable types, and a visible world, containing lots of particular tokens, which are what they are in virtue of 'participation in' the types.

My letter **e** analogy contains a pun, because the token-type distinction and typography are not the same, but maybe the pun can be helpful. A digitally-displayed page of text is an affair of **type**, in that it mostly consists of letters. But it is also an affair of **types**, in that the things you see, letters and shapes, are constructed with reference to things you don't see: abstract sets of digital instructions for making as many copies of that kind of thing — the letter **e**, a dancing cow — as you might want. Etymology may help: 'type' comes from the Greek for **strike** or **dent**. A **type** of thing is a thing punched out of a mold or pattern. Until typewriters went out of fashion, the connection was obvious. **That** bit of ink-covered metal strikes the page and leaves a mark resembling itself. **Type**-writing is shapes on paper participating in reusable patterns. Of course, if you're quite sure you've typed your last letter, you can throw your typewriter away. You won't be needing it any more; your last words can stand on their own. Tokens of this type are independent of the writers that produce them.

So let's shift back to the computer case, because we want to imagine a case in which such participation is not one-off but on-going. Digital word-processing is also **type**-writing. But if you trash your word processing application, font files and operating system after composing your final document, no one will be able to read what you wrote. On your computer desktop, files and folders **look** discrete and self-contained. This makes for an intuitive interface. But the visual metaphor is misleading (if you took it too seriously.) Documents consist of instructions that say, informally, 'go **there** to get instructions about how to construct the **type** of thing that is supposed to appear **here**.' And the software and hardware scurry off to a font file, or an image file, and come back with instructions about which pixels to light up to make an **e** — or a dancing cow.

Plato's Theory of Forms says **our** world works the way the computer does. The individual tokens you see around you in the visible world — that man, that woman, cow, horse, piece of gold, rock, tree — look like discrete, self-contained entities. But, in fact, this visual interface is a lie. Really these are highly relational entities that are what they are in virtue of participation in behind-the-scenes data resources. Plato's usual word for these behind-the-scenes things is translated 'Form' or 'Idea'. (It gets capitalized, in English, to make clear this is a technical use.) The Greek is usually **eidos**, whose original meaning is something like **shape** or **outline**.

So: according to Plato, a cow is a cow (rather than a dog or a cat or a rock) in virtue of participation in (brace yourself for an awkward phrase) the **Form of Cow-ness**. A dancing cow is what it is (rather than being a **sleeping** cow or an **eating** cow) through participation in the **Form of Dancing**. So every particular thing you encounter in the visible world is what it is in virtue of sitting at a crossroads of data pathways (to use another technological metaphor.) All roads lead to the intelligible world. This participation of tokens in abstract resource types is ongoing, as in the computer case. But, according to Plato, this participation is also highly imperfect, which brings us back to the typewriter case. The things of the visible world are like letters from a banged-up old typewriter with a worn-out ribbon.

You've never seen a Real Cow!

Yes, you read that right! The cows we see are very imperfect copies of the **real** Cow. Why would you think **that**? There does seem to be a sense in which Plato conceives of these imperfections as inevitable by-products of mechanical reproduction. That is, he just takes it to be obvious that copies are always a bit off. But I think we are better off trying a new analogy.

When you took geometry your textbook contained illustrations: circles, triangles, lines, squares. At some point you got frustrated, couldn't figure out the answer and were tempted to take out your compass and just **measure**. Your teacher said you couldn't. Why not? Isn't taking measurements with scientific instruments a fine method? Not in this case, because the figure you were told to investigate could not be the same as this ink on paper. Why didn't the publisher print it more accurately? Because it couldn't be done.

Geometrical objects are intelligible, not visible. Strictly speaking, a point has **no** extension. Your textbook may have introduced the concept **point** by representing points as small black dots. But, strictly, being extensionless isn't a matter of being very, very small. It isn't even **like** that. It is not the case that, as printing technology improves, geometry textbook publishers get better and better at representing extensionless points for what they really are.

At a certain point you, the student, made the leap across a conceptual gap, leaving textbook illustrations behind. The visible drawings helped you, in the end, not by encoding the information you needed, but by suggesting that you needed to look elsewhere for what points, lines and circles really are. A **real** point, line, circle is something you can only grasp with your mind, not see with your eyes.

Plato thinks the things around us in the world we live in — men, women, chairs, rocks, trees, cows, stars in the sky — are like so many illustrations in a geometry text. As with the illustrations in the geometry book, we should look at them, understand them, by looking **past** them with our mind's eye, seeing what they are all trying to be, what they ought to be. We should understand the **intelligible** world, of which this visible one is a mere copy.

We are all — every one of us, and every rock, every tree — sadly fallen from our true natures, striving to get back to that ideal condition. That is the point of making the Form of Forms be the **Form of the Good**. Ultimately, the Forms are the way they are because it is good for them to be that way. Our world is an inferior copy. Our world is, in a sense, unreal. **Less** real. Shadow of the real. We are all, in a weird way, cheap knockoffs **of ourselves**.

This sounds like a metaphor at best, madness at worst. A dancing cow on-screen is what it is because it participates in an abstract data structure or resource — a file on some hard disk, saved as **dancingcow.jpg**. That makes sense. But a **real** cow doesn't work like that. Cows come from cows, not from some abstract Form of Cow-ness. What would it even mean to assert the contrary?

The geometry example makes a certain sense in its own terms. But **everything** isn't like geometry. We understand the sense in which a geometry illustration is 'trying to be' pure and abstract. Here 'trying to be' is shorthand for a teaching function. But **cows** aren't trying to be pure and abstract, let alone geometrical. It seems especially obscure to suggest that solid, material cows — cows you can see and touch — could be, in any meaningful sense, less real than the Form of Cow-ness, if there **is** such a thing.

8

Let's make the correspondences with elements of the Cave myth explicit. In **Republic** VI, two other famous metaphors are advanced — Sun and Line. Often Sun, Line and Cave are taken as a set. Here's a picture (but don't expect to get it right away.)

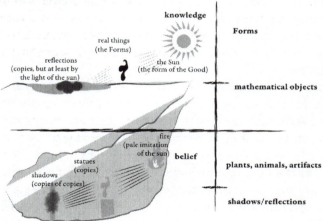

Sun, source of light and life, is an appropriate metaphor for the Form of the Good, root of all Being, all knowledge of Being. The Sun gives us the division between intelligible and visible, which is worked out more elaborately in terms of the so-called 'Divided Line', which refers to a fourfold division of modes of cognition and their corresponding objects. The better the mode, the more real its object. There are many problems interpreting this. It is more than reasonable to suspect that Plato — straining to make out that many different problems are really **one** problem — has generated incoherent clutter. Let me confine myself to sorting out one major difficulty. The major division on the Line is the distinction between belief and knowledge. What **is** the difference? Plato (Socrates, if you prefer) asserts that the difference is this: knowledge is of what **is**; belief is of what **is and is not**. That is, different modes of cognition are different in virtue of being about different things.

But surely this is confusion. Belief may be true or false; knowledge is true by definition. But that is not the same as saying my belief, or the thing my belief is about, is both true and false, ergo not the same thing my knowledge would be about. I believe I have $20 in my wallet. Either I do or I don't. I can check. But I don't **both have it and not**, before I check (as if my money were Schrödinger's cat.)

What can Plato be thinking, asserting the opposite? How can belief and knowledge have different objects? If I know I have $20 in my wallet, but you merely believe it, my knowledge and your belief are about the same thing, right? My money? If we talk about what I know, and you believe, we aren't talking past each other about different things. But apparently Plato thinks otherwise? Why?

When we can answer these questions, we will be on our way to understanding one of the deepest — not necessarily wisest — motivations for Plato's belief in Forms. But let's start from a different angle. Let's try to motivate belief in the Forms by watering down the view to something a bit less extreme-sounding.

Philosophers use 'platonism' — lower-case, to indicate not all versions of the view are Plato's — as a name for the view that abstract entities exist.

Like what? A ghost? More like the number 3: abstract, not located in space or time, not subject to growth, decay; not causally interactive in a natural, physical sense. The number 3 is not identical to the **numeral** 3, written on any page. You could burn all the math books, every scrap on which '3' has been physically scratched, without burning the number. 3 itself is not identical with three apples, three oranges, three cows. You might suggest that the number 3 is what all potential sets of three things have in common. But that is not obviously right; and, in any case, does not make the number 3 any less abstract.

The number 3 is not identical with ideas, in a human psychological sense. When I assert **2 + 3 = 5** this is not a roundabout way of asserting an empirical proposition about what people **think** 2 + 3 is. Arithmetical method is not a method for taking opinion polls about math.

What about the color blue? You could destroy all blue things in the universe without destroying **blue-ness**. For that matter, you could kill all the cows without destroying the concept of a cow — that is, the Form of Cow-ness.

The poet William Butler Yeats asks: "How can we know the dancer from the dance?" A platonic philosopher might answer: easy! Imagine no dancer.

Dance (n.)
series
of movements
matching
musical tempo
& rhythm.

The word 'dance' is meaningful. It refers to an abstract property that may or may not be exhibited by (instantiated in) anything. Particulars are 'sensible', things you might perceive. Properties are 'universals'. They are not identical with any particular and can be many places at once. So you've never seen **the** Dance, as opposed to dancers, only **known** of it. After the cows go home, after the dance has ended, sentences containing the word 'cow' or 'dance' can go on being meaningful. Thoughts about cows and dances are **about** something, come and go what may, cow and dance-wise. We live in a world in which cows and dancing don't mix (on an easy social basis.) But we can think about it, talk about it. How do we manage to **mean** things that we can't point to, because they don't exist? Maybe by reaching up into the realm of Forms, to mix a few ingredients.

Perhaps these ideas all turn out to be subtly extravagant nonsense. Strange metaphysical dream. Still, questions like 'do numbers exist?' seem meaningful and even simple. It looks as though the answer should be 'yes.' Numbers exist. Over and above the domain of sensible objects we have reason to believe in a separate domain of abstract objects.

9

Still, it seems doubtful that such considerations support the conclusion that cows themselves — those **moo**ing things — are less real than, let alone inferior to, the abstract Form of Cow-ness. Two further features of Platonic Forms deepen the difficulty. First, Plato's Forms are unchanging and inert: they neither move nor shake. How, then, are we supposed to conceive of them interacting with the sensible world around us? Johannes Gutenberg introduced **moveable type** to Europe in the 15th Century. He figured out a method for manufacturing little pieces of metal for pressing — typing on — paper. Plato introduced **Immovable Types** to Europe in the 4th Century BCE. I have tried to give you some inkling how the latter works by analogy with the former. But, then again, Plato's Forms must be the exact opposite of print technology. Plato's Forms don't 'dent'. They do what they do in virtue of the fact that they **don't** — do **anything**, that is. Plato's Immovable Types are as far from moveable type as a dot on a page is from an extensionless point. If we are going to understand the Forms, a conceptual leap must be made past typewriters and computers … and we haven't made it yet.

Second, Plato insists that the forms are self-predicating. The Form of Cow-ness is, itself, a cow. The Form of Blue is blue. The Form of Circularity is a circle. But how to conceive this? The Form of Cow-ness is just a … very spiritual Cow, with all mere mortal cows radiating imperfectly around it? At best this is a metaphor, and a rather silly-looking one. Plato will object that we should look with our minds, not our eyes. Corny cow puppets are not good guides to the nature of the Forms. But what would be?

10

Why buy Plato's Theory of Forms? The obvious reason is that you are already independently convinced something of the sort must be right. To pick a possibility highly relevant to Plato's posthumous career: you might be a Christian. If you are convinced that, behind the mire of this existence, this vale of tears, there must be a transcendent, eternal, all-powerful, all-good, non-physical, non-visible Being that is, in some sense, the reason why everything is as it is, and why this way must be for the best — well, then the Allegory of the Cave will seem like a beautiful anticipation of a truth religion has subsequently revealed.

But Plato is not a Christian. What is **his** reason — his allegedly rational reason — for thinking the picture his Cave allegory presents us with is, in some deep, metaphysical sense true? I would not discount the possibility that the doctrine is, ultimately, mystical. But we should try a little harder than that to find an argument that might be Plato's.

Let me offer one. Here is its major premise: **things that don't make sense can't be real or true.** Say you are living in a city, making your day-to-day way with a vague sense of overall geography. One day something knocks you off your path, makes you stop and **think** where you are going. Suddenly the pieces don't fit. That neighborhood you thought of as 'to the west'? — it can't be. And if that neighborhood isn't west …? You sit down, study a map, discover how poor your sense of direction has been. The city you thought you lived in, the map in your head, was not just unreal but absurd — yet somehow **half** real. You were living in **it**. In your mind. Plato thinks we are all living in a dream in that sense. Our workaday concept-maps of the things around us — men, women, cows, trees, rocks, the stars — are not just mistaken but incoherent. Shot through with contradiction; ergo these things must be, at most, semi-unreal. But, as in a dream, we don't notice, so we mostly don't try to wake ourselves up.

You might think the response to this argument should be short and sharp. You don't conclude the **city itself** is unreal just because you lost your sense of direction. If Plato concludes that cows themselves are unreal because our ideas of cows are confused, surely **he** is the confused one. This is a strong response. But sometimes it **is** the case that our concepts prove **so** confused we are forced to conclude the things we thought we were thinking about sort of don't even exist. If you are thinking about a round square, for example. Plato thinks our ordinary thoughts about holiness, virtue, justice, are like that. About **something**, yes; but maybe also about **nothing**. As to the things around us? Things that change, yet stay the same things? Does that even make any sense?

Let me introduce Heraclitus, a Greek thinker who died around the time Socrates was born. His most famous saying (**if** he said it): you never step into the same river twice! What does **that** mean? Maybe: there are only **tokens**, no **types**. Let's take it from the top. How many cows?

Again, you might answer one or **three** but are more likely to say three this time. These cows are not the same — not exactly — only **similar**. But, come to think of it, even in that first case the three cows were only **very** similar. To the naked eye three cows might be indistinguishable, but a closer look would reveal differences in print or display quality. Any three biological cows are going to be different in small ways, even if they are clones. Even if we waive that point, three cows are always going to be located at different points in space-time. So, they are three, not one. Conclusion: 'the same' is only ever a sloppy way of saying similar. Two never equals one. Thus, if we talk about types, let alone some pure Form of Cow-ness shared across cow cases, we are not discovering some fabulous, intelligible realm, which our eyes are too weak to see. Rather, we just plain have weak eyes. We are overlooking differences that are always really there. The truth is: there are only **particulars**. The river may look the same today as yesterday, but it's not. That particular configuration of individual molecules is not coming back this way again. You never step in the same river twice.

A Socratic mini-dialogue, in response to this Heraclitean argument:

Imagine those flickering shadows on the cave wall as a flowing river. Can you see it? — Yes.

Now imagine we are fish. — These are funny looking people.

The fish, they say, is last to know he is in the water. Presumably he is last to know he is a fish. Same goes for those who live in caves. — Whatever you say. (Yawn.)

Maybe the fish can escape from the river. It would be very tiresome, but it might be worth it. — Zzzzzzzz.

Platonists think it is possible to go against this Heraclitean flow. Anyway, a river needs a bank. Change itself must be conceptualized against background constancy. Parmenides (a few decades older than Socrates) may go so far in this constant direction as to deny that you can step into a **different** river even **once**.

Slow down! What does that mean? Depending how you read Parmenides, he may argue that reality must be a strict unity. That is, there can really only be **one** thing, and that thing must be unchanging. (It's hard to know how to draw this, so just contemplate the round shape of the fish plate. Circles are a symbol of one-ness.)

Only one thing? Again, what could this mean?

Let's water Parmenides down, so the position is a bit less incomprehensibly strange. Once again: how many cows?

Suppose you decide to humor me by getting into the Parmenidean swing of things — swing of **Thing**. Only one cow? How so? Are your eyes so bad you don't see the differences between the tokens? No, you are wisely inferring something about how the image was constructed. I made the image using software. At some level, the lines of the cow cartoon are defined, mathematically, as curves. At some level, there **is** just one cow (vector cow-function). To look at these three and see One is not a case of slurring similarity into identity. It is case of knowing what is going on behind the scenes (behind the seens).

But could it be true to say that these cows are 'the same', despite appearances? They are, at least, **similar**. Similarity (come to think of it) is just as abstract a quality as **identity**. What is it that makes these three cows similar? Something **abstract**. Something they share. So similarity is just a **kind** of identity. We need a concept of identity to understand similarity, ergo we can't explain away identity as mere similarity. More fundamentally: distortion by design isn't distorted design. Predetermined change isn't really change. You wouldn't say this book is changing or distorted, just because that third cow looks changed and distorted from the first. Both cow images are aspects of the one, unified, unchanging way this book **Is**. Now see the world that way.

To sum up: Heraclitean thinking emphasizes difference, particularity and change. Parmenidean thinking emphasizes unity, sameness and constancy.

Plato's metaphysics — his theory of reality — would appear to be an attempt to combine the two.

Starting to get the picture?

The Myth of the Cave might say: Heraclitus is right about the domain of appearances, the so-called Realm of Becoming; Parmenides is right about reality, the so-called Realm of Being.

11

But I still haven't answered the question: why buy Plato's Theory of Forms? Because it synthesizes Heraclitus and Parmenides. But why buy **that**? Let's be specific. What is a good reason for thinking our ordinary thoughts — about cows, say — are not just confused, which would not be too surprising (no doubt a cow is complicated) but **so contradictory we should** conclude the thing I think I am thinking about **doesn't really** — or fully — exist?

Here's a bit more Heraclitean wisdom, fresh bend in the river metaphor. "All is in flux, and opposites are always combining." What's that supposed to mean? It may assert that a condition of the possibility of material, sensible change is that all material, sensible objects exhibit strictly contradictory properties.

Perhaps this not a good interpretation of Heraclitus, but it seems to have influenced Plato. If you thought material objects had to be, by nature, self-contradictory, you might conclude material objects are, by nature, somewhat **unreal** — mere appearance, dreamworks — since contradictions can't possibly be true.

But why would you think that all sensible objects exhibit contradictory properties?

Take a few cells of my little cow cartoon. Cut them apart. Overlay them. What do you get?

A blurry mess, **that's** what. (I warned you: the picture quality in Plato's underground cinema is going to be lousy.)

Suppose the cartoon is a long one. Young cow grows up to be old cow. Dancing episode is one of many. The final cell shows a skull and a few bones. Overlay them. What properties does the cow have? Contradictory ones. Young and old, healthy and sick, alive and dead, standing tall and bending over. Dancing, standing, sitting. Moving, still, graceful, clumsy.

Yes, but you aren't supposed to watch
the show **that** way. You aren't supposed
to look at all the cells at once. (What a
stupid theory of how to watch cartoons!)

But in talking about 'the cow' we are
talking about all the cells — hence thinking
about all the cells — at once. The cow **is** all the
things it ever is or will be (or might be.) Any general claim of the form 'the cow is x' is therefore
likely to be true **and** false. The cow is a concatena-
tion of opposites; that is, a contradiction in terms.

How do we respond to this? Here's one possibility.
You bite the bullet and deny that there really is such
a thing as the cow. The truth is: you never watch the
same cow twice.

If this is the Heraclitean theory of cartoons — of
film — it isn't half bad. (Forget digital stuff for a
moment.) You never view the same frame twice.
So: if we have sketched Heraclitus' theory of reality
rightly, it basically says the world is a film-like parade
of particulars — a movie. There's nothing more to it. Each
moment is unique and comes around only once. How could it be otherwise?
If you insist on thinking otherwise; if you try to think the cow as a thing that
endures, self-identically through change (through time, across frames) you
commit yourself to contradiction. You are falling victim to a blurry optical
illusion of identity. Yours eyes are telling you that 2 = 1.

Here's the Parmenidean/Platonic retort: the assumption that 'the cow' talk
is meaningful — even to say 'the cow' is a combination of opposites!' — pre-
supposes there **is** an enduring it, beyond or behind the passing show. Ergo,
Heraclitus' own way of talking denies his own way of thinking.

There are enduring things and also **kinds** of things, above and beyond
passing particulars. But then: the fact of there being such things will constitute a different level of reality than any mere particular.

Also, at least some talk about sameness and equality and identity **is** absolutely valid: 2 + 2 = 4. (2 + 2 isn't just **similar** to 4.) We work out from this point.

Whatever makes it be the case that all these frames are **of** the cow can't just
be one more frame among many. One more frame would just compound the
mess. Whatever cleans the mess, explaining how **many are really one,** must
be abstract — intelligible, not visible, different in kind from any particular.

Pushing the film analogy one step beyond: in order for a film to show, there needs to be a constant source of **light** — and **order**.

That is, there needs to be another kind of light behind that light. Some mind must have thought it would make sense, be good, for the show to show up this way. Parades of particulars don't just **happen**. Individual frames don't pop into existence without rhyme or reason. There needs to be something underpinning change: a constant reason why things are as they are.

On the other hand, Plato's Theory of Forms is hardly a self-evident explanation for this passing show we call 'reality'.

Chapter 4   How To Read This Book, Part II:
Reason & Persuasion

1

NOW I'VE GIVEN you a cartoonish Platonic synthesis of Heraclitus and Parmenides: the Theory of the Forms; Being and Becoming. Objections have occurred to you. I would not be surprised if they turn out to be good ones! I will be quite properly shocked if I have succeeded in converting you to Platonism on the basis of cow cartoons! (How many cows? Give the dancing cows a rest!)

Our three dialogues do not explicitly address metaphysical issues about the Forms and/or possible divisions between visible and intelligible realms. Why, then, have I belabored these issues at such length?

Because if you read these dialogues, you can't help wondering what Plato is getting at. They all end with unanswered questions. We want answers!

I won't leave the reader in the dark. I think Plato's answer is: we won't get answers until we embrace something like his Forms. But once we **do** accept such a view, we **can** expect answers. We can hope to arrive at definitive accounts of the likes of holiness, virtue and justice. These subjects will become technical; not mathematical, but like mathematics: sharp-edged, conceptually pure, precise. But if the theory of Forms seems speculative and implausible, this is disappointing. It would seem these classic works of philosophy by Plato exist to cajole us into believing something we probably aren't prepared to believe. This chapter will try to do better, not so much in terms of metaphysics and epistemology but in terms of the character of ethical problems themselves.

The former prisoner descends back down into the Cave to help his fellows, allegedly turning new-won metaphysical insight into political wisdom. Socrates predicts this individual is in for rough treatment. "Wouldn't he be mocked at? Wouldn't it be said that his upward journey had wrecked his eyesight, that this showed it was not worthwhile even to try to travel upward?"

If there is one element of the Cave myth that is surely spot-on, this is it.

Plato is, of course, one of the most famous and influential thinkers in history. He is in no danger of outright neglect. Yet it is common for readers to react negatively, dismissively. The Theory of Forms is not **the** problem but exemplifies it. And, please note: Plato anticipates the problem.

What **is** the problem?

A friend comes over to your house. 'I'm worried my dad may have murdered someone. What should I do? Should I go to the police?' Minus his self-righteous self-confidence, this could be Euthyphro. Naturally, you tell your friend: 'Well, let's sit down and define 'holiness'. That will provide you with an answer.'

No, of course you don't say that!

Why would you think you could define 'holiness'? Even if you could, why would pulling down the dictionary from the shelf help your friend in a life crisis?

That's the problem. There is something about Plato's whole approach that seems so pedantic, hence head-in-the-clouds wrong-headed! It's **so** wrong, it's hard even to **say** what is wrong with it! (Many people feel this way.)

Partly it's that incessant demand for definitions. But what's wrong with demanding definitions? Suppose, instead of coming to you, your friend went to see a trusted lawyer-friend. 'You think your father murdered someone and you don't know what to do? Well, let's consider very carefully how the law defines 'murder'.' You may think this approach to the problem sounds a little cold and calculating, but it is not crazy. Definitions are often useful, sometimes necessary. Legal cases are one sort of context where this is typically true. Science is perhaps an even clearer case. Scientists don't always need definitions, but sometimes they need the very sharpest ones.

Maybe, then, what seems so odd about Plato is that he thinks ethics could be a technical subject for experts — a science. But suppose your friend went to his priest for advice. Hardly an odd thing to do. Isn't a priest a kind of technical expert? Why can't there be technical expertise about ethics? (The root of 'science' means **know**. You **know** right from wrong. Right? So **you're** an ethical scientist. Sort of?)

It still seems crazy to try to solve these problems by defining 'holiness', doesn't it?

2

Let me frame this problem in terms of another substantial passage from Plato, from the dialogue **Symposium**. It isn't about anyone named 'Symposium'; it isn't about an **academic** symposium — seminar-style discussion of some intellectual subject. In Greek the word means **drinking party**. That's the dialogue's dramatic setting: a drinking party, at which various guests are giving speeches in praise of love.

The speaker I will quote is Alcibiades, a very real, very controversial figure in ancient Athens. Let me introduce him briefly: handsome young aristocrat; born to rule; brilliant military leader — until he betrayed Athens. It's a long and tangled tale. Alcibiades apparently committed acts of recreational vandalism against certain holy things. Then, when called back from Sicily, where he was leading the army, to stand trial for these impious acts, he went over to the enemy, the Spartans.

And one more thing: Alcibiades was a 'student' of Socrates. Plausibly this is one of the motivations for Socrates' denial, in **Apology**, that he teaches. Alcibiades' handsome face is exhibit A in any argument that Socrates corrupts the youth. Here he is, drunk as a lord:

I'm going to try to praise Socrates, gentlemen, by means of comparisons. He may well think I'm doing this to make fun of him, but this comparison is for the sake of truth, not mockery. For I say he resembles those Silenus figures you can see standing in the statuary shops, the ones the craftsmen have made holding pipes or flutes, and when you open them up they are seen to contain beautiful images of gods. And I also say he resembles the satyr Marsyas. As to your resembling these in external form — even you yourself won't contradict that, Socrates, but I'll go on and say that you are like them in every other respect as well! You are a lewd, insolent person, are you not? If you won't admit it, I've got witnesses right here. And aren't you a pipe-player? One much more extraordinary than the satyr?... (215b)

Satyrs are goat from the waist down, man from the waist up, with leering goat-face and horns. They are goatish in their appetites, especially from the waist down.

It is indeed true that representations of satyrs look astonishingly like representations of Socrates. And satyrs are followers of Dionysus, beautiful god of wine and madness. So Socrates at a drinking party seems in character as a satyr-like figure. Silenus is another follower of Dionysus: satyr-faced — broad, flat-nosed, thick-lipped, big-eared but human-legged and a drunk.

A bust of Silenus with pipe and flute, satyr instruments, would be indistinguishable from the bust of a satyr. (Perhaps there was a tendency to conflate the two? In some versions satyrs are Silenus' children.)

At any rate, Marsyas was a satyr who (in some versions) challenged Apollo to a music competition and (in all versions) was flayed for his presumptuousness. He was skinned alive. If you imagine the ugly outer face of these statues as Marsyas, the symbolic act of cracking them open, peeling their surface back, looks a bit sinister. If Alcibiades is comparing Socrates to Marsyas, is he dropping hints about — or foreshadowing — Socrates eventual, unhappy fate?

We don't know what these statues Alcibiades refers to were like. Nesting dolls, with a Dionysus inside? A clay piggy-bank (goaty-bank?) you cracked to get at some treasure? Some later writers seem to think these **silenoi** were hinged boxes of some sort.

In place of this image that has been lost, let me offer an image that has been preserved. Our 'satire' descends from an early Greek comedy form — so-called **satyr plays**. We have ancient representations of beautiful young actors gazing, like Hamlet at the skull, at what appear to be flayed satyr/Socrates skins: namely, the masks they will wear in the performance. Picture Alcibiades that way, addressing Socrates. Maybe.

Skipping a few sentences ahead, he continues:

For example, when we listen to anyone else — even someone who is quite a good orator — giving a speech, it has practically zero effect on us. But when we hear you speak, or hear your words spoken by someone else — even if the speaker is a rather poor one, and be the listener woman or man or youth — we're thunderstruck and entranced. In fact, gentlemen, if it weren't that it would make me seem completely drunk, I'd tell you all under oath about the extraordinary experiences I've been put through by his words, things I still feel even now! For whenever I hear him, I'm worse than some religious fanatic. My heart skips a beat and tears spring to my eyes listening to his words, and I see many other people having the same experiences. Listening to Pericles, or to other skilled orators, I thought: He speaks well. But nothing like this happened to me, my soul wasn't cast into turmoil or compelled to follow along like a common slave. Our Marsyas here, on the other hand, has often put me in such a state that I thought my life wasn't worth living as it was. And you can't say any of this isn't true, Socrates. Even now I'm conscious that if I were willing to open up my ears to him I wouldn't be able to withstand him, and would suffer the same things all over again. He forces me to admit that, inadequate as I am, I neglect myself while I attend to Athens' affairs. So I stop up my ears by main force and flee as if from the Sirens, because otherwise I'd sit down beside him till I was an old man. And there's one experience I've had, only with this man, something no one would expect in me: I've been made to feel ashamed. He is the only man before whom I feel ashamed. When I'm with him I'm aware that I can't do anything other than what he tells me to, but as soon as I leave him I'm a slave to the honors of the multitude. So I become a runaway and flee him, and when I see him I'm ashamed about the things we had agreed on. Often I think it would be a better world without him among us, but then, if such a thing were to happen, I know perfectly well I would feel much worse than ever. The result is that I really have no idea what to do with the man… (215d-216c)

...There are many other marvelous things for a person to praise in Socrates, and though you might well liken most of his doings to those of another, on the whole he's like no other man on earth, past or present, and that is the truly astonishing thing about him. For someone might say that Brasidas and others are like Achilles, or Pericles like Nestor and Antenor, and there are many others one could make the same comparisons about. But of this singular man, both in himself and with respect to his words, you will find no likeness at all, whether you search among men of our time or of the past — unless, as I did, you compare him and his words to the Silenoi and Satyrs. Because I skipped over it earlier, but it's not just in his person that he resembles these. His words also are extraordinarily like the Silenoi that open up. When someone hears Socrates' speech, it seems totally ridiculous at first: he wraps himself up in words and language that are like the skin of some lewd Satyr — for he talks about pack-asses and smiths and shoemakers and tanners, and he seems to be saying the same things all the time, so that an inexperienced or igno-rant man will probably laugh at everything he says. But when they open up and you can see what's inside, you'll see that they are the only words with meaning inside of them, and are the most divine, having beautiful images of virtue inside, and also having the widest relevance — in fact, being completely suffi-cient for the study of anyone who wants to become a good and honorable man. (221c-222a)

You don't need to know who Brasidas or Nestor or Antenor are to get the point. Warriors, wise men and leaders are familiar from myth, legend, story and song. You even see a few around town! But Socrates is singular. Let's work backwards from the end — from the point Alcibiades says he should have started with. Not just the man, Socrates, but his **arguments** are super-ficially ugly. They seem so crude and coarse!

That is, even though Alcibiades begins by saying he — and everyone else — feels more affected by Socrates' speeches than by those of any orator, it is also the case that Socrates does not **immediately** have this affect. At first you are put off by the sheer crudity of the approach.

What thought could flip you across that con-ceptual divide? From dismissing Socrates as a comic goat to venerating him as a golden god?

3

Let's try to get clearer about what it is that typically **bothers** people about Plato — about Socrates. In **Republic**, one of Socrates' friends — Adeimantus, a sympathetic fellow — attempts a diagnosis:

No one can contradict the things you say, Socrates. But each time you say them your audience has an experience something like this: they think that because they are inexperienced players of the game of cross-examination, they are tripped up by the argument — a little here, a little there, at each of your questions. When all these small concessions are added together in the end, they find they fall flat, fallaciously contradicting their own starting points. Just as novice game players are in the end trapped by masters, and cannot move, so this lot are trapped and have nothing to say in this different sort of game, played not with counters but with words. Yet they aren't the least bit inclined to accept the conclusion for all that. (487b)

But why does it **seem** this is just a game? Why would the words Socrates worries about seem like mere counters — like a checker or a pawn? We **really use** these words in everyday life. 'Justice'! That's no toy. If you say 'that's not fair!' and I inquire why not, and you say something about 'justice', and I show you your answer implies something you yourself cannot possibly believe, what then? Apparently you are somewhat confused. No one forced you to answer in a way that implied something false or nonsensical. **You should** conclude that you should probably modify **your beliefs about** fairness and/or justice. How can you **not** take **this seriously?**

Still, Adeimantus is right. Plato obviously knows it. Socrates has little effect on people, not permanently **anyway. Why** not?

Let me answer by means of a passage from **a famous phi**losopher — not Plato this time, but Dale Carnegie, **author** of **How To Win Friends and Influence People** (1936). In fact, much of the rest of this chapter will **be about** Carnegie. But how can Dale Carnegie teach **me** to read a book about Plato?

Carnegie is the Plato ... of the self-help section of the bookstore. These shelves and shelves of 'how to' and 'success' are footnotes to him. And yet Carnegie is, to an impressive degree, perfectly **anti**-Platonic. So if you can just get **him** (he isn't **so** hard to understand) you simply add a 'not': you've got Plato.

I know! Carnegie is not considered a philosopher. Bear with me. One of the things that makes these play-meets-problem-set-with-no-answer-key dialogues puzzling is that Socrates is arguing with non-philosophers. Euthyphro is a priest. Meno, an inspirational speaker and aspiring public figure and military man. (Part-time dreamer, full-time schemer.) Cephalus and son, immigrant businessmen. Thrasymachus is a sophist. (Like Dale Carnegie, although Thrasymachus' book would probably have a less friendly title.)

It would be strange to read, say, a modern chemistry textbook written in dialogue form. But it would be even stranger to read one in which the author puts forward technical ideas about chemistry by engaging in semi-hostile, mock-dramatic debate with fictional opponents who aren't even chemists. It would be strange for someone who didn't know about chemistry to **want** to engage in hostile debate with a chemist about chemistry. It would be frustrating to watch, if what you wanted was to learn chemistry — although it might be funny. There might be a train-wreck fascination. This, in effect, is what Plato gives us. And there surely **is** a reason: namely, this is how philosophy goes and, perhaps, has to go. Because, unlike chemistry, everyone **thinks** they know about philosophy, because everyone has ideas about life and how to live it. There isn't any boundary between philosophy, as a special field of study, and the attitudes of ordinary men and women. Philosophy is bound to be not just a matter of philosophers talking academic shop with philosophers. It is a matter of philosophy arguing with non-philosophy (because non-philosophy often **is** philosophy.) But how do you stage such an encounter productively? Isn't this just going to devolve into comedy?

Speaking of 'arguing': it's a funny old word. Let's get on with the story.

4

Dale Carnegie recalls being a foolish young man at a party, hearing another guest misattribute a quote. Young Carnegie was eager to jump in. (It wasn't the Bible! That was Shakespeare!) An older friend kicked him under the table: "Why prove to a man he is wrong? Is that going to make him like you? Why not let him save his face? He didn't ask for your opinion. He didn't want it. Why argue with him? Always avoid the acute angle." This was much-needed advice to a young loud-mouth.

During my youth, I had argued with my brother about every- thing under the Milky Way. When I went to college, I studied logic and argumentation, and went in for debating contests … Later, I taught debating and argumentation in New York; and once, I am ashamed to admit, I planned to write a book on the subject. Since then, I have listened to, criticized, engaged in, and watched the effects of thousands of arguments. As a result of it all, I have come to the conclusion that there is only one way under high heaven to get the best of an argument — and that is to avoid it. Avoid it as you would avoid rattlesnakes and earthquakes.

Nine times out of ten, an argument ends with each of the contestants being more firmly convinced than ever that he is absolutely right.

You can't win an argument. You can't because if you lose it, you lose it; and if you win it, you lose it. Why? Well, suppose you triumph over the other man and shoot his argument full of holes and prove that he is **non compos mentis**. Then what? You will feel fine. But what about him? You will have made him feel inferior. You have hurt his pride. He will resent your triumph. And —

> "A man convinced against his will
> Is of the same opinion still."

…Real salesmanship isn't argument. It isn't anything even remotely like argument. The human mind isn't changed that way.[1]

Carnegie is giving perfectly sound advice: you catch more flies with honey. (Gadflies? Get a flyswatter.) Yet what he is saying is absurd. He is making an argument against the possibility of making good arguments. This looks like a job for…Socrates!

 My good Carneges, no doubt you are right and I am dull not to see it, but I have one little question. What **is** an argument, according to you? You say you have witnessed thousands, and have just offered one yourself, so you must know…

1) Dale Carnegie, **How to Win Friends and Influence People**, (Pocket Books, 1981), pp. 116-7. The reference is to the current edition, but the passage is from an older edition. The revised edition omits the final lines: "Real salesmanship… the human mind isn't changed that way."

Despite the fact that what Carnegie is getting at is plain sense, there isn't a good way for him to define his subject without contradicting himself. This is not just because sharp definitions are hard to come by. The problem is ambiguity. **Carnegie uses 'argument' to mean verbal fight**. But 'argument' also means **set of premises and conclusions, in which the premises are grounds for accepting the conclusions**. This is more elaborate (although you might want to polish it further, for a formal occasion.) But it is a perfectly ordinary use of 'argument'. Arguing is reason-giving. An argument, in this sense, has nothing to do with fighting. It doesn't even have to do with **doing**. It doesn't have to do with **people** — no more so than an abstract truth like **2 + 2 = 4** has to do with people.

Why do we have one word that means (1) verbal fight; (2) those highly abstract things you meet in math books and scientific texts? They don't seem the same at all. Why do they have the same name? You know what ambiguity is: the thing that lets us make puns, which aren't usually deep puzzles. 'Bank' refers to the sides of rivers and to financial institutions; 'duck' means a bird and a thing you do to avoid getting hit on the head. The ambiguity in 'argument', on the other hand, is no accident. It grows out of an ambivalence we humans feel about … arguments (for lack of a better word).

Let's start with etymology. You might think the root, 'arg', comes from the sound people make when you try to prove they're wrong: **'Argh!'** But no. It's the same as **argent, silver**. The original meaning was something like **shine, be bright, white, clear**. In Latin **arguere** means **clarify, show**. But the frequentative of that verb — the thing you are doing if you argue a lot — is **argutare: babble, talk nonsense**. We think of intelligent people as bright. But, at least as English speakers, we have no positive word for the character

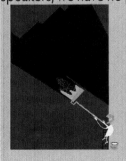

trait of **practicing brightness** — that is, habitually clarifying. Just plain old figuring out what's what. What we have is 'argumentative': word for people who get in fights; which, as Carnegie will tell you, is not a bright way to live. Getting back to Carnegie, let's call the argument-types he doesn't like — the fights — **AF's**. Let's call the justificatory structures **AJ's**. Carnegie offers an AJ to the conclusion that AF's are a waste of time.

His argument no longer looks necessarily self-undermining. But is it good?

> It seems, my dear Carneges, that when you taught me to "avoid arguments, like rattlesnakes and earthquakes", you did not teach me correctly. For, unlike those other things, these things, the arguments, are sometimes good, sometimes bad for a man. And when they are good, even if such cases are but one in ten, as you say, they are among the most precious. For arguments are the very things for teaching which things **really are** good and bad. Your own argument is a perfect illustration. You **do** think your argument is a good one? — Yes, Socrates. — And that it is about what is really good, and what is not? — Yes. — If we knew a small number of precious items lay concealed in a great pile of dirt, wouldn't it be worth our while to sift the pile, to find this treasure? — Certainly. — Then, instead of butting heads, shall we put our heads together, to see if we can sort out which is which in our case, and in every other case we might encounter?

But you can't just separate out the AF's from the AJ's, like sorting trash from treasure. Why not?

Sometimes we say people are 'arguing' when they are, literally, just screaming abuse, like monkeys in the zoo. That could be pure AF.

Some of the things printed in science texts, on the other hand, may count as pure AJ. Proofs in mathematics might be the very clearest cases.

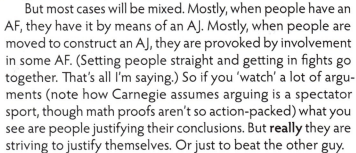

But most cases will be mixed. Mostly, when people have an AF, they have it by means of an AJ. Mostly, when people are moved to construct an AJ, they are provoked by involvement in some AF. (Setting people straight and getting in fights go together. That's all I'm saying.) So if you 'watch' a lot of arguments (note how Carnegie assumes arguing is a spectator sport, though math proofs aren't so action-packed) what you see are people justifying their conclusions. But **really** they are striving to justify themselves. Or just to beat the other guy.

Arguing is a dominance display. Deer grow big antlers, the better to butt heads. The brighter sort of monkey grows grand, elaborate philosophies, for much the same reason. Thus, the subject matter of any given argument (politics, culture, some headline, who forgot to take out the garbage) is not what is **really** at issue, not at the human level.

Arguments are opportunities to display and enforce our sense of status and self-worth. From another Carnegie book: "Our so-called reasoning consists in finding arguments for going on believing as we already do." And: "They had chosen their topics because these topics permitted oratorical development. They had no deep, personal interest in the arguments they were making. And their successive talks were mere exercises in the art of delivery."[2]

5

Let's step back. What is the point of an AJ? What should it be? To **justify**; that is, establish whether (to what extent) a given conclusion is true (warranted by reasons/evidence.) The point Carnegie is making by his anti-argument argument might be expanded and summarized — a bit provocatively — as follows: people don't care about that thing AJ's are good for. People want to know **that** they are right, which is not at all the same as wondering **whether** they are. Or it's just a game for them. The debater's motto: **my conclusion, right or wrong.** This seems like a very cynical view of what people are up to when they are apparently trading reasons to believe. But it would be hard — pointless — to deny that there is a good deal of truth to it. But is it the whole truth?

Hardly. Scientists construct arguments, to justify theories and claims. Nothing Carnegie says about "avoiding argument as you would rattlesnakes and earthquakes" could apply to working scientists. "Real salesmanship isn't argument." This fails to consider the (surely obvious) possibility that there might be cases of argument that aren't supposed to constitute acts of salesmanship. Carnegie seems to have forgotten that sometimes people make arguments in order to figure stuff out. Furthermore, if we are so worried about personal rivalries and squabbles over beliefs-as-property, it is worth pointing out that scientific discoveries — truths about the world, valid arguments, sound theories — are paradigm cases of what economists call 'non-rivalrous goods'. Once you've got them, everyone can share in the goodness. We needn't rake Carnegie over the logical coals, forcing him to concede this logical point. He will surely grant it. He is in favor of science, always adopting a respectful tone when he mentions famous scientists by name. He doesn't think science is just egghead nonsense. So why did he formulate his conclusion too broadly?

2   Dale Carnegie, The Quick and Easy Way to Effective Speaking (Pocket Books, 1962), p. 139,140.

Probably Carnegie would reply that no one is going to mistake a book called **How To Win Friends and Influence People** for a treatise on scientific method. There is no danger that he will corrupt scientific youth into not bothering with all that 'knowing what you are doing' stuff. The need for competence at whatever you do is a truth that needs no reinforcement. Yes, there are incompetent people, but no one thinks that's good, **per se**. By contrast, there really are people who want to develop better 'people skills', who think speech and debate might be a good way to do that. They aren't wrong. Confidence is key. Being able to speak effectively to groups is necessary for anyone who aspires to be any sort of leader. But these people need reminding that aggressive habits they may have, that may be reinforced in the process of confidence-building, are bad, producing results the opposite of what we really want. In short: don't argue with everyone!

So if we will just read Carnegie's anti-argument argument as aimed at the type of reader it **is** aimed at — aspiring sellers/leaders who might take speech-and-debate tactics a bit too far — all will be well. This makes a lot of sense. But some pieces still don't fit. Carnegie says he is "ashamed" he once thought of writing about "logic and argumentation." Carnegie is almost never rude — disdainful, dismissive. But here he is, rude to all the world's logicians. Why go so far out of his way to drag them into his seminar on salesmanship, just to (falsely) accuse them of being bad salesmen? The fact that Carnegie doesn't actually think there is anything shameful about being a scientist or technical professional only makes this more mysterious. Where's the harm in teaching what you yourself admit is necessary? Pushing the point: it's not as though there's a bright line, or even a gray line, between **those** people — the ones who need to be able to think things through — and regular folks. As Carnegie himself emphasizes, a key ingredient of personal success, whatever you do, is cultivating the capacity to stand back, to reflect and analyze in a detached, objective, moderately impersonal manner.

Everyone needs to be a little bit of a scientist, at least some of the time. **You**, for example!

You have a **problem**! (It's like you've known me all my life, you cry!)

What should you do? Stop wasting nervous energy, for starters. Tossing and turning all night is not the way. State exactly what the problem is. What's the worst that could happen? Good. Now suppose it does. How bad is that? It's probably not the end of the world. Once you've seen that life will go on ... life can go on. But we don't want the worst to happen, do we? Now that we've calmed ourselves down a little: how do we ward off the worst case? Break the problem down. Figure out what you want. Assemble the facts. Settle on a course. Pursue it. If you are wrong, you're wrong, but at least you've done your best. Agonizing more wouldn't have made it any better.

This is all common sense, certainly not rocket science (however hard it is to remember that at 3 AM.) Instead of worrying, think it through. But that might as well be: argue. Arguing just **is** thinking through. **Stop worrying and start arguing.**

Why didn't Carnegie write a book with that title, instead of peddling this anti-argument argument nonsense? At this point Carnegie might want to wipe the 'argument' slate clean, if we are just going to get hopelessly hung up on this one word. In **How To Stop Worrying and Start Living** he has a chapter about "How to eliminate fifty percent of your business worries." In **Win Friends** he makes a related point: "Dealing with people is probably the biggest problem you face, especially if you are in business. Yes, and this is true if you are a housewife, architect or engineer." He cites research suggesting that, even in technical fields, "about 15 percept of one's financial success is due to one's technical knowledge and about 85 percent is due to skill in human engineering—to personality and the ability to lead people" (xiv).

I don't know about those numbers. But let's grant for the sake of argument (that word again!) that there's plausibility to it. It just goes to show, **not** that we can separate people into 50/50 or 85/15 piles—persuasion professionals vs. people who need to understand what's going on; rather, that we can't. There are times when everyone needs to be both reasonable and persuasive. That's fair enough. But everyone needs persuasion more than reason? We're going to need an argument!

6

Let's try this. You might assume some of Carnegie's books are for everyone who wants to lead a happy life—that is, everyone. Others, like **Win Friends** and **The Quick and Easy Way To Effective Speaking**, are for 'persuasion professionals', i.e. sales and marketing people, leaders; those whose job is to stand in front, bringing others around to their way of thinking. But Carnegie would say that's not right. When he says arguing isn't salesmanship he's **not** just advising the marketing department. Success in life **is** salesmanship. The products may not be literal goods for sale. But life is a matter of getting people to buy **your** goods. What **you** think is good. Your first good is **you**! You want your life to be worth something. How do you propose to drive the price up and keep it up?

But why buy **that**? Maybe even the most rational philosophers, with their elaborate arguments, can be viewed as bringing their goods to the market of ideas (their Form of the Good, in Plato's case). But it doesn't follow that selling is all there is to it. Or that selling is the stage of the process that demands most care. As if writing a good book were the incidental part, marketing it the only truly deep, essential problem. (Who would buy a book, let alone write one, if everyone thought that way?) Also, in shifting ground like this, we appear to have gotten ourselves completely turned around.

At first it made sense to denounce argument, even though scientists need it, because Carnegie was addressing salespeople, not scientists. Now it turns out the real reason it made sense to denounce argument, even though scientists need it, is that everyone is mostly a salesperson, including the scientists. So which is it? Do we need two senses of 'salesperson', to go with our two senses of 'argument'? Two senses of 'scientist'?

7

Back to the drawing board! At the start of **Stop Worrying** Carnegie quotes the French thinker, Paul Valéry. "Science is a collection of successful recipes."

That's an interesting thought.

Valéry is hinting that science is both broader and shallower than we may tend to assume. It's broad in that there is no sharp division between scientific activities and more everyday ones. It's shallow in that the reason why it's broad is that Plato's picture of science (see Chapter 3) is exactly wrong: science is **not** a special form of cognition distinguished by its concern with a special class of objects or truths outside of the realm of ordinary experience.

This isn't **just** Plato's picture, please note. There's something Platonic about the popular stereotype of the scientist as solitary brainstormer who ascends into rarified, exclusive realms of ideas, or digs deep down, to grasp and pull up hidden truths by the roots.

This stock image of the Nutty Professor, brilliantly out of touch with everyday life, can do double-duty as a paradigm of science itself. Not every scientist is Einstein, but they must all be like him in some essential way.

Conclusion: science is a special, highly distinctive, non-ordinary way of knowing.

Ergo, a scientist is **not** just a jumped-up cook!

No (Valéry will reply), science is a knack, a trade you pick up, hanging around others who picked it up by hanging around others, back to their fathers' fathers (like any trade.)

The scientific method is a grab bag of what has worked and will, presumably, continue to do so — until it doesn't, which also happens. Success in science is a matter of messing about with what you think you know until, if you are lucky, you hit on something new. Then in the bag it goes.

Let's subdivide this point. (Please note: we aren't saying it is right, only worth thinking about.) The science we know consists of reproducible results. If it's not reproducible, it's not science. But if it **is** reproducible, it's a recipe. The science we don't know consists of things out there on the frontiers of discovery and invention. They aren't science yet (otherwise they wouldn't be out there, they'd be in here.) Discovery/invention is experience, guess-work, tinkering, a pinch of **a-ha!**, a lot of sniffing around what's promising and turning up one's nose at what isn't, and a dollop of dumb luck. This isn't a recipe because it isn't **even** a recipe. (It should be so lucky!)

Maybe this gives us some sense as to why reason — "logic and argument" — could turn out to be less important than we might have thought, even in science. But, then again: no. The point isn't that scientists don't need to know what they're doing, but that the nature of their knowledge might turn out to be different than thinkers like Plato dreamed. Humbler, perhaps. But that still doesn't make persuasion the key. It makes no more sense for a cook to read Carnegie than a scientist, seemingly. It's not as though you can persuade that burnt dinner to un-burn itself by making friends with it — no more so than you can flatter a refuted theory into un-refuting itself.

Why **does** Carnegie quote Valéry? First, he wants to emphasize what he teaches is as 'scientific' as anything. Because it works! Carnegie's results are, he claims, reproducible. But now we've gotten turned around again. First, salespeople were not scientists, different species entirely. Next, scientists were just a species of the salesperson genus. Now, salespeople are sprouting up a species of scientist. So which is it?

Here's a clue. Carnegie admits — emphasizes — that none of his recipes are new. We hereby arrive at the rather comforting thought that we can all be great scientists, not without difficulty, but without special **intellectual** difficulty. Great science can just be obvious stuff we already know. From the introduction to **Stop Worrying**:

You and I don't need to be told anything new. We already know enough to lead perfect lives. We have all read the golden rule and the Sermon on the Mount. Our trouble is not ignorance, but inaction. (xx)

We know enough to lead perfect lives! Think about that. Do you think the man is right? (Half right? Has he got a point?) Is this fortune cookie foolishness. Plain common sense? Or **a** bizarre paradox that undermines our cherished assumptions about the value of knowledge? Is it comforting? Vaguely depressing? (Both, on alternate days?) Will this thought inspire you to get up and go, or make you lazy and complacent? Are Carnegie's claims crude on the outside but golden on the inside? Or golden on the outside, crude on the inside?

Let's crack the case, best we can. Carnegie is compressing at least three levels of argument to the conclusion that argument is — not useless (we've seen that's too strong.) Better: **minimally** useful.

Let's go back to assuming you've got a problem. You need to stop worrying (as opposed to thinking.) I could prove it, from premises you would accept. But it's not intellectually difficult to grasp that tossing and turning all night, to no good end, wastes energy. So you need to undergo a serious mental shift, get your head on straight. Turn your gaze away from those nervous shadows on the black cave wall of worry. The thing casting those shadows is your problem. Turn around and face it. Then crawl up past it to the sunlit world of effective action — Life itself! The Good!

And yet: this spiritual shift, migration from the cave into the light, will only amount to reminding yourself of what you always knew, all along! Intellectually, it's trivial.

Don't tell me my problems aren't serious! I didn't say that. Intellectually, it's trivial. First, it's interpersonal. (How did I know? There's no trick. Unless it's medical, most problems are interpersonal.) Now that you have stopped worrying, have seen your problem for what it is, you should basically know what to do. Don't yell at them, recriminate or fling abuse. Put down **Stop Worrying** and pick up **Win Friends**. The best way to deal with enemies is to eliminate them. Make friends.

How do you do that? Don't nurse grievances or hold grudges. Don't hate. Such things don't pay. Turn the other cheek. Judge not, lest ye be judged. See from the other fellow's point of view. Now: do the right thing. (Wasn't that easy?)

Was that really three levels into one? Yes. 1) Turn worries into problems; 2) think it through; 3 do the right thing.

Carnegie runs the three together because the basic techniques are the same at each level: our habits, analytical methods, the practical steps we take. These are aspects of the same basic, simple, known-it-all-along truths. The Golden Rule — harmonious reciprocity — goes a long way toward stopping worry. It disciplines you to step back from yourself. It is also an analytical tool, because empathy — seeing from the other fellow's point of view — is a crucial source of facts you need to understand problem situations. (Why is this person not doing what I want?) Then, with the facts in, the proper response is probably a straightforward application of the Golden Rule. Do unto others as you would have them do to you. The customer is always right because I am always right.

The Golden Rule and the Sermon on the Mount aren't usually shelved with all those other bright, glossy sales and marketing pamphlets in the self-help and success sections. But for Carnegie these moral teachings amount to time-less techniques for closing (as the salesmen say.) Of course, they should not be seen as **mere** marketing gimmicks. Carnegie is not setting out to trivialize some of the deepest ethical wisdom the world's great religions and cultures and civilizations can provide. He's doing his best to move in the opposite direction. You basically have to spend your life selling yourself, if nothing else. Find some way to make salesmanship a rich, full, satisfying, career ethos. If this is life, philosophize it!

And please note: Carnegie isn't just giving advice for dealing with **other** difficult people. Some of the most difficult people are **me**. Techniques for interpersonal closing are techniques for intrapersonal closure.

Stop worrying and start living!

8

But isn't all this just utterly, perfectly ridiculous? Nobody thinks a statue of Carnegie gets to sit up there on the Great Sage shelf next to that bust of Socrates. (Maybe Valéry gets to go there? He kept getting nominated for the Nobel Prize, although he never won.) Successful self-help author, sure. Great Philosopher?

But what higher form of philosophy could there be than successful self-help? Yes, but there's a world of difference between helping yourself by selling a ton of books and **truly** being successful at 'self-helping' others (whatever you call it when people help people help themselves).

Are you saying "stop worrying and start living" is bad advice? Carnegie's books have nothing helpful to say on the subject?

Well, no… But pretty much only the sales and marketing people seem to like him much. Isn't that sort of a bad sign? Put it like this: to 'win friends' (that's Carnegie's game) is to treat **people** like **things**, like pawns. We say of a selfish personality: he's a **user**. Stay away from people like that! To teach someone to be more like that? That sounds like teaching bad people to be worse. To earn money selling books that make bad people worse sounds like one of the worst things you could do with your life. Dale Carnegie is a salesman. Salespeople are manipulative. They play on our emotions, mess with our heads, nudge us toward the shelf with the things **they** want us to buy. At best, this is annoying; at worst, enraging. What if everyone were like that?

Surely the fact that Carnegie is a user who teaches people to be users should be Carnegie's secret shame, not that he once liked logic.

But here comes Carnegie's predictable — blandly sensible, folksy — reply. Look here, friend! Nothing wrong with making friends! That doesn't mean molding them like clay in your hands. Of course it's an affair of emotion, not reason. (You want life to be an affair of pure reason?) If your dear wife asks whether she looks alright, and you think her dress is not so nice, but it's too late for her to change, the correct thing to say is 'dear, you look lovely!' That's not mind-control or disrespect. Complimenting your wife, on appropriate occasions, is a time-tested recipe for reproducibly pleasant results. Marital science in action!

But surely there's more to life than telling white lies in trivial social settings!

You think a happy marriage is a trivial setting? Making 'reciprocity' your watchword makes you some moral monster?

— Well … no.

What's the problem?

— That's it! You don't seem to see real problems! Social justice! Politics! Nothing wrong with being an agreeable, empathic person. But suppose two customers are in a heated argument. Are they **both** right, just because 'the customer is always right?' How can you say 'no!' when the time comes, if you only say 'yes' to everyone?

But Carnegie has a reply. Take these two fighting customers (if they interest you so much.) Either they are reasonable people, in which case we should emphasize the ways in which they are both potentially right. Or at least one isn't reasonable. If so, all the more reason not to bother trying to reason with him.

We should call the police, or the hospital, or just ask him to leave. Maybe you can't smooth the world's troubles away by making friends. But for sure you can't **refute** the world's troubles!

Now, I think, we are near the core of Carnegie's anti-argument outlook on life. Life is hard, but the formula for a good life, insofar as there is one, isn't intellectually difficult. People are people. Of course, saying it like that doesn't mean problems go away. But figuring out what you should do — all the figuring you can do — is mostly a matter of keeping in mind a few simple things everyone already knows but most forget just when it matters most.

Man is the animal who forgets what kind of an animal man is. We're so smart we're dumb like that. What about all the genuine technical problems, above and beyond that? Here an important qualification is necessary. If you have good people skills you can procure the technical assistance you need. On the other hand, if all you have is technical specialization in some area, that won't be sufficient. That area, whatever it is, isn't Life. But you've got your life to live! Conclusion: people skills are the only true master skills. They travel across all fields, applying equally in public and private. Everywhere you go, those at the top — those who are successful, happy — have these skills.

If specializing in Life is what philosophy aims at, the true philosophers are the 'people people' — which is to say, the salespeople.

9

I think we have pulled up the root of Carnegie's hostility to "logic and argumentation." He wouldn't object to contributions to any other technical field; wouldn't be ashamed of having thought of writing a chemistry textbook, for example. But logic and argumentation, unlike chemistry, seems to hold out the promise of **technical achievement that is also completely general.** Logic and argument is about everything, so if it breeds success, it breeds success at **everything**. This is a mistake. Good human relations skills — nothing else! — afford that sort of general leg-up. Logic's domain of use is narrower.

But don't you need logic and argumentation wherever you go? (Haven't we gone over this already?) Yes, but only an ordinary, healthy capacity for thinking through — nothing so fancy that you might need a book on the subject. True, you can be a persuasive fool and a failure, but those who are persuasive successes do not succeed through superfine capacity for logic-chopping, let alone through technical training in that sort of thing.

How do we **know** that? We know it because (write this down!) **we know that we already know everything we need to lead perfect lives**! But everything isn't perfect, is it? Look around! Ergo, we've got a leadership gap to fill, not a knowledge gap. We need to work on our persuasion skills — people skills.

But do we know this thing Dale Carnegie is sure we **know** — about knowing everything that we need to know, that is? Let me put it less confusingly (although it is educational to see the number of times you need to keep saying 'know' to gauge Carnegie's indifference to the value of knowledge.) Let me also remind you how we got off on this tangent. The puzzle was this: why doesn't anybody listen to Socrates? As Alcibiades says: at first everyone thinks his arguments look like ugly toys. As Adeimantus says: when Socrates refutes people, they feel it is just a game. They may be amused or annoyed, but it never crosses their minds to **change** their minds. Why not?

In part, the explanation must be the one Carnegie offers in the passage I quoted. People are proud, don't like to lose, don't like feeling forced. But that can't be the whole story. When people lose at chess they don't refuse to admit it, even if they don't like it. At least some of the rest of the story seems to have to do with other things Carnegie hints at as well. How could I (of all people!) be wrong — how could it all fall apart for me — at a basic conceptual level, when it comes my wise thoughts on **justice, virtue**, or **holiness**? It just doesn't seem possible that any mere mousetrap of an 'if you accept A and B you must give up C or D' technical combination could trap me (**me**, of all people!) where ethical questions are concerned. But why not?

Because **I already know it all**, at least right from wrong. There can't be intellectual surprises in this area. So the more devastating my dialectical defeat at Socrates' hands, the less plausible defeat seems, quite apart from my bruised pride.

10

Furthermore — here we make a significant, sudden shift: new idea strides onstage! — **no one knows about this stuff anyway**. The human mind isn't built for it, or maybe it's the world. Human affairs are too rough yet subtle — too complex, contextual and ... plain **practical** for any of these toy arguments to have force. The fact that Socrates acts as though it is possible to know it all, tidying up life like a geometrical diagram, shows he can't know a damn thing about it.

Where did this new thought come from, all of a sudden? **No one knows?** Is that supposed to follow from other stuff? — because it sounds as though it doesn't follow at all. Surely Plato/Socrates can't be wrong **both** because we already know it all about Life, **and** because no one really knows anything.

No, that doesn't sound quite right. Still, despite the fact that these thoughts don't seem to fit, they work together very effectively to preclude serious consideration of, so to speak, technical possibilities.

What does that mean? Technical matters are things I can be ignorant of and/or wrong about. There can be experts who know a lot better than I do, to whose judgment I am happy to defer, and even pay for the privilege. This could be anything from shoemaking to nuclear physics. But (to repeat): I can't be completely ignorant of, or completely wrong about, ethics — the meaning of life; basic questions of how I should live. Also, life problems never get solved to three significant decimal places. Conclusion: ethics can't be technical.

What does Plato think? Perhaps the opposite, all down the line. We certainly do **not** know enough to lead perfect lives. We might be capable of coming to know enough to lead perfect lives, at least better ones than we are leading — but only if we can bring ourselves to admit we don't know **yet**. And only if we can bring ourselves to admit that the move from ignorance to knowledge may very well be technical. Or, if that makes it sound too much like we need to build a machine: ethics may be crucially a matter of **thinking through**, using logic and argument — those things Carnegie is ashamed of — to look for potentially surprising answers to our questions about life, about everything.

Alcibiades marvels that Socrates is unlike anyone who came before. His arguments, too. And yet: maybe nothing else makes sense. Plato wants to urge this as at least a possible view, not just of his teacher but of ethics generally — of philosophy generally. Carnegie emphasizes the Golden Rule. Maybe it doesn't make much sense to hypothesize that the Golden Rule could be just plain wrong. Still, perhaps Golden Rule 1.0 is best regarded as a buggy beta. It might well need upgrading to Golden Rule 2.0, a more stable application — less liable to crash.

11

Why write philosophy as a cross between a play and a problem set with no answer key? My answer, in a nutshell, is that the dialogue form allows Plato to construct arguments (in the justification sense) while considering what arguments (in the fighting monkey sense) are like; how they go. How do these levels interact? What happens when (transcendent, angelic, robot-like) logic crash-lands onto primate anthropologic?

$- (P \& -P)$
$\& -p$

There may be no more serious question in all of philosophy.

The way to read Plato is, simply: take the arguments seriously, in the abstract logic and argumentation **and** the anthropological senses. But this advice isn't easy to follow. So answer instead: who do you agree with? Who do you trust? Plato or Dale Carnegie?

I don't mean to set up Carnegie as a straw man, as if obviously the great Plato must be the wise one and your job is to see that. Most people think more like Carnegie. Most people might be right. It's not as though Carnegie lacks for sensible-seeming things to say about dealing with difficult people and disciplining yourself to stop worrying in unhelpful ways. I also don't mean to set up Plato and Carnegie as though they are the only two philosophers who have ever lived. What is important to see is what a deep problem the likes of Carnegie poses for Plato. The Carnegies of the world may be what drives Plato to compose these odd hybrids of pure abstraction and human drama: **dialogues**. Plato wants to argue with (and exhibit what it is like to argue with) people who are not just skeptical about the merits of his arguments but are fundamentally — yet oddly intermittently — skeptical about the merits of argument itself. Yet inclined to argue!

12

Let's step back for a second look at that strange new thought that occurred a moment ago. Where did 'no one knows anything' pop up from, all of a sudden? Let me finish out this chapter by answering that question, which may help the reader think about who is more right, Plato or Carnegie.

Let's turn back to the point where the following objection was made to Carnegie: you don't seem to see **real** problems. 'Be agreeable' is good advice but doesn't, in itself, answer anything. 'Stop worrying, analyze, then do the right thing' is not a formula for figuring out what the right thing is. At best, you've cleared a space for thinking, but you haven't filled it. And you seem strangely hostile to any attempts to fill it, theoretically. Why is that?

What does an ethical problem look like, theoretically?

Problems in ethical theory are often made vivid, particularly in introduction to philosophy classes, as hypothetical dilemmas. To take a classic example (due originally to a philosopher named Philippa Foot):

> A trolley car is out of control. In its path are five people who will be killed unless you throw a switch, sending the trolley down a different track where, unfortunately, another person — but only one — is sure to be killed. What should you do?

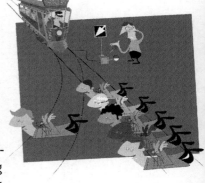

There is no Carnegiesque solution. Oh yes, it's a 'people problem', if you want to call it that; but not one that can be smoothed by people skills or salved by advice to avoid worry.

What factors are we forced to weigh and balance in such a case? On the one hand, it seems reasonable that the good of the many should outweigh the good of the few. So I should throw the switch. On the other hand, it seems categorically wrong to kill. Perhaps letting five die, doing nothing, is more permissible than actively killing one, even if the results are worse, absolutely? So I shouldn't throw the switch. But how can it be better to act in a way that produces worse results overall? So I should throw the switch. But how can I possibly have the right, and authority, to decide who lives and who dies? So I shouldn't throw the switch.

Theoretically, the 'you should count consequences and act to maximize the good' view is **consequentialism** (also called utilitarianism.) The alternative theoretical stance that you have (or might have) absolutely strict duties, perhaps including a duty not to kill, is known as **deontology** (from a Greek root that basically means **that which is binding**; hence, duty.)

So which theory is right?

That is the signal for the trolley car of ethical theory to leave the station! It rattles and puffs down the tracks — should/shouldn't/should/shouldn't. We don't know which track it will end up on. We hope it doesn't just go round and round forever.

But in any case, Carnegie has failed to catch the train of thought. He has nothing to contribute to ethical theory in this sense.

Shouldn't he have at least something to say?

Before hearing Carnegie's reply, let's push another objection against him. Carnegie obviously thinks the 'human engineering' skills he teaches are basically non-technical. That's what makes these skills so marvelously portable. For example, you can be the leader of a team of technicians without having to understand all that stuff yourself.

This is already problematic: how can you know better than a group of experts how to do their jobs unless you at least **know** how to do their jobs? But let's grant there might be some sense to the notion that leaders lead **people**. If you are heading up a team of engineers, constructing a bridge, you don't have to know how to build a bridge yourself, without having it fall down. You only have to know how to hold a team together, without it falling apart. You need to understand engineers, not engineering. There might even be some Socratic table-turning at this point: the secret of leadership is being wise in ignorance.

But aren't people complicated? Don't they have lots of twitchy, moving parts that easily get out of balance and proper alignment? Isn't an engineer who can build a bridge that won't fall down at least as complicated as the bridge he builds, only in a different way? So management — leadership — must be technical, since it's about a complex subject matter. And you, Mr. Manager-Leader, whichever it is: you are people, too! Mustn't management be **self**-management, in the first place, hence self-knowledge? Mustn't **that** be technical, given the complexity of the subject? Shouldn't we expect a lot of crucial logic and argumentation to come first about what parts make up a person, how they should interrelate and function? This **can't** be common sense. It's obviously **not obvious** how people work. You have a book titled **The Leader In You**. But there's a little scientist in me, too. I'm not **sure** I shouldn't be trying to grow him instead of the leader — or in addition.

Either Carnegie really has some theory about how people work, in which case he should argue for it. Or he doesn't, in which case it's hard to take him seriously as a practical expert on 'people skills', since he isn't obviously a qualified technical expert on people.

13

Let me give what I think would be the Dale Carnegie response to both challenges, which is really very simple.

These philosophers, with their toy train sets, toy people tied to toy tracks, and little toy switches you can throw! It's like they think philosophy should be a book entitled **How To Start Worrying Without Starting Living**.

Either you really have to throw switches like that or you don't. If you don't, it's a game. Play as you like, so long as you don't take it too seriously. But if you have to throw real switches, toys don't help. Of course we know life is full of dilemmas. In **Stop Worrying**, I discuss cases of military leaders called upon to make awful decisions. Here is Admiral Ernest J. King, of the US Navy, during World War II. "I have supplied the best men with the best equipment we have and have given them what seems to be the wisest mission. That is all I can do. If a ship has been sunk, I can't bring it up. If it is going to be sunk, I can't stop it. I can use my time much better working on tomorrow's problem than by fretting about yesterday's. Besides, if I let those things get me, I wouldn't last long" (6). **There's** the solution to your toy trolley problem. Do what seems wisest.

King, behind his desk, had to deal with any number of highly technical problems — equipment, intelligence, logistics, politics, and the enemy was no push-over either. Mostly he delegated technical problems to 'the best men', and rightly. Equally surely, he faced any number of ethical dilemmas: what should I do with these lives in my hands? That doesn't mean he faced, let alone attempted to solve, technical ethical problems.

Is it 'right' to send one ship on a suicide mission in the hopes of saving that convoy of five? That's harder even than the trolley problem because there are no pat, story-problem guarantees. You might lose all six.

If you pick up a book of academic moral theory, selling some consequentialist or deontological set of principles, some moral mathematics, you'll probably just doze off. The alternative is worse. You'll worry yourself sicker, when you might have done something useful. If you don't succeed in worrying yourself sicker, even with all that ethical theory weighing on your stomach, that just goes to show that these toy arguments are nothing even you yourself take too seriously. You might as well have worked the crossword puzzle, if you like word games so much.'

14

We can generalize this point and thereby respond to the second criticism as well. The way the admiral commands his ships is the way you should command **your** ship — that is to say, your soul. Carnegie opens **Stop Worrying** by quoting Sir William Osler (founder, Johns Hopkins School of Medicine; Regius Professor at Oxford; knighted by the King of England; subject of a 1466 page biography.) What words did Osler live by? "Our main business is not to see what lies dimly at a distance, but to do what lies clearly at hand." That's Thomas Carlyle. Carnegie proceeds to quote Osler himself from a speech delivered before a crowd of young male aristocrats who would one day be prominent public men and leaders of the **polis** — that is, Yale undergraduates. Osler tells them what they need to know to be as successful as he has been. He begins by confessing, cheerfully, that he has brains of "no special quality," of "only the most mediocre character." Scratch **that** bright idea about how to get ahead!

What is Osler's secret? He calls upon his experience crossing the Atlantic in a magnificent ocean liner. The captain has a control panel with buttons that seal sections of the ship off from others, in case of flood. Osler turns this into what we might call (in a Platonic mood) The Myth of Ship and Soul:

> Now each one of you is a much more marvelous organization than the great liner, and bound on a longer voyage. What I urge is that you so learn to control the machinery as to live in 'day-tight compartments' as the most certain way to ensure safety on the voyage. Get on the bridge, and see that at least the great bulkheads are in working order. Touch a button and hear, at every level of your life, the iron doors shutting out the Past — the dead yesterdays. Touch another and shut off, with a metal curtain, the Future — the unborn tomorrows. Then you are safe — safe for today! ... Shut off the past! Let the dead past bury its dead ... Shut out the yesterdays which have lighted fools the way to dusty death ... The load of tomorrow, added to that of yesterday, carried today, makes the strongest falter. Shut off the future as tightly as the past ... The future is today ... There is no tomorrow. The day of man's salvation is now. Waste of energy, mental distress, nervous worries dog the steps of a man who is anxious about the future ... Shut closed, then, the great fore and aft bulkheads, and prepare to cultivate the habit of a life of 'day-tight compartments'. (4)

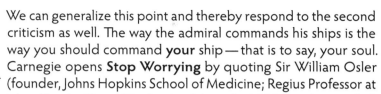

This is a mixed metaphor, but richly mixed. The ship is your life and your person and your world. You have to avoid looking too far outside yourself — forward or back in time, presumably not too far around you in space either. No more than necessary. But you also have to avoid prodding too deeply **inside**.

Where Socrates teaches that the unexamined life is not worth living, Osler teaches that the examined life is practically unlivable. Where Plato proposes that philosophy means broad analysis of the whole **polis** — the whole political, social order — complemented by rational examination of all parts of the soul, the better to manage and harmonize self and society, Osler teaches that this sort of examination is probably unmanageable therefore positively hazardous. You are better off **not** knowing what is sloshing around in the bilge of your soul. You probably couldn't do much about it.

So the only switch you should worry about in the trolley case is the one that keeps you from feeling bad about whichever switch you throw?

That's **it**?

Is Osler selling a glib, shallow, know-nothing philosophy?

In case it isn't obvious, I don't think it is so **obviously** bad. Osler, like many an eminent medical man before him, going back to the ancient Greeks, is a skeptic. That means he thinks the deepest wisdom consists in realizing that our knowledge is limited, and appreciating those limits, respecting and living within them. Really **knowing** you don't know is important information (lack-of-news you can use!) This **is** a Socratic view in its way. **Know yourself**, advises Socrates. Plato wants us to achieve that by escaping from the Cave. Osler and Carnegie want us to achieve that by getting us to embrace our natures as natural-born troglodytes — day-tight compartment dwellers.

Doing so has at least two advantages. First, if it really is impossible for us to leave the Cave, because that would mean becoming different than we essentially are, knowledge-wise, then trying is a waste of energy. Second, the cave-dweller who sees he is in the Cave has the advantage over his fellows. Here again, this sounds like living a life of fooling our fellow cave-dwellers. And it may be. But it needn't be. At any rate, it isn't **just** about that.

We've turned Carnegie around a few times already. Here we go, one last go-round.

15

I quoted this earlier: "You and I don't need to be told anything new … Our trouble is not ignorance, but inaction." That makes it sound as though that is a philosophy of action, as opposed to thinking. But in a sense the opposite is the case. When asked "what is the biggest lesson you have ever learned," Carnegie's answer is as follows:

> By far the most vital lesson I have ever learned is the importance of what we think. If I knew what you think, I would know what you are. Our thoughts make us what we are. Our mental attitude is the X factor that determines our fate. (113)

There's more to the life of the mind than knowledge; there's belief.

There is appearance and reality, and the important thing is to achieve knowledge — of appearance.

Notice how, in an odd way, we are reintroducing that strange division we met with in Plato's Cave. Somehow the objects of belief and the objects of knowledge aren't even the same objects. You can't study the way things are, but you can study how they seem. You can gauge what effect the show is having on the audience. Carnegie titles this chapter of his book "eight words that can transform your life." He quotes them from the Roman stoic philosopher, Marcus Aurelius: "Our life is what our thoughts make it." If we think happy thoughts, we will be happy. If we think failure, we will fail. He quotes Norman Vincent Peale: "You are not what you think you are; but what you **think**, you are." He then anticipates the objection that this is absurdly optimistic, as if wishing makes it so. He replies that he knows this doesn't make life easy. Still, a positive attitude is the single most valuable character trait you can cultivate. He goes so far as to quote, approvingly, Mary Baker Eddy, founder of Christian Science: "I gained the scientific certainty that all causation was Mind, and every effect a mental phenomenon."

16

At this point we have left common sense a good distance behind us (but somehow that always happens when you try to say what common sense comes to.) In the process of trying to move as far away as we can from the Platonic idea that we need to solve for X

in some realm of Mind, we seem to have arrived back **at** the view that we are stuck in an X-factor realm of Mind. Let's be ancient Greek about it. Let X = Xenophanes, a 6th Century BCE poet and thinker, best known as a critic of popular religion. He remarks that, for some strange reason, the Greeks think the gods look and dress like Greeks, whereas Ethiopians think they look like Ethiopians. The Thracians imagine them looking and talking rather like Thracians.

Xenophanes concludes: if horses and oxen had hands and could draw, they would represent the gods as looking like horses and oxen. As the sophist Protagoras puts it: "Man is the measure of all things."

If so, people skills are the **practical** measure of all things. Things that matter to us, anyway.

If, on the other hand, you were to take mathematics for the measure of all things — of ethics, say, or religion — you would only succeed in depriving yourself of self-knowledge (the very thing you were most concerned to acquire!) You won't see your own face in the mirror of your every thought. But only because you have blinded yourself! In seeking to abstract away, purely, from the human element, you only make ethics a pure game. Verbal coins are not genuine currency unless stamped with a human face.

So what are human faces like?

Each is different, and they have many moods and expressions. Plato often strikes readers as insensitive to the anthropocentric, relative, situational, case-by-case character of ethical problems. Philosophy is about Life! Life is a grey business. There is a reason Aristophanes titles his play about Socrates **The Clouds**. In the play, the Clouds are a chorus of goddesses, but **you** know what clouds are like: everyone sees something different. (That one looks like a cow, no, a fish, no, a man in profile!) Nothing stands still. But if this is the foundation of our philosophy, something else follows. To be Xenophanic about ethics is to be a Heraclitean. Since "man is the measure of all things," and men are always at odds, changeable, changing their minds, "opposites are always combining." In terms of Carnegie's formulation: if the thing you know about is **belief**, then the objects of your knowledge will be contradictory. They don't make sense, and they aren't really going to. So logic and argument are not much use.

But why think Plato misses this? Isn't the challenge posed by this view a big part of what the dialogues are about? Aren't they attempts to portray the dynamic fluidity of the drama of human thinking? Plato nods to the

Protagoras point in Book 5 of **Republic**: beautiful objects are ugly — from different perspectives, to different viewers. Holy things are also unholy. Just things also unjust — under different circumstances, from different points of view. Euthyphro says it is holy to prosecute his own father. But, by the terms of his definition, it is holy **and** unholy to do so. Cephalus (you'll meet him in **Republic**) says it is just to speak truth and pay your debts. But, Socrates points out, if it is a case of a friend who has gone mad, it wouldn't be just to give back the weapons he left with you. You should lie; say you don't have them any more, for his own good. So telling the truth is both just and unjust. Judgments of ethics are relational, relative, situational, perspectival — human.

Nothing appears to us as good at all unless it is part of this great but changeable river of human life. Might as well go with the flow. Plato doesn't buy it, but he gets why this would seem like an attractive, plausible view.

17

But is 'go with the flow' satisfactory? Take the admiral again: it is certainly implausible that some One True Solution can preserve him from ever doing the wrong thing. Still, it would be going too far the other way to deny he faces hard ethical dilemmas. The following argument is surely no good. P1: If there's no real solution, it can't be a problem. P2: There's no real solution. C: This admiral's got no problems! (He just needs to stop worrying!)

No, the admiral surely has to wrestle, painfully, with consequentialism vs. deontology, not necessarily under those seminar room headings, but in **some** way. He has to achieve good consequences; he probably thinks there are other things he must and can't do. Waging war itself needs to be justifiable or every individual decision about how to wage it might go down with the whole ship. There is no way wielding the power of life and death can fail to be ethically problematic. How can a Carnegiesque style of thinking admit this, while holding out against the Platonic view that real problems need real, rational (if not seminar-style) solutions? Let's try a different angle.

Confronted with any moderately complex ethical scenario, forced to justify a course of action in the most general terms, I can probably be convicted of inconsistency. I have my reasons, my rules. But in tough cases, and even in apparently easy ones, these principles of mine have a habit of implying things I am unwilling to accept — at which point I usually start sweeping under the rug. Consider a remark by John Stuart Mill, from Chapter 1 of his book, **On Liberty**:

> The peculiarity of the evidence of mathematical truths is, that all the argument is on one side. There are no objections, and no answers to objections. But on every subject on which difference of opinion is possible, the truth depends on a balance to be struck between two sets of conflicting reasons.

What sorts of other subjects would these be? Mill says: "Morals, religion, politics, social relations and the business of life." In **Euthyphro**, Socrates asks the title character what sorts of things even the gods fight about, and suggests a similar answer: "justice and injustice, beauty and ugliness, good and bad" (7d). Probably I should be ready to fight with even myself about this sort of stuff.

But now let us muster a bit of Platonic skepticism. "Balance of conflicting reasons" is just a polite way of saying **contradiction**. Combinations of opposites are contradictions; contradictions can't be true. So it **can't** be the case that the truth depends on a balance of conflicting reasons. What can't be true can't be real. This "business of life", at least as we live it, must be a kind of illusion. Not that there is no such thing as right, justice or religion! But what these really are is going to be different — different in **kind** — from what Mill takes them to be. Because something that necessarily **doesn't** make sense is different in kind from something that necessarily **does** make sense. Beneath the Heraclitean flux of Millian "conflicting reasons" there **must** be something solid. The fact that men like Carnegie and the admiral have an evident psychological need to build day-tight compartments shows they **feel** it.

'Merrily, merrily, life is but a dream' lasts until something **real** has punched through your hull below the waterline. Carnegie-style advice is good not because Plato is wrong but in case he's right. The unexamined course is not worth sailing. Not if you value your life.

In the last chapter I presented a metaphysically maximalist Platonism that involves strange commitments: Platonic forms. But perhaps there is a minimalist Platonism that is more negative — more Socratic? Plato just says: things have to make sense. If they don't, that means we're out of touch with reality, hence in danger of reality getting in touch with us, painfully. Applying this to ethics: either there is a **rational** method for resolving conflicting 'reasons' or there isn't. If there **is**, there can be no conflict, ultimately. If there **isn't**, then what is the point of reasoning about ethics or the business of life at all? There is no point even to 'balancing reasons' if the notion of balance isn't, at bottom, reasonable. This is just code for: say what you want.

To be sure, sometimes you are splitting the difference just to get the other side to come to the table. Negotiation isn't about absolute right or wrong, it's about what people will say 'yes' to. Carnegie is the King of Yes, so we can understand Mill's point in a Carnegiesque spirit. On the other hand, if you think it **ever** makes sense to argue about right and wrong, not as haggling, but because you want or need to figure out what the right thing to do **is**, then reflexively splitting the difference and muddling through can't be automatically right.

Can it? Reasoning about what I should think or do is not just a matter of haggling with **myself** about what I'm actually willing to think or do. Is it?

In thinking through ethical problems, we think through the implications of our beliefs. If we see an implication that doesn't make sense, we should take that as a sign that there is some submerged error in the sea of our mind. But if, in the end, not making sense is not an objection — it just comes down to 'balancing' — then in what sense can I reason about what I should do at all? What am I even **doing** when I reason about what to do, if I am allowed to contradict myself?

18

This chapter is supposed to be about how to read Plato. I said at the start of Chapter 1 that these dialogues are like a cross between a play and a problem set with no answer key. I think I have said enough about puppet theater by this point. In what sense could these dialogues be like problem sets?

We shouldn't neglect the obvious possibility: they are intended to be worked through by students. Speaking of Plato's Academy, what was it like? To a surprising extent, we have no idea. The author of rather a good book on the subject makes this basic point and remarks that, in the absence of reliable information, the mind plays its usual tricks.[3]

The English have figured out Plato's academy must have been like a proper English school. The French know it must have been rather French in spirit, and the Germans that it must have been impressively Germanic. And if oxen and horses had homework to do, they would no doubt have figured out that Plato's Academy was the original Cow College.

We have a few stories about Plato's Academy, passed down the centuries. So they say, at the door was an inscription, 'no non-geometers allowed'. A math prerequisite for higher education admissions is not so strange. Maybe this was just a way of saying: no non-arguers allowed. If you enter, you will be required to show your work, the steps leading to your conclusions.

That said, Plato **does** seem to over-value mathematics as a model. In our readings this is particularly clear in **Meno**, in which Socrates seems simply to assume in passing (85d) that **all** learning will be like the geometry lesson he conducts. There are also — though our ears don't hear them today — religious echoes in this formula. At the threshold of a sacred site, in Plato's day, you might read, 'let no unclean/unjust/uninitiated person enter.'

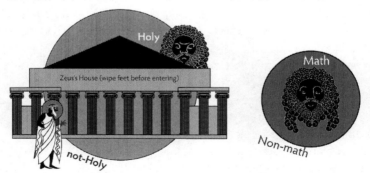

3   Cherniss, Harold F., **The Riddle of the Early Academy** (New York , Russell & Russell, 1962), pp. 61-2.

We'll hear more about this when we get to **Euthyphro**. (The title character is worried dad has dirty hands.) But this only makes the 'no non-geometers' exclusion peculiar in a different way, by putting geometry on the same footing as religion and ethics, as if abstract proofs could be the source of the sorts of values and guidance people think religion and righteousness should provide.

Who thinks the purity of geometry could be **personally** purifying?

Let's combine this concern with another the reader may have been nurturing for some time. In section 10, I suggested, off-handedly, that maybe we need to upgrade from Golden Rule 1.0, which may be buggy and crash-prone, to the more stable platform of Golden Rule 2.0. But this sounds more like mockery than a sketch of a plausible program. How could 'do unto others as you would have them do to you' be buggy? It's so simple and obvious. Bugs hide in software that is maybe millions of lines of code long. There they have a place to hide.

But even one line can have thousands or millions of implications. Who knows what odd behaviors lurk in that undiscovered country? Also, there is a non-trivial question as to which is preferable, the Golden or instead the so-called Silver Rule: 'do **not** do unto others as you would **not** have them do to you.' Do you see how that might have quite different implications?

I could also point out that the Golden Rule is ambiguous. It articulates an impersonal value (perhaps expressible as an abstract right of all people to equal moral consideration.) It is also a compressed piece of self-interested practical advice: it's unwise to punch people in the nose because they are likely to react the way **you** would react if **you** were punched in the nose. That is wisdom even an immoralist — someone who doesn't care about right and wrong — can fully appreciate (assuming only that he dislikes being punched back.) So does the Golden Rule appeal to my self-interest or to my sense of impersonal duty? Both! (That's what makes it so golden. But gold isn't clear.) Does self-interest **always** track ethical duty, and vice versa? This issue will be explored in Plato's **Republic**, in particular.

Let me offer some final pictures that may serve to express the difference between Carnegie's and Plato's general approaches.

Do you see that negative space between the facing figures? Let's hope this effect produced by two people facing off (exchanging, arguing, persuading) is harmonious and balanced, because — to the extent that we are like these figures — that negative space comes to quite a lot: society, culture, politics, economics, war and peace. The world, in short.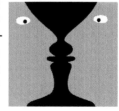

Carnegie more or less leaves all that to take care of itself, apart from incidental expressions of optimism that prudence and ethics go together. His advice doesn't extend into that space between. He tells you what the other guy is probably like (he's pretty much like you) hence what you should do to get what you want. He doesn't theorize what society should be like, much less tell you how to build an ideal republic. Maybe Carnegie is a bit like Socrates at least to this extent: his negative method is preoccupied with care of the self. But Plato is more inclined to theorize that space in a positive way. Can we represent what an ideal harmony between people would look like, rather than letting a practical sense of what people are like negatively define our sense of the shape of what goes between?

What is the best — as opposed to most prudent, given how things actually are — way to live? What would an ideal politics, culture, society be like? This is getting pretty Big Picture.

What does it have to do with what Plato's Academy might or might not have been like? In section 3 I remarked that we don't really have a term for the activity of 'practicing brightness'; that is, going around constantly working out what's what, clarifying, thinking through. We have 'being argumentative', which means being disagreeable. But we actually do have a more positive term. We have 'doing science'. Some scholars think Plato's academy was, in effect, the first scientific institute, with specialists working on problems and projects in mathematics and astronomy, perhaps other subjects. Whether this was so (we truly do not know), let a (cartoonish) image of science as the impersonal, potentially collaborative quest for truth — for knowledge of things that will make everyone's lives better — be a first sketch of a positive thing to fill that negative space.

Carnegie speaks well of scientists and has no doubt that science is real and valuable. But his ethics generates a blind-spot for it — for the possibility of it. Which gets us back to Golden Rule 2.0. We may not imagine philosophers as scientists in white coats, solving ethical equations to three significant digits. But could there be a better, more Platonic way for even Carnegie to get what he wants: better picture of harmony and the good life? Is it possible to sketch what ideal human social order would be like, without baiting-and-switching that question for different ones, i.e. how best to aim at what **I** want, given that everyone is elbowing each other in my vicinity? If **how should I live?** is a real question, admitting of sensible answers, then **how should everyone live?** should have an answer, too. A rational answer. That is to say, an answer that makes sense.

19

Having talked down Plato's Theory of Forms at the end of Chapter 3, let me conclude Chapter 4 by talking up the good of these dialogues, on the grounds of their self-contradictory qualities. Many readers — I would include myself in this group — prefer the earlier, more Socratic dialogues, in large part because we are more drawn to Plato's questions than his answers. Alcibiades' parable of the Silenus statue can get turned inside out. We like to give the radiant, Golden God of Western Philosophy, Plato, a good crack, to get at that satyr-faced plaster saint of critical thinking he hides inside.

But there is more. 'All of Western philosophy is just footnotes to Plato.' The danger in a line like that is that it sounds like one of those things people say to be friendly, before they get started, get serious. You stand before the monument politely. In such a mood, we may not consider that it might be **true**.

A. N. Whitehead (author of the 'footnotes' quip) adds that one of the secrets of Plato's success is he makes a point of 'writing out all the heresies in advance'. That's very true! Plato writes about everything: metaphysics, epistemology, ethics, politics, art, science, religion, economics, culture, education, technology, mathematics, logic, psychology. More: he considers all these topics from a variety of angles. He gives us Socrates on trial, declaring the unexamined life is not worth living. He gives us two blueprints for Utopia, both authoritarian. Plato is the first spokesman of free speech **and** censorship. He writes movingly of the value of truth. He is a dutiful servant of **logos**. Then he tells myths and advocates 'noble lies'. He is a rationalist yet a mystic. He strikes readers as crude. His arguments seem like toys. His characters are not quite life-like. Then he turns around and displays astonishing shrewdness and delicate verbal artistry. His feet are on the ground. He's just lighter on them than he looks. He's serious, yet a comedian. Perhaps one of his most impressive achievements of breadth is to be a complete generalist and also one of world's first narrow-minded academic specialists. (Think of the skill it takes to pull **that** contradiction off.) I don't think there is any point denying that many of Plato's arguments are plain bad. As his pupil Aristotle says: Plato is dear, but truth is dearer. (They fought, those two.) But some of Plato's arguments really are as subtle and sophisticated as his interpreters obviously want them to be (hence keep finding them to be.)

If, like Mill, you think the truth about 'the business of life' will always be a balance of conflicting reasons, not some pure, simple, final thing, be aware that Plato is keenly aware of your reasons. But he thinks the opposite. (Don't you think the opposite, too? Sometimes?)

Chapter 5   Euthyphro:
                                    Thinking Straight,
                                    Thinking in Circles

1

PHILOSOPHICALLY, PLATO'S **Euthyphro** appears to consist of a series of failures by the title character to answer one of Socrates' signature **what is X?**-style questions. In this case, **what is holiness?** But let's start more practically.

Plato's **Euthyphro** is about a pending court case — two, actually. Socrates and Euthyphro meet because they both have business with the **archon basileus**. (I explain who this official is in section 13.) But mostly the dialogue focuses on the ethical implications of the title character's deter-mination to prosecute his father for murder. Euthyphro sum-marizes what he takes to be the essential facts of the case: on their family farm a drunken servant assaulted and killed a slave. Euthyphro's father sent a messenger to Athens to get religious advice about what to do. Meanwhile, the servant was bound and thrown in a ditch, where he died of exposure. Euthyphro takes his father to be responsible for the man's death (3e-4e).

This seems bound to get complicated, despite Euthyphro's insistence that the matter is straightforward. But the dialogue is not about forensic inves-tigation or criminal intentions. (What **was** dad trying to do?) The dialogue isn't even really about what should happen to the father now. The down-to-earth question, from which the philosophy takes flight, is: what should Euthyphro do about it? Of course 'do about it' depends on **it**, so all that other business comes right back. But the question that sends Socrates and Euthyphro down their **what is X?** path seems largely independent of all that.

Euthyphro insists that his father is guilty but is also standing up for a procedural principle (one wishes he were clearer about this.) If there is probable cause (as we might say) to think a man caused another's death, wrongfully, a trial should be held. If he did wrong, he should be punished. If not, his name will be cleared. The demand that the justice system handle such cases is independent of specific determinations of guilt or innocence. On the other side, we find Euthyphro's family insisting the father is innocent,

but also standing up for a different procedural point. Even if the father were **manifestly** guilty, it would not be Euthyphro's place to prosecute.

So guilt is disputed but is not the crux of the dispute.

So what **is** it? What are Euthyphro and his family fighting about?

2

Let me add a bit of biography and report a literary coincidence. Euthyphro was, it would seem, a real person. In another dialogue, **Cratylus**, set years earlier, Socrates refers to 'the great Euthyphro', apparently a self-styled expert on religious etymologies. He sees meaning in the names of the gods. ('Great' would seem ironic, since what Socrates is doing at this point in **Cratylus** is offering what he himself clearly knows are far-fetched etymologies.) So let's take a page from Euthyphro's book. Let's over-interpret his name. The primary sense of the root — **euthu** — is **straight**, either horizontally or vertically. It can also mean straight in a temporal or proximal sense: straightaway, direct. Add '**phron**', from **phronēsis**, which is **wisdom**. **Euthyphron** means **straight-thinker**; by extension, **right-minded**.

Now, the coincidence. Confucius' **Analects** contains a famous passage: "The Governor of She said to Confucius, 'In our village we have one Straight Body. When his father stole a sheep, he the son gave evidence against him.' Confucius answered, 'In our village those who are straight are quite different. Fathers cover up for their sons, and sons cover up for their fathers. In such behaviour is straightness to be found as a matter of course.'"[1] In another translation the son is 'nicknamed Upright-Kung'. So we have two straight-up guys — straight mind, straight body — prosecuting their own fathers. Plato and Confucius have independently arrived at the conclusion that this is an important kind of case. So what's the common denominator of a stolen sheep and a dead servant in a ditch?

3

We are going to have to abstract away from the bloody, woolly details to something more general and universal. Suppose you meet a strange person who subscribes to a moral theory expressible in terms of three principles:

1   **Confucius: The Analects**, 2nd ed., trans. D.C. Lau (Chinese University Press, 2000), XIII.18, p. 127.

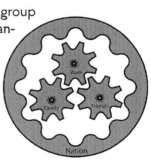

1) In any dispute, side with anyone who is within 10 meters of you.
2) If no one is within 10 meters of you, side with anyone within 20 meters.
3) Take no sides in disputes involving parties all of whom are at least 30 meters from you.

There are three problems with this odd view:

It is potentially **incomplete**. There are things you might need to know that it doesn't tell you. What about time and change? People move. Am I supposed to switch sides or once I have settled do I stick where I am?

It is potentially **inconsistent**. Suppose both parties are within 10 meters of me. What am I supposed to do? Take **both** sides?

It is **crazy**.

The thing to do in a dispute is take the **right** side. Spatial proximity to me is not a reliable index of right and wrong. It's not even a half-decent rule of thumb. (Nothing special about this one spot of earth I'm holding down.) To subscribe to any form of this theory would be absurd, even if you patched up 1 and 2 to the point where the game was playable, which it does not appear to be as it stands.

And yet: we all think like this very strange person. So we must all be crazy. We decide **what should I do?** in (we're going to need a name for a big class of cases) 'circular' style. When questions of right and wrong arise, we side with those in **our** circle; with those closer, not necessarily in space, but along more social axes. We think we owe family more than we owe friends and neighbors. We think we owe fellow citizens more than citizens of other countries. In anthropological terms, we side with our in-group against any out-group. Family, nation, race, economic class, religion, tribe, clan, club, party, neighborhood, team, association, school. Family values is a broad category.

Up to a point we may be able to impose concentric tidiness. But life is complicated. If my mom is fighting with dad, whose side do I take? At some point we are likely to find ourselves wondering which group commands our primary loyalty. The philosopher Jean-Paul Sartre considers the case of the son who wants to go fight for the French resistance, who knows this will mean neglecting his aged mother. The novelist E.M. Forster declares: "If I had to choose between betraying my country and betraying my friend, I hope I should have the guts to betray my country." Maybe

you hope you would have the guts to betray your friend. Opinions differ, but the style is the same. Circles **matter**.

These examples make it all sound tragic and life-wrenching, which it may be. But in little ways these problems crop up everyday. They complicate office politics, start fights between friends, lead to uncomfortable silences around the dinner table.

Let me generalize the pattern one circle further — in, that is. The one closest to me is: **me**. **I owe it to myself** to be self-interested. 'Egoism' is the standard name for this view. It may look like the very opposite of group loyalty but, in a sense, is just an instance: tribalism for a tribe of **one**.

In **Republic**, Book 1, Socrates argues with Thrasymachus, who advocates pure egoism, so we will be hearing more about this view. For now, let me simply note that adding this possibility fits many more familiar types of ethical dilemma into this circular template.

I want to do one thing. My family/friends/boss wants me to do something else. Which circle commands my true loyalty?

If that sounds hard to decide, what's the alternative?

Thinking … straight?

An upright person sets personal ties aside. Good judgment is impartial. A man has been killed. "It is ridiculous, Socrates, that you think it makes a difference whether the victim is a stranger or a relative" (4b).

Euthyphro doesn't do much to develop this. But it sounds good as it stands. The great Greek orator Demosthenes asks: "what should we all most earnestly pray shall not come to pass, and in all laws what end is most earnestly sought?" He gives a simple answer: "That people may not kill one another" (D.20.157-8).

"that people may not kill one another."

Impersonal, sure; but that sounds good in this connection. Justice is blind, after all, not because she doesn't know the relevant facts of the case but because she doesn't let herself see any irrelevant facts. She doesn't

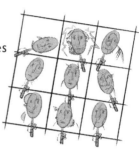

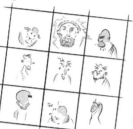

Relevant Facts
Relevant Facts
friends family nation
race co-worker

see father, mother, friend. She sees, for example, one who has killed another.

Killing **anyone** is **bad**.

On the other hand, sometimes killing is **justified**. That's relevant!

So what is justice?

Maybe we can't say, but it seems like its portrait won't be a family portrait of **my** family. It will be a picture of everyone — but in which everyone appears to be no one in particular. (Does that look about right?)

4

Let's hear a rebuttal. That **some** circular schemes are silly or ethically insane does not prove **all** such schemes are. Impartiality isn't everything. As Confucius says, uprightness may be a matter of partiality. Ethics is a function of attachments to family, friends, community, country. These ties that bind are the very things that make life meaningful. Justice cannot mean cutting all such ties. Abstracting up and away into an imaginary ideal world in which everyone is no one in particular is idiocy, not insight. Treating parents or children as if they were 'equal' — if that means regarding them as no different than strangers — would be morally monstrous. You **aren't** everyone. You're **you**. Surely there is no more relevant consideration, for purposes of answering **what should I do?** than **who am I?**

Maybe it has occurred to you that you aren't prepared to give up either of these ways of thinking. You want judges to be **impartial** in court; children to be **partial** to parents at home (and vice versa.) It can't be a matter of purging either of these ways of thinking. Rather, they must be combined. But you see the problem. Superimpose a straight grid on a set of concentric circles. Looks like a great way to get your wires crossed.

Be it noted: my metaphors of straight and circular
are not really views at all. A number of different
theories or views, any number of justifications for
them, could be 'straight' or 'circular', maybe both,
depending how you look at it. I've dropped a few
hints about likely arguments, but the point of the
schematic cartooning is not to guide your life, let
alone ground your reasoning, but to give you an intuitive sense of a characteristic type of difficulty that promises to crop up in all sorts of contexts. The
advantage of 'circles vs. straight', so far, is not how much but how **little** it says.
To repeat: we have two pictures we like. They aren't going to fit together
coherently. We don't really know what it means if they don't fit. Probably:
trouble. What to do? What to think?

But this much is clear. **Circles vs. straight** is why Plato writes about a dead
man in a ditch; why Confucius is worried about a stolen sheep. Or maybe:
why Plato makes a point of **not** writing much about a dead man in a ditch.
Instead, he spins us round and round **what is holy?** Euthyphro stumps for a
straight-up straight view. Socrates mock-innocently tosses this straight man
curve after curve. Is that because he's trying to convert him to the circle view?
He doesn't say so. "Hercules! I imagine, Euthyphro, most men don't know
how things ought to be. I don't think just anyone would be able to do what
you are doing. This is a job for one far advanced in wisdom!" (4a). Does the
dialogue make such advances?

5

In Chapter 4 I invited you to imagine a friend at your door, seeking advice.
'I think dad may have murdered someone. What should I do?' Obviously
you would sit down with your friend, pull down the dictionary, and attempt
to build up a definition of 'holiness'.

No, **not** obviously. Obviously **not**. But if no one in their right mind turns
first to the dictionary for advice about life, why presume that answering some
Socratic-style **what is X?** question will help Euthyphro figure out what to do
with his life? If your car won't start, you need a mechanic not a dictionary
entry for 'car'. It seems strange to assume ethics will be more definition-based,
even if we grant the potential existence of ethical expertise.

Second, why this specific X? The Greek is **hosion**, translated **holy** or
pious. Wouldn't it make as much sense, maybe more, to ask what is right or
just or even just legal? It is unsurprising that Euthyphro—a **mantis** (no, not
a bug; see section 16)—is quick to suggest religious answers to ethical and

even legal questions. Certainly it isn't unusual for people to think their religion informs their ethics. Still, isn't it assuming a lot, putting all the weight on holiness in this case?

We can answer the first question at least to some extent by diving right in. The second will have to wait, but eventually the dialogue implies an answer, even if it is not stated in so many words. (Yes, it probably would have made more sense to ask one of those other questions instead, or in addition.)

6

How does Euthyphro **know** he is right and everyone else is wrong? The specific ethical issue concerns an alleged duty of filial piety. Prosecute dad or not? Euthyphro says he knows he is right because he understands what piety is all about. He is a holy man.

So we are, from the start, on the semantic track we stay on. It's a religious question because its about how to relate to father figures claiming authority.

In English a linguistic accident makes it easy to migrate from family feud into theology without noticing how we got here. Ask anyone what piety is all about and they will say: religion. But the piety in 'filial piety' is not religious. We don't think it is important to respect parents because they are **gods**. (Do we?) Why **do** we call it 'filial piety'? Because 'piety' once meant **duty**. The term is a time-capsule, preserving ancient notions of how far duty extends: to god(s) and kin. Ancient practices of ancestor worship made it easy to conflate parents and gods in ways that seem extreme to modern minds; even modern religious minds; even the modern minds of religious people who really respect their parents and think of God as a father-figure.

In response to Socrates, Euthyphro says what he is doing, and things like what he is doing, are holy. In prosecuting his father for wrong-doing, he is like Zeus, who punished his father, forcing him to cough up five unjustly swallowed siblings. (Rather harsh to compare your own dear dad to Kronos!)

Socrates objects that a few examples do not a definition make. But first he makes a slightly different point, having to do with the wild, violent character of the myth:

So you believe that the gods really go to war with one
another, that there are hateful rivalries and battles between
them, and other things of this sort, like the ones narrated
by the poets, or represented in varied ways by our fine
artists — particularly upon the robe that is carried up to
the Acropolis during the great Panathenaic festival, which
is embroidered with all these sorts of designs? Should we
agree these things are literally true, Euthyphro? (6b-c)

Robe carried up to the Acropolis?

A bit of background: the highlight of the Panathenaic festival — **the** major
religious event in Athens — was a procession. An embroidered **peplos** was
carried up the Panathenaic Way on its way to the temple.

The parade will pass within a few meters of the spot where Euthyphro and
Socrates are now sitting, in fact.[2] A **peplos** is a one-piece, belted robe worn
by women. Possibly there were two different festival robes: a more or less
regular-sized one for the yearly festival, suitable for dressing a certain statue
of Athena. And a big one — big as a sail, hung from the mast of an actual
trireme rolled along the road. This would have been for the greater festival,
celebrated only every fourth year, which attracted visitors from all over the
Greek world. No fewer than three other Platonic dialogues are incidentally
framed by the Panathenaic festival, which gives some sense of how civically
significant this event was (or how much it meant to Plato.) The title character
of **Ion** has come to compete in the music competition. In **Parmenides** the
title character is in town for the festival. The debates in **Timaeus** take place
during the festival.

Getting back to the peplos: it will be embroidered with depictions of
gigantomachy, war between the gods and giants. What's the story?

2   An excellent source is Jenifer Neils (ed.), **Goddess and Polis: The Pana-
     thenaic Festival in Ancient Athens** (Princeton University Press, 1993).

The giants — vaguely Thracian, barbarian lot — start lobbing boulders and torches up Olympus, protesting against the Olympian overthrow of the Titans, their kin. (So this story is tied into the whole Zeus-punishes-Kronos narrative: divine intergenerational strife.) The gods need Hercules' help, due to a peculiar rule that these giants can only be killed by a mortal. Hercules is hampered by the fact that the giant's leader springs back up if killed on his own land, so Hercules has to drag him across the border before clubbing him properly. (Arbitrary rules about spatial proximity again!) The Fates themselves — who you might think would watch from the sidelines — get in the mix, swinging pestles, cracking giant skulls. Not the least dramatic tactical contribution is made by Athena, who defeats Enkelados by throwing Sicily on him. Yes, **that** Sicily. (I'll bet she had the advantage of surprise!)

By some accounts, Enkelados is the spirit still grumbling beneath Aetna, the volcano. (Others say that is Typhon, the hundred-headed one. Or Briareos, the hundred-handed one. And it was Zeus who buried ... whoever it was. Heads, hands? Who can keep it straight?) Oh, and there's an invisibility helmet and an invulnerability herb. There's a funny bit where Eros shoots a giant with a love arrow so that, instead of trying to kill Hera, at least he's only trying to have sex with her.

None of these festival robes survive. None of the surviving, ancient representations of gigantomachy feature Enkelados looking up in amazement as Sicily falls on his poor head. Even so, "Yes, Socrates, and even more astonishing things as well — things that most people don't know" (6b) is rather rich. (Euthyphro has maybe heard some story about a giant buried under **two** Sicilies? Some titan with **200** heads or hands?)

One wonders whether being a sincere literalist about myths was common in Euthyphro's day. In another dialogue, **Phaedrus**, Socrates remarks that it is fashionable to explain away myths as **allegories of natural events**. The god of the North wind kidnapped and raped a mortal, Orythia. Maybe, Socrates suggests, she just got blown off the rocks — hence 'taken by Boreas.' But just because it was fashionable for the smart set to debunk or naturalize stories like this doesn't mean it wasn't considered a bit scandalous, even impious.

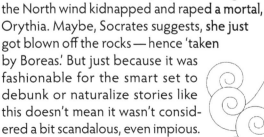

Sophisticated intellectual fashion's no fun if there aren't old-fashioned folks to get their peplos in a knot, as it were.

The point is this. Given Euthyphro's penchant for citing myths to rationalize his ethical position, it seems he ought to be more sensitive to how rationalism can corrode religion. It ought to cross his mind that maybe the rational thing to do is suspect that — just maybe! — it **didn't** literally happen. But the tall-tale quality of the gigantomachy is not even its worst feature, for Euthyphro's purposes.

Suppose it all **did** happen, crazy as it sounds. Now suppose you ask the average Athenian on the street what the point is — robe as rigging, theatership on rollers, the whole rigmarole. This citizen will most certainly say the point is piety. How not? But how so? For a person to become pious is presumably for that person to acquire an increased capacity to do what is holy, not what is unholy. Doing the right thing need not be **just** a matter of knowing. Still, you need to know what you're doing. How is looking at pictures of gods fighting giants supposed to make me better? Even if it all really happened?

The gigantomachy doesn't sound silly only because I narrated it briefly. Robert Graves writes that "the farcical incidents of the battle are more characteristic of popular fiction than myth."[3] But aren't myths popular fiction? Well, never mind — you see his point. This story seems more fun than fundamental. What, then, do we make of the fact that the ceremonial focus of the most important religious festival in Athens is a robe featuring pictures of gods fighting giants?

Festivals are **supposed** to be fun! They have to be spectacular, otherwise people won't come from all over Greece. Stands to reason! Yes, but how does spectacle make us more likely to act rightly, less likely to act wrongly?

7

Socrates pushes the point:

> I asked what essential form all holy actions exhibit, in virtue of which they are holy. For you did agree all unholy actions are unholy and all holy actions holy in virtue of some shared form ... Tell me then what this form is, so that I can pay close attention to it and use it as a paradigm to judge any action, whether committed by you or anyone else. If the action be of the right form, I will declare it holy; otherwise, not. (6d-e)

3   Robert Graves, **The Greek Myths: Complete Edition**. (Penguin, 1993), p. 131.

At this point Euthyphro might have been better off promising to provide better examples — stories later scholars might certify as 'properly' mythic. But he doesn't, and that line would have its own problems. Myths that teach moral lessons usually do not try to teach us complicated, surprising, subtle truths we've never thought before. (The exception that proves the rule may be Plato's own brand of obscure myths.) Myths are not for intellectual fine-tuning or original investigation; rather, they are for conventional reinforcement. It's easy to tell a story about why murder is bad. **In the end, the murderer was punished by Zeus!** It's not so easy to come up with a myth about why a complicated legal case should be decided in such-and-such a way. Myths that teach, teach simple truths. So if your only ethical tool is the hammer of Thor, as it were, every ethical problem starts to look like a nail — simple, that is. Euthyphro's problem, his case, his family situation, is not simple. So it looks like he's got the wrong tool for the job (and/or he **is** the wrong tool.)

Socrates' signature demand for an answer to a **what is X?** question is starting to look a bit more reasonable. How so? Sometimes you can teach by example. You say 'this is a chair, and other things like this are chairs.' That seems to work most days (not that Plato admits it. But it's true.) People pick up the concept. But 'this is holy, and other things like this are holy' actually doesn't work. People still fight about it. So we need, not a handful of examples plus a fancy robe, but a reasonable procedure for resolving serious, complicated, deep-seated religious-legal-moral disputes.

Yes, but does the procedure need to be a definition?

8

Let me be a bit absurd about it, but there will be a point. At the start of the dialogue, Socrates says what brings him before the **basileus** is that he stands accused of 'fabricating gods.' (The Greek says **make**, but it seems appropriate to translate with a term that splits the difference between technology and fakery. Socrates isn't being charged with unlicensed manufacture of **authentic** divinities.) Euthyphro sees this as a charge of religious innovation.

So let's get innovative! Here on the Socratic factory floor we have designed and prototyped a **Hosionotron** — a device for sorting the contents of the universe into two piles: **holy, not-holy**. People, gods, actions, trees, days of the week, events, character traits, animals, artifacts, rituals, books, ideas. You name it! Toss it onto those holy rollers, which convey every item into the brain of the machine, where they are worried about rigorously. One of those two lights goes on. **Holy. Unholy.** Your answer! Wonderful!

But how do you fabricate a **Hosionotron**?

That's tough, but this much seems right. We can't just wrap it in a robe. We need to program its innards. There needs to be some property Y that the machine's various detectors detect, or fail to. Every X exhibiting Y goes in one pile. Everything not-Y goes in the other. So what we need is a precise, technical expression of Y.

I can see you are starting to look doubtful. Does all this sound like a great deal of bother, at best? But look at it this way: do you have any idea how hard it is to embroider an extra-large robe with nice pictures of gods fighting giants? No one said the best things in life would come easy or cheap.

But what if there just **isn't** any such Y — to say nothing of further engineering difficulties we are sure to encounter?

Then we can't construct our wonderful **Hosionotron**, alas.

Isn't that the likeliest outcome, after all?

No, because — allegedly — we've **got** one. Behold, the **Euthyphrobot 399**!

Perhaps you've seen this fantastic tool, the latest model (to hear it tell the Holy/not-Holy tale.) If you agree a general algorithm would be needed to detect holiness, then it must be possible to have such an algorithm because, to repeat, we've got it. "If you did not know precisely what is holy, and what unholy, you would never have undertaken to prosecute your aged father for murder on behalf of a servant" (15d). Yet here he is! If the Euthyphrobot were not programmed to test for a reliable criterion of holiness, surely it would behave like the useless **Socratic Daemoninator**; which, as you may know, only ever spits out one answer: **invalid input, abort procedure**.

But surely Euthyphro isn't 'well-programmed'. Bit of a fool, isn't he?

Probably. But even bad programming has to run some way. The question of how people **do** think may be as interesting as the question of how they **should**. Put the point this way: it's all well and good to point out that if your car won't start, you need someone who understands how cars **work**, as opposed to a dictionary definition of 'car'. A good mechanic is not the one who can sort all the contents of the universe into two piles: car, not-car. That's asking for not enough, also for too much. But the word 'holiness' **is** a device for sorting all the contents of the universe into two piles: **holy, not-holy**. A car goes from A to B. A word sorts A's from B's. So to ask what the word means **is** just to ask how this practical unit of sorting work is accomplished.

So how do people work, who are, seemingly, doing this work?

If **you** know how to construct a functioning **Hosionotron** — or even a malfunctioning **Euthyphrobot** —without coding in a holiness algorithm, we'd all love to see the plans. Because, admittedly, we are running into a few … complications.

Shifting away from silly robots, the better to see the serious point: it does seem possible, admittedly, that we might theorize the nature of linguistic meaning and the nature of conceptual content in ways that work around any demand for strict, verbal definition. Maybe people who use the word 'holy' on a regular basis aren't following any rule, **per se**; let alone consciously applying a verbal formula. But it is not obvious how regular behavior that isn't 'encoded' as a rule is possible; or why, if the machine (person) isn't following a rule, we should trust its operation. So it may be best to start by at least trying to come up with an ideal rule, which will basically be a definition.

Let me say it again: neither Plato nor Socrates is the least bit interested in constructing divine robots — fabricating gods, whatever that means. What I have just done is present what is basically a very simple idea: to use the word 'Y' is to grasp a concept **Y**, is to possess something like a general rule (paradigm, call it what you will) for picking out Y's.

The point of thinking about robots is that you already are one, in effect. Your thinking works some way, for better or worse. What **is** that way?

```
ELIZIAN MYSTERY PROGRAM

(Hello, my name is Socrates.
+What brings you to the King-Archon's
    Court?
(Never mind about me. What brings you to
    the King-Archon's Court?
+I am prosecuting my father for murder.
(Do you think it is normal to be
    prosecuting your father for murder?
+Yes, I believe what I am doing is holy.
(Why do you believe what you are doing
    is holy?
+Because the gods act the same way.
(Do the gods act the same way?
+Yes, and what the gods do is holy.
(What is holy?
■
```

9

Having accepted Socrates' challenge to provide a general account of holiness — a definition, in effect — Euthyphro proceeds to set up three candidates, which Socrates bats down with ease. Much of the dialogue is devoted to Socrates' efforts in this regard. The logic is mostly rather straightforward, so I will be fairly brief.

First Definition: Holy = what is loved by the gods

And what the gods hate is unholy.

The problem is the gods fight, and not just with giants. Zeus loves turning himself into a bull and seducing mortals. Hera, his wife, hates that. Poseidon and Athena fought over who got to be divine patron of Athens. Athena won. Poseidon is still sore. Euthyphro says Zeus will love anyone who does as Zeus did when he punished his father. Kronos might disagree. Lots of things are shaping up to holy **and** unholy. Euthyphro admits this is awkward. He opts to modify his definition.

But it is worth pausing to ask: holy **and** unholy? Is this an **absurd** result?

Greek mythology is a great place to get stuck between a divine rock and a hard place. Maybe that's the answer. Later in the dialogue (9d) Euthyphro accepts, at least in passing, that things might be both holy and unholy, if loved and hated by different gods. But here at the start he shifts ground instead.

Second Definition: Holy = what is loved by all the gods

This is supposed to fix the trouble. Trouble is: it isn't obvious **all** the gods would agree about any of the cases concerning which we might bother to consult them. Euthyphro says all gods will be against murder. The question is whether his father is guilty, not whether murder is bad. The point made above about myths and morals applies again. Myths can be tools for reinforcing simple notions like **don't murder**. They are not obviously instruments for investigating what ought to count as murder.

By this point modern readers who are themselves religious may feel a bit frustrated, thinking that, with friends like Euthyphro, religion doesn't need enemies, whether Socrates is one or not. Stipulating that all the Greek gods agree is Euthyphro sticking a band-aid on a fatal flaw in his whole outlook. Modern readers who believe in God don't believe in any colorful, soap opera superhero cast of Olympians. When we want to see an action hero fighting a big villain, we have our own version of a big-screen peplos. Our people call it 'going to the movies'. Whether we are religious or not, we don't confuse going to church with taking in a summer blockbuster.

Modern readers aren't ancient Greek polytheists. If they are religious, they are likely to be subscribers to a monotheistic religion: Christianity or Islam or Judaism. But let's not forget Hinduism and Buddhism. That's more than a billion living counter-examples. Don't write off non-monotheist religions as relics! But maybe Plato is driving at the conclusion that monotheism makes sense. If there is only one God, there is no problem with gods fighting; no risk of the gods handing down an inconsistent command structure, thereby crashing the moral program.

10

But the next stage of the dialogue between Socrates and Euthyphro pushes past these problems to a more fundamental one. The initial problems stand revealed, in retrospect, as symptoms. The real problem is an incoherent order of explanation.

> S: Consider this: is the holy loved by the gods because it is holy, or is it holy because it is loved by the gods?
>
> E: I don't know what you mean, Socrates.
>
> S: Let me try to explain more clearly. We speak of something carried and of a carrier; of something guided and a guide; of something seen and one who sees. You understand that, in every case of this sort, these things are different from one another, and how they are different? (10a)

Socrates' examples sound odd and may, in fact, make things **less** clear (in part this is a problem with translating things that run more smoothly in Greek.) The full passage is recommended to the interested reader as an exercise in verbal disentanglement. But let me try to state, plainly, what the point is; why it matters.

It's a chicken-and-egg puzzle. **Do the gods love it because it is good; or is it good because the gods love it?** This is a famous hinge in the dialogue, often called 'Euthyphro's Dilemma'. Why Euthyphro's, in particular? He wants to justify prosecuting his father. He does so by elevating a standard of impartial justice over family loyalty. (Grid vs. circle.) He justifies this stance by asking, in effect, WWZD: **what would Zeus do?** (Let's leave the other gods out, for simplicity.)

Zeus, he claims, favors impartial justice. But, supposing so, why — in what way — should we care? To explain, Euthyphro needs to solve the chicken-and-egg puzzle. No solution satisfies. Let's examine our options.

Suppose goodness 'comes first'. That is, there is some god-independent, reason-giving standard of holiness — of right conduct. On this picture an ethically-minded individual might cut out the middle man (Euthyphro) and middle god (Zeus.) Taking your cue from wise Zeus' love puts you on the right track, sure. But, if **murder is wrong** makes sense, independently, you can figure it out yourself without asking Zeus; just as you can do your calculus homework without praying to Zeus for the solutions. Even if Zeus gave you an answer key, that wouldn't turn calculus into a branch of Greek mythology. Ethics will be like that. It just makes sense!

That's the first horn of the dilemma. Here's the second. If there **isn't** an independent, prior standard of holiness (goodness), it must be that god(s) create right and wrong (good/bad) by liking/ ordering some things, not others. This is often called 'divine command theory'. What the god says, goes. Could there be a simpler picture? It's pretty straightforward. Still, there is a problem. Zeus hates murder. But why?

Don't murder!

Isn't it obvious what's hateful about it? He hates it because it's wrong!

No, that gets us back to the first horn of the dilemma. Think of it this way: could Zeus make murder right if he got up on the wrong side of bed some morning? Or like this: do you have any reason to dislike murder **besides the fact that it is wrong**? Strange question. (Do gods dictate values the way mortals pick car colors. We say, 'I like it! Do you have it in red?' They say: 'I like it! So we'll have it in right!')

How are we supposed to understand Zeus' moral preferences if we can't wrap our heads around his (by hypothesis pre-moral) reasons for having them?

Could it all be random? There is a key scene in Homer's **Iliad** in which Zeus watches the fight between Achilles and Hector. He raises his golden scale and places a 'doom' for each warrior in the pans. Hector's goes down. He is to die. Zeus' scales do not suit our case perfectly. They don't make it be the case that Hector **deserves** to die. They do not determine right and wrong, only life and death. But if we imagine Zeus using his scales as a device for randomly generating values, then we might envision a world that is, ethically, as arbitrary as the course of the Trojan War is, militarily. But the conceptual disadvantages of divine command theory go deeper than mere fluke of fate (or fog of war.) It is not clear that we can **reason** about ethics on this view, something Euthyphro definitely wants to do. Zeus could command us to prosecute all murderers **and** never to prosecute our own fathers. An inconsistent set of demands can't all be met. But that doesn't mean they can't be made.

11

Euthyphro is attracted to something like divine command theory; but he wants ethics to make sense. But that first horn won't save us if we flip back now. It isn't just that you don't need Zeus' help if you can figure out right and wrong for yourself (like math.) If ethics is delinked from potentially arbitrary god-love, to ensure its good sense, there is no reason religion — the gods — must remain ethical rather than unethical.

Here is Adeimantus from **Republic** (we'll meet him when we get there.) He is speaking for Plato, I expect; and — who knows? — he might be thinking about poor Hector, who hardly deserved his fate.

> What is said about the gods and virtue is the most incredible thing of all; namely, that the gods themselves inflict misfortune and misery upon many a good man, while the opposite fate awaits the opposite sort. Begging priests and prophets darken the doors of the rich and persuade them they possess a god-given power to stage a pleasant festival

of sacrifice and prayer, thereby expiating any crime the rich man or one of his ancestors may have committed. Not only that, but if one wants to make trouble for some enemy, then — for a very reasonable price — this lot will contrive to harm the just and unjust alike; because they have incantations and spells for persuading the gods to serve them. (364b)

Selling salvation like soapsuds! (Or soapsuds like salvation?) Either way, **that** can't be right! Let's check back in with our heroes, Socrates and Euthyphro.

As mentioned, the Panathenaic festival parade will pass within just a few meters of where they are sitting now, proceed up the road, up the hill to the temple. It's the most wonderful event — exciting, entertaining! You get to admire the designs on the peplos. Of course it costs the city a pretty penny, but that's a small price to pay for automatically becoming a better person just by meeting a few ritual obligations. Also, all those tourists buy stuff while they're here.

Adeimantus is complaining about low-end private operators in the holiness line, not the high-end civic version (which I expect he supports.) But the model is kind of the same, right?

12

But what does this have to do with Euthyphro?

He may be a self-righteous idiot. (You be the judge.) But, in his defense, he doesn't seem to be in it for the money. And he doesn't work for the city.

Let's see how it ends. Euthyphro is stumped by chicken-and-egg: **is it holy because the gods love it, or do the gods love it because it is holy?** He wants it both ways, but Socrates won't let him have it. But things get scrambled up in two final ways.

First, Socrates finally raises the issue of justice (better late than never!) He asks, in effect, whether 'just' and 'holy' just mean the same. One or two? "Is all that is just holy?" (11e). This sounds odd. Euthyphro doesn't get it. Socrates makes it simpler, hands Euthyphro a better idea on a platter. "Is it rather that where there is holiness, there is also justice, since justice is not coextensive with holiness — holiness is a part of justice?" (12d). And, completing the thought: where there is justice, there is not necessarily holiness.

Oh, **that**!

Yes, of course, there's justice and then there's holiness. Of course not all questions of justice are settled just by asking what is holy.

This is sensible enough. But it highlights the oddity of the performance to this point. Why didn't Euthyphro think of this before? His case against his father is, on the face of it, a question of justice — a legal issue.

Maybe we should examine it in those terms, rather than flying straight up to Olympus for our answers?

13

There actually **is** an explanation for Euthyphro's determination not to consider his own legal case in terms of justice, rather than holiness.

Let's turn back to the beginning of the dialogue. Socrates and Euthyphro meet on the steps of the **archon basileus' stoa**. (Open-sided, colonnaded building, like a stand-alone porch.) Who is this man? There are nine **archons** in Athens, elected officials who serve terms of a year. (One archon, the **polemarch**, is selected less democratically. But never mind about the man in charge of the army.) The **basileus** — the king — oversees religious affairs. It's an archaic title, as befits the venerable character of his duties, making sure that peplos gets made on time and that other aspects of the Panathenea are properly conducted. There are temples to keep up, sacrifices to be arranged. The basileus is busy, keeping books for all that.

Beyond that, his most significant duty is hearing cases concerning alleged religious crime. Socrates' case is before the basileus because he is charged with impiety. Why is Euthyphro here? Because murder is a religious matter. Athens is like Euthyphro: it distinguishes justice and holiness. Then, having done so, it thinks about murder in terms of holiness. The basileus hears about, "that part of justice concerned with the care of the gods, while the part of justice concerned with the care of men comprises the rest" (12e). I'm quoting Euthyphro on holiness but it is also a nice and accurate formulation of the basileus' delimited domain of legal authority.

Think about what it means that this domain includes murder. Euthyphro comes upon the dead servant in the ditch. He responds as any pious citizen would. 'Great Zeus needs my help! He stands in immediate need of my care

and assistance. Call the city official in charge of taking care of the gods so
that he and I can work together to take better care of Zeus!'

And the shade of the dead servant looks up from Hades and adds: 'And
I'm not feelin' so good neither.'

How does such an absurdity work its way into the justice system? Via
Euthyphro's dilemma (so it isn't **just** his.)

It is absurd to suppose the reason we care about murder is **only** because
Zeus cares. Obviously the idea is supposed to be that Zeus has a reason to
look down, angrily, and judge, 'this man has been mistreated!' But if that's
the case, it's a case of 'care of men', after all. So we should cut to the chase
and just plain **care** about , hence for, the man in the ditch. (That's what Zeus
would do. We want to be like Zeus.) We are back on the first horn of the
dilemma. If you've figured out what makes sense, regarding care of men,
what do you need Zeus for?

14

There is more to the murder-as-religious-crime story. Euthyphro explains at the
start that he is concerned about being 'polluted' by his father, being forced
to be under the same roof. The Greek for this is **miasma**, a term we now use
for the 'bad air' associated with a swamp. We understand, intuitively, what it
means to be stained by sin. We understand why people want to 'clean up their
act'. But the Greeks apparently took this idea literally. Miasma is contagious.

Guilt is catching? Like the flu?

It might seem this strange notion makes merely figurative sense. By staying
under the same roof, Euthyphro is implicitly condoning his father's actions.
The Greeks held all murder trials in the open air, by law. If Euthyphro's case
comes to trial, no one will be willing to be under the same roof as his father
for the duration, so to that extent they will be ratifying the son's apparently
excessive notions about sanitary housing. Still, symbolism matters. The notion
that bad behavior infects by contact may not be superstition but a way of
condensing plausible thoughts about social dynamics. Condoning wrong-
doing causes it to spread. But there is more. The orator Antiphon:

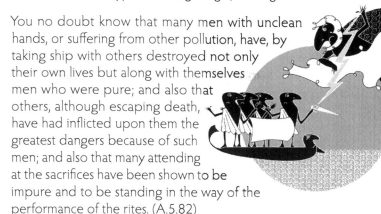

You no doubt know that many men with unclean hands, or suffering from other pollution, have, by taking ship with others destroyed not only their own lives but along with themselves men who were pure; and also that others, although escaping death, have had inflicted upon them the greatest dangers because of such men; and also that many attending at the sacrifices have been shown to be impure and to be standing in the way of the performance of the rites. (A.5.82)

The ship case is nice because it solves for the variable of intention, also for any 'collective guilt'. I can feel ashamed of something my country has done, my family, my in-group. But if the stranger you happen to sit next to on the boat turns out to be a fugitive murderer, it can hardly be your fault. Still, you can catch your death from miasma. The moral of this story is that pollution, in this ancient Greek sense, is not strictly a **moral** story.

There are guilty people who are not polluted. Note how when Euthyphro lists things that count as 'wrong-doing' he lists, "murder or temple robbery or anything else" (5d). 'Anything else' would seem to cover: robbing a merchant, breaking a contract. Doing all that is wrong, right? Yes, but what Euthyphro is trying to get at is the sort of wrongdoing whose prosecution counts as **holy** (because it cleans miasma.) So even at this early stage, where he is just listing a few obvious examples, not yet offering bad definitions, he is already mis-speaking. He is conflating justice with holiness, via 'wrong-doing'. Conversely, there are polluted people who are not guilty. New mothers are polluted; soldiers who kill in battle. There is no moral guilt associated with giving birth or defending your city. A highly but not strictly common denominator in these cases is blood. There are rituals for handling blood; places you don't go until cleansed. Call it superstition, contagious magic, hemophobia, innate disgust response, metaphor, religion, moral confusion. Whatever it is, it is the basileus' business. He's the divine sanitation engineer for the city.

He cleans up spilled blood.

So murder, qua miasma question, isn't pure fairness-and-justice. Or it is **and** isn't. Anyway, facts are facts: Zeus cares about miasma, so we have to care about him caring about it, 'fair' or not.

Thus, we appear to be back on the second horn of Euthyphro's dilemma. What is holy and unholy only determines what counts as polluted. Care of the gods is shaping up to be ethically arbitrary. But that can't be right. Right?

15

But what exactly does this have to do with Euthyphro? Is all this exotic ancient Greek cultural background supposed to point us to some solution to his problem? What **is** the relationship between holiness and justice? (Also, wasn't there a suspected money trail around here?) Let's forge on to Euthyphro's final stab at an account (12e):

Third Definition: Holy = Care of the gods

But Socrates manages to make it all sound like sordid haggling.

He doesn't do this by highlighting the hazards of miasma-spill. He considers more happy accidents. How have we managed to strike such a favorable balance of trade with the gods? They give us a lot, don't ask for much in exchange.

Funny story in Plutarch (later Roman writer, but the style of thinking is the same.) Jupiter (Zeus) offers King Numa a deal: in exchange for a moratorium on lightning strikes, he wants 'heads' — that is, human sacrifice. Numa figures he can satisfy the letter of the contract by providing onion heads. How do we humans keep finding all these bargains and loopholes? Euthyphro tries to moralize the picture. Somehow care of the gods is inherently linked to doing the right thing. But he only manages to stick himself back on the horns of the dilemma. Our religious acts — our sacrifices and services — are "pleasing to the gods." That is what makes them holy. But why do the gods want us to do these things, rather than something else? Is it because these things are good in themselves? Or is it because … ? Round and round we go.

16

By way of filling out this point, let me report another Greek-Chinese coincidence, and ponder the significance. In a classic discussion of ancient Chinese thought, **The Way and Its Power**, Arthur Waley hypothesizes that around

400 BCE attitudes shifted.[4] (This attempt at dating is not precise. Societies don't flip attitudes like a light-switch. But I like that Waley picks almost the exact date of Socrates' meeting with Euthyphro.) Before this time, sacrifice had been understood to be the offering of proof to the divine ancestors that their descendants are prospering. (So says Waley. It's not clear this line is satisfactory. But the ancient Chinese would not deny this was **a** point of sacrifice.) The shift Waley describes really amounts to thinking this thought through with elementary consistency. Since prosperity of the living is the point, sacrifice (signaling prosperity) comes second. The gods are far away but man is near. Indeed, take care of men and care of gods very nearly takes care of itself (since these gods we care about so much care so much about us.)

Do you see the connection with Zeus and the man in the ditch?

Waley calls the old perspective 'pre-moral'. He wants to contrast it with the moral 'care of men' perspective he sees coming on. He picks this term because, at this stage, all the moral words have primitive meanings that look, to us, non-moral, or not clearly moral. 'Moral' meant **customary**, as did 'ethics'. 'Virtue' meant **power**. 'Just' may have meant something like **ritually appropriate**. 'Holy' meant **inviolable** (not touched or penetrated); perhaps this was just an extension of **healthy** (clean?) These are Indo-European examples. The Chinese cases follow the same pattern. At bottom we find power and ritual and conventions enforcing social solidarity. Waley admits 'pre-moral' is not a good term. He prefers 'auguristic-sacrificial' (although it's a mouthful) because, as he says, ancient ethics-talk revolves around religion, and religion-talk revolves around two things: augury — that is, the establishment of channels of privileged communication with divine beings. And sacrifice: ritual, devotional acts intended to placate/win favor of divine beings.

Euthyphro is teetering on the edge of just such a shift. He is sometimes called a priest. But he doesn't have a human flock — and not just because he's unpopular. He might be a preacher, spreading the Hades-and-brimstone word of Zeus. But, to the extent this is true, it underscores how strange Euthyphro's behavior is in the eyes of his fellow Athenians. Ancient Greek religion isn't doctrinal. It is not a matter of sitting through righteous sermons but of making right sacrifices. And augury. Euthyphro is bitter that all his prophecies have come true, yet still he gets no respect!

What Euthyphro really is, is a **mantis**!

4   Arthur Waley, **The Way and Its Power: Lao Tzu's Tao Te Ching and Its Place in Chinese Thought** (Grove Press, 1994), p. 21 and following.

Like a bug?

In Greek, a **mantis** is not a bug but a religious person who wears many hats, potentially: seer, sooth-sayer, priest, prophet. 'Mantis' is related to all our words ending in 'mancy'. A wizard hat, then?

Euthyphro is, if you like, a self-styled **logomancer**.

Magic + logic. Provoking conjunction!

But let's get back to Waley and allegedly pre-moral points of view. That 'pre-moral' isn't really the word for it is shown by Waley's own illustrations.

He quotes a tale from **The Book of History** about the Duke of Chou [Zhou], who bargains for his dying king's life, striking a deal with the spirits of the ancestors. It is a story of augury and sacrifice. The Duke makes special contact and negotiates a mutually beneficial exchange of goods and services. But the story is clearly intended to showcase the Duke's exemplary righteousness, not his superlative skills as supernatural haggler. He is doing the 'done thing', behaving in a ritually appropriate manner. But, even more, he is doing something courageous and exemplary.

The Duke bravely offers **himself** to the spirits, to serve in place of his dying king. The spirits, evidently moved, spare the king. Noble, uplifting tale!

But — this is key — the story has no vocabulary for referring specifically to the Duke's especially admirable moral qualities, let along theorizing them. There is only auguristic-sacrificial religious talk. The Duke has advanced tele-communications gear (discs of jade, in case you are wondering how the magic is done) and exchange goods to offer. All such stuff is instrumental. Even the Duke himself, offering to serve the spirits, is a trade good. It is all means, as opposed to moral ends. Hence the story is not so much pre-moral as non-moral.

Of course we smell the difference between pure, noble self-sacrifice and cut-rate **Miasmaway** brand commercial-ized cynicism. We instinctively distinguish the Duke from those 'begging priests'. Still, there is nothing in the story that explicitly articulates what the difference comes to. Exactly what moral rule is the Duke following? (Don't say anything about discs of jade this time.)

Obviously it is the selfless quality of what the Duke does that seems so admirable! He is altruistic, hence moral!

Yes, but Euthyphro is on track to sacrifice not just himself but his whole family on the altar of justice — or holiness.

Is that noble?

Or idiotic?

Or morally reckless?

Is Euthyphro just making a spectacle of himself, to embarrass his father, or to enhance his personal religious fame? Surely there is such a thing as ethically-misguided self-sacrifice.

How do you tell the difference?

17

Let me underscore this point with another Greek example, by way of Latin etymology. **Augur** is uncommon in English. (You know 'oracle'? Same thing.) Possibly the job title came from **augere** — increase. (Same root as 'augment'.) Priests were in charge of making sure the gods gave us the goods. Alternatively, the job title meant 'bird talk' (**avis + garrire**). The Chinese had oracle bones and discs of jade. Greeks and Romans preferred to study entrails and flight patterns of birds. So let's talk birds. Aristophanes — the comedian who stuffed Socrates in a basket in the clouds — wrote **The Birds**. A pair of idiots find themselves in the country of birds, where, to save their skins, they end up feathered and winged, organizing the birds into a political power. They start a bird-centric religion. The newly self-confident birds build a mighty fortress, Cloud Cuckooland, between the human world and Olympus, so they cut into the lucrative augury-sacrifice trade route. The gifts humans give the gods — vaguely conceived of as aromas rising up out of the fires — are embargoed. A deputation of Olympians (and one Thracian god, who can't speak Greek, or get his clothes on straight) come to Cuckooland on a diplomatic mission. They **need** this stuff they are used to getting from mortals on a regular basis!

In effect, it's all a **reductio** on auguristic-sacrificial approaches to religion and ethics. To see what's absurd about such talk, just imagine that it literally works the way the talk implies. Holiness is telecommunication and trade. Fine. But then the line can be cut. But surely a trade embargo/denial-of-service attack on piety is absurd.

Also, when the humans-turned-birds find their new condition convenient, they reflect on why this is so. If you have powers
no ordinary mortals do — in this case, flight — they can't touch
you. Obviously you will get up to all sorts of unethical stuff, if there
is no threat of punishment. Here we touch on a very simple thought
about the relationship between holiness and ethics. We don't want
them to come apart, but there is actually a reason to think they will be, not
just imperfectly aligned, but negatively correlated. If 'holy' means **inviolable**,
the bird-men have become that. They are untouchable. But power corrupts,
and absolute power corrupts absolutely. Is there any reason to think someone
like Zeus will always do the right thing, if the only thing we're really sure of
is that he has nearly absolute power?

18

Generally readers have a poor impression of Euthyphro, hardly the sharpest knife in the drawer of sacrificial implements. One can't help wondering
whether he has some dubious motive, conscious or unconscious. It must
have stung Euthyphro that dad didn't consult **him** about how to handle the
murder on their farm, instead sending off for advice from the city. Is this a
father-son struggle for authority and dominance (like Zeus had with dad,
in his day?) Is the trial, or the threat of the trial, some publicity stunt? Or
maybe, as sacrificial technicians go, he's just a bird-brain, off in some eccen-
tric Cloud-Cuckooland of his own invention?

Still, some readers are impressed by the moral clarity and forthrightness
of Euthyphro's basic stance: set aside personal ties and **do the right thing**.
That sounds good. Socrates' too-clever-by-half chicken-and-egg trouble-
making can look frivolous, unserious by comparison.

Why doesn't Plato, or Socrates, tell us whether Euthyphro is doing the
right thing? Maybe because that isn't the point. The point is: whichever it is,
'care of the gods' talk will not help us settle which it is. Worse, such talk will
take up all the verbal room so no better style of thinking can get a word in
edgewise.

This is Euthyphro's problem, and this is Socrates' problem with Euthyphro:
he is ethically inarticulate. **Maybe** he's doing the right thing. But even if he is,
for all he knows he isn't. Worse: he has all sorts of stories that effectively paper
over the gaps in his thinking. He can talk endlessly about his case without it
so much as crossing his mind that he is not actually managing to talk about his
case at all. To adapt Nietzsche (talking about someone else): Euthyphro has
one significant advantage over his own views on holiness. He's interesting!

How can Euthyphro **even think** his approach to this issue is going to work? That's an interesting question. Now let me make things worse for him, by way of emphasizing how, at his very worst, Euthyphro is probably kind of like us.

If I asked you 'what are the three most important religious values?' you might answer in various ways. (Faith, hope and charity? I leave it to you.) If I asked what the three most important religious values were to the ancient Greeks, you might say (on the basis of what you have read in this chapter): augury, sacrifice and myth. But I think there is something to be said for adapting an old joke about real estate. The three values that mattered most, for ancient Greek religion, were: **location! location! location!** The one thing you absolutely could not do without was — not a book, not even a belief; but an altar, centering a sacred space. All ancient Greek religion is local. How local? Well, how many Athenas? Counting statues up on the Acropolis: **Athena Polias** (she beat Poseidon, to become patroness of the city. The peplos is hers); **Athena Promachus** (military lady and, at nine meters, no push-over); **Athena Parthenos** (virgin, even taller.)

But these are just representations of **the same** goddess, right?

In a sense, every shrine to Athena has its own goddess, since every altar is its own bit of real estate.

But there's **one** goddess, right?

What part of 'location, location, location' did you not understand?

Obviously this threatens to make the 'many gods' problem potentially much worse. Maybe something will be loved by **Athena Parthenos**, hated by **Athena Promachus**? Loved by **Zeus Meilichios**, hated by **Zeus Olympios**?

Then again, since 'many gods' was fatal enough when we only had one Zeus to worry about, why belabor the point? Doing so goes to show how far

Euthyphro has to go. If you try to read a religion consisting of ritual localism as impartial moral theory — misreading a table of real estate values as statements of universal, ethical value — it will come out arbitrary, hence absurd. (Remember the guy who drew such arbitrary lines in the sand — 10 meters, 20, 30? We don't want Zeus to be that guy.)

To be sure, there is something appealing about building morals up out of local circles: me/us/them. Family first sounds good. Holy circles map family values (for a broad value of 'family'.) But if, like Euthyphro, you aspire to something more impartial, universal, sensible? It is hard to square a circle. Euthyphro's attempt to project universal, abstract doctrines out of local, grounded non-doctrines is, at best, a heroic effort to go against the grain. His level best is confusion about whether the many is somehow really one. And there, but for the grace of Zeus, go all of us!

People think in this confused way all the time. Let's work up to modern manifestations via another ancient source, Isokrates' **Areopagiticus**. He is an orator, a generation younger than Plato, nostalgic for the good old days of virtuous democracy when men were wise and Socrates was put to death (OK, to be fair he's thinking about a slightly earlier period.)

> Where, pray tell, could one find a democracy more stable or more just than this [during the good old days], which appointed the best men to have charge of its affairs while giving the people authority over their rulers? Such was the constitution of their politics and from this it is easy to see that also in their day-to-day conduct they never failed to act appropriately and justly. For when people have laid sound foundations for the activities of the whole state it follows that in the details of their lives they must reflect the character of their government. (I. 7.27)

It's self-defeating of Euthyphro to imitate Zeus by asking WWZD (because, if you think about it, **Zeus** never asks what Zeus would do.) Venerating ancestral democrats as divinely infallible is, likewise, silly. They did not decide what was just and unjust by sitting down, democratically, and announcing 'let's devoutly imitate **ourselves**.'

What **made** those ancestral democrats just? Obviously the way to answer is to rattle on at great length about 'care of the gods', augury and sacrifice. I'm kidding. Isokrates is not. Let's read on:

First of all, as to their conduct towards the gods — for it is right to begin there — they were not haphazard or irregular in worship or in the performance of rites. They did not, for example, drive a procession of three hundred oxen to the altar, when it entered their heads to do so, while omitting on a whim sacrifices instituted by their fathers. Nor did they lavishly lay out for foreign festivals, whenever those went together with a feast, while selling to the lowest bidder the contract to perform the sacrifices demanded by the holiest rites of their religion. For their only care was that no institution of their fathers should be destroyed, and nothing introduced which was not approved by custom, for they believed that reverence consists not in extravagant expenditures but in disturbing none of the rites their ancestors had handed down to them. And so also the gifts of the gods were visited upon them, not fitfully or irregularly, but seasonably both for the plowing of the fields and for the harvesting of its fruits.

But if we are supposed to do as the ancestors did; then, if the ancestors instituted rites, shouldn't we imitate them by instituting rites of our own? If the point is to do the right thing, we should do **that**. Or if the point is to do what the gods want — again, why dog-leg through the ancestors? Also, what does any of this have to do with the virtues of democracy? Why vote on any of it, if we know the answers, or know who knows the answers? (Athena's right there! Just ask **her**.) Last but not least, if the point is to get a job of work done, what actually is the problem with contracting out "to the lowest bidder?" Why pay more?

Why bother giving speeches like this one by Isokrates? It's not as though we have stopped. Think about the American veneration of the Founding Fathers; the US Constitution and its Framers. (You aren't American? Then substitute some document, institution or tradition your people hold especially dear and sacred. I'm sure you can think of something.) Suppose it comes to an argument — a fight. (Needn't be politics. "Justice and injustice, beauty and ugliness, good and bad" (7d). Any of these hot topics will do.) Your instinct is to argue — that is, justify yourself — with authoritative reference to some traditional things. But what are you **really** saying? That you know tales of the ancestors?

Surely you know this thing you are venerating is a household god. Maybe just a neighborhood shrine to a national god? And you have more than one. (Everyone has lots of circles! If circles are holy, we are all polytheists.) Yet your local notion is so wise, so you say, that you can presume to project it, over everything, for everyone? And you trust the results will be coherent?

Is it right because it's Constitutional, or is it Constitutional because it's right? You finesse it: there is wisdom in tradition. If it worked before, it probably won't kill us. But, even so, this doesn't remove the dilemma. From the inside, tradition always feels reasonable. But from the outside, you look like a circle pretending to be a straight line. (Am I saying you are stupid, because you are like Euthyphro? I'm hinting you might be a bit on the normal side, yes.)

19

We are effectively done with **Euthyphro**. But let's circle back to some lines tried out at the start. Remember circles vs. straight? Chicken-and-egg aside, the real dilemma should, by rights, be this one: which ethics is best?

1. **I must be 'straight' with everyone: fair, impartial.**
2. **I must favor, be partial to, those in my 'circle'.**

If I want a bit of both, how do I square the circle so it doesn't turn out a mess? What might Plato be prodding us to think of 1 & 2, even if he isn't saying much?

Euthyphro would strike his fellow citizens as ethically outlandish. Socrates' mock-shock is in line with conventional attitudes. But, in a sense, this shouldn't be the case. By rights, Euthyphro's dilemma ought to be recognized as a hometown tradition in its own right (or rite.) It is the self-same problem Athenians solved for Orestes. It is the great pride of the Athenian homicide court system that it **can** handle these cases well — better than the gods themselves, in fact!

Who's Orestes? What kind of **case**?

Obviously you are not an ancient **Athenian** or you would know.

The **Oresteia** is a trilogy of plays by the great playwright Aeschylus (a contemporary of Socrates): **Agamemnon, Libation Bearers,** and **Eumenides**.

Let me tell you just the end of the story of the royal house of Atreus — how its heavy crown dripped **miasma**. How it turned out OK. It's an old story. Homer told it. Aeschylus' version is fuller, more philosophical in its implications, and was especially beloved by the Athenians of Plato's day.

It's a revenge tale. Three generations are confronted with a dilemma of the following basic form: duty to family both requires and forbids the killing of someone else in the family. You can imagine how this will go. Vendettas, in their nature, are self-perpetuating. You killed one of ours. We kill one of yours. When this trouble arises within a family, the practical difficulties of endless killing are compounded by ethical paradoxes. Everything is right **and** wrong.

The final figure in this line is Orestes, son of Agamemnon and Clytaemnestra. She killed her husband (her motives were multiple, but ritual sacrifice of their daughter would surely top the list.) Apollo commands that Orestes kill his own mother, to punish her for murdering his father. There is a (what's the word?) pregnant moment when Orestes' mother asks him if he can kill her, of all people.

He has a friend, Pylades, who was with him when he went to Apollo's temple and is with him now. He now tells Orestes to kill her not as his mother, but as 'one who has done wrong.' Be impersonal about justice. In short, Orestes is ordered to think like Euthyphro. But it doesn't work. Clytaemnestra ends up dead. Orestes end up covered with **miasma**, hounded by his mother's Furies (**Erinyes**). Some further mythological explanation is now in order. Furies are old gods — goddesses, rather — and here we find another connection to Euthyphro's case. The Furies belong to the generation of Kronos, prior to that of Zeus and the Olympians. (Athena and Apollo are the two other members of this young generation who figure in these plays.) The Furies are said to have sprung up from the familial blood shed when Kronos castrated his father, Ouranos, for wrong-doing. Alternately, they were, literally, 'born from the night'. The thematic significance is this: you might think that if you want to figure out how it can be just to prosecute your own parent, the first person you should ask is Zeus. But, in a sense, what Aeschylus' play suggests is that, precisely because Zeus did the same thing, he and his generation are going to be the last people to be able to help. As Socrates says, if the gods fight about anything, they fight about the same things we do, so we get a regress, no solution. Zeus' lofty impartiality can't be regarded as disinterested about impartiality. He has too obvious a personal stake in a case so much like his own (noble son punishes wrong-doing royal parent.)

On the other side stand the Furies with their own biases. Traditionally Furies punish oath-breakers and murderers. Homer says they are "those from

beneath the earth who punish a false oath."
In Aeschylus that role is modified. Oaths
become associated with the sky — Zeus,
Apollo, Athena. The new gods stand for
impersonal justice — law, contracts, abstract
law and order. The old gods are always for
vengeance on behalf of the ones closest
to you, in terms of blood. Often the Furies
have been depicted as rather sexy young
huntresses, but Aeschylus goes for hideous
and snake-haired. The furies are also tradi-

tionally depicted as winged, sometimes specifically bat-winged and cave-
dwelling (like certain modern crime-fighters one could name.) In Aeschylus
they are described as "like harpies, but without wings" and as "falling heavily"
on wrongdoers. They are earth spirits, made heavy with gravity by the playwright. They smell **miasma**. Basically, they are anthropo-bat-snake-morphized
vengeance, just as miasma is chemicalized guilt.

Orestes tries the standard tricks to get the Furies off his
scent. Sacrifice an innocent animal. A young pig. Get its
blood on you, just as you might smear yourself with something strong-smelling to throw dogs off your scent. You
are, in a sense, trying to fool the spirits of vengeance.
But you are also exhibiting, symbolically, your desire
to clean up your act. Apollo told him this would
work but it doesn't. Orestes is chased from Argos
to Delphi, Delphi to Athens.

Let's pick up the action at the point
in the third play where he is on his
knees, clutching the statue of Athena,
claiming sanctuary. (Location, location, location!) The Furies heave and
wheeze in at the gate, saying that they
are extremely tired from walking all
that way, but they smell blood.

Today is a good day for man-killing!

Orestes protests that he has made
the right sacrifices. His hands are now
clean. Athena appears in shining armor.
She is polite.

'Long time no see, Furies. What brings you to Athens?' 'We're here to punish a matricide, Athena.' 'Is that him?' 'That's the one. He killed his mother.' 'That's it? He killed his mother? He didn't, for example, have a **reason** to kill his mother? This sounds like half the argument, Furies.' 'Fine, **you** be judge. See if what we say isn't right.' 'It wouldn't be right for me to decide the case by myself, goddess though I am,' says Athena. 'I will empanel a jury of twelve Athenian citizens, good men and true. And they will decide. If there is a deadlock, I will cast the deciding vote for conviction or acquittal.'

At this point Apollo shows up to be Orestes' defense lawyer. Athena declares the trial open. Apollo and the Furies engage in faintly ridiculous lawyerly dialectic, with Orestes getting a word in edge-wise at a few points when asked to testify. You can imagine how it might go. It's Euthyphro vs. his family — circles vs. straight lines. Apollo and the Furies make some conspicuously absurd arguments. First, the Furies argue that it isn't **so** unholy for a wife to kill a husband, because there is no blood relation, just a broken contract, in effect. In response, Apollo argues that it actually isn't **so** bad for a son to kill a mother because really sons aren't related to mothers, only to fathers, just as the plant that grows is only related to the seed that was planted, not to the earth in which the seed was planted. (The gods are such confabulators!)

The jurors split six to six. Athena breaks the tie in favor of Orestes. Since she herself is a woman who only had a father and no mother (since she sprang full-grown from Zeus' brow) she is always for the male and Zeus' side in such a case. The Furies are, predictably, furious. For this they will blast the ground of Athens, making it so that nothing grows! They start ranting and raving! Just wait and see what the old, much-abused earth gods can still do to a city like Athens that is so dear to the sky gods!

And, now, in the final scene of the third play, Athena does a funny thing. She bargains with the Furies.

Henceforth, if the Furies wish, they will be especially honored in Athens.

They will, as she says, win first fruits in all matters concerned with children, and marriage. The people of Athens will worship them and they will go from being cast out earth spirits from the previous generation to being honored goddesses of the land around Athens. They will cease to promote private

vengeance. They will unite citizens, serving public
justice, protecting against external threats,
sharing patron status with Athena herself.

The Furies take the good deal. They become
Eumenides —meaning **good spirits**. Everyone
is happy and exits the stage in a big parade.

And how are these new mother-figures for the
city described in the final lines of the play? They are
praised as **euthuphrones**! Took me a while to get to
the punch line, but we've squared Euthyphro's circle for
him, mythico-dramatically at least. A family-centered practice
of sacrifice (purification) has turned abstract doctrine of impartial justice, at
least at the civic level. As Isokrates puts it, in that very speech I was quoting:
the Athenian homicide courts are so well constituted even the gods prefer
the judgment of these juries to their own, divine wisdom!

20

By the way, what would have happened if Euthyphro's case came to trial?

Did it?

We have no idea. But just suppose!

But why bother speculating? Even if we can be fairly confident how ancient
Athenian justice worked in general — never mind one case — we couldn't
be sure enough to know what Plato expected readers to know, hence might
intend them to recognize them as legal background for this one dialogue.

Taking the second point first: it seems safe to say Plato's intended readers
would be legally sophisticated. Hearing about Euthyphro's case, as we do
at the start, the sorts of thinkers and students Plato would have had in his
Athenian Academy could naturally leap a few steps ahead: what a weird
case! How might it play out?

The Athenians were inveterate court-watchers.
It was a national pastime. There is a play about
it, Aristophanes' **The Wasps**. An old man,
Philocleon, is addicted to the courts. That is,
he is addicted to serving as a juror. There
are lots of cases. Juries are large. They
need lots of citizen bodies to fill those
seats. Philocleon is paid a small amount,
but — better than that — he feels flattered
by the attention. All these fine and eloquent

speeches, all aimed at swaying his opinion! His son, in desperation, tries to lock dad in the house, eventually giving him a job judging cases like: which family dog stole the cheese? Inanimate objects are called in to testify as witnesses.

So pardon me as I play modern Philocleon, in my amateur-expert way, presuming to stage a mock Euthyphro trial. But where's the profit in make-believing a case that, maybe, never even happened?

We'll get to that. For now: even if we can't be sure, we can make out certain outlines. The courts are supposed to be about justice but there's also spectator sport spirit; status anxiety; swarming, stinging savagery. Winners and losers; insiders and outsiders. So much, so clear from **The Wasps**. Euthyphro is status-consciousness. He is sore about being ignored, an outsider, in the Assembly. Now he's nursing some ambition of playing to the jury, rhetorically, in the murder trial of the century! Father vs. son! Just like Zeus himself!

But how is this **not** going to get messy? Even if some twists and turns I am about to sketch are debatable, it seems clear Euthyphro's fond dream of a 'straight' answer, vindicating him, won't come true. The Athenian homicide court system is set up badly to handle such a case — an Orestes-type case. And, by calling it that, I emphasize that this is potentially embarrassing not just for Euthyphro but for Athens herself.

Without further ado, a whirlwind tour of the courts.[5]

21

We begin, again, at the stoa of the **archon basileus**. He won't judge the case himself. He will hold a preliminary hearing to determine what the issue is — the so-called **euthydikia**. Large juries, or bodies of judges, can't debate what cases are really about. They can only give a straight vote, up or down. The basileus must predetermine what 'straight justice' that straight vote will concern. He makes both parties swear, accordingly. The trial will, in a sense, be about which party has 'sworn straighter'.

5   See Edwin Carawan, **Rhetoric and the Law of Draco** (Oxford UP, 1998); Douglas M. MacDowell, **Athenian Homicide Law In the Age of the Orators** (Manchester UP, 1966). In what follows I sound more certain about how the system worked than scholars can be today. Even if we can be sure how it was supposed to go in principle (which often we can't be), it doesn't follow that we know how the wheels of Athenian justice ground through in procedural practice. A lot of things you could only know by attending and participating in lots of trials, like old Philocleon, have surely been lost.

Oaths duly extracted, the basileus ushers the case on to one of five venues.

And, by the by, as he is not really the judge, he presumably does not have authority to dismiss a case a citizen is determined to bring. So even if he thinks Euthyphro is a maniac, if he's a maniac who is willing to swear to, we've got a case.

Which of five straight pillars of the legal system gets the case?

First, the alleged murder of the slave by the servant happened on the family farm on Naxos. So what? So this means Euthyphro and his father were part of the Athenian cleruchy there. That is, they were colonial occupiers of an island some distance from Athens. They must have been part of a group of Athenian citizens settled there to ensure the Naxians stayed within the sphere of Athenian naval hegemony, the so-called Delian League. But Athens lost the Peloponnesian War, and its empire, in 404 BCE. Our dialogue is set in 399, because Socrates' case is just coming to trial. This means the case Euthyphro means to bring against his father is at least five years old, maybe older. It concerns events that happened in territory over which Athens no longer claims jurisdiction.

We hear none of this in the dialogue, but it would be obvious to Plato's readers that Euthyphro is stretching things, across time and space.

It all happened long ago, and in another country.

On the other hand, murder is murder.

Remember the guy from section 3 with the weird moral theory? Side with people within 10 meters? That's crazy, because it means drawing an arbitrary circle in the dirt. Who cares which side of some line it happened on. Wrong is wrong. But courts, of course, often care very much which side of some line it happened on.

Since the **cleruchy courts** that might once have heard this case haven't existed for years, we had better move along.

Cases of alleged intentional homicide are handled 'on **the Areopagus**'; that is, by the Areopagite council composed of ex-archons. They do not hear cases in which victims are slaves or non-citizens. Suppose the victim was a citizen, as seems possible. Did Euthyphro's father intend to kill the man? It's hard to say what he was thinking, ditching him like that. We aren't even sure what he asked the **exegetes** — those religious experts whose advice he sought, perhaps to the annoyance of his allegedly expert son. Maybe he took it for granted that, far from Athens, colonial justice would be rough. He wasn't seriously going to haul that servant all the way back to Athens, to stand trial. Maybe all he was worried about, in asking advice, was how to clean up the miasma that was now polluting his farm?

Let's move on. If the Areopagus is not the proper venue, the **Palladion** might be better. The **ephetai**, jury of 51 (respectable old men) hear charges of unintentional homicide and 'planning'. There are a number of ways of being charged with a lesser crime than intentional killing. You can be involved, or conspire, without actually being the guy who sticks the knife in.

Charging Euthyphro's father with 'manslaughter' or 'negligent death', as we would say, makes intuitive sense. Is there any absurdity in trying the case here?

Two, actually. First, per above, the case concerns events that happened before the restoration of democracy, in 403 BCE. There has been an amnesty. That would cover Euthyphro's father, except that the amnesty excludes cases of 'homicide with one's own hand'. If dad is guilty of killing **with his own hands**, he can be tried.

Suppose, as is plausible, dad is at most guilty of 'planning'. He ordered the servant to be tied and ditched. (He's old, Euthyphro says. He has people to throw people in ditches for him.) Will the trial hinge on whether the father himself laid physical hands on the victim in a forceful way? And, if so, whether causing death by throwing someone into a ditch constitutes, not just causing death by letting die, but causing death by letting die with one's own hand? (Is there even such a thing as the crime of **letting die with one's own hand**? That's pretty passive-aggressive.)

Remember that classic moral dilemma, from Chapter 4, section 12? The trolley is out of control and five innocents will die unless you throw a switch, shunting it onto the other track, killing a single innocent person?

Here's an interesting fact. When asked, most people say they would be willing to throw the switch. Saving five seems to be worth killing one. But there is a standard variant, the so-called Footbridge Case, that gets a different response.

Would you push someone off a bridge, if that were the only way to save five others? (We have to draw the guy big. You have to imagine you can't heroically throw yourself off instead. Only **that** guy will do as a trolley-stopper.) People are much less willing to say they would push a living person off a bridge than to throw a switch. But it comes to the same. Psychologically, the explanation seems to be this: the application of personal force sets off emotional alarm bells in our moral brains.[6] It's like we are programmed to believe in miasma, in 'dirty hands', if we push someone to his death. But, on reflection, how can this pattern of moral alarmism make sense? Euthyphro's father's case is a perfect illustration. If the case comes down to the question of whether he pushed the victim, himself, **by hand**, rather than arranging things indirectly, that seems arbitrary.

And, as I said, there's a second absurdity. The punishment for unintentional homicide is exile. When the victim is a non-resident non-citizen, this doesn't make a lot of sense, since the point of exile is to get you away from the victim's family — lest you pollute them by your unwelcome presence. This is a good point at which to shift to our next venue, the **Phreattro**. Exiles wishing to plead to return home may do so 'in Phreattro', from a ship drawn near the shore. Should Euthyphro's father be convicted, and later plead to return home, he may have to take elaborate, pointless precautions to avoid stepping on Athenian soil — pointless because probably the dead victim's family is in Naxos.

The **Delphinium**, next stop, is also presided over by the ephetai. Here admitted killings alleged by the defense to be legal are judged: accidental killing of a fellow soldier in battle; accidental death in sporting events; doctors whose patients die. It might seem dad would be on fairly solid ground here. He feels he acted justly, binding the murderer and throwing him in the ditch. But, of course, one cannot argue **both** that a killing was unintended **and** that it was intended to be just. (A bit like the old lawyer joke. Lawyer borrows something from you. You ask for it back. He says: I never borrowed it and, anyway, it was broken. Furthermore, I returned it in perfect condition.)

6   See Joshua Greene, Moral Tribes: Emotion, Reason and the Gap Between Us and Them (Penguin, 2013), chapters 4 and 5.

Euthyphro might have to be careful, too. Even if his father killed justly, there should still be a trial. That's the point of having this court. But it would be uncomfortable for Euthyphro to argue that he is, wrongly, swearing his own dad is guilty of unjust killing, so dad can, rightly, get purified for a just killing. Who is more righteous? The father who killed justly, yet illegally? Or the son who prosecuted legally, yet unjustly?

And now things get weird.

Our final stop is the **Prytaneion**. The Athenians had a court for trying unknown killers, inanimate objects and animals. This one is presided over by the basileus and an assistant. How does it go? A stone is thrown and kills a man, say. The 'doer' may be convicted, even if unknown. A tree falls and kills a man. The tree itself may be convicted. (This is getting as silly as Philocleon trying the dog for stealing the cheese, calling the bowl and pot as witnesses.) The tree will be carried and cast beyond the border. (Again, very arbitrary lines are being fetishized as morally significant.) By modern standards holding a trial for an inanimate object is strange, to say the least. It is probably best to think of this court's function as located at the juncture of ritual, contagious magic, criminal forensics and public health and sanitation.

It would be bold, but, if hailed into one of the other courts, Euthyphro's father could move for a change of venue. The Naxian weather is the man you want! Or: the ditch did it. Sounds silly, but, in all seriousness, part of the appeal of the ditch option, from the start, is surely that dad wants the guy dead, but doesn't want to have killed him. He wants to keep his hands clean. (How did the Greeks dispose of unwanted infants? They exposed them. Left them on some hill, or in the woods. That way you can feel you didn't do it — kill a human child. You 'let it happen'.)

Our tour is done, but we shouldn't end it without noting the most signifi-cant non-stop along the way: the public prosecutor's office. There isn't one. From our modern perspective, Athenian justice, for all its many courts, is curi-ously lacking, due to its semi-private, semi-public character. Private citizens must prosecute on behalf of themselves, their family, **phratry** [clan] or friends.

Can a citizen sue his own flesh and blood? Can a son prosecute a father?

Obviously if a crime has been committed, **someone** should prosecute. We have plays like Aeschylus' **Oresteia**, positively celebrating the moral neces-sity of a son prosecuting a parent, in an extreme case. And again: Euthyphro is standing up for the principle that a suspect should stand trial, even if he is found innocent. The process purifies. Euthyphro may understand this in religious terms that are a bit strange to us. But we get that the justice system isn't just for punishing the guilty. Innocent people need to 'clear their names'.

But, again, the Athenian system is ill-equipped. Consider the oaths that must be sworn for the basileus, to get this ball rolling. Here is Demosthenes, explaining how that goes 'on the Aereopagus' (perhaps in other courts, in some form:)

> First the man who accuses someone of such a deed [murder] will swear an oath calling down doom on himself and his family and his house, and it will be no common oath, but one sworn concerning no other thing, while standing over the cut pieces of a boar, a ram, and a bull, which have been slaughtered by the proper persons on proper days, so every sacred obligation has been fulfilled as regards both timing and participants. And even then, after all this, the man who has sworn this solemn oath is not to be trusted, but if he is proven to be a liar he will bring perjury home to his children and his family and will not gain anything by it at all. (D 23.67-8)

The defendant swears the same. So, obviously, if both Euthyphro and his father swear, their house is, literally, damned if he did, damned if he didn't. Far from affording an opportunity for the family to clean up pollution under its roof, any trial is doomed to rain miasma on everyone.

22

The point isn't that Euthyphro's summary of his case should trigger precisely this cascade of legal speculations in the minds of readers. But, plausibly, Plato does intend readers familiar with Athenian justice to see complications.

Like Euthyphro, the court system is a mix of the rational and irrational. It's modern in some ways — five courts! — primitive in others. (Plato, whose teacher was convicted and sentenced by an Athenian jury of 500, obviously has his concerns about the competence of Athenian juries.)

So the trouble isn't just one Zeus-bothering, manic mantis.

Even a true philosopher would have trouble navigating this legal system in pure pursuit of the straight lines of rational justice.

This gets us ahead of our story, to **Republic**, in which the move is explicitly made from the individual to the social system. You can't understand what justice is like unless you see it, ideally, in both City and Soul. For now we can say this much. In **Republic** some of the concerns raised in Euthyphro are implicitly dealt with.

Zeus!

For example what do we do about stories of the gods behaving unethically, rewarding the unjust or punishing the just? We don't let poets tell such stories.

What about Euthyphro-type dilemmas? Cases in which a son is called upon to prosecute a father? Plato advocates (perhaps not fully seriously) that a kind of communism should be instituted. Children (at least of the ruling class) will be raised communally and will not know who their biological parents are. That's **one** formula for straightening the curves.

23

In Chapter 3 I sketched Plato's Theory of the Forms because, so I said, the reader deserves an answer to a simple question: where is all this going? But did I give the right simple answer? I don't think many scholars would dispute that **Republic** Book I is headed for Books V-VII, in which the Theory of Forms is presented, or that certain elements of the **Meno** foreshadow the Theory of Forms in ways that can hardly be accidental. But **Euthyphro** might be a different case. It is a very early dialogue. Perhaps it is more purely Socratic. Perhaps Plato has not come up with anything like his Theory of Forms yet.

There is no answering this question. But, once again, let's speculate. If we look for anticipation of mature Platonic epistemology in **Euthyphro**, where might we find it? It seems to me we are likeliest to find it in the sheer, frustrating irrelevance of what we are seeing to the thing we are supposed to be thinking about.

In The Myth of the Cave, the walkers on the wall carry their statues — statues of the gods included, I presume. The shadows of these flicker for the prisoners to see. In the Myth we hear that something causes a certain prisoner's head to turn. But what? What does Socrates (Plato) say about what might actually induce us to turn our heads around and look in that backwards direction? What might we be seeing, in front of us, that would make us look behind? Here is Socrates, explaining to Glaucon:

Among our sense impressions there are some that do not call upon the intelligence to examine them because what is delivered up to the senses is sufficient, while other cases certainly summon the help of intelligence to examine them because the sensation does not achieve a sensible result.

You are, he said, obviously referring to things appearing in the distance and to shadow-painting.

You are not quite getting my meaning, I said. — What is it then?

They do not call for help, I said, if they do not at the same time give a contrary impression. I describe those that do as calling for help whenever the sense perception does not point to one thing rather than its opposite, whether its object be far or near. You will understand my meaning better if I put it this way: here, we say, are three fingers, the smallest, the second, and the middle finger. — Quite so.

Assume that I am talking about them as being seen quite close. Now examine this about them. — What?

Each of them equally appears to be a finger, and in this respect it makes no difference whether it is seen to be at the end or in the middle, whether it is white or black, thick or thin or any of that sort of thing. In all this the common sort of soul is not compelled to ask the intelligence what a finger is, for the sense of sight does not indicate to it that the finger is the opposite of a finger. — Certainly not.

Therefore this sense perception would not be likely to call on the intelligence or arouse it. — Hardly likely.

What about big and small? Does the sense of sight have a sufficient perception of them, and does it make no difference to it whether the finger is in the middle or at one end? Or thick and thin, hard or soft, in the case of the sense of touch? And do our other senses not lack clear perception of these qualities? Does not each sense behave as follows: in the first place the sense concerned with the hard is of necessity also concerned with the soft and it declares to the soul that it perceives the same object to be both hard and soft. — That is so.

Then in these cases the soul in turn is puzzled as to what this perception means by hard, if it says that the same thing is also soft; and so with the perception of the light and the heavy, the soul is puzzled as to what is the meaning of the light and the heavy, if sense perception indicates that what is light is also heavy, and what is heavy, light.

Yes, he said, these indications are strange to the soul, and need investigation.

Probably then, I said, in these cases the soul will attempt, by means of calculation and intelligence, to examine whether each of the things presented to it is one or two. — Of course. (523b-4b)

Was that hard to follow? Socrates' three fingers are my three cows (from Chapter 3) all over again. Also, all those Athenas up on the Parthenon. Is she one or many? And Euthyphro's dilemma. One straight way looks like two horns. Surely seeing holiness as a dilemma means suffering double-vision. We need a resolution that reduces an appearance of two to a reality of one.

But Euthyphro can't manage. "I can't possible explain to you what I have in mind because every time we advance some proposition it runs around in circles somehow, refusing to stay where we put it" (11b).

Socrates replies that such propositions must be "like the works of my ancestor, Daedalus." Daedalus was a mythical artist-inventor (allegedly an ancestor of Socrates: divine beings and long dead family proving, once again, hard to distinguish.) His statues were so lifelike they got down from their pedestals and walked around. Socrates says that Euthyphro can't credit him, Socrates, with having inherited this magical power, because these are Euthyphro's propositions coming to life. Socrates didn't make them. Euthyphro replies that he does indeed think it is all Socrates' fault. "They would have stayed put if it were up to me" (11d).

This Euthyphro — who, so he says, would be no better than the ordinary man on the street if he did not have "accurate knowledge of all such things" — would seem to be, alas, no different from the ordinary man on the street. He keeps seeing two related things (justice and holiness) and thinking he is seeing one (holiness), so of course there is an optical illusion of motion.

24

Returning to the Cave, it is a bit of a puzzle where the walkers along the wall come from and where they go. I imagine their platform wall as circular. They go around the back of the fire and come round again. (This would conserve the supply of walkers.) In Chapter 3 I made the inevitable film comparison. The walkers are like individual film cells passing before the projector's light. But I have always imagined that the Cave projection mechanism as more like a zoetrope. Or, to be precise, a late-model praxinoscope, which is like a cross between a zoetrope and a magic lantern (but who's counting? Perhaps this is not the time for a history of precursors to modern cinema.)

Do you know what a zoetrope is? They are simple toys. I'll show you how to make one. Do you see that picture below? Cut it out. (Photocopy it first. Don't ruin your nice book.) Cut out all those little slits — the white vertical bits. Wrap the ends around so it makes a cylinder. You want the pictures to be on the inside.

Now figure out some way for it to revolve. (**You** figure it out. Maybe tape it to a toilet paper roll.) Gaze through the slits at the figures. If I've drawn the pictures exactly right (honestly, I haven't!) it should look like the little statue-man is running and jumping. Do you know who invented the zoetrope? Apparently it was invented in China almost 2,000 years ago. But it was independently reinvented in 1834 by a man named William Horner.

Do you know what he called it? A 'daedalum'. I think maybe it was Plato who really invented the first one. He might have called the technique **euthy-phrotoscoping**. (Only animation buffs are going to get that one!)

25

Am I arguing that Plato is already narrating the Myth of the Cave, anticipating his Theory of Forms, as early as **Euthyphro**? No. I don't think it would be surprising if it turned out Plato was thinking certain thoughts years before committing them to paper, but I can't say how likely that is. What I do think is that Plato's mind works in funny ways, making him hard to follow. Your nearest emergency exit may be behind you. Except he doesn't bother to put up signs that say so, in so many words.

Let me complete the Cave analogy. If Euthyphro is in the Cave, the set-up is as follows.

Euthyphro sees **holiness** running in circles like a statue of Daedalus because he is seeing two as one: holiness and justice. He ought to turn around and see two things as two.

So is that the answer? Does this somehow solve Euthyphro's dilemma?

Once we have seen holiness and justice as two things, not one incoherent thing, we keep going, climbing up. There will come a point at which these two become one again. When we have apprehended the Form of the Good we will see why holiness and justice cannot really come apart, or conflict, even though they are distinct. Euthyphro was right all along to want to see them as one, but he was looking in the wrong direction. But turn him around and the unpleasantness of feeling unity dissolve keeps him from fighting through to a recovery of real unity.

Do you see the similarity between the lowest and the highest levels of intellectual development, according to Plato? Watching a film — peeking through the slits of a zoetrope — is tricking your eye into seeing the many-as-one. 2 = 1 is the soul of cinema, its Heraclitean trick. 2 = 1 is the soul of Plato, too, in a sense. His Parmenidean truth.

This is why Plato hates movies. They trick people into thinking they are getting what only philosophy truly provides. In the movies it runs together, but in illusory, contradictory ways. By contrast, going to the Not-Movies, **thinking** the many-as-one, is the highest intellectual achievement. It all comes together, in real, non-contradictory ways.

To repeat points made in Chapter 3: the Form of the Good is like the light shining out of the projector. It is the unitary, constant condition of the possibility of apparent change and multiplicity. The Form of the Good is also like the light of your own mind. Or of Mind. Plato thinks it is important to realize the ultimate source of the passing show is not outside but, in a sense, inside. Or deeply akin to what is inside you. A strange enough thought that we should probably set it aside until it is placed front and center in **Meno**.

Euthyphro, of course, is moving off too soon. "Some other time, Socrates. I am in a hurry, and I really have to go now" (15e).

Chapter 6
EUTHYPHRO

Summary of Sections

On the Steps of the Court:
Socrates' Case

[2A-3E]

Introductions. We meet Socrates, Euthyphro, the absent Meletus (Socrates' prosecutor) and — stretching a point — the citizens of Athens. Socrates explains about his case. He is accused of corrupting the youth by introducing new gods into the city.

Euthyphro's case:
Ought a Son to Prosecute a Father?

[3E-5A]

Euthyphro explains about his own case. His father caused the death of a servant, who was himself a murderer. The question: ought a son to prosecute a father? How to know? Euthyphro's first stab: family ties don't bind in these matters.

Holy Enroller:
What is Holiness?

[5A-6E]

Socrates enrolls as Euthyphro's pupil. What is holiness? Speculation about the nature of the gods. A condition on possible answers: not just examples; a general form or idea must be produced.

First Attempt at Definition:
What the Gods Love is Holy

[7A-8A]

Euthyphro's first attempt at definition: what the gods love is holy; what is unloved by them is unholy. Awkward consequence: some things will be both holy and unholy.

Injustice Must Be Punished;
Second Attempt at Definition

[8A-9D]

E: No one denies that unjust killings must be punished. S: But there is disagreement about what counts as unjust. How does Euthyphro know what the gods will make of his particular case? And, again: what is the definition of 'holiness'. Will it be: what all the gods love?

Do the Gods Love It Because It Is Holy?
Divine Orders; Orders of Explanation

[9E-11B]

Modified definition: what all the gods love is holy; what they all hate is unholy. But is the holy loved by the gods because it is holy, or is it holy because it is loved by the god? Either the good (holiness) comes first, inducing love, or love induces the good qualities (holiness). E: The gods love things because they are good (holy). Therefore, Euthyphro's definition cannot be correct. It implies a contradiction: if A is prior to B, and A = B, then B is prior to A.

Statues of Daedalus;
Containment relations

[11B-12E]

Euthyphro's claims are like statues of Daedalus, running around in circles. A fresh start: all that is holy is necessarily just. But: is all that is just holy? Comparison with the case of fear and shame. Holiness is only one part of the domain of justice. But which part?

Care of the gods;
Inconclusive conclusion

[12E-16A]

Holiness is the part of justice concerned with the care of the gods. But what sort of care do the gods require? And why? Shrewd consideration of the balance of trade sustaining the divine service industry. Return to the proposition that what the gods love is pious. Inconclusive conclusion.

2A　EUTHYPHRO: WHAT'S NEW, SOCRATES? Something out of the ordinary, since it has dragged you from your usual haunts in the Lyceum to hang around the archon basileus' court. Surely it can't be that you, like me, have a suit pending against someone before the basileus?

SOCRATES: The Athenian term for what brings me here is not suit but indictment, Euthyphro.

E: What? Someone must have indicted you, then.
2B　There's no way **you** have indicted someone else.

S: No indeed.

E: But someone has indicted you?

S: That's just it.

E: Who is it?

S: I don't really know the man myself, Euthyphro. He seems to be a young man, and still unknown. He's called Meletus, I gather. He belongs to the Pitthean deme, if you happen to know anyone from there by that name — long hair, thin little beard, rather pointy nose.

2C　E: Doesn't ring a bell, Socrates. But what's the charge he brought against you?

S: What charge, you ask? No mean one, as I see it, for it is no small thing for one so young to have figured out such a serious situation. He says he knows how, and by whom, the young are corrupted. More likely than not the man is wise, so when he sees my dull ignorance corrupting his whole generation, he is provoked to denounce me to the city like a child running to its mother. I think he is the only
2D　one of our public men to make a proper start in politics. One's primary concern really ought to be for the young, so they will become

good men — just as it's reasonable for a good farmer to tend young sprouts first, looking after the rest later. In just this way Meletus will start off by uprooting weeds — such as myself — that damage the tender shoots of the young, as he says. Later he will obviously turn his attention to older men, thereby making himself a source of bounty and fruitful blessings for the city; a likely fate for anyone who sets out from a starting point as good as this one.

3 A

E: I hope so, Socrates, but I'm afraid it may be just the opposite. By trying to hurt you, it seems to me he makes a very crude start, cutting at the very heart of the city. But tell me, what does he say you do to corrupt the young?

S: It sounds like an outlandish business, my friend, when you first hear it. He says I fabricate gods. He indicts me, so he says, on behalf of the old gods, whom I don't believe in, since I'm busy making new ones.

3 B

E: I see, Socrates. This is due to the divine sign you say comes to you now and again. This man has written out his indictment against you as against an innovator in divine matters. He comes to court to slander you, knowing such matters can easily be made to appear in a bad light before the crowd. That's how it is with me, too. Whenever I speak up concerning divine matters in the assembly, and foretell the future, they laugh me down as if I were crazy. Yet I have never made a prediction that didn't come true. They envy those of us with such gifts. But you shouldn't pay any attention to them. Just face them head-on.

3 C

S: My dear Euthyphro, maybe being laughed at isn't such a big deal. The Athenians, it seems to me, don't care much about whether so-and-so is brainy, as long as he doesn't **teach** his peculiar brand of wisdom. But if they start to think someone is bringing others round to his way of thinking, **then** the Athenians get riled up — either out of jealousy, as you say, or for some other reason.

3 D

E: I certainly don't have any desire to put their feelings towards **me** to the test.

S: Perhaps they take you for someone who is stingy with himself, and not unduly eager to teach your personal wisdom. But I'm worried that my fondness for people makes them think I am ready to pour out whatever wisdom I have to anyone and everyone — not just for free, but maybe with a little something extra tossed in, happily, if anyone is willing to listen to me talk. Well then, as I said just now, if they were just going to laugh at me, as they laugh at you, 3 E   there would be nothing unpleasant about the prospect of a day in court, spent laughing and having fun. But if they are serious about it? Well, in that case the outcome is somewhat obscure — except to prophets like you.

E: Perhaps it will all come to nothing, Socrates, and you will bring your case to a gratifying end, as I trust I will mine.

S: WHAT ABOUT YOUR CASE, Euthyphro? Are you defending or prosecuting?

E: Prosecuting.

S: Who?

4A   E: One whom I am thought insane to indict.

S: Why? Is he a flight risk?

E: He's far from able to flee; he's actually quite old.

S: Who is it?

E: My father.

S: My dear sir! Your own father?

E: Exactly so.

S: What is the charge? What is the case about?

E: Murder, Socrates.

S: Hercules! I imagine, Euthyphro, most men don't know how things ought to be. I don't think just anyone would be able to do what you 4B   are doing. This is a job for one far advanced in wisdom!

E: Yes, by Zeus — **very** advanced, Socrates.

S: Is it a case, then, of your father killing **another** relative? But I suppose that much is obvious. You certainly wouldn't be prosecuting your father for killing a stranger.

E: It's ridiculous, Socrates, for you to think it makes a difference whether the victim is a stranger or a relative. One should only consider whether the killer acted justly or not. If he acted justly, let him alone; if not, prosecute even a killer who shares **your** hearth and home. You are just as polluted **if you** intentionally remain under the same roof with a person like that, instead of purifying both yourself and him by bringing charges. The victim was a dependent of mine, and when we were farming in Naxos he acted as our servant. In a drunken rage, he killed one of our household slaves, so my father bound him hand and foot, threw him into some ditch, then sent a man here to inquire of a religious advisor what should be done. In the meantime, he didn't show any consideration to the man as he lay there bound, and neglected him, thinking that as he was a murderer it wouldn't be a big deal if he were to die — which is just what happened. He died from hunger, the cold and his bonds before the messenger came back from the religious advisor. Now my father and other relatives are furious that I am prosecuting him for murder on behalf of a murderer — when, they say, my father didn't even murder him! And besides, even if he **had** just **completely** murdered him, the dead man, being a murderer, doesn't deserve a second thought. They say it is impious for a son to prosecute a father for murder — that's how wrong they are, Socrates, about how things stand in the divine realm with respect to holiness and unholiness.

S: You on the other hand, Euthyphro, think your knowledge of the divine, of holiness and unholiness, is **so** accurate that — by Zeus! — given that it all happened just as you say, you have no fear of acting impiously now by bringing your father to trial?

5A   E: I would be of no use at all, Socrates — there wouldn't be any difference between **Euthyphro** and the man on the street — if I did not have accurate knowledge of all such things.

S: THEN THE BEST THING that could possibly happen to me, admirable Euthyphro, is to become your student and, before the suit from Meletus starts, go offer to settle with him. I would say to him that even in the past I thought it was very important to know about divine matters, and now, since he says I do wrong by treating religious subjects carelessly and innovating in them, I have enrolled myself as your
5B   pupil. I would say to him: Meletus, if you grant that Euthyphro is wise in these matters, then grant that I have correct beliefs too, and don't drag me into court. If you don't grant it, sue my teacher, not me, for corrupting the old — both me and his father — by teaching me, and by admonishing and punishing his father. If he won't buy it, and doesn't either drop the charge, or else pin it on you instead of me, I'll try out the same line of defense in court as I did in my settlement offer to him.

5C   E: Yes, by Zeus, Socrates! And if he should try to indict me, I would find his weak spot, I think, so that talk in the court would sooner be about him than me.

S: I'm well aware of that, my dear friend, which is why I'm so eager to become your pupil. I know that neither Meletus nor anyone else

seems to cast you so much as a glance, whereas he has seen through me so sharply and easily that he has indicted me for impiety. So tell me now, by Zeus, that thing you just maintained you knew so well: namely, what is the nature of righteousness and unrighteousness, regarding murder and everything else. I take it holiness always   5 D
consists in some **one** thing, with regard to every action; and unholiness is always the opposite of holiness, and the same as itself. For everything unholy always appears to us in the same form — namely as a form of unholiness.

E: Most certainly, Socrates.

S: Tell me what you say, then. What do you say holiness is, and what unholiness?

E: I say holiness is doing what I'm doing now — namely, prosecuting wrong-doers, whether the crime is murder or temple robbery or anything else, and whether the culprit is your father or mother   5 E
or anyone else, and not prosecuting is unholy. And please note, Socrates, that I can point you to a certain proof — one which I have already offered to others — that this is the law and that it is right for things to turn out this way, and that we must not let a wrong-doer escape **no matter who** he might be. As it happens, these people themselves believe that Zeus is the best and   6 A
most just of gods, but they admit that Zeus bound his own father for the injustice of devouring his sons — and that he in his turn castrated his father on similar grounds. Yet they're angry at me for prosecuting my father for wrongdoing! And so they contradict themselves in what they claim about the gods and about me.

S: Indeed, Euthyphro, isn't this just the sort of business that has landed me in legal trouble, because I find it somehow hard to accept it when

6 B

someone says such things about the gods? Someone is likely to say I am going wrong on this very point. Now, however, if you — who know all about this stuff — believe these tales, then I must, it seems, give way. What else can I say, since I freely admit I know nothing about it? Tell me then, in the name of the god of friendship, do you really believe these things happened?

E: Yes, Socrates, and even more astonishing things as well — things that most people don't know.

6 C

S: So you believe that the gods really go to war with one another, that there are hateful rivalries and battles between them, and other things of this sort, like the ones narrated by the poets, or represented in varied ways by our fine artists — particularly upon the robe that is carried up to the Acropolis during the great Panathenaic festival, which is embroidered with all these sorts of designs? Should we agree these things are literally true, Euthyphro?

E: Not only these things, Socrates. As I was just saying, I will, if you wish, relate many other things about the gods that I'm quite sure will astound you when you hear them.

6 D

S: I wouldn't be a bit surprised. Someday — when you've got time on your hands — you must tell me all about it. In the meantime, try to speak more clearly about what I was asking just now. Because, my friend, you did not teach me adequately when I inquired as to what holiness is. You told me that the thing you happen to be doing at the moment — namely, prosecuting your father for murder — is holy.

E: And what I said was true, Socrates.

S: That may be. But there are lots of other things, Euthyphro, that you would also claim are holy.

E: Yes, there are.

S: Keep in mind, then, that this isn't what I asked you to do — to give me one or two examples out of the many holy actions. Rather, I asked what essential form all holy actions exhibit, in virtue of which they are holy. For you did agree all unholy actions are unholy and all holy actions holy in virtue of some shared form, or don't you remember?   6 E

E: I remember.

S: Tell me then what this form is, so that I can pay close attention to it and use it as a paradigm to judge any action, whether committed by you or anyone else. If the action be of the right form, I will declare it holy; otherwise, not.

E: If that is how you want it, Socrates, that is how I will give it to you.

S: That's what I want.

E: WELL THEN, WHAT THE GODS LOVE is holy; what is unloved by them is unholy.   7 A

S: Magnificent, Euthyphro! You have now answered in just the way I wanted. Whether your answer is true — that's a little something I don't know yet. It's obvious, though, that you are going to show me that what you say is true.

E: Oh, certainly.

S: Come then, let us examine your words. A man or deed loved by the gods is holy. On the other hand, a man or deed hated by the gods is unholy. They are not one and the same — in fact, they are diametrical opposites: the holy and the unholy. Isn't that so?

E: It is indeed.

S: This seems to you a sound proposition?

7 B   E: I think so, Socrates.

S: Haven't we also declared, Euthyphro, that the gods exist in a state of discord, that they disagree with each other — indeed, that they hate one another. Haven't we said this, too?

E: We did say that.

S: When hatred and anger arise, Euthyphro, what sorts of disagreements are likely to be the cause? Let's look at it this way. If you and I were to get into an argument about which of two numbers was greater, would this difference of opinion turn us into enemies and 7 C   make us furious with each other, or would we sit down, count up, and quickly smooth our differences?

E: The latter, certainly.

S: Likewise, if we had a fight about the relative sizes of things, we would quickly end the disagreement by measuring?

E: That's so.

S: And we would employ a scale, I think, if we disagreed about what was heavier and what lighter?

E: Of course.

S: What sorts of things might we argue about that would make us angry and hostile towards one another, if we couldn't reach agreement? Maybe you don't have an immediate answer, but let me 7 D   suggest something. See whether it isn't these things: justice and injustice, beauty and ugliness, good and bad. Aren't these the very things for causing disputes which, when we are unable to reach any satisfactory agreement, make people become enemies, whenever we do become enemies — whether you and I or anybody else?

E: That's just how it goes in arguments about such things, Socrates.

S: What about the gods, Euthyphro? If in fact they get into argu- ments, won't they be about these sorts of things?

E: That must be how it is, Socrates.

S: Then according to your argument, good Euthyphro, different   7 E
gods consider different things to be just, beautiful, ugly, good, and
bad — for they wouldn't be at odds unless they disagreed about
these things, would they?

E: You are right.

S: Each of them loves what each considers beautiful, good, and just,
and each hates the opposite of these things?

E: Certainly.

S: But now the very same things, according to what you say, are
considered just by some gods but unjust by others. It's because
they disagree with one another about these things that they quar-   8 A
rel and war with one another, isn't it?

E: It is.

S: The same things, then, are loved by the gods and hated by the
gods, and will be both god-loved and god-hated.

E: It seems likely.

S: And the same things will be both holy and unholy, according to
the terms of this argument?

E: I'm afraid so.

S: So you didn't answer my question, you man of mystery. I did not ask you for something which, while remaining one and the same, is both holy and unholy. But it appears what is loved by the gods is also hated by them. So it won't be too surprising if the thing you're doing now — namely, punishing your father — is pleasing to Zeus but hateful to Kronos and Ouranos; is pleasing to Hephaestus but hateful to Hera. And the same goes for any other gods who may disagree with one another about the matter.

8B

E: I think, Socrates, that here we have something no god would dispute: whoever kills anyone unjustly must pay the penalty.

S: Well now, Euthyphro, have you ever heard any man arguing that one who has murdered or otherwise acted unjustly should not pay the penalty?

8C

E: There are endless disputes about this sort of thing, both in and out of the courts, because wrongdoers will say and do anything to avoid getting punished.

S: Do they admit they have done wrong, Euthyphro, but maintain that, **even so**, they should not be punished?

E: No, they don't admit it at all.

S: So then they don't say or do just **anything**. For they don't presume to claim that, nor do they deny that they should pay the penalty **if** they did wrong. I think they just deny their guilt, don't they?

8D

E: That's how it is.

S: Then they don't dispute **this**: wrongdoers must be punished. Maybe they just disagree about who did wrong, what they did, and when.

E: You are right.

S: Don't the gods have the same experience — if indeed they are at odds about justice and injustice, as your argument maintains? Some say some have done wrong, while others deny it? For surely, my friend, no one, either among gods or men, goes so far as to say a wrongdoer should not be punished.

8E

E: Yes, that is basically true, Socrates.

S: So parties to a given dispute, whether gods or men, dispute about each separate action — if in fact the gods ever dispute. Some say the thing was done justly, others unjustly. Isn't that how it goes?

E: Yes, indeed.

S: Come now, my dear Euthyphro. Tell me, that I may be the wiser 9A for it, what proof do you have that all gods deem this man unjustly killed — this servant-turned-murderer, bound by the master of his victim, who died in bondage before his captor learned from the seers what was to be done about him — and that all gods consider it right for a son to denounce and prosecute a father on behalf of such a person? Come, try to show me clearly that all the gods 9B definitely believe this action to be right. If you can demonstrate this adequately I will sing the praises of your wisdom forevermore.

E: Perhaps this is no small task, Socrates — though I could show you very clearly indeed.

S: I quite understand that you think I'm dull-witted compared to the jurors, since obviously you are going to show **them** that these actions are unjust and hated by all the gods.

E: I will show them **very** clearly, Socrates, if only they will listen to me.

9C   S: They will listen so long as you seem to be speaking well. But something occurred to me while you were talking, a thought I am even now turning over in my mind. Suppose Euthyphro does show me conclusively that all the gods consider such a death unjust. To what extent will he thereby have taught me the nature of holiness and unholiness? That such a deed is hated by all the gods — so much would seem to follow. But a definition of holiness and unholiness does not, for what is hated by the gods has also been shown to be loved by them. So I won't keep pressing the point. Let us grant, if
9D   you like, that all gods consider this thing unjust and hate it. Is this, then, the only correction we wish to make to our account — namely, that what all gods hate is unholy, whereas what they all love is holy, and what some gods love and some hate is both or neither? Is this how we now wish to define holy and unholy?

E: Is anything stopping us, Socrates?

S: Not as far as I'm concerned, Euthyphro, but consider your own position. See whether this proposal will pave the way to the instruction you promised me.

9E   E: I WOULD CERTAINLY SAY the holy is what all the gods love, and the opposite — what all the gods hate — is unholy.

S: Then let us examine, once again, whether what we have here is a sound proposition. We could, of course, just let it pass. Whenever we — or anyone — say something is so, we could simply take it to be so. Alternatively, we could look and see what it all means.

E: We must look and see, but I really think what we have now is a sound proposition.

S: And soon we will know better about that. Consider this: is the holy loved by the gods because it is holy, or is it holy because it is loved by the gods?

E: I don't know what you mean, Socrates.

S: Let me try to explain more clearly. We speak of something carried and of a carrier; of something guided and a guide; of something seen and one who sees. You understand that, in every case of this sort, these things are different from one another, and how they are different?

E: I think I do.

S: Similarly, isn't there something which is loved and something which loves, separate from it?

E: Of course.

S: Tell me then whether the thing carried is carried because some- 10B
one carries it, or for some other reason.

E: No, that's the reason.

S: Likewise, the thing guided is guided because someone guides it, and the thing seen is seen because someone sees it.

E: Of course.

S: It isn't that someone sees it because the thing is seen. It's the other way round: it is seen because someone sees it. Likewise, something's being guided doesn't cause its guide; the thing is guided because of a guide. Nor do carriers come to be by things getting carried; instead, things are carried because someone carries them. Is what I 10c
am getting at clear, Euthyphro? I mean this: when something comes to be, or undergoes some effect, it doesn't come to be because it's in a state of becoming. Rather, it is in a state of becoming precisely

because it is coming to be. Likewise, effects don't happen because things undergo effects; effects happen because of **causes**. Or don't you agree?

E: I do.

S: Either the quality of being loved — belovedness — is something that just comes about, or it is something brought about by someone's love?

E: Certainly.

S: So this case is analogous to those just mentioned: the thing is not loved because of its belovedness; rather, it is beloved because of one who loves it.

E: Necessarily.

10D S: What then do we say about holiness, Euthyphro? Surely that it is loved by all the gods, by your account?

E: Yes.

S: Is it loved because it is holy, or is there some other reason?

E: There is no other reason.

S: It is loved then because it is holy, but it is not holy because it is loved?

E: So it seems.

S: And because the gods love it, it becomes loved by the gods and god-beloved?

10E E: Of course.

S: What is loved by the gods is not, then, identical to what is holy, Euthyphro, nor does 'holy' mean god-beloved, as you maintain. These are distinct things.

E: How so, Socrates?

S: Because we agree that what is holy is loved because of its holiness. It isn't holy because it is loved. Isn't that so?

E: Yes.

S: And, on the other hand we agree that what is god-beloved is so, just because the gods love it — that's just what it is to be god-beloved. It's not the case that they love it **because** it's god-beloved.

E: True.

S: But if that which is god-beloved and that which is holy were one and the same, dear Euthyphro, and if the holy were loved because 11A it was holy, then what is god-beloved would be loved by the gods because it was — god-beloved! And if the god-beloved were god-beloved because it was loved by the gods, then the holy would also be holy because it was loved by the gods. But now you see we have two quite opposite sorts of cases here — very different from one another. We have someone who loves a thing, making it be loved; and we have a lovable thing, which makes someone love it. I'm afraid that when I asked you what holiness is, Euthyphro, you didn't want to make its nature clear to me. Instead, you told me about one of its properties — namely the property holiness has of being loved by all the gods. But you have yet to tell me what 11B holiness is in itself. Now, if you please, stop hiding things from me and start over again from the beginning, telling me what holiness is. Never mind whether it is loved by the gods, or has some other such quality — we won't argue about that — but tell me freely what holiness and unholiness are.

E: BUT SOCRATES, I CAN'T possibly explain to you what I have in mind, because every time we advance some proposition it runs around in circles somehow, refusing to stay where we put it.

S: Your propositions, Euthyphro, seem like the works of my ances- 11C tor, Daedalus. If it were **me** stating them and setting them forth, you might make fun of me, saying that, due to my relation to him even my works in words run away from me and won't stay where they're put. As it is, these propositions are **yours**, so we need some other joke — they really won't stay put, as you yourself have noticed.

E: I think that joke suits our discussion well enough, Socrates, because **I'm** not the one making these things wander around and fail to remain in one spot. I think you're the Daedalus here, because they would have stayed put if it were up to me

11 D

S: Then it looks as if I must be even **more** terribly clever than Daedalus, my friend, since he set only his own creations in motion, while I have apparently animated both my own and those of others. And the pinnacle of my genius is that I am clever without wanting to be, for I would give up the wealth of Tantalus as well as the cleverness of Daedalus, if only my words would stay and remain fixed in one spot. But enough of this. Since you seem inclined to slack off, I'll have to share my excitement with you so that you can teach me about holiness somehow. So don't give up before you find a way! Consider whether you think all that is holy is necessarily just.

11 E

E: I think so.

12 A

S: So, then, is **all** that is just holy? Or is it rather that while all that is holy is just, not all that is just is holy, but some is and some not?

HOLY?

JUST?

E: You lost me there, Socrates.

S: And yet you outshine me as much in your youth as you do in wisdom! As I was saying, your rich diet of wisdom has made you sluggish. Pull yourself together, my good man, because the thing I'm saying is not that hard to grasp. I am saying the opposite of what that poet said, who wrote:

12 B

Zeus, who has brought all that to pass, and made it grow, you will not name/ For where there is fear there is also shame.

I disagree with the poet. Shall I tell you why?

E: Please do.

S: I don't think that where there is fear there is also shame, for I think many people who fear disease and poverty and many other things feel fear but are not ashamed of what they fear. Don't you agree?

E: I do indeed.

S: But where there is shame there **is** also fear. For is there anyone who feels shame and contrition about some matter, who does not at the same time fear and dread a reputation for wickedness? 12C

E: He will fear it.

S: Then it isn't right to say, where there is fear there is also shame, rather that where there is shame there is also fear. But shame is not everywhere that fear is, since fear covers a wider area than shame. Shame is **part** of fear, just as odd is part of the concept of number — from which it follows that it isn't true that where there is number there is also oddness. Rather, where there is oddness there is also number. Do you follow me now?

E: Absolutely.

S: This is the kind of thing I was asking about before: where there is justice, must there be holiness? Or is it rather that where there is holiness, there is also justice, since justice is not coextensive with holiness — holiness is a part of justice? Shall we say so, or do you think otherwise? 12D

E: No, that's fine; I think what you say is right.

S: See what comes next: if holiness is part of justice, we must, it seems, find out what part of justice it might be. Now if you asked me a similar question about the thing I just mentioned — what part of the concept of number is even, and what kind of number it was, I would say: a number which can be divided evenly, rather than unevenly, by two. Or don't you think so?

E: I do.

12E S: Try to give me a similar account of what part of justice holiness is, so that we can tell Meletus not to wrong us any more, and not to indict me for sacrilege, since I have learned enough from you to be able to tell the difference between what is sacred and holy and what is not.

E: I THINK, SOCRATES, that piety and holiness are that part of justice concerned with the care of the gods, while the part of justice concerned with the care of men comprises the rest.

13A S: What you say seems excellent, Euthyphro, but I'm still unclear on one **tiny** point. I don't yet know what you mean by 'care', for you don't mean care of the gods in the same sense as care of other things. We say, for example — don't we? — that not everyone knows how to take care of horses, only the horse-breeder does.

CARE OF GODS

MEN JUSTICE

E: Yes, I do mean it that way.

S: So the art of horse breeding is the care of horses.

E: Yes.

E: Nor is it the case that everyone can care for dogs, but the hunter knows how.

E: That is so.

S: So the art of hunting is the care of dogs.

E: Yes.   13B

S: And that of cattle-raising the care of cattle.

E: Quite so.

S: So, the art of holiness and piety is the care of the gods, Euthyphro. Is that what you mean?

E: It is.

S: Doesn't each of these types of care aim at the same result? I mean something like this: it aims at some good or benefit to the thing being cared for. Just as you see that horses, when they are cared for, gain some benefit and are made better. Or don't you think so?

E: I do.

S: So dogs are benefited by the art of hunting, cattle by the art of   13C
cattle-raising, and so on and so forth. Unless you have some notion that care aims at harming the thing cared for?

E: By Zeus, no.

S: It aims to benefit the object of
care?

E: Of course.

S: Is holiness then — being the care of the gods — also a benefit to them, something that makes the gods better? Would you agree that when you do something holy you improve some one of the gods?

E: No, by Zeus, I would not!

S: I didn't think that was what you meant — quite the contrary — but that's why I asked what you meant by 'care of the gods'. I couldn't   13D
believe you meant this kind of care.

E: Quite right, Socrates. I didn't mean this kind of care at all.

S: Very well, but what kind of care of the gods would holiness be?

E: The kind of care, Socrates, that slaves take of their masters.

S: I understand. Holiness is shaping up to be a kind of service to the gods.

E: Exactly.

S: Could you tell me: what is the **goal** that service to a doctor serves to bring about? Don't you think it would be health?

E: I think so.

S: What about being of service to shipbuilders? What goal would
13E   that service aim to accomplish?

E: Clearly, Socrates, the building of a ship.

S: And as to being of service to housebuilders: the goal would be houses?

E: Yes.

S: Tell me then, my good sir, what is the point of the service men provide to gods? You obviously know since you say that you, of all men, have the most complete knowledge of divinity.

E: And I speak the truth, Socrates.

S: Tell me then, by Zeus: what magnificent result is it that the gods achieve when they employ us as servants?

E: Many fine things, Socrates.

14A   S: And the same goes for generals, my friend. All the same, you would not have any trouble telling me that the main point of what they do is to achieve victory in war. Isn't that so?

E: Of course.

S: Farmers too, I think, produce many fine things, but still, the main point of what they do is to bring forth goods from the earth.

E: Quite so.

S: Well then, what is the main point of the many fine things that the gods achieve?

E: I told you just a little while ago, Socrates, that it is no easy matter to arrive at precise knowledge of these things. Nevertheless, to put it simply, I say that if a man knows how to please the gods in word and deed — with prayer and sacrifice — then his are holy actions that support and sustain private houses and public affairs alike. The opposite of these pleasing actions are unholy, and overturn and destroy everything.

S: You could have been much more concise, Euthyphro, if you wanted to, by answering the main part of my question. You're not exactly dying to teach me — that much is clear. You were just on the point of doing so, but you turned aside. If you had given that answer, I would already be well versed in holiness, thanks to you. But as it is, the lover of inquiry must chase after his beloved, wherever he may lead him. Once more then: what do you say that the holy is, or holiness? Don't you say it's a kind of science of sacrifice and prayer?

E: I do.

S: To sacrifice is to give a gift to the gods; to pray is to **ask** them for something?

E: Definitely, Socrates.

S: Then holiness must be a science of begging from the gods and giving to them, on this account.

E: You have grasped my meaning perfectly, Socrates.

S: That is because I want so badly to take in your wisdom that I concentrate my whole intellect upon it, lest a

single word of yours fall to the ground. But tell me, what is this service to the gods? You say it is to beg from them and give to them?

E: I do.

S: And to ask correctly would be to ask them to give us things we
need?

E: What else?

14E   S: And to give correctly is to give them in return what they need
from us? For it would hardly represent technical skill in giving to
offer a gift that is not needed in the least.

E: True, Socrates.

S: Holiness will then be a sort of art for bartering between gods
and men?

E: Bartering, yes — if you prefer to call it that.

S: I don't prefer to, if it isn't true. But tell me, what good do the gifts
the gods receive from us do them? What they give us is obvious
15A   enough. There is no good we enjoy that does not come from them.
But how is their lot improved by what they receive from us? Or have
we gotten so much the better of them in our barter that we get all
their blessings, while they get nothing back in return?

E: Do you really think, Socrates, that the gods receive some benefit
from what they get from us?

S: What else could these gifts from us to the gods be, Euthyphro?

E: What else, indeed, except for honor, **reverence**, and that thing I mentioned just now, gratitude?

S: Holiness, then, is pleasing to the gods, Euthyphro, but not beneficial or dear to them?

15B

E: I think of all things it is most dear to them.

S: So the holy is once again, it seems, what is dear to the gods.

E: Most certainly.

S: After saying that, will you be astonished that your arguments won't stand still but start wandering off? And will you accuse **me** of being the Daedalus who makes them walk — though you yourself are far more skillful than Daedalus, since you can actually make things run in a complete circle? Perhaps it has escaped your notice **15C** how our argument has revolved and come right back where it started? You surely remember how, a little while ago, we said that holiness and what is loved by the gods were not the same, but distinct from one another. Or don't you remember?

E: I do.

S: Don't you see that now you are saying that what is dear to the gods is what is holy? Is this the same as what is loved by the gods, or isn't it?

E: It certainly is.

S: Either we were wrong about what we agreed to before, or — if we were right then — we're wrong now.

E: That seems to be so.

S: So we have to begin again at the very beginning, to investigate what holiness is. And I won't willingly give up before I figure it out. Don't think me unworthy; instead, concentrate your attention to a **15D** supreme degree and tell the truth. For you know this thing, if any man does, and so I will clutch you as tightly as if you were Proteus himself, until you tell me. If you did **not** know precisely what is holy, and what unholy, you would never have undertaken to prosecute your aged father for murder on behalf of a slave. You would have been afraid to risk the wrath of the gods, in case you should be acting wrongly, and you would have felt shame before your fellow men. As it stands I am

15E   certain you believe you know **pre-cisely** what is holy and what **not**. So tell me, my good Euthyphro, and don't keep secret what you think it is.

E: Some other time, Socrates. I am in a hurry, and I really have to go now.

S: What are you doing, my friend? Will you leave, and **cast** me down from the high hope I **had**, that by learning from you what is holy and what not, I might have escaped Meletus'

16A   indictment? I hoped to show him that — thanks to Euthyphro — I have become wise in divine matters, and that I no longer proceed carelessly through my ignorance, nor make innovations with regard to them, and most of all that I will live a better life from now on!

Chapter 7

Meno:
Reason, Persuasion & Virtue

1

OF THE THREE DIALOGUES in this book, **Meno** gives modern readers most difficulty. **Euthyphro** has cultural, legal and religious backstory that is easy to miss or misunderstand, but the basic arguments are extractable without that. Anyway, it's short. **Republic**, Book 1, is long and involved, but Thrasymachus is a good villain. If you lose track of the argument, you can watch him chew the scenery. It seems intuitive why such a person poses a challenge. But **Meno** loses readers. It's long, with an odd, three-part structure: virtue; then, a geometry lesson; then, more virtue.

The obvious question — who got geometry in my virtue? or, who got virtue on my geometry? — has no obvious answer.

Twists and switchbacks are scarcely sign-posted. Consider the juncture at which we shift from virtue to geometry (82a). Meno has made a peevish argument that it is impossible to inquire about anything. Socrates responds by going off on what looks like a tangent. He passes along mystery hearsay about reincarnation. Meno asks how Socrates knows such things. Socrates proposes that a geometry lesson, of all things, will provide an answer. But can you argue for reincarnation by investigating the area of a square? **That** doesn't sound right.

It's not just hard to track the argument, it's hard to see what the human point could be. Meno is a sophist, but the dialogue isn't a critique of sophistry (nor an advertisement for geometry, nor a promise of reincarnation.) Better: it targets the common denominator of the sophist, Meno, and the anti-sophist, Anytus (sturdy citizen with a walk-on part near the end.) But these two look like opposites, so what — who? — would the opposite of both be?

In **Meno** we confront 1) a survey-resistant sprawl of diverse content elements — characters, topics, ideas, arguments; 2) too few of which are likely
to strike contemporary readers as intuitive. This chapter addresses 2), at
the risk of recapitulating 1). I walk through **Meno**, seeking, point by point,
the **point**. I try to find contemporary coordinates for ancient oddities. But,
as Lewis Carroll jokes in **Sylvie and Bruno**, a map the same size and shape
as a whole country will have drawbacks, for navigation purposes. Let me, in
the next section, offer a pocket guide to complement the **Meno**-sized-and-
shaped map this chapter on **Meno** shall shape up to be. Let me close this
section with a word of advice. Reading **Meno**, before this commentary, or this
commentary, before **Meno**, may be frustrating. Still, 'you can't get there from
here,' is needlessly despairing counsel. A bit of **Meno**, a bit of commentary;
more **Meno**, more commentary, might be the ticket. I hope the next section
will also convey a preliminary sense of why the trouble might be worth it.

2

If **Meno** is about one thing, it is not virtue nor geometry but knowledge.
Specifically, **half**-knowledge (but 'what is half-knowledge, Meno?' sounds
funny.) You could also say the dialogue is about the split between ideal ways
of thinking and actual ways of thinking. Virtue and geometry are cases in
point, as are Meno and Anytus.

It is best, with Plato, to have some sense of how interlocutors interlock with
arguments; how personalities suit problems. What **is** the common denominator of a slick sophist (Meno) and a stiff anti-sophist (Anytus)? They both
think they know it all; **and** that no one really knows. About virtue (big, fine,
vague word.) These views contradict, hence should collapse. But that's not how
the mind works. Perhaps you yourself have at times been extremely morally
self-certain, yet prepared to roll out a spot of convenient relativism if your
opinion is challenged. **I know it all, and nobody knows
anything anyway, so don't tell me I'm wrong!**
Taken together, these attitudes form a double-
shield against what Socrates is pushing: what
if we **are** wrong yet we could, potentially,
know better?

The human tension in the dialogue
stems from difficulty Meno and Anytus
have accepting this. Couldn't we learn
better? This sounds so modest, yet they are
incapable of processing it. They would have

to stamp on their strongest habits, bite their rhetorical tongues. Admitting they could learn means admitting they could be wrong means admitting threats to status. These are men whose status depends on projecting an air of effortless superiority — innate virtue. Can't march into battle looking confused!

Let me shift to consider that moment when virtue meets geometry (82a). You can meet a man like Meno every day, and it would be hard to walk through a crowd without bumping into several copies of Anytus. (By contrast, you don't meet Thrasymachus everyday, although I suppose everyone has a **little** Thrasymachus in them.) But the geometry lesson seems out-of-place, by design. Plato is provoking with incongruous juxtapositions, just as Socrates is provoking Meno. Meno complains he feels dumb and numb. The geometry is, partly, Socrates' way of saying this is a healthy sign. Of course, reassurance that mental paralysis is quite normal does not alleviate the discomfort of the symptoms.

How does the story end? If, in the end, Plato were pushing an alleged rational proof of a grand, unified theory of virtue, the stakes would be so much clearer. **You said you knew it all (and nothing can be known.) But here is something new and knowable! You are refuted!** But Plato has Socrates advance no such theory, not in **Meno**. So is he resting his case on a mere maybe? **Maybe** we can rationalize virtue (whatever that means!) only we can't see how yet? Such a maybe may be irrefutable; but, by the same token, disappointing. Such a long, difficult dialogue! May there be more than maybe at the end, to pay us for our pains! We pray it is so.

It is hard to say more until the reader reads more, but let me drop one last hint. In this chapter I discuss self-help; then, positive psychology. These are intended as analogs for aspects of **Meno**. But there is more. I discuss the psychologist Jonathan Haidt. He is a scholar and popular author, and he makes the following claim: ironically, Plato's desire to illuminate everything by the light of the reason blinds him to the nature of reason itself. Haidt summarizes Plato's view (in **Republic**, but it could be **Meno**): "reason must rule the happy person. And if reason rules, then it cares about what is truly good, not just about the appearance of virtue." The trouble, Haidt says, is this:

> As is often the case in moral philosophy, arguments about what we ought to do depend upon assumptions — often unstated — about human nature and human psychology. And for Plato, the assumed psychology is just plain wrong.[1]

1   Jonathan Haidt, **The Righteous Mind: Why Good People Are Divided By Religion and Politics** (Vintage 2013), p. 85-6. Hereafter, RM.

Wrong how? "People care a great deal more about appearance and reputation than about reality." Haidt thinks Plato misses that real people think like — well, like, Meno and Anytus, to pick picture-perfect Haidtian specimens. The fact that people think like those two falsifies Plato's psychology, according to Haidt. Holed up in his Academy, head in the clouds, doing geometry, dreaming of Forms, Plato misses how the man on the street thinks. But obviously Plato gets it about Meno and Anytus. He has written this long dialogue, in which he perceptively dramatizing the ways in which this pair predictably cares about — and for — the appearance of virtue, not its reality, despite Socrates' best efforts to rub their noses in the latter.

In the end, Plato does not offer a rational theory of virtue. But he is on the lookout. In the meantime, he's out on the street, coming to constant grips with the thing Haidt is so sure he comprehensively misses. It's as if Plato is counter-arguing in advance: my theoretical ambitions may meet with success or failure. But if I am wrong, it won't be because I am clueless about psychology. I know how people think; how the style of theory I seek is at odds with all that. I see my geometry lesson sticking out like a sore thumb. Who could miss it? My ideas paralyze ordinary patterns of thinking without (yet) offering obviously workable alternatives. Does that prove I'm wrong?'

No point scoring a debate before starting it, of course.

3

Let me start by addressing an even more basic source of confusion than the dialogue's strange, three-part structure. Take Meno's question: "Can you tell me, Socrates, is virtue the sort of thing you can teach? Or is it not the sort of thing you can teach, but you could pick it up by practicing it? Or maybe it's neither: virtue is something that naturally arises in men, or they get it some other way?" (70a).

The Greek is **aretē**, which the dictionary tells you means **excellence** or **virtue**. 'Virtue' will do, but does a so-so job of conveying what Meno is getting at. In contemporary English, 'virtue' means admirable personal character. But the term connotes concern for moral self-restraint; specifically, sexual restraint, especially for women. Virtue is paradigmatically a matter of rightly **not** doing something you are selfishly tempted to do. These connotations are totally off the mark in Meno's case, so if 'how is virtue acquired?' puts you in mind of primly edifying Victorian matrons on pedestals of sexual propriety, kindly wipe that picture from your mind.

Also, in academic philosophy virtue ethics is often identified as one of three main currents of normative theory, the other two being consequentialism and deontology (I mention these theories in Chapter 4.) It is certainly appropriate to coordinate **Meno** with academic virtue ethics, but not to construe Meno, the man, as concerned with it. He isn't enough of a theorist, in the academic sense; or enough of a moralist, in an ordinary sense. So even academic philosophical readers may take the mismeasure of Meno, if not of **Meno** as a whole.

4

When Meno asks whether virtue is teachable, what he is getting at is basically this: can you teach **success**? Take the title of a well-known best-seller, **The Seven Habits of Highly Effective People**, by Stephen R. Covey. Meno is interested in **that**: being highly effective. The way he launches in, without introduction, ticking off candidate positions — nature? nurture? something else? — shows his awareness that this is not just an issue but an established debate topic. For Meno, this **is** the debate-worthy aspect of ethics: how to get ahead.

One thing Socrates does in this **dialogue** is urge Meno to say what he really thinks. (He's the sort to pick a position just for fun or profit.) So let me ask you, dear reader, what **you** really think about this 'highly effective' business. Can you buy a book, read it, and expect to become ... highly effective?

For the price of an over-priced coffee you can turn your whole life around? For real? What a deal!

The title of Covey's book by itself reports a result, if it is one: effectiveness a function of habit. It would seem to follow it is not something you know, theoretically, or are born with. It's something you practice. But then: can a book provide it? Perhaps it can tell you what to practice. But what is the scope of 'effective'? Effective at **everything**? (That would be a lot!) If only some things, which? Does effectiveness equal success, or do I need to take additional steps to ensure the effects of my effectiveness aren't **bad**? Seems to be some risk of means-ends slippage.

When you see a book with a title like Covey's, what do **you** assume it is about? Covey is shelved under self-improvement, inspirational, success, business, 'health & mind'. Different bookstores have different notions, it seems. But Covey is never shelved in the (less popular!) academic philosophy section, where you find, for example, the Plato books. How far we've come, since Meno's day!

Academic philosophers don't have much to say about the likes of Covey. He doesn't take note of academic philosophy. It is not much of an exaggeration to say we have Plato to thank (or blame), as much as anyone, for this bookstore segregation. His academy was the first attempt to secure a separate shelf for Plato's preferred sort of pure intellectual product. But Plato wants his own shelf as an independent platform from which to argue against the likes of Covey. Not that arguing against Covey is **all** Plato wants to do! But it is by no means the least thing. If Plato has won over academic readers to the point where they read dialogues like **Meno** without thinking about the likes of Covey, Plato may have academicized philosophy too well for its own good.

What is it Plato wishes Covey and co. could see? Let's try this. When Meno asks how virtue is acquired, imagine he and Socrates are in a modern bookstore, in the self-help section: 'what do you think, Socrates?' Socrates doesn't say. Instead, he drags Meno on a roundabout tour through other sections — here, the math books; there, natural science; psychology, (academic) philosophy; religion, myth! So much, all in all! If we doubt self-help books can **really** help, as much as their titles promise, that may be because we have a sinking suspicion wide-scope success must be success at **all this**. I can't be 'highly effective', period, unless I'm effective all over. How will self-help authors like Covey save me from not knowing **everything**? Covey might deflect the question: so what's **your** bright idea, Plato? Work geometry problems all day? Admittedly, that doesn't sound so good. We'll have to think.

5

Who are the ancient Athenian analogs to Covey? I mentioned them in Chapter 2. They are the **sophists**: teachers who, for a fee, promise to impart the knowledge and skills you need to get ahead. Prodicus, one of these, is mentioned at a few points in **Meno**. In another dialogue, Socrates claims to have attended his one-drachma lecture (he couldn't afford Prodicus' full course on 'the uses and meanings of words.') Meno is a student of Gorgias, who has his own Plato dialogue. Meno himself is an aspiring inspiring speaker. As he tells Socrates, no doubt padding the numbers: he must have given a thousand lectures on virtue (80b).

Truth!
Beauty!
Virtue!
Justice!

When Socrates says he doesn't even know what virtue **is**, Meno is shocked. Didn't he meet Gorgias when he came to town? Why should Gorgias know, of all men? Because Gorgias' claim to fame is that he can make you **effective**. Effective at what? Riding horses? Piloting a ship? Unclogging drains? No. Gorgias will make you ... **persuasive**.

As Socrates says (70b), Gorgias is famous for challenging all-comers to ask any question. He had stored up/could concoct on the fly, confident, authoritative-sounding responses to anything. I don't suppose anyone thought he just plain **knew** everything. He didn't have a brain of gold but a tongue of silver. This was speech-and-debate as street theater. Staging this show was a way of self-advertising as the man with the bag of effective talk tricks (with sundry other stuff tossed in for good measure.) Students want **that**. They think they can use it to become ... **effective**.

Anyway, if you want a portrait of virtue as Meno sees it (to replace that be-pedestaled Victorian frump) imagine what he sees in the mirror.

"When you look in the dictionary under 'virtue', you see **a** picture of **me**, baby!"

See, I **told** you! You've met this guy before!

But there's more to virtue than a winning smile. What sorts of slick talk tricks are we talking?

6

Note how Meno brightens up when Socrates mentions Empedoclean efflu-ences [**aporrhoē**] as a possible explanation of human perception (76c). This part of the dialogue sounds like proto-natural science. When I see a red tomato, something must be 'flowing off', striking my eye. These effluences are like keys that unlock only my eyes, not my ears; which will, of course, be fitted by a different set of keys. Not much, as science goes, but it's a start, looks like.

But Meno, one guesses, is not thinking how you could get started, testing and refining this hypothesis in the lab. He is thinking 'effluence' is a fine-sounding, two-drachma word. The theory as a whole is ripe for adoption and adaptation. No obvious flaw (check); concrete enough to be vivid, abstract enough to be creatively applied to many different subjects (check). Has an authoritative ring and famous name attached (check). So if someone asks you why the sun is brighter than the moon, whip up something about how there are more powerful streams of effluence flowing off the sun. Maybe there could be a spin-off series of self-help titles: **The Law of Effluence**. And: **Who Stole My Oar? How To Get Moving When Things Aren't Flowing Your Way**. 'Effluence' could be like 'synergy': a word that might mean something, but whose most typical use is to sound as though it means, roughly, everything, thereby getting someone off the hook of having to know, roughly, anything.

Socrates' skepticism about Empedocles is the flip-side of Meno's enthusiasm. Socrates denigrates his own effluence-based answer as 'theatrical' (76e). Why? Sure, Meno is probably scheming marketing angles. It is understandable that Socrates is skeptical about **that**. But the hypothesis is not **made** for that. Empedocles sounds more like an ancestor of modern science than modern marketing. Why not regard the existence of effluence as an admittedly speculative, preliminary hypothesis?

7

Ah! But preliminary **to what**?

Neither Meno nor Socrates (nor Plato) has any notion of empirical science as a paradigm of success in its own right. (Seven habits of highly **scientific** people? Hasn't been written!) They can't point to individuals, methods or institutions with a track record of taking plausibility and refining it into solid, reproducible results. Yet this elusive virtue of replicable success is the focus of the final section of the dialogue. Why can't virtuous fathers pass all that on to their sons, consistently (93a-95a)? This may seem, therefore, a perfect occasion to usher the scientific method onstage. Instead, empirical science turns out to be a dog that doesn't bark.

There is, however, one clear counter-example to my claim that neither Socrates nor Meno knows about science. They know about math. But if you aren't planning to make math a tool for natural **science**, what are you thinking it is for? Consider this. If you want to make Gorgias squirm up there on his soapbox, what question would be best? How about math? Not that Gorgias is innumerate. But if he happens not to know, it's going to be hard to bluff through with guff about 'flow'.

8

Let's finish filling out our preliminary thoughts about virtue and success. Back to the self-help bookshelf! Meno is content to paddle in effluence of plausibility. What is it that makes this **seem** like such a solid formula? I like Covey's title, but we might do better to turn back to our original self-help authority, Dale Carnegie. He is more in the Gorgiastic mold. (But friendlier.)

In Chapter 4, I cast Carnegie as a Midwestern Xenophanes — practical Protagoras, healthy Heraclitus. Man is the measure of all things, so go with the flow. 'People skills' are master tools. I critiqued this line. How can Carnegie be sure **selling** is the soul of living? We need an argument!

This ethical dilemma turned out to be, at bottom, epistemological. How can you respond, practically, to awareness that awareness is limited. How is it possible to plan a successful life of seeming — of frequently false belief, as opposed to knowledge? How can getting comfortable in the day-tight compartment of your Cave produce security or reliability?

How can you be an effective leader if you know you don't **know** what you are doing?

Let's work backwards. Carnegie says leadership has two components: vision; the capacity to communicate your vision to others. Communication first. People are credulous. Planting the seed of an idea means growing a sprout of belief — so long as nothing else squashes it. Let me quote from a chapter entitled, forcefully, "How To Be Impressive and Convincing". "Aristotle taught that man was a reasoning animal — that he acted according to the dictates of logic. He flattered us. Acts of pure reasoning are as rare as romantic thoughts before breakfast. Most of our actions are the result of suggestion." Thus:

> It is easy to believe; doubting is more difficult. Experience and knowledge and thinking are necessary before we can doubt and question intelligently. Tell a child that Santa Claus comes down the chimney or a savage that thunder is the anger of the gods and the child and the savage will accept your statements until they acquire sufficient knowledge to cause them to demur. Millions in India passionately believe that the waters of the Ganges are holy, that snakes are deities in disguise, that it is as wrong to kill a cow as it is to kill a person — and, as for eating roast beef… that is no more to be thought of than cannibalism. They accept these absurdities, not because they have been proved, but because the

suggestion has been deeply imbedded in their minds, and they have not the intelligence, the knowledge, the experience, necessary to question them.

We smile ... the poor benighted creatures! Yet you and I, if we examine the facts closely, will discover that the majority of our opinions, our most cherished beliefs, our creeds, the principles of conduct on which many of us base our very lives, are the result of suggestion, not reasoning ...

Prejudiced, biased, and reiterated assertions, not logic, have formulated our beliefs.[2]

We stand at a crossroads. On the one hand we see the difficult way, hard road of doubt. You could toil to acquire knowledge and critical thinking skills; study logic and argumentation to eliminate prejudice and bias; encourage others to do the same. On the other hand, an easier path: ever-flowing, ever-changing, ever-meandering river of belief. Don't apply the skeptical lesson home. You might lose your religion, then your friends. (Obviously Carnegie would never write such insulting things if he thought devout Hindus, as opposed to Christians, might be buying his books. Think how he would sound if he were consistent.) Instead, **sell**! Now that you understand your true, innate nature — man is not the rational but the suggestible animal — you know how. In the land of the blind, the man who **sees** he can't see is king!

With that sort of keen insight, you are prime **leadership** material!

This perhaps explains Meno's tendency to conflate leadership with mastery of the grey arts of product differentiation and market segmentation (70e-71a).

2   Dale Carnegie, **Public Speaking and Influencing Men in Business** (World's Work, 1945), p. 218, 9. A version of the book, lacking the chapter in question, is more recently in print: Dale Carnegie, **How to Develop Self-Confidence And Influence People By Public Speaking** (Pocket Books, 1956).

But let's step back. I'm saying Carnegie and Meno are much the same. I'm hinting that there's something dubious and ironic about the idea(s) they have in common. But what, exactly? In a sense, it's obvious. Stock techniques for winning friends and influencing people will largely overlap the contents of the Gorgiastic bag of tricks for answering all questions asked. To be persuasive, make people like you and **want** to believe what you say. That's 90% of the job done right there.

The irony is a bit harder to pin down.

On the one hand, we see old-fashioned notions superceded by slick and polished persuasion professionalism. (One such old-fashioned notion is Anytus. He's grumpy about his downgrade.) **But what new thing does the customer want? Virtue, naturally! But that's old. So what sort of new-fangled, old-fashioned 'virtue' does the customer really get?**

Is Carnegie a radical or a conservative? And doesn't he worry that his is a philosophy for benighted creatures, living by exploiting weaknesses of others? To hear him tell it, the key to teaching virtue is knowing about human nature, ergo it is not so much a matter of knowing about virtue as vice: suggestibility. (Not even a **major** vice, which is almost more embarrassing. Thus, when you loftily lecture Man, the suggestible animal, about virtue, for profit, maybe skate over that awkward bit.)

9

But seriously: Meno isn't worried about being badly in the wrong, dispensing 'virtue' viciously.

Why not? Like most people, he's normal. That is, he figures he's exceptional. Remember this? "I imagine, Euthyphro, most men don't know how things ought to be" (4b). Euthyphro agrees! Who wouldn't? But who would think to apply the lesson home? Per Chapter 4, Carnegie alternates between attitudes that make it hard to see where he's **really** coming from. The same goes for Meno. Thus, when it comes to ethics, both Carnegie and Meno assume:

1. **Everyone already knows it all (enough to lead a perfect life.)**
2. **No one knows anything (there's just belief.)**

2) is suggested in the Carnegie passage quoted above: belief about right and wrong is a function of suggestibility, bias and uncritical acceptance, which are hardly likely to be truth-tracking. But then 1) reassures you life in the Cave will not be **so** bad. Let's review Carnegie's argument for 1), from Chapter 4.

> **P1:** **You know the Golden Rule.**
> **P2:** **The Golden Rule basically couldn't be wrong.**
> **C:** **You know right from wrong, basically.**

What about good from bad? Again, you know the basics. What do people **want**? Carnegie makes a list: 1. Health (life). 2. Food. 3. Sleep. 4. Money and material goods. 5. Salvation (afterlife). 6. Sex. 7. A good life for one's children. 8. A feeling of importance. This list appears in a chapter of **Win Friends** entitled "The Big Secret of Dealing With People". The secret, such as it is, is that item 8 is the real challenge for most people. Carnegie isn't naive about the possibility that those other things might be lacking. His point is that, in any environment in which the basics are secure, a disproportionate amount of effort is expended on 8. There will never be enough of me being the important one to go around. A lot of those other things tend to be 8 in disguise.

Think about the gap between being and **feeling** important. Lucky for Carnegie, people aim at the latter. Otherwise, supposing there were — oh, say — some Form of the Good, above and beyond the stream of human affairs, you would have to come to know it, to sell people real Goods. But precisely because it wouldn't be in the stream, knowing wouldn't **do** you any good. In the stream, goods are **feel** goods.

When I went fishing, I didn't think about what I wanted. I thought about what they wanted. I didn't bait the hook with strawberries and cream. Rather, I dangled a worm or a grasshopper in front of the fish and said: "Wouldn't you like to have that?"

Why not use the same common sense when fishing for people?[3]

3   Dale Carnegie, How to Win Friends and Influence People, revised. (Pocket Books, 1981), p. 32.

Think how eager Euthyphro is for status in the eyes of his fellow citizens (4a-6b). Socrates could have sold him **anything**, so long as it fed that hunger. Instead, Socrates disrespects him. No sale!

Supposedly, Plato gave one public lecture on 'The Good'. He flopped. Attendees found the mathematical parts a snooze. Plato should have told them how above-average all Athenian gentlemen are! That's the sort of moral math audiences **like** to learn! Might this explain why there is so much geometry in the middle of **Meno**? Plato just doesn't get it that readers are unlikely to want to sit through a whole math lesson? I don't doubt Plato has his failings, not infrequently in the PR department; but I'm confident he's aware what he's selling could be a drag on the market. We will return to this point.

10

The fact remains: 1) **everyone knows** and 2) **no one knows** can't both be true. Which does Carnegie truly think? Is he a convicted skeptic or a complete dogmatist? Neither, probably. I'll bet the same is true of Meno and Anytus. But how so?

Let's go back to the beginning. Socrates mock-innocently confesses he doesn't know what virtue is (71a). He adds, off-handedly, that the whole town is in the same sorry state. Meno is shocked. But why should he be? Hasn't he read Dale Carnegie (or Gorgias?) Socrates is just saying the citizens of Athens are like people everywhere. They have opinions, but those are likely to be baseless hearsay. Most people's opinions about the most important things are, after all.

Suppose a reporter went around town, asking the opinion of the man on the street about the burning issues of the day. Suppose everyone answered 'I don't know' (unless the question was something really simple — elementary math, say.) But obviously they wouldn't. People may or may not suffer from a knowledge gap, where virtue is concerned, **but they** don't have a belief gap. 'Do you think Pericles has been **an excel**lent leader during his term in office?' 'Do you think Socrates is corrupting the youth?' 'Do you think the sophists teach virtue?' Anytus answers the last one with complete confidence, despite the fact that he admits he has never met any of the people he is denouncing, and none of 'his people' have either (92b-c).

Anytus is obviously not psychic but crazy; that is, normal.

Now turn the point around. Near the end of the dialogue, Socrates remarks that if people were virtuous by nature, we would identify the good ones and guard them — more carefully than gold — until they were old enough to run the city (89b). This picture is, if anything, even sillier than the prospect of a 'what do you think?' opinion poll netting a 100% 'don't know' response. Virtue isn't the sort of thing you can securely stockpile, like gold! But notice what follows. Give up the idea that we can pick out the good ones on sight (thanks to our psychic powers or scientific instruments) and you give up the idea that we **know** how to lead perfect lives — know what that would even look like. Apparently we feel we know virtue when we see it, even when it's too far away to see. And we wonder if we know it, even when it's right in front of our noses.

It is looking increasingly likely that we **do** suffer from a knowledge gap where virtue is concerned. But not just a gap between what we believe and the truth. There's a gap between what we say and think. Anytus' suggestion that anyone who wishes to learn virtue can pick it up from any gentleman he happens to meet (92e) illustrates this. It isn't plausible every adult male citizen in Athens is excellent, as if the city were some extreme version of Lake Wobegon, where 'all the children are above average.' Then again, it isn't plausible Anytus seriously thinks this. What could Anytus' solid picture of the moral universe be: boys (no girls, I'm sure!) standing on the shoulders of Athenian gentlemen, on the shoulders of other Athenian gentlemen? After that, it's Athenian gentlemen all the way down?

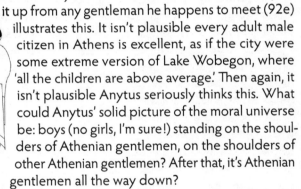

For real? (Anytus will be one of Socrates' legal prosecutors, so he's really mad at Socrates, so it seems. But that doesn't really answer this question.)

Neither Meno nor Anytus can admit to being badly in the wrong about ethical basics. Faced with that status threat, they instinctively shift from foot to foot: **I know it all already; anyway, no one really knows.**

How can we call a halt to this self-protective shiftiness, which resists anyone else potentially knowing **better**? What more inquiring view will be appealing to such status-sensitive epistemic sensibilities? How about this? We **sort of** know what virtue is. Some of our beliefs are likely to be improvable even if it's hard to believe they are all utterly erroneous as they stand.

This sounds sensible, moderate, difference-splitting. Who could deny it?

But how to proceed on this basis? How can you start in the muddy middle of half-knowing what we are even talking about?

11

The main reason the geometry lesson seems doubtfully relevant, erupting in the midst of discussion of virtue, is we all surely remember this much from geometry class: you build up proofs from self-evident starting points. Meno tries this line of attack, experimentally, suggesting Socrates should be forced to define everything (75c). Socrates pushes back. This is not necessary if this is a friendly discussion, as opposed to a competitive, point-scoring debate.

But isn't it hypocritical for Socrates, of all people, to be so easy-going about definitions when it suits him? How come he's allowed to invoke common notions when convenient? He never lets anyone else do so, apparently.

How can we tell when definitions are truly necessary, at least helpful, and when demanding them is a debater's trick or waste of time? It stands to reason we need an account of the essential nature of something if we are disputing about that something and the dispute hinges on disagreement about its nature. But that still leaves us with a methodological problem. It's quite predictable that trying to move from ordinary notions of virtue to sharp definitions will lead, at best, to a regress. If you and I disagree about virtue, and I propose a definition, it will predictably employ some term that itself is potentially problematic. When we get to **Republic**, Thrasymachus seems to be making this complaint right at the start (336d).

I say 'justice' is about 'right' or 'good'. Seeing where this is going, you predictably dig in your heels about **that**. In this way, our dispute is pushed back.

Of what use, then, are definitions for settling ethical disputes between disagreeable people who only half-know what they are talking about?

How could doing geometry ever — **ever** — be a model for making advances in ethics?

The worry is that Plato is barking mad, or barking up the wrong tree.

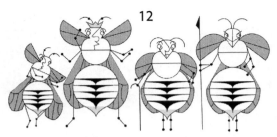

12

Let's read on, while trying to keep our minds open. Initially Meno says it is easy to say what virtue is. There is virtue for a man, a woman, old man, child, so forth (71e). I already mocked Meno as a promoter with an instinct for placing product in every market niche. Socrates mocks him, too. His "swarm of virtues" is likened to a swarm of bees. Socrates points out that saying bees come in different shapes and sizes, although true, does not amount to offering a general account of what a bee is.

This is two objections in one. First, examples are no good. We need a general account. Second, a general account needs to say what all X's have in common, not what may distinguish various X's from each other.

A standard rebuttal to this Socratic line is likely to occur to the reader. Offering examples is an excellent way to teach general concepts, so why not teach what virtue is by example? Children would hardly learn anything if this method did not work. If you had to wait until a child could read the dictionary to teach it anything, it would never learn what 'mommy' means, never mind 'virtue'. More deeply, there is no reason to assume, if we know X is Y, that we must be in possession of something like a formal, linguistically articulable definition of Y-ness. If I know this buzzing thing is a bee, why assume I must be able to **define** 'bee', verbally? This alleged mistake is sometimes called 'the Socratic fallacy'. Still more deeply: there is no reason to assume that, for every concept X, there is **any** essential feature, Y, that is necessary and sufficient for X-ness. It's not just that I might be competent to pick the bee out of a bug lineup without being competent to give verbal expression to the essence of **bee-ness**. There might be no such essence.

This objection is associated (all three levels of it) with a 20th Century philosopher, Ludwig Wittgenstein, but is so widely subscribed it is probably misleading to associate it with any individual critic of Plato at this point. The objection cuts deeply against the metaphysical picture presented in Chapter 3 (the view that the things of this world are imperfect copies of their ideal Forms.)

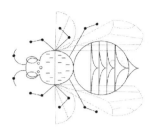

Bee-ometry needn't be like geometry. This condenses the concern that **Meno** (the dialogue) goes wrong as soon as Meno (the man) concedes he owes a definition. On this view, the geometry lesson is a symptom of the disease of thinking virtue must be definable. But let me now make suggestions about how to find **Meno** interesting and insightful even if you think a basic misstep is, in fact, taken right at the start.

13

Could Meno say what it is that all bees have in common? Meno confidently declares he could (what good student of Gorgias would promise less?) From a scholarly commentary on this part of the dialogue:

> [Meno] could perhaps. But some doubt is permitted on this point. To tell what is common to all bees, and, by the same token, what differentiates all bees from anything else, that is, to "define" what "bee" is, is not an easy task. Quite apart from the difficulty that "queens" and "drones" pose in this case, such "defining" presupposes the agreed acceptance of a much larger frame within which the defining takes place — as all known classifications of living beings show — and ultimately perhaps agreement on the structure of the entire universe. Does Socrates want us to understand the immensity of the problem by picking bees as an example? The difficulty of defining is hardly lessened in the case of "human excellence".[4]

If "structure of the entire universe" seems to cast the net wider than necessary, consider that your view of the nature of bees is conditioned by whether you believe animals evolved through a blind process of natural selection or were designed by a divine Creator. It sounds silly, but if someone asks you what a bee is, there would be a certain sense in replying that first we have to figure out whether God exists. Also, the difficulty posed by queens and drones and workers should not be set aside. Bees illustrate the weakness of what we might call 'sample thinking' as opposed to 'system thinking'. If you understand what a thing is in terms of a sample — allegedly exemplary, singular token — your thinking may be partial and confused. You cannot hold up any individual bee — which will be a queen, worker, or a drone — and say, '**this** is what bees are like; judge the excellence of bees by **this**!'

---

4   Jacob Klein, **A Commentary on Plato's Meno** (University Of Chicago Press, 1998), p. 48.

Anyone who thought doing good bee biology meant writing Great Bee biography would be crazy. You cannot understand the 'function' of an isolated bee. A queen exhibits 'excellence' in a well-ordered hive. A hive consisting of queens would not be the most excellent hive. Excellence for bees is ill-defined except against the background of a normative conception of healthy bee ecology. What any bee is, is a function of how all bees ought to be. Looking forward to **Republic**, the labor divisions of social insect societies might be regarded as a hint of things to come: ideal, three-level class structure. But sticking with **Meno**, it says something that Meno's thinking — and ours — is so sample-bound, where virtue is concerned.

Consider how easily Meno goes from invoking all the different sorts of virtues to saying (this is his first stab at actual definition) that virtue is, "the power to rule over men" (73d). Socrates points out that Meno can hardly think women, children and slaves should rule. Why is Meno incapable of remembering something he himself emphasized a minute earlier? Obviously he isn't interested in giving lectures for women and children — that would not befit his manly dignity as leader of men! Analytically crucial cases slide from view. His imagination is dominated by images of successful men. Public men! Men with power to rule over men! For Meno, investigating virtue means figuring out how to make himself one of those, in part by making himself someone who can talk persuasively about what makes one of those. All the same, it is as senseless to envision a human society populated exclusively by effective male leaders as a beehive stuffed with queen bees.

English 'virtue' has (through a series of Victorian accidents) become narrowed in its connotations. We know the word does not apply only to sexually-restrained females but somewhere along the line the picture became a picture of that. This is ironic. The root is the same as in 'virile' — manly. It seems we humans have a hard time thinking about human excellence without forgetting about half the humans. Indeed, 99.99% of them. Think about how the success shelf at the bookstore is dominated by biographies of successful leaders. Everyone wants to be Steve Jobs, it looks like. But not because everyone thinks **everyone** should be Steve Jobs, presumably. What would that even look like?

'What order and interrelations of types is optimal for a hive?' is not the same as 'who gets to be queen?', much less 'how can I get to be queen?' If we run these together, assuming an answer to the last is an answer to the first, we are going to back into a nonsensical pseudo-theory. This is particularly ironic in light of the fact that a clear vision of what the group should be like as a whole is what leaders presumably need. Welcome to the mind of Meno!

14

When it comes to defining 'virtue', Socrates has not the least trouble tripping Meno up, mostly by laying traps concerning parts and wholes, means and ends. Partly it's Meno's preoccupation with getting ahead (as opposed to getting his head straight.) Partly it's the word, the concept itself. If someone were to write a self-help book entitled **The Seven Virtues in Virtue of Which Virtuous People Are Highly Virtuous**, it would be easy to get turned around concerning which sense(s) of the key term are operative, sentence by sentence. Partly it's the world itself (if that's distinct from the concept.)

There is virtue, then the virtues. This is genus-species; then again, apparently not. Lions, tigers and (domestic) cats are all cats. It is potentially confusing that we use 'cat' as a name for a class and one member of the class. 'Virtue' could be like that. Courage, moderation and justice are virtues. But we also say (Meno does) 'justice **is** virtue'. Is this harmless? Or indicative of confusion? Also, you don't make a cat by combining a lot of smaller cats. But you do make virtue by combining a lot of virtues, it seems.

Is virtue like a jar into which virtues get poured? If there is more internal structure to it, does one or more of those things that go in (justice, maybe?) function to structure all the others, or does the jar do the structuring? If justice does the structuring, maybe the jar **is** justice (see 73b, 79b)?

I leave the outlines of Meno's dismantlement to the reader, but consider: Socrates places the accent on justice. Justice, whatever its virtues as master virtue, is an especially likely candidate for highlighting Meno's vices as master thinker. 'Virtue' tends to be a sample word, i.e. it encourages us to see some individual on a pedestal. 'Justice' is a system word. Justice is blindfolded against seeing persons. Her symbol is the scale. We don't imagine anyone in particular weighed in the balance. Meno is in favor of justice. He isn't an immoralist like Thrasymachus. But he's weak on pictures that are nobody in particular's portrait.

Virtues? other external goods? riches generosity courage cleverness moderation

Virtue!

15

Thus, even if Socrates isn't right that we can and should demand definitions for all key ethical terms, he's right not to let Meno prop up a few busts, for 'virtuous' inspiration, and leave it at that. He sees how Meno's character, and that of the subject, demand the introduction of something more, yet resist its introduction.

But consider a strong counter-argument. Meno is like one of those blind men in the parable, feeling only part of the elephant, fighting with the others about what it's like. (You've heard the story, I trust.) He mistakes part for whole and misses the Big Picture. Still, the solution is the opposite of the one Socrates is hinting at, and outright asserting by the time we are done. What the blind men need to do with their big elephant is keep groping around until they've felt all over, reporting partial results to each other, disconfirming wrong hypotheses, until they arrive at an adequate, unified, empirically-grounded overall survey. The worst thing they could do, to resolve their little 'it's a snake, no it's a spear, no it's a bunch of trees, no it's a wall' dispute is sit down, fold their hands, and get into an ingenious, logic-chopping Socratic debate about the semantics of 'elephant'. You can't figure out what an elephant is just by thinking about it. Why should you be able to figure out what virtue is just by thinking about it?

What would it look like to study virtue the way Meno wants to — concretely, in its embodied variety — but rigorously? Less theatrically? Let me quote Jonathan Haidt, describing empirical research conducted by a pair of scholars, Martin Seligman and Chris Peterson, in the field of positive psychology. What is that?

> It is nothing more than the scientific study of ordinary human strengths and virtues. Positive psychology revisits "the average person" with an interest in finding out what works, what's right, and what's improving. It asks, "What is the nature of the efficiently functioning human being, successfully applying evolved adaptations and learned skills? ... Positive psychology is thus an attempt to urge psychologists to adopt a more open and appreciative perspective regarding human potentials, motives and capacities.[5]

5   Quoted by K. Sheldon and L. King, in W. C. Compton, **Introduction to Positive Psychology**, 2nd ed. (Wadsworth Publishing, 2004), p. 3.

Why do psychologists need urging? Crudely: psychology finds crazy people fascinating. But normal, healthy people are important, too. How can you recognize, let alone repair, malfunction if you don't know proper function?

Here is another definition of 'positive psychology', which Haidt himself approves: "the scientific study of optimal human functioning. It aims to discover and promote factors that allow individuals, communities, and societies to thrive and function" (4). Whichever definition you prefer, it is obvious positive psychology is what Meno is interested in. Indeed, it would never occur to Meno to talk about much of anything else, where 'virtue' is concerned. That is a measure of his distance, hence of the dialogue's, from Philosophy 101 moral theory, which usually isn't positive psychology.

Haidt describes Seligman and Petersen being initially assured by anthropologists that there was no prospect a universally valid characterization of virtue and the virtues, such as they sought, could be distilled out of the differences exhibited by all the world's various peoples. But these researchers persevered. Here we have an attitudinal mix of Meno and Socrates, be it noted: belief in the importance of concrete cases plus insistence on seeking the abstract general case.

> Petersen and Seligman surveyed every list of virtues they could find, from the holy books of major religions down to the Boy Scout Oath ("trustworthy, loyal, helpful, friendly … ") They made large tables of virtues and tried to see which ones were common across lists. Although no specific virtue made every list, six broad virtues, or families of related virtues, appeared on nearly all lists: wisdom, courage, humanity, justice, temperance, and transcendence (the ability to forge connections to something larger than the self). These virtues are widely endorsed because they are abstract.[6]

As with the elephant, eventually everything **does** come together.

More or less. The elephant of virtue doesn't come together like a geometrical figure. Virtue is, and remains, a 'family resemblance' concept. That term is Wittgenstein's, which makes a nice connection with our concern about the possibility of definitions. How is it possible for me to know that X is Y, if I can't define Y? Well, perhaps I have picked up the practical knack for recognizing what sort of family the Y family is: a looser, rougher identity criterion than would satisfy Euclid, but functional for everyday use.

But Plato is not driven from the field. When things come together, they get abstract. But what does an **abstract** family portrait look like? Let's see.

6   Jonathan Haidt, **The Happiness Hypothesis: Finding Modern Truth in Ancient Wisdom** (Basic Books, 2006), p. 167. Hereafter, HH.

The six families are next subdivided into 24 "character strengths." Justice, for example, is subdivided into citizenship, fairness and leadership. Here is Haidt's comment on the complete list:

> Odds are that you don't have much trouble with the list of six virtue families, but you do have objections to the longer list of strengths. Why is humor a means to transcendence? Why is leadership on the list, but not the virtues of followers and subordinates — duty, respect, and obedience? Please, go ahead and argue. The genius of Peterson and Seligman's classification is to get the conversation going, to propose a specific list of strengths and virtues, and then let the scientific and therapeutic communities work out the details. (HH 169)

What is striking here is that, in fact, the conversation Peterson and Seligman have got going is **exactly the same** as the one going on in **Meno**. Haidt is noticing what was pointed out above: everyone aspires to be/admires the queen (leader), no one aspires to be/admires the drones (followers). But it isn't the case that, ideally, **everyone** leads. Is it clear we **should** have no trouble with the list of six virtue families?

The list assumes justice is one virtue among many. Why shouldn't it be? For the reasons Socrates gives. Imagine a semi-Socratic exchange, like so.

Do you admit someone can be a virtuous Nazi?

— That doesn't sound like the sort of thing I would want to admit, exactly.

But you **do** admit there could be an intelligent, perceptive, courageous, self-controlled Nazi who cares for his children, is loyal to those above him, inspires loyalty in those under him, has a sense of humor and love of music, allowing him to relax after a day of murder, so he can get up and do it again tomorrow?

— No one quite like that answered our survey. We get a lot of 18-year old college students, although we try our very best to ask other people, too.

The strained possibility matters because it brings out our willingness to acknowledge that Nazis might be 'virtuous' in one sense: **effective at X**. A flexible capacity to negotiate life's interpersonal obstacles is something we value. Yet 'virtue' as a whole — the general label — is a term we withhold from Nazis and psychopaths. Highly effective moral monsters are more monstrous, not more moral.[7] So justice **is** virtue! At least first among equals. If the other virtues collectively conduce to justice, we get virtue — part and whole; means and end. If not, no amount of generic 'effectiveness' will add up to virtue.

I don't mean to say Haidt would be blind-sided by this socratic trap. Nevertheless, it is not clear carrying on the conversation past this point is a job for empirical surveyors as opposed to socratic questioners ("members of the therapeutic community?") It's not clear what experimental data could enlighten us further. Data tell us what **is**. Ours is an **ought** question. That doesn't prove it can't be studied empirically. A biologist who thinks biology is blind evolution, no Divine Plan, is not contradicting herself if she says a bee with a broken leg is not 'supposed' to be like that. But it isn't clear the virtue case is like that. Our sense of what counts as 'positive', i.e. virtuous, in humans may not reduce, cleanly, to some mixed function of what is biologically normal and/or adaptive. It seems we might need to do some conceptual analysis, above and beyond data collection. But you can't analyze half a concept. What's a crutch for conceptually crippled beings, like us, in a state of half-knowing what's good for them?

16

Luckily we have **Meno**, which turns out to be about half-knowing at every broken-looking twist and turn!

My virtuous Nazi challenge is just an intensified version of an argument Socrates uses to confound Meno (79a). Is it virtuous to acquire the good things in life in an unjust way? Meno hastily concedes it is not. This is part of Socrates' critique of Meno's second proposed definition of 'virtue': to want the best things in life, and to know how to get them (77b). That is, "to find joy in beautiful things, and have power."

The problem is that Meno forgets to add the third leg to the stool: morality. Virtue is readily regarded as a sturdy tripod of beauty, power and goodness (righteousness). Alas, it is not clear these three automatically go together. You can have might without right, and vice versa. Are the best things sometimes a bit ugly on the outside (the best arguments?) But there is a more basic problem. Socrates attacks the first clause of the definition — "to want the best things" — by suggesting, not that it is wrong, but trivial. No doubt Meno means something like 'aim high!' 'dare to dream!' 'visualize success!' But

7   The inevitable self-help title has, however, been written. Kevin Dutton and Andy McNab, *The Good Psychopath's Guide To Success: how to use your inner psychopath to get the most out of life!* (Apostrophe, 2014).

Socrates takes him more flatly (because he did ask for a definition, not a poster slogan.) Does anyone **not** want good things? Does anyone want what is **bad**? Meno concedes no one does. Everyone who is trying to get something bad is confused. They are going after the bad thing under the misapprehension it is good. This is a crucial kind of case. It comes up in **Euthyphro** (8c). Does anyone argue injustice should be done? Yes, lots of cases about this in the courts! Ah, but those aren't, strictly, cases of people advocating **wrong, per se**. Dale Carnegie, too, finds this sort of case so significant he puts it right on page one of **Win Friends**. He quotes a letter, hastily penned by a murderer in the midst of a gun-battle with police. "To whom it may concern, under my coat is a weary heart, but a kind one — one that would do nobody any harm." Carnegie's point: accusing people of being in the wrong is a waste of time. Not that arresting killers is a waste of time. But don't bother trying to shoot holes in their ethical delusions.

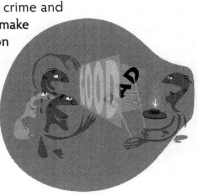

Go For The Gold! BEE all you can BEE!

It is striking how easy it would be to draw a diametically opposed conclusion. It is possible to be profoundly deluded about right and wrong. So many are! Ergo, **I** might be. Ergo we should examine ourselves — and those around us — to see who is **really** right. (Maybe the cops have the wrong guy?)

"To whom it may concern" is thoughtlessly formulaic yet oddly perfect, with guns blazing, both sides convinced they are good and would do nobody any harm. It concerns all of us. Murder is a state of mind. You can't be guilty of murder unless you exhibit, to use the legal term, **mens rea** — evil mind, wicked intent. Otherwise it's some lesser charge. So: **does** anybody? If no one wants what is bad, and murder is bad, no one wants to murder, ergo no one is a murderer. In **Republic**, Socrates sells a highly medicalized view of wrong-doing to Polemarchus (335d). 'Bad' men need help, not harm.

Even if we are not concerned with crime and punishment, we should wonder how to **make** sense of our own capacity for delusion and weakness. Take a simple case. I am on a diet but crave sweets. So sweets are bad — for me (let's say.) Do I **want** what is bad? Certainly. So the conclusion of Socrates' 'no one wants what is bad' argument is refuted.

But what do I really think is going on in me in such a case? Plausibly, part of me wants sweets while another does not. Plausibly, part of the murderer — the part writing the letter — wants to do no harm. Unfortunately, some other segment of his soul is an evident threat to public safety.

I am two (or more) selves in one, but I identify with one more than the other. This foreshadows themes in **Republic** — image of the soul divided. For now, since I have brought in Haidt, since we already have the right sort of beast bumping around in the dark, let me borrow a metaphor Haidt has popularized: your conscious, rational mind is an elephant rider. The rest of your mind **is** the elephant. Disciplining yourself to think, respond, **feel** appropriately, is training and steering an elephant, an often stubborn beast. Arguing with the elephant doesn't do much good; engaging it in socratic dialectic is a total waste of time. It's not much of a talker and no philosopher. The elephant's problem, when it has a problem, is that it doesn't **know** enough. It moves toward what it thinks is good, away from what it thinks is bad. Too often (but not as often as you might think!) it is wrong.

So Socrates is not refuted, after all. When I appear to want something bad — say, I am drinking far too much, straight from the bottle — that is always a case of a part of me wanting that thing, thinking it is good. The part of me that knows it is bad genuinely doesn't **want** the bad thing but isn't in control.

17

This picture of the divided self is not explicit in **Meno** but is Platonic and the most natural way to make sense of the superficially absurd 'no one wants what is bad' conclusion — which Haidt, by the by, buys. "Why do [people] fail to control themselves and continue to do what they know is not good for them" (HH 3)? Because their selves are divided. Haidt and Plato are agreeing nicely, so where does the disagreement come in?

Near the end Socrates hypothesizes that "virtue then, as a whole or in part, is a matter of mindfulness" (89a). (Note how 'whole or in part' qualifies, in case the hypothesis doesn't pan out.) 'Mindfulness' translates **phronēsis**, which the dictionary says is **wisdom** or **prudence**, so our translation is non-standard. But 'mindful' has the advantage that it gets 'mind' in fully, maintaining clear contrast with narrower mental powers. 'Mindfulness' sounds Buddhistic. Plato is no Buddhist, but what he has in mind is similar enough to what Buddhists mean that the echo is enlightening, not erroneous: a power of memory, plus attention, enabling undistractable correct perception. (Don't assume **phronēsis** still means this when you get to Aristotle, however!)

Socrates' argument: virtue is necessarily good, but character traits like courage, goods like wealth, honors, status, are none of them **necessarily** good. They are good or bad as well or ill-used. Take mental quickness. It means learning quickly; or never having to admit you are wrong. Take strong memory. It can allow you to retain knowledge; or turns your mind into a lumberyard of rhetorical bits and pieces. These examples are not random. The dialogue is an implicit critique of the damage Gorgias does to students, diverting native quickness and memory to bad, sophistical ends.

The only trait that is necessarily good is **mindfulness** — rational right direction. Ergo, only mindfulness can equate to virtue (88e). On this view, Meno's nearly blind second shot — justice **is** virtue — hits the bulls-eye. (This foreshadows Socrates' point that guessing right is as good as knowing; also, that it doesn't last.) If justice is mindful balancing, it is the master virtue. Also, that justice seems to us more a social than individual virtue may fit with the expansion of subject matter implied by the definitions of 'positive psychology'. Students of virtue must turn sociologists. Or turn philosophers.

Anything for Haidt to object to in all this? Yes! 'Virtue is mindfulness' can be read as highly absurd if we take Plato to be proposing that we should strive for total, rational self-awareness; as if the way to win a sprint were to become hyper-conscious of exactly where you place each foot with each step; as if you wouldn't trip over your feet if you tried. Man is mostly an instinctive beast. That's the whole point of the rider/elephant metaphor.

Haidt's tag for the Platonic Rationalist view is 'the Promethean Script', after the titan who steals fire from the gods to give to mankind. Plato would play Prometheus, spreading the light of reason over the whole mind, driving back the dark. But must we read 'virtue is mindfulness' as a formula for hyperconscious hubris? Consider: practice doesn't make perfect. **Perfect** practice makes perfect. Behind every champ stands a coach, mindful of what the athlete does. **Virtue is mindfulness** is not crazier than **athletes need coaching.**

A passage from the dialogue **Protagoras** (320c-28c) might lend credence to Haidt's line that Plato denies the animal in us more strongly. We hear how Prometheus and his brother, Epimetheus were tasked by Zeus with making humans and beasts. Epimetheus — his name means **afterthought** — carelessly uses up all the good bits on his animal projects: teeth, claws, fur, wings, etc.

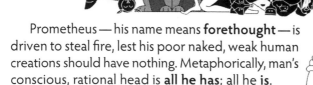

Prometheus — his name means **forethought** — is driven to steal fire, lest his poor naked, weak human creations should have nothing. Metaphorically, man's conscious, rational head is **all he has**; all he **is**.

'The Epimethean Script' is an even better name for what Haidt critiques: the notion that I essentially lack a (backwards) animal nature. But the myth is put in the mouth of Protagoras. Socrates challenges its wisdom on rather Haidtian grounds (328d). Protagoras is too flattering to our rational natures, hence his political thinking is over-optimistic.

In general, if Plato thinks Reason can micromanage all workings of the Soul he ought to advocate downsizing its divisions. Fire all workers except the Boss! Instead, he advocates harmony as his ideal. This is explicit in **Republic**, implicit in **Meno**. In Haidt terms, the rider can't replace the elephant. Still, the rider has to steer wisely. Is Plato so far from Haidt?

Or suppose Plato **is** saying perfect virtue means having only rational beliefs, plus deliberate control of all internal states and dispositions. So long as you add that humans don't have it, this might be fine. The final section of the dialogue contains arguments suggesting humans aren't virtuous. They just look that way, while their dumb luck holds. If this is Plato, he is pessimistic, not Promethean.

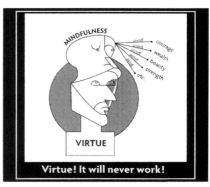

Virtue! It will never work!

Haidt might at this point adjust his complaint: Plato's problem is he won't settle for second-best. (So he is, by turns, despairingly pessimistic and hopelessly optimistic about first-best Rationalism.) In economics, the so-called 'theory of the second best' tells us sometimes our second-best option is a slight knock-off of first-best. By all means aim high, but be prepared to hit lower. But sometimes second-best looks very different. If your first-best dinner is steak garnished with a sprig of parsley, and you forgot the parsley, plain steak is plausibly second-best. But if you forgot the steak itself, a peanut butter sandwich might be second-best. There is a point at which abandoning the original plan is better than downgrading it. A sprig of parsley, on its lonesome, is **too** inferior, as a steak dinner. In Plato terms: ideally, human minds would be something like general purpose Reason engines. But reality is so far off from that! Telling people to try to be perfectly logical is very bad advice. They'll ignore you, if you're lucky; put you to death for introducing new gods and corrupting the youth otherwise. Plato needs to give up what he can't have (rational purity) and accept second-best, which he can't avoid, which is quite different in kind (instinctive, social and appearance-minded.)

Putting the point another way: **ought implies can** means you shouldn't define 'virtue' in such a way that no human can exhibit it (just as bee scientists would be foolish to model an 'ideal' queen, to get a heuristic handle on biological function, then conclude there aren't any queens, if no real bee measures up to the toy model.) In **Meno**, the best evidence that Plato is mismodeling the mind, then reproaching reality for failing to live up to his error, is the geometry lesson. I leapt over it, to get to 'mindfulness'. Let's backtrack, to see what we can see in this interlude between bouts of virtue-seeking.

18

What is the point of putting the boy though his geometric paces (82d-5c)?

Not to find the length of the side of a square twice the area of a 2x2 square, **per se**. I'll assume you took geometry and know how and why the answer is √8. But Plato isn't hinting virtue is √8. Here's a better clue: a seemingly simple and concrete problem (just scratches in sand, how hard could it be?) is harder than it looks; yet not too hard, once you've made the paradigm shift to irrational numbers. The boy is on the cusp of a fundamental discovery about the nature of number itself.

Could virtue be like that? Not the square root of anything, but, like an irrational number, intellectually surprising, the first time you meet one?

If you know a bit about Pythagorean philosophy, which influenced Plato, you may object I should not be so quick to turn the math into metaphor here. The Pythagoreans attributed moral values to numbers (even=bad; odd=good.) If, as Aristotle says, they believed 'all is number', ethics should follow suit. Someone who reads number mysticism into **Meno** might be onto something.[8] But let me try to steer clear. Whether or not math is holy, it's funny. Funny **strange**. It's 'all in your head', so it shouldn't contain surprises. But intrepid explorers venture forth into that jungle of number and return bearing strange gifts. Could there, likewise, be new moral truths lurking in the abstract interstices of our **ought** thoughts, however humble our daily to-do lists look?

Virtue seems down-to-earth. But so did geometry when it consisted of techniques for measuring the most down-to-earth thing: the earth. Then it matured into a pure, abstract field. Then it got interesting! You'll never discover the strange stuff so long as geometry is mostly for real estate professionals. (Euclid's first three postulates are not: location! location! location!) Could Plato on virtue be like Euclid on geometry? You won't discover the truly strange truths until the subject is taken out of the hands of the 'practical' men? The reader who answers 'maybe?' agrees with what Plato is getting at in **Meno**. The reader who answers 'definitely not!' disagrees.

8   I am confident the appearance of Empedocles, Persephone and geometry together in **Meno** means Plato is deliberately, persistently referencing traditions of Orphic mystery religion, with which Pythagoreanism was associated. Whether this is just a 'theatrical' literary joke, running through the dialogue, or affords a glimpse of the mystical headwaters of Plato's thought — or both — I cannot say. For a fascinating, formidable, non-standard view, see Peter Kingsley, **Ancient Philosophy, Mystery, and Magic: Empedocles and the Pythagorean Tradition** (Oxford, 1995), especially pp. 160-5.

19

The geometry lesson is staged in response to Meno's argument that inquiry is impossible. Socrates summarizes it (80e): you cannot inquire about X because either you know what X is like or you don't. If you know, you cannot inquire. (Can't start a job that's done.) If you don't know, you cannot inquire. (You don't know where to start.) But the geometry lesson is not, then, a rebuttal to this argument. Socrates' direct response is, oddly enough, to report hearsay about priests and priestesses, plus a pinch of Pindar. Let's trace it out.

The obvious response would be that what makes inquiry possible is the possibility of **half**-knowing. But, come to think of it, how **is** it possible to half-know X? Isn't half-grasping a concept like being half-pregnant? Judo-style, Socrates uses the strength of Meno's argument against him. It's true! You never learn! What seems like learning is 'recollection'. If so, we may have a model of half-knowledge: knowledge in absent-minded, amnesiac disguise.

Meno's argument is sophistical, but with a kernel of skeptical plausibility. Socrates' response seems wild, but there might be a grain of commonsense here, too. Let me quote Nicholas Taleb, arguing along Menoesque lines:

> This point [Meno's, roughly — although Taleb is not discussing Plato] can be generalized to all forms of knowledge. There is actually a law in statistics called the law of iterated expectations, which I outline here in its strong form: if I expect to expect something at some date in the future, then I already expect that something at present.
>
> Consider the wheel … If you are a Stone Age historical thinker called on to predict the future in a comprehensive report for your chief tribal planner, you must project the invention of the wheel or you will miss pretty much all of the action. Now, if you can prophesy the invention of the wheel, you already know what a wheel looks like, and thus you already **know how** to build a wheel, so you are already on your way …
>
> But there is a weaker form of this law of iterated knowledge. It can be phrased as follows: **to understand the future to the point of being able to predict it, you need to incorporate elements from this future itself.** If you know about the discovery you are about to make in the future, then you have almost made it.[9]

Taleb isn't modeling inquiry but prediction. Not the same. Yet there is an 'either you know it or you don't' sharpness to Taleb's picture that corresponds, instructively.

9   Nassim Nicholas Taleb, **The Black Swan: The Impact of the Highly Improbable**, (Random House, 2007), p. 172. (Emphasis in the original.)

Taleb's idea is that the bolded bit of the passage means you mostly **don't** know. But, on a bolder reading, any genuine ability to predict the future could be an indicator of a deep harmony between oneself and the universe. If I can know some essential feature of the universe, I **am** it. This brings us to the alleged wisdom of Socrates' priests and priestesses (81a-e), who preach a doctrine of innate ideas, based on a doctrine of reincarnation, which is also a parable of redemption-through-purification. Souls do not simply circulate eternally but, per the Pindar poem, can in some sense atone for (epistemic?) sins. In the dark, prepare to see the light! The first step is admitting you have a problem: **I don't know!** That's the proper catechism for cave-dwellers.

Meno likes this, despite the fact that, as a student of Gorgias, 'I don't know' is not in his vocabulary. He is happy to reverse his sulky 'inquiry is impossible' line, getting back on inspirational track with a 'no pain, no gain!' tale of kings winning superpowers from Persephone.[10] But these details are wild enough even Meno would like to hear a bit more before buying. Hence we get the geometry lesson (82a-86c), which is supposed to serve as something like proof-of-concept for the reincarnation concept.

20

But before we get to the question of how a geometry lesson can prove the possibility of endlessly recycled souls, a more basic question.

Does Plato himself buy this Persephonic soul-stuff Socrates is selling?

Plato believes something akin, I'll bet. He believes in souls with the capacity to grasp Being (Chapter 3). He may be a Pythagorean mystic, perhaps a sincere devotee of some Orphic religious tradition (now my shots are getting wilder, more speculative.) Still, it seems reasonable to suppose he knows very well that passing along poetic hearsay, by itself, is something between a bad argument and none. Reasons there may be, but Socrates isn't providing them here. Can it be right for Socrates (Plato) to argue so badly?

10   The Pindar reads 'swift/rushing strength' (81c) but I like Jacob Klein's portmanteau epithet, 'lightning-like strength' (p. 95): power, speed, 'Eureka-like!' enlightenment, the retinal afterglow of sudden glory; a nice contrast with the Socratic stingray's dull, paralyzing stun.

Maybe we are seeing an ironic appreciation of the wisdom of settling for second-best, after all. Entrancing Meno with Persephonic mystery science theater might be a case study in motivated irrationality.

How so? (What's motivated irrationality?)

Sometimes you put your alarm somewhere dumb so you won't roll over, turn it off, go back to sleep. How is this like the Meno case? Well, maybe Socrates is worried when his argument goes off like an alarm — warning Meno he is doing it wrong: living, that is! — Meno will go back to sleep. So Socrates is being rather round-about, devising a bad answer that might keep him awake.

Rags-to-riches metaphysics, with a touch of poetry! As Carnegie says: "why not use some common sense when fishing for people." It's common sense that people like things that don't sound commonsensical. Being let in on some esoteric Mystery makes you special. Socrates sometimes seems like he's got only his stingray sting, to combat Meno's fishy arguments. He can only stun and paralyze. But here maybe he shows he knows very well what people are like. He is giving Meno the sort of shock he might **like**.

'Even if I'm not sure all this stuff is true, it's better for you to **believe** it' (81e). Power of positive thinking! Meno likes this style! To readers today the weird, murky Mystery of Socrates' reincarnation myth is off-puttingly opaque. But think about how a lot of self-help writing today gets jazzed up with alleged cutting-edge science. 'How the power of mirror-neurons helps CEO's close the big deals!' 'What evolutionary psychology tells you **not** to put on your next job application.'

I totally just made those up. But this is the kind of thing someone might click. What Socrates is saying may click with Meno as **sellable**. It seems strange that someone would want to detour through the brain, or through evolutionary history — or an endless wash-and-rinse cycle of soul reincarnations — to get ahead in business, but people are funny that way. It's inspiring to see ordinary aspects of our lives from a cosmic perspective. Even if it's maybe nonsense. (Even if it's not true, it's inspiring to believe it!)

Maybe, all things considered, it would be better if Meno went around giving sketchy speeches to large audiences about the power of geometry. Maybe kids would be inspired! Make math glorious! If a few kids graduate from the rhetorical theatrics to the real deal, maybe it will have been worth it.

WHEN I FELL INTO THAT VAT OF GEOMETRY, I THOUGHT I WAS DONE FOR! BUT IT GAVE ME THE LIGHTNING-LIKE POWER TO FIGHT FOR GOOD!

Speaking of strange geometrical results: here is a creature — a boy — with a mind so constituted that, miraculously, it seems pre-attuned to the basic structure of the universe itself. It is an infinite knowledge box. It only needs to be appropriately triggered with a little bit of logic and argumentation. Provoke it with a math puzzle and watch it learn (excuse me: recollect!) the most astonishing things!

True, this creature can also be tricked into buying a brand of soap basically indistinguishable from other brands on the market. Here, too, a simple triggering is all that is required. ("Miasmaway Soap is the **Best** Soap!" Repeat, repeat, **repeat**!) **Your** idea — Meno, Gorgias, Dale Carnegie — is we ought to pursue the second path, **not** the first? You have a boy who could 1) be initiated into wonderful mysteries; 2) be tricked into buying stuff. You say 2) is the true path of virtue? Surely more heroic exploration is in order before we settle down in such a sorry Cave, forevermore!

On the other hand, isn't it ironic to trick Meno into not settling for selling soap . . . by selling him soul soap? Pindarian-Persephonic placebo to cure his addiction to Gorgiastic patent medicine?

Maybe it's poetic justice to fight tricks with tricks. But is that **justice**?

It could be hubris. Plato presumes to say who's got their head on straight, and to straighten it for them, with or without their consent. He's the guy with the right to lie! Does this mean Haidt is right? What a Know-It-All Plato is!

But Haidt's criticism is not, properly, that Plato was personally arrogant, to the point of pushing ideas on others in sneaky ways. The charge is that Plato wrongly advances the false proposition that it is possible to Know It All, by pure Reason. **That's** the suspect script: Rationalism with a capital-R.

Set aside mythic framing and suspicions about personal arrogance. What's left in the text that speaks to Plato's delusive dream of pure Reason?

Just a geometry lesson that is really a cognitive science experiment. How do humans learn math? Let's look and see. As experiments go, it exhibits at least one minor and one fatal flaw. The minor flaw is it is very poorly controlled (even apart from actually being fictional.) Socrates says he is not telling the boy the answer, but isn't he dropping hints? "Doesn't a line drawn from corner to corner cut each of these figures in two" (85a)? Still, this is consistent with rehabilitating the case into what is known today as a 'poverty of stimulus' argument. If I drop one coin in the slot and ten come out the bottom, there must have been coins in the machine the whole time. Perhaps we can regard the hints Socrates drops as triggers for the release of an absolutely greater volume of mathematics 'inside' the boy.

But this only gets us to the epistemic elephant in the room. Socrates' inference that what is true in this case will apply to the learning of "every other subject" (85e). Surely false! From the fact that I can 'recollect' all of geometry it doesn't follow I can 'recollect' what is going to happen tomorrow. Socrates is committing an extreme version of the fallacy he himself sees: **not every mental capacity is a master capacity.** Being quick doesn't make you comprehensively mindful; nor does having a good memory; nor, however, does being able to ace geometry pop quizzes.

GEOMETRY! It isn't the BEE-All and End-All.

21

So Plato seems like the proverbial drunk, looking for his ethical keys under the streetlight of geometry, though he lost them in the alley of emotion, because 'the light is better here.' That's Rationalism all over! (Haidt would say.)

Ah, well. Smart people outsmart themselves every day. It fits with that story (from Chapter 4) about how Plato set up his academy, hanging 'no non-geometers allowed' over the door. Whether that legend is true or not, it seems likely that Plato can't envision a non-geometrical model working. Remember the problem with **elenchus** (Chapter 2)? How can testing for consistency be enough? Only if we had ethical axioms could dialectic be a positive method. Since Plato is committed to dialectic, and the goal of knowledge, he is holding out for axioms in ethics that will work like those in math.

Here we may see the negative side of the power of positive thinking. Plato over-optimistically backforms a model mind to go with his model institution, which fits his abstract vision of an idealized structure of knowledge. He hereby traps himself in a hopeless dead-end, when these ideals collapse and cascade back down in a series of failures. The mind **can't** work that way.

But are we **so** sure Plato is making this mistake? Didn't we decide, back in section 16, that Plato isn't naive about how we humans are mixes of rational and non-rational bits? Yet here he is, sounding wildly over-optimistic about geometry as a model for All-Knowing. And knowing is the model for ethics, for living. So which Plato is the real one? Naive, Rationalist geometer, or shrewd psychologist rhetorician?

Back to Haidt. Elephants are well and good; but, for zoological variety, and domestic familiarity, I introduce the reader to the emotional dog and its rational tail. Haidt is an 'intuitionist', so it should be 'intuitionist dog'. But 'emotional' will do. It's intuitive.[11] When it comes to moral psychology our minds are emotion engines. We know what we like and don't. Ethical reasoning just backs that up, like Gorgias, concocting plausible answers on the fly. This solves puzzles we started with. Why would Anytus think he knows the sophists are bad if he's never met them (91c)? Because he **wants** them to be bad. If sophists teach virtue, Anytus, the gentleman, isn't as good as he thinks. That's unacceptable! Desire, not reason, holds up the roof of Anytus' moral house.

The basic reason we suffer no belief gap, regarding ethical questions, whether we have a knowledge gap or not, is we have no emotion gap. Dogs are full of feeling; the tail is a tell-tale. But the tail doesn't wag the dog. Thus is born a rich metaphor. Reason is the tail. What people argue for, morally, is a tell as to what they want; but telling people your moral argument seldom changes a moral mind. The foundation is emotion.

I hope this gives a feel for what 'intuition' means, for Haidt: a kind of cognition, but not rational; perception-like. Another clue is the importance Haidt places on disgust responses. This subject seems far-afield from ethics, hardly the seat of wisdom. Nevertheless, Haidt argues it is central. You are revolted by something! Instantly reason is on the case, like a Gorgiastic lawyer, confabulating reasons why revulsion makes sense. Maybe: 'Zeus hates it!' (Sound familiar from **Euthyphro**?) Ethical reasoning mostly consists of **post facto**

rationalizations of gut responses. The practical takeaway is: you have to take people as they are, as emotion-driven. (If even the gods fight about right and wrong, probably we can see it in their facial muscles.)

If Haidt opened a school of positive psychology in ancient Athens, maybe he would commission the architect to carve canine caryatids topped with wag-tail, pseudo-acanthus capitals, to remind students of their true natures. Reason as ornament! Emotion is load-bearing! But Haidt could still use a sign over his door. 'Curb your dog!' Students will conduct double-blind experiments, offer blind peer reviews of each others' research, to keep bias at bay. If someone submits a psychology research paper, saying she has no evidence for

11   Jonathan Haidt, "The Emotional Dog and Its Rational Tail: A Social Intuitionist Approach To Moral Judgment." **Psychological Review** (2001), 108:4, 814-834.

her conclusion, but her 'emotional dog' is wagging its tail, Haidt will reject it. He emphasizes how heuristically reliable our emotional responses are in most situations. Still, he's a scientist; that is, a rationalist.

Emotional dogs must be kept on leashes.

In science, just **feeling** you are right isn't nearly good enough. But Haidt is opposed to Rationalism, on scientific grounds. So what gives? Is he for or against reason?

Consider a famous saying of Jean-Jacques Rousseau: political philosophy takes men (people) as they are, laws (politics) as they might be. Science is like that, too. It institutes procedures, like double-blind protocols, as crutches for biased brains. Ethics, too, takes us as we are **and** might be. When Aristotle says 'man is a rational animal' it is unfair of Carnegie to say he is just wrong. This neglects the aspirational quality of the thought and opens Carnegie to an equal-and-opposite critique. We humans are not perfectly rational, yet not lacking in reason either. Thus we are drawn back to the central question of **Meno**: how does half-rationality work for the mentally mongrel likes of poor old us?

22

Let's parse 'half-rational'. 'Rationalism' denotes a descriptive view and a normative view. Descriptively, people **are** rational. Normatively, they **should be**. (We should say 'science', 'belief', 'knowledge' in addition to 'people'. But just plain people are enough to keep us busy for now.) Consider four statements:

1) **People use reason to figure stuff out.**
2) **People are irrational.**
3) **People should try to be rational.**
4) **If people try to be perfectly rational, they fail badly.**

It would be hard to find anyone who denies 1-4. Yet 1) is descriptive rationalism; 2) is descriptive anti-rationalism; 3) is normative rationalism; 4) is (probably) normative anti-rationalism. We all buy all of them, it seems!

Maybe Plato fails to give 4) enough emphasis, but his divided soul model implies any human attempt to be purely rational must be, at best, aiming high, expecting to hit lower. Certainly Plato is a subscriber to 2), per the parade of incompetent interlocutors in his dialogues. By contrast, Haidt can sound shaky where 1) and 3) are concerned. He is forever quoting the 18th Century philosopher, David Hume: "Reason is and ought only to be the slave of the passions." What Hume means are things in the vicinity of 2) and 4).

Still, Hume would never dream of denying certain senses in which 1) and 3) are obviously true. Nor Haidt. Nor any scientist.

Haidt is a scientific rationalist who defends intuitionism. Plato is an intuitionist selling rationalism. But if Haidt misses how much Plato is working the same side of the street as he is, that may be Plato's fault, too. Only a bad craftsman blames his tools. The tools of thinking are embodied human brains, with all their deep, animal, non-rational, non-conscious layers. Plato seems to blame the flesh, which does not put him in the best frame of mind for appreciating its positive potential. Meanwhile, Haidt is working with what he's got in a steadier, second-best style. It really is a very interesting architectural puzzle. How to build solid, rational structures (be they intellectual or institutional) on such weak foundations as we humans seem to be. Still, I will now argue Plato does not neglect the challenge. **Meno** contains two attempts to build on the second-best sand of our semi-rationality

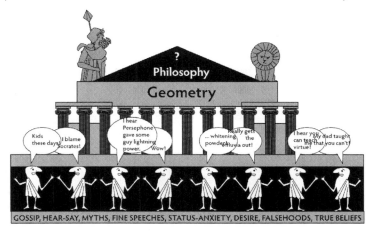

23

The first is aspirational, a bit vague; the second is technical, obscure and a failure, but perhaps it will shift our sense of where Plato is coming from.

A simple question (not a math puzzle, but a puzzle about math): can a geometry proof change your life? Probably not, but don't rule it out. At the ripe old age of 40-something the 17th Century philosopher Thomas Hobbes first encountered Euclid's **Elements**. He was (he said) thunderstruck at the realization that this sort of thing is possible. His style of philosophy changed. There is room for debate about whether Hobbes became a king, with lightning-like strength. But he did write a book, **Leviathan**, certainly one of the greatest, most influential works of political philosophy in the English language. But — fair enough! — Hobbes was probably an intellectual outlier.[12] Best to get them before they sprout whiskers. Kids' minds are more malleable. The 20th Century philosopher Bertrand Russell has an essay, "The Study of Mathematics", about the ethical value of math study for children. It reads like one long gloss on Socrates' odd-sounding allegation that all these opinions the boy has expressed are 'his own' (85c).

In what sense 'his own', and does this determination of intellectual property rights matter? We are right to connect the phrase with cognitive science debates about innate ideas, but that isn't quite Russell's notion. He thinks mathematics at first seems authoritarian. Teachers lays down rules that seem arbitrary. What teacher says, goes.

illustration credit:
Violet
Holbo
(age 9).

But, with luck, a paradigm shift may occur. Reason rules here, not teacher! Reason can be identified with one's own thought-processes. If reason rules, and I reason, I rule! It is liberating to think so. Math is the opposite of an arbitrary, external political structure. It is internal, non-arbitrary, non-political (if politics is defined in terms of interpersonal conflict.) Does increased respect for reason improve understanding of words like 'good'? Russell ends on a utopian note. It is healthy to call models of perfection before the mind's eye.

12   See Andrew Clark (ed.), 'Brief Lives', chiefly of contemporaries set down by John Aubrey, between the years 1669 & 1696 (Clarendon, 1898), Vol 1, p. 332.

Don't presume to cure Russell's rationalist naiveté! He jokes he is still looking for evidence man is a rational animal and singles out 'boys can learn math' as a conspicuously weak argument that Utopia is just around the corner. You can be a Rationalist **and a** political realist **and** a shrewd psychologist. There is **no** contradiction. Russell thinks you should know what **you want,** ideally, not that you should be deluded about the **likelihood** that you will get it, in practice.

Still, isn't his pedagogy impractical? This shift **Russell hopes** for is unlikely to occur. Most kids will not emerge **from** math class as Russellian rationalists/utopians. But math **does** impress its distinctive intellectual character on a **small set** of human characters — whose size might be increased **by** targeted pedagogy.[13]

The reader will not have failed to note how, in section 21, 1-4 were true because so indefinite. Sure, 'people' are rational **and** irrational. But maybe some people are a bit unusual. There could be rare breeds of emotional dog.

> People may at times reason their way to a judgment by sheer force of logic, overriding their initial intuition. In such cases reasoning truly is causal and cannot be said to be the 'slave of the passions.' However, such reasoning is hypothesized to be rare. (819)

Haidt hereby concedes rationalist rarities may manifest, "among philosophers, one of the few groups that has been found to reason well."

Do Russell or Plato need more than that?

This question of the many vs. the few brings out a tension between normality and virtue. Excellence is not averageness, but when we talk about biological function, we equivocate between what is typical and what is tip-top. The same goes for virtue. We sort of think everyone's got it **and** that only a few do. Recall the proposition that, "positive psychology revisits 'the average person' with an interest in finding out what works, what's right." Does this assume the average person is in working order as-is; is 'virtuous'?

Do we **want** to assume that?

13   "The Study of Mathematics" appeared in Bertrand Russell, **Philosophical Essays** (Longmans, 1910), re-issued as **Mysticism and Logic** (Allen & Unwin, 1919). Readers looking for Russellian barbs about bias and irrationality might sample **Unpopular Essays** (Routledge, 1950).

24

Let me turn to the technical fix that is, I am afraid, little better than a suggestive failure, yet worth noting. **Meno** contains not one geometry problem but
two. The first, the boy's, is so simple I omitted explanation. The second is so
complex I cannot provide one. Socrates mentions a hypothetical method.
"For example, if someone were to ask [geometers] whether a certain area
can be inscribed as a triangle in a given circle, one of them might say, I don't
yet know whether **this** area has **that** property, but I think I have a hypothesis that will move us forward with the problem" (87a). The details are hard
to follow. Socrates may be talking shop in an attempt to entice Meno, who
is always shopping for technical talk — as stage props; with the result that
scholars are confused about what properties Socrates is staging. But geometry is just an analogy. Perhaps it is good enough to say Socrates' point here
is that we need some way to proceed rigorously, yet hypothetically.

I call this a failure because I am sure Plato is not dreaming of getting half
hypothetical enough to model the workable half-knowledge empirical science has shaped up to be in the modern era. Recall Taleb's point about
the stone age thinker who either knows about the wheel, in which case he
doesn't need to predict it; or doesn't, in which case he can't predict much.
Plato's Cave (Chapter 3) is caveman stuff, in this sense. Plato mocks the notion
that having, "the best head for remembering which shadows usually come
earlier, later, and simultaneously — thus enabling predictions of the future"
(517d), is some prize possession. He grossly underestimates how effective
this method will prove to be. Record regularities; hypothesize continuation
in ignorance of underlying causes. Still, give Plato half-credit for a wrong
hypothesis (rather than none) about how scientific hypotheses should go.

The important thing is not to half-salvage Plato's reputation from the
charge that he's half-savage. The point is that there is a balance to be struck
between rejecting too-strong Rationalism, in some senses, assuming trivial
rationalism in others, all the while exploring possible middle ground. Where
do Plato and Haidt stand in this middle ground they somewhat share?

Haidt thinks Plato's brand of Rationalism entails denial of Haidt's psychological claims (hence the empirical truth of these claims refutes Plato.)

> A rationalist can still believe that reasoning is easily corrupted, or that most
> people don't reason properly. But ought implies can, and rationalists are
> committed to the belief that reason **can** work this way, perhaps (as in Pla-
> to's case) because perfect rationality is the soul's true nature. (RM, 392)

This is a fallacy. Haidt says you can't believe in pure reason unless you believe humans can, potentially, reason purely. This is as bad as inferring that psychologists are thinking illogically, from the fact that they study illogical thinking. But maybe Plato is committing the opposite fallacy (so Haidt is right to see him slip, even as he slips himself). Put it this way: natural science could have been based on geometry. Serious thinkers proposed geometry as the theoretical basis for mathematical physics. This didn't pan out, but it wasn't a bad bet. But reading that stuff, you get a lot of unhelpful conflation of how the mind must work with how science will look, ideally. But the brains of scientists were never going to turn into pure geometry engines, even if physics has shaped up to be a pure, geometrical discipline. Science might just work differently than scientists. Would that be **so** surprising?

The problem, basically, is that 'reason' is ambiguous between a pure factor, which we isolate in logic and math, and a human capacity, which is never a pure factor. Confusion about this causes arguments. You get dueling justifications; also a lot of genuinely angry fights. People get pretty worked up.

To illustrate, I quote Taleb again (although the line of thinkers eager to get in anti-Platonic licks is long.) He quotes Galileo, a very Platonic thinker:

> The great book of Nature lies ever open before our eyes and the true philosophy is written in it … But we cannot read it unless we have first learned the language and the characters in which it is written … It is written in mathematical language and the characters are triangles, circles and other geometric figures.

Taleb retorts, indignantly.

> Was Galileo legally blind? Even the great Galileo, with all his alleged independence of mind, was not capable of taking a clean look at Mother Nature. I am confident that he had windows in his house and that he ventured outside from time to time: he should have known that triangles are not easily found in nature. We are so easily brainwashed.
>
> We are either blind, or illiterate, or both. That nature's geometry is not Euclid's was so obvious, and nobody, almost nobody, saw it. (257)

Plato sees himself as a lonely thinker in a Cave crammed with shadow-chasing Talebs. Taleb knows himself to be, to the contrary, a lonely seer in a sea of Platos. "We seem naturally inclined to Platonify." Is Platonism a tacit assumption of the silent majority or a minority conclusion, silenced by the majority? Who's right about the sociology, do you think?

Next, a spokesman for the Platonic side. John Barrow, astronomer, begins a popular book on mathematics with a dramatic passage (but some might say this opening is too ... theatrical.)

> A mystery lurks beneath the magic carpet of science, something that scientists have not been telling: something too shocking to mention except in rather esoterically refined circles: that at the root of the success of twentieth-century science there lies a deeply 'religious' belief — a belief in an unseen and perfect transcendental world that controls us in an unexplained way, yet upon which we seem to exert no influence whatsoever ...

> This sounds more than a trifle shocking to any audience that watches and applauds the theatre of science. Once there was magic and mysticism, but we have been taught that the march of human progress has gone in step with our scientific understanding of the natural world and the erosion of that part of reality which we are willing to parcel up and label 'unknowable'. This enterprise has been founded upon the certainty that comes from speaking the language of science, a symbolic language that banishes ambiguity and doubt, the only language with a built-in logic which enables communion with the innermost workings of Nature to be established and underpinned by thought and actions: this language is mathematics.[14]

This is Platonism, with a twist.

In **Meno**, Socrates suggests what goes for geometry goes for all things; Barrow relies on our sense of the uniqueness of mathematics. Where does Haidt stand? At one point he asks:

> Do people believe in human rights because such rights actually exist, like mathematical truths, sitting on a cosmic shelf next to the Pythagorean theorem just waiting to be discovered by Platonic reasoners? (RM, p. 38)

It sounds like Haidt **might** credit a cosmic shelf, at least for triangles. (But once you install such a shelf, for any storage purposes, the deepest objection to accepting transcendent ethical truth — i.e. I'd **love** it! but where would I put it? — falls away.) I am sure Haidt does not suppose he has fMRI [functional magnetic resonance imaging] data, demonstrating the non-existence of **abstracta** in the lab. But he thinks he can refute Plato in the lab. But can you refute someone, empirically, if you don't think you can refute the allegedly non-empirical basis for their position?

14   John D. Barrow, **PI in the Sky: Counting, Thinking, and Being** (Back Bay Books, 1992), p. 3.

Let me give you **my** opinion. Unlike Taleb, I don't think you can refute platonism by looking out the window. Unlike Plato, I don't think platonism about mathematics is fit to do the one job you would ever want it to: namely, explain.

25

What **is** distinctive about mathematics? We know 2+2=4 without having to test the additive function on apples, aircraft carriers and anacondas; without having to travel to Australia to make sure math works there, too. That's math. But consider a more challenging calculation. Shall we say: 2248+3678=?

There must have been a time when no member of our species could solve this, or clearly conceive of what it asks. Rationally, we have come a long way. If you don't know the answer off the top of your head, you know there is one. To do math is not to be purely rational. Don't tell mathematicians intuition plays no role in math thinking! Yet (intuitive) discovery and (rational) proof are sharply distinguished. There is a purity and certainty to the subject itself, which our primitive ancestors can hardly have conceived of, but which we help ourselves to on a daily basis. Still, saying this is due to our reaching up and grasping items off some cosmic shelf is no explanation whatsoever.

Let me pull things together with a pair of jokes. (If I had an argument, I would offer it instead.) The Balkans, Winston Churchill said, produce more history than they consume locally. Plato's Heaven does the same for metaphysical mystery.

I also have a funny animal I like almost as much as Haidt's dog. There is an old American saying, 'independent as a hog on ice'. I always assumed it was a wry way of calling someone helpless. Top-heavy, frictionless trotters, getting nowhere fast. (Get the picture?) 'Plato's Heaven is independent as a hog on ice,' I would say. But it turns out I was wrong. My meaning wasn't standard. The phrase means: self-assured, prideful. That might fit Plato. Still, since a pig on a slick surface would be anything but self-assured, some explanation is in order. The best hypothesis seems to be it has to do with the Scottish game of curling, in which stones are scooted across ice towards a target, as in bowling. These stones are 'hogs' if they come up short.[15] I can play with that.

Plato's Heaven

empirical reality

15 Charles E. Funk, A Hog On Ice & Other Curious Expressions (Morrow, 2002), pp. 3-14..

Plato's Forms are like stones that
didn't make it where Plato tried to
launch them. Now they sit, inert,
blocking you, never helping?

If I were to found a school for
the study of moral thinking, I might
settle on asymmetrical architecture.
Honestly, I just don't see how metaphysics, reason and emotion fit.

Approaching from one side, reason is thought **is** the brain; from the other,
it's a pure abstraction, hence certainly not identical with the brain. Whether
or not 'everything in Nature is akin' (81d) the mind seems like it must be akin
to its platform, also its objects, including triangles and ethical truths.

What one thing is like all these things?

It's like those blind men and their elephant. Different approaches to the
nature of moral thought produce such divergent 'results' that different inves-
tigators don't just disagree. They are incredulous of each others' reports.
Haidt cannot imagine what Plato is, if not a bad psychologist. But Plato, for all
his faults, isn't a bad psychologist. (I've said it so many times by now. I hope
you believe me!) This should give us pause; make us try to see both sides.

Haidt is trying to distinguish reason from Reason. Lower-case-r reason is
healthy. Upper-case-R Reason is illusory. But at what point does the good stuff,
for everyday household use, tip over into Reason-worshipping hubris? No
doubt there is room for debate. Still, as the judge said about pornography:
I know it when I see it! Exhibit A, to illustrate the pornography of Reason,
could be Socrates' preposterous allegation that 'all nature is akin', and the
Soul its rational mirror, ergo you can 'recollect' all facts, including moral ones,
like doing geometry. Ridiculous!

I could object that it is not clear Socrates is serious. That's true, hence
important for interpreting **Meno**. But I waive this defense. The interesting
question is: what if he **is** serious? If so, must the error be due to Plato pushing
from view a fact that he knows but doesn't like: namely, we humans are emotional dogs at heart, especially when it comes to moral judgment?

Here is an analogy to suggest why not. Theoretical physicists debate the
prospects for a GUT [Grand Unified Theory]. They dream of a formula that
would, in a sense, encode all Truth about the physical universe. (A capital-T
seems the least we can deploy, to celebrate such a revelation.) Ideally, this
formula will be not just true but somehow self-evident. We would like to
know not just **that** it is true but **why**. (That last step is a doozy, yet desirable.

If you have a formula, and it contains an apparently arbitrary constant, **k**, you have to ask: why not **k'**? Any arbitrary element cries out for explanation! It seems natural for physics to push on any seemingly arbitrary front indefinitely, in the hopes of finding non-arbitrary answers.)

It seems likely that GUT is too much for our mortal brains. Maybe reality itself isn't made for it. My amateur sense is that enthusiasm for GUT, among professional physicists, peaked at roughly the same time-t as did public enthusiasm for placing unread copies of Stephen Hawking's **A Brief History Of Time** (1988) on coffee tables. All the same, I would not presume to cite a literary fad as evidence that a particle physicist, struggling to unify the electromagnetic, weak and strong interaction forces, should give it all up as a bad job. People surely **feel with their gut** when dreaming of GUT, but that is neither here nor there with respect to the question of whether GUT research is worthwhile. Remember: not all scientific failures are, in retrospect, failures due to Reason-worshipping hubris. You win some, you lose some.

There is a sense in which doing natural science is profoundly 'unnatural'; not a thing our species evolved to get good at. There is a sense in which reasoning well goes against the grain of the brain. Haidt would not propose giving up science, although going against the grain does make us liable to run against limits and make mistakes. Science is hard. Deal with it.

In **Phaedrus**, Plato likens the soul to a chariot drawn by two horses: the bad one, a shaggy, unruly beast; and a noble, winged steed. Haidt retells this Myth, to explain Plato (but he leaves off the wings.) He sees here, once again, hubris: presumption of rational control. I see that. But I also see down-to-earth shrewdness. No aviation authority is going to OK take-off in that contraption! No self-respecting civic authority will license you even for city driving. If that is me, I'm hardly god-like. I'm an accident waiting to happen. It will be tough to buy insurance.

Lucky for us, the final section of **Meno** is about how tough it is to buy insurance!

26

What became of Meno (the real man, not our fictional character?) Apparently he went on to become a military leader of Greek mercenaries in the pay of a throne-seeking Persian prince. In **Anabasis**, Xenophon (another writer of Socratic dialogues, and a military man himself) writes disapprovingly about how this unprincipled, ambitious rogue, Meno, would do anything to get ahead. He kept his troops in line by indulging and participating in their bad behavior. He came to a bad end, tortured to death slowly over a period of a year by Ataxerxes of Persia, after the attempted coup against him failed.

How predictable, with good old 20/20 hindsight!

In another version of the story, however, Meno was the only general spared, because he was the only Greek willing to betray his fellow Greeks. Only the slipperiest eel slips away! Makes total sense! I buy it!

Either way, we have what Taleb calls a 'black swan': a highly consequential, essentially unpredictable event that looks strangely explicable in retrospect. Taleb is concerned with markets and views financial crises, in particular, through this lens. How can you prepare for the unpredictable? The term derives from a philosophy of science case. So long as Europeans hadn't seen any black swans, it seemed reasonable to say all swans were white. Then they got to Australia where there are black swans: cautionary lesson in how it goes. Any bit of empirical science that looks law-like is a guess that hasn't gone amiss. Some things in nature are black swans because everything in nature is ultimately a black box. We don't have access to any ultimate reasons why.

Plato invented them, of course: black swans. They are those shadows on the Cave wall that, predictably, no one predicts. Then the fools go right on predicting, even though their regular failures really ought to give them pause as to whether they are capable of predicting accurately.

What does this have to do with **Meno**?

Meno's response to life's unpredictability seems skeptical. If you don't know what tomorrow will bring, just seize the day with a bit of help from the fact that no one else knows any better. Taleb takes a more circumspect approach, advocating strategies for hedging bets. Plato seems to take a third line: we have to try to prevent black swans by penetrating to that elusive, deeper level of rational reasons why. There are surprising results in math, but no black swans. If we take math as our model for ethics, maybe we can at least avoid having lousy moral luck. Whatever else goes wrong, I can know I am a virtuous person!

The final section of **Meno** is all about black swans. Of course, the term does not occur in the text. But the final section is about 'vision' — that second component of leadership, for Carnegie. (You thought I forgot all about that, after section 8, but no.) Black swans are that which shows the limits of vision and inspiration. So that's the connection.

Let's go back to the self-help section for one final sweep of the shelf. Here's a funny title: **Leadership for Dummies.** Joke writes itself. No more anti-Platonic title can be conceived. Yet there is something Socratic about the whole "For Dummies" series. Admitting you are a Dummy — **knowing** you don't know — is a virtue. Leadership is, plausibly, a matter of knowing how best **not** to know. How to act as head when you aren't sure where you're headed. That's **every** leader's real problem, most days.

The first line of this book reads: "Anyone can be a leader, but all leadership is temporary." A quote from Napoleon backs this up: "Every French soldier carries a marshal's baton in his knapsack." These soldiers would hardly be willing to keep invading Russia if their heads weren't stuffed with dreams of glory and advancement! Here's a famous saying by Napoleon these authors don't quote: 'don't send me a **good** general, I want one who is **lucky**!' Absurd, but it raises the question: is leadership luck? That would explain why it has to be temporary. What **is** leadership? "The set of qualities that causes people to follow. Although this definition may be circular, it does demonstrate that leadership requires at least two parties, a leader and a follower."[16] And yet there is no 'followership for dummies' volume. Remember Haidt's puzzle about the virtue list. "Why is leadership on the list, but not the virtues of followers and subordinates — duty, respect, and obedience?" Obedience for dummies seems at least as sensible but will never sell.

Note that leadership, as our authors define it, is no **virtue**. (Suppose someone asks you whether pointing guns at things is a virtue. You'd ask what things they plan to point at, wouldn't you?) Causing people to follow you is good or bad, depending on whether you are leading them somewhere worth going. So, to repeat: is **good** leadership a matter of **luck**? Is **virtue** luck?

16   Marshall Loeb and Stephen Kindel, **Leadership for Dummies** (For Dummies, 1999), p. 9.

27

Let's back up once again. After the geometry lesson, Socrates argues for 'virtue is mindfulness'. Then he reverses course. I'll be brief, since Socrates' argument concerns that eternal education debate: reformers say traditionalists are ruining kids' minds. Traditionalists say reformers are ruining kids' minds. Why can't we figure this stuff out? What works and doesn't, educationally?

A big part of the reason is that such debates are highly moralized. How best to teach gets entangled in who we want (our kids) to be. Socrates makes the point that if we can't agree who is a teacher of virtue, or even whether there are any competent ones, it is unlikely virtue is a stable candidate for mindful attention. If we agreed on what we wanted, we'd know whether it's taught. So we must not even know what we want. (I think this is the hint.)

If virtue would be mindfulness, if anything, but no one is, Meno starts to wonder whether there are any good men (96d). Socrates suggests we need to consider the distinction between true belief and knowledge. True belief is as good as knowledge. The good men we see around us — these public men who have achieved great things for themselves, and for the city — had true beliefs about what to do. So they didn't go wrong. But, like prophets and seers, they didn't **know** what to do. They had a vision and communicated it (Carnegie's two conditions!) but didn't know what they were talking about (99d).

The problem with true belief is not that it is wrong but temporary. You can guess right but can't **keep** guessing right. If thousands of people flip fair coins repeatedly, a not inconsiderable number will amaze us by flipping heads over and over. Some of them will come to believe they have the knack for tossing coins that come up heads. They might teach the 'craft' to others. Hence, Socrates focuses on virtuous fathers who can't teach it to their sons, which offends Anytus (93b-95a). The father-son relationship is generalizable. My future selves are my children. Am I able to predict what will make future-me successful? If I seem to be doing OK today, I feel I know what I am doing. Do I?

It's perfect that we don't know what became of Meno (even if Plato could hardly anticipate our ignorance.) It's like in **Euthyphro**. We aren't told Socrates thinks Euthyphro is doing the wrong thing. Or the right thing. Saying which action would really be right would distract from the dialogue's real point: namely, whether he's right or wrong, he could be wrong **for all he knows**.

TODAY

TOMORROW

28

Socrates speaks in mock-admiration of the 'inspired' ones, who receive this 'gift from the gods', virtue. Meanwhile back on earth, no one in their right mind calls dumb luck 'virtue'.

QED: there is no virtue.

At this point we should re-raise the objection that it is all very well to advocate mindfulness — always doing the right thing for the right reason. Still, this is possibly the least practical **practical** advice ever peddled. There may or may not be a craft of leadership but there definitely isn't a craft of just plain always doing right. It is fair, in my opinion, to accuse Plato of thus making the perfect the enemy of the good (that is, making The Good the enemy of second-best goods.)

Still, he has a good point about the tendency to misconstrue answers to **what's a good way to get made leader?**-type questions as answers to **what makes a good leader?**-type questions. Someone who makes this slip, regularly, is probably not even your second-best pick.

Who/what **is** the best fallback pick, then?

To answer a question with a question (one we asked, but didn't answer): could ethical truth be weird, like a surprising proof result in math? Could the right way to live be totally different from what I feel it to be? Consider: there's a slave boy in this dialogue! Today we regard that as beyond the moral pale. For the ancient Greeks it was normal. I would like to think Plato is making a subversive point. Here is a boy whose mind is as fine as any, yet unfree! But I doubt it.

What do we know that the Greeks didn't, enabling us to see what they missed. Slavery is wrong! How can our moral normal be loftier than Plato's dream? Are we just smarter? That seems unlikely. Is 'slavery is bad' a complex result, akin to higher mathematics undiscovered in Plato's day? That seems unlikely. If the Greeks could be so wrong about the rightness of slavery, it seems we could be just as wrong about something we think is right. Could **you** be a moral monster and not know it?

And another question (which may answer the first.) Is anything left of 'virtue is mindfulness' at the end? "If, then, virtue is something in the soul, and necessarily useful, it must be a matter of mindfulness" (88d). No mindfulness in the soul, no virtue for people? But wait! Does it have to be **your** mind doing the minding? Maybe there's a solution if we stand back, take in the larger social scene.

Doing so will allow me to pull together points from Chapter 4 as well: the trouble with typical approaches to personal virtue — of the 'win friends' and 'stop worrying' self-help sort — is that 'the personal is political.' These approaches suffer from a failure of the sociological imagination. This is really a restatement of the point that asking how I can get ahead is not the same as asking what it would be like if society as a whole got its head on straight.

Speaking of which, let me quote the final paragraph from **The Sociological Imagination**, by C. Wright Mills:

> Do not allow public issues as they are officially formulated, or troubles as they are privately felt, to determine the problems that you take up for study ... Know that many personal troubles cannot be solved merely as troubles, but must be understood in terms of public issues ... Know that the human meaning of public issues must be revealed by relating them to personal troubles — and to the problems of the individual life.[17]

Meno doesn't see it this way. So if society is run by Menos, the results may not necessarily be bad. But if they are good, they will be so by chance. Whether or not there is any craft of 'being effective', there needs to be a craft of thinking through what's good, not just for me but others. And not just as things are, but as they might be. The selfish, ambitious, honor and status-seeking, sloganeering spirit of excellence that dominates the self-help shelf may need to be supplemented with a theory of the good society. And we shouldn't just assume ours already is that society. Mills is an empiricist, no Rationalist star-gazer or triangle-monger. He is under no illusion that cultivating a sociological imagination promises invulnerability to error and uncertainty. But it's **necessary**. That makes Mills a Platonist ... partly.

At another point Mills writes: "Were the 'philosopher' king, I should be tempted to leave his kingdom; but when kings are without any 'philosophy', are they not incapable of responsible rule?" (180).

THE GOOD

Mindfulness?

Virtue!

Virtue!

Virtue!

17   C. Wright Mills, **The Sociological Imagination** (Oxford UP, 2000), p. 226.

29

This gets us to **Republic**, Book 1.

To pave the way, finishing off **Meno**, being fair to Haidt (whom I have criticized a lot), let me turn back to that first thing I quoted Haidt saying in section 2. "For Plato, the assumed psychology is just plain wrong."

That got us started. I've batted it back and forth. Plato is quite shrewd about how people actually think. But he does have strange notions about recollection and reincarnation. He may overestimate the aptness of geometry as a model for other sciences. But he is not obviously serious, or dogmatically insistent, about some of this. And we must distinguish between the potential existence of pure rational subjects, like mathematics, and the proposition that we humans **are** pure rational subjects, because we can do math. We shouldn't deny the former, just because we doubt the latter.

Suppose Haidt takes one last crack, like so: 'I didn't mean that Plato is dumb about rhetoric and persuasion. I mean he is wrong to think the part of me he thinks of as my 'true self' could be **simple**: rational, pure, unchanging, eternal. I can forgive him for not having read Darwin, but I can't see rightness in any theory of the mind that doesn't allow for how we are, at bottom, complex animals. It is false that we could rise above our animal natures, even in theory, hence wrong to aspire to that, normatively.

In response, let me narrate two myths from Book 10 of **Republic**. First, the Myth of Glaucus. Once upon a time there was a mortal fisherman named Glaucus. He ate a magic herb of immortality, went mad, dove into the sea, became a prophetic sea god. In other versions he's a sailor, or diver, part of Jason's crew on the Argo. The common denominator of these stories seems to be: mortal who becomes divine. Yet in the process of becoming higher than a man he also becomes, paradoxically, lower, more beast-like. Fish-like. In the water he is a man in beast's shape. He is also consistently characterized as a powerful prophet. More than a man, yet less. Very betwixt and between, this poor divine amphibian.

Socrates brings up Glaucus because he has made an argument that the soul is immortal and indestructible (so there's the connection to Haidt's complaint.) Earlier in **Republic** he has argued that the soul is a three-part compound. It's got rational, honor-loving, and appetitive parts. (More about this in Chapter 9. But it explains why the chariot from section 25 looks so hard to steer.) But now Socrates objects to his own view: things that are compound can be broken down. If the soul were complex, it could decompose. Ergo, it wouldn't be eternal and unchanging, after all. So which is it? Complex or unchanging?

But to see the soul as it truly is, we must not study it as it is while maimed by association with the body and other evils — as we were doing before — but as it is in its ideal state. That is how to study the soul, thoroughly and by means of logical reasoning. We'll then find it is a far finer thing than we supposed, and that we can see justice and injustice as well as all the other things we've discussed far more clearly. What we've said about the soul is true of it as it presently appears to us. But the condition in which we've studied it is like that of the sea god Glaucus, whose primary nature can't easily be made out by those who catch glimpses of him. Some of the original parts have been broken off, others have been crushed, and his whole body has been maimed by the waves and by the shells, seaweeds, and stones that have attached themselves to him, so that he looks more like a wild animal than his natural self. The soul, too, is in a similar condition when we study it, afflicted by many evils. That, Glaucon, is why we have to look elsewhere in order to discover its true nature.

— To where?

To its philosophy, or love of wisdom. We must realize what it grasps and aspires to relate to, because it is akin to the divine and immortal and what always is, and we must realize what it would become if it followed this aspiration with its whole being, and if the resulting effort lifted it out of the sea in which it now dwells, and if the many rocks and shells were hammered off it — which have grown all over it in a wild, earthy, stony profusion as it feasts on the supposedly happy fruits of the earth. Then we'd see what its true nature is and be able to say whether it has many parts or just one and whether or in what manner it is put together. (611c-612a)

Haidt would, I presume, take this as strong confirmation that he is exactly right about how Plato is wrong. This image of Glaucus is **almost** spot-on. (Plato gets so close!) Our moral minds **are** ancient things, mostly submerged from view; brain region on brain region, built up by waves of ocean-like selective pressures over time, making us seem like wild animals.

Because that is precisely what we are! There is no eternal, pure, rational **me** hidden underneath all that. I am it. It is me. In all its complexity!

Plato could reply that imagining Glaucus scoured of all that scurf is just like a biologist positing that the broken limb of a bee is not 'supposed to be' broken. Proper function is distinct from an entity's potentially highly mutilated material condition.

But that really doesn't get at the radical abstraction of Plato's posit of a pure, eternal, unchanging soul. Let's try another myth from Book 10, the so-called Myth of Er.

Who, or what, is Er?

He is a man who dies, remains curiously undecomposed, gets to see the set-up in the afterlife, returns to tell about it.

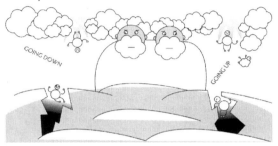

Here's the story. When you die, you stand between a pair of judges. Above them are two entrances into the heavens, all bright. Below, two entrances into the earth, dark and forbidding. Souls are coming up on the right — that is, going up into heaven and climbing up out of the underworld. On the left they are descending from heaven and descending into the underworld.

As you might guess, heaven is a reward, the underworld is punishment. There's also a cycle. Those coming down from heaven and coming up from the underworld are preparing for another go-round in the world. This is a reincarnation myth, like in **Meno**. And at this point Plato imagines something kind of funny. Everyone gets to choose their new life. There are all these lives just lying around in a field, and you shop around, pick one — examine it, select it. Congratulations! It's yours! Your lot in life. The only thing you can't see is: what the effect of your type of soul, in that type of life, will be. (Oh, and your memory will be wiped in a second, so you won't remember any of this. Ah, well. People never learn.)

A lot of the souls that just got released from the underworld pick wisely and well. Paying for their crimes was educational. But a lot of the souls that come down from heaven choose badly. They only got into heaven that first time due to a kind of dumb moral luck, not any real virtue in their souls. They happen to have lived relatively blameless lives, just because — due to circumstances — they somehow weren't tempted to mess up. There weren't opportunities to mess up in heaven, so they didn't learn any better when they went to their reward. Heaven is no school of hard knocks! So, of course, a lot of these souls make bad choices, when given a real, hard choice.

Plato's message seems mixed. On the one hand, happy circumstances, hence good institutional design, can keep people's rather dumb natures in line. Nothing wrong with nudging people, around the margins, if they have no hope of getting their ideas all justified and straight.

Haidt can sign on to modest paternalism of that sort, and that's not nothing. But maybe he would doubt the next bit. Or regard it as unscientific.

You can't tell what's good or bad for people just by looking at how they actually live. They **could** live all sorts of ways, including ways no one has **ever** lived. It's easy to say the place for a bee is in a happy hive. Bee nature seems fixed, hence happy bee social structure. But humans, like Glaucus, are a bit more … amphibious-souled. A change could do us good.

Whether you call it my 'true self' or not, the best thing for me is to live in a way, and in an environment, that will bring out the best in me. I want optimal relations between my Soul and my Society, between the parts of me and those around me. (Did I just defend Plato against Haidt? Not really. I hinted how aspirations like Plato's might sidestep certain objections to Plato. But that doesn't make these high aspirations rational, even if they are **for** Rationality.)

On that harmonious note, we turn, finally, to **Republic**. (Or, if you haven't read **Meno** itself yet, just this commentary, you might read that next, to double-check that everything I just said makes sense.)

Chapter 8
MENO

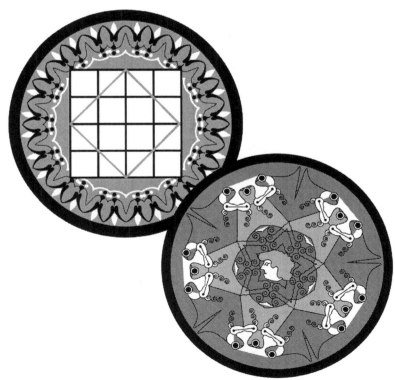

Summary of Sections

The Question:
Is Virtue Teachable?

[70A-71D]
Socrates and Meno; Gorgias the sophist; Thessaly vs. Athens. Meno's question: is virtue teachable? Socrates: first we'd better find out what it is. Meno: Gorgias knows. Socrates: tell me what **you** think.

The Swarm of Virtues;
Request for a Definition

[71E-73C]
M: there are many different sorts of virtue. Socrates demands a definition. Comparison of virtue to strength and health, to establish the plausibility that all cases share a common form. Meno is skeptical of the analogy. S: virtue seems always to involve moderation and justice, suggesting that the virtue case is not so different than those of strength and health.

Virtue & Rule; Color & Shape;
Genus & Species

[73D-75A]
M: virtue is the ability to rule. S: but some rulers are not just, and for some people it is just not to rule. M: justice is virtue. S: is justice virtue or is it one kind of virtue? An analogy to shape and color helps explain the genus-species problem.

Definitional Detour:
What Is Shape?

[75B-77B]
M: what is shape? S: shape invariably accompanies color. What if I don't know what color is? How such disputes should be handled — and a touch of geometry: shape is the limit of a solid. M: but what is color? A touch of Empedoclean physics: color is an 'effluvium' off of objects. Socrates discounts the value of this answer as 'theatrical'.

To Want the Best, and Get It;
No One Wants What Is Bad

[77B-79E]
M: virtue is to want the best and to be able to get it. S: no one ever wants bad things. So it comes down to the getting, by fair means or foul. Meno admits the good things should be gotten justly. We are back to virtue-as-justice. Meno is guilty, again, of genus-species conflation.

The Stingray:
Learning as Recollection

[80A-81E]
Meno complains that Socrates has numbed him like a stingray. As to virtue: how can you look for something if you don't know what it is? Socrates holds forth on priests, poetry and Persephone: no pain, no gain. Also: learning is recollection.

The Geometry Lesson, I:
The Consolations of Confusion

[81E-84C]
M: in what sense is learning 'recollection'? How could one prove it? The slave boy's geometry lesson: descent into darkness of perplexity. It is better to be confused and know it than to be confused and not know it.

The Geometry Lesson, II:
Inquiring into Being in Earnest

[84C-86C]
The slave boy's geometry lesson, part II: into the light. The lesson from the lesson: the man who does not know has within him true opinions about what he does not know. Knowledge is recollection.

An Investigation by Hypothesis:
Knowledge Should Be Teachable

[86C-89C]
Back to the original question: is virtue teachable? An investigation by hypothesis. Q: what would virtue have to be like to be teachable? A: knowledge. Therefore, if virtue is knowledge, it is teachable. Virtue is good in itself. So: is there anything good in itself that isn't knowledge? No. Virtue is mindfulness. Two sub-arguments: 1) if virtue were innate, it would be recognizable, but it is not; 2) since virtue is mindfulness, i.e. knowledge, it should be teachable.

Counter-argument:
No Teachers & Anytus No Help

[89C-95A]
Counter-argument: if virtue were knowledge, there should be teachers and students. But there do not appear to be. Anytus appears and is questioned: who should Meno go to, to learn virtue? The sophists? No. Rather, any Athenian gentleman. But why, then, have so many of these gentlemen failed to teach their sons virtue? It seems virtue cannot be taught.

Are the Sophists Teachers of Virtue?
Virtue Can & Cannot Be taught

[95A-96D]
Are the sophists teachers of virtue? M: I don't think so. Gorgias: you should turn people into clever speakers. Contradictory hints from the poets: virtue can, and cannot, be taught. There seem to be no teachers of virtue, therefore no learners. Virtue cannot be taught. How, then, do good men come to be?

Knowledge Vs. True Belief;
A Gift from the Gods

[96D-100B]
Knowledge versus true belief. The advantage of the former is that it doesn't 'run away', like a statue of Daedalus. The importance of being lucky: success in public affairs not a matter of wisdom but of divine inspiration. Virtue: a gift from the gods.

MENO: CAN YOU TELL ME, Socrates, is vir-   70A
tue the sort of thing you can teach? Or is
it not the sort of thing you can teach, but
you could pick it up by practicing it? Or
maybe it's neither: virtue is something
that naturally arises in men, or they get
it some other way?

SOCRATES: Thessalians used to be famous
and greatly admired among Greeks, Meno,
for being such good riders and for being so   70B
rich. Nowadays, it seems, they are famous for
wisdom also, particularly your friend Aristippus'
people, the citizens of Larissa. The credit goes to
Gorgias, for when he moved to your city he con-
verted the leading men of the Aleuadae — your
lover Aristippus among them — into lovers of wisdom, and the other
leading Thessalians as well. And in particular, he got all of you into
the habit of answering any chance question put to you in a confident
and magnificent manner — just in the manner of those who truly
know. This is because he himself is always ready to answer any Greek   70C
who chooses to question him, on whatever subject they wish to ask,
and he has an answer for absolutely everyone. On the other hand,
here in Athens, my dear Meno, it's just the opposite. It's as though
there were a wisdom drought. Maybe the wisdom has all drained
away from these parts to where you come from. So if you want to ask   71A
this sort of question to one of the folks around here, there isn't one
of them who won't laugh and say: Good stranger, maybe I seem to
you to be an especially gifted man, one who knows whether virtue
can be taught or how it comes about. But I'm so far from knowing
whether virtue can be taught or not that I don't know what the thing
in question — virtue — even is at all. And I myself, Meno, am just   71B
as badly off as all my fellow citizens in this regard, and I blame no
one but myself for my utter ignorance about virtue. And if I don't
know what something is, how could I know what it's like? Unless
you think it's possible that someone who has no idea who Meno is
could know whether he is handsome and rich and a real gentleman,
or rather the complete opposite? Do you think he could?

71C   M: No I don't. But, Socrates, do you really not know what virtue is? Should I bring this report about you to everyone back home?

S: Not only that, my friend. Tell everyone back home that I have never yet met anyone who **did** know, in my opinion.

M: What? Didn't you meet Gorgias when he was here?

S: I did.

M: Didn't you think then that he knew?

S: My memory is not so good, Meno, so I cannot tell you now what
71D   I thought then. Maybe he did know, and you know what he said. So you remind me of how he spoke. Or if you wish, you may speak for yourself, for I'm sure you agree with everything he says.

M: I certainly do.

S: Then let's leave Gorgias out of it, since he's not here right now. Meno, by the gods, what do you yourself say virtue is? Speak up and don't spitefully hold out on me, so that when I said that I never met anyone at all who knew, I will turn out to have told the happiest lie imaginable — if it should turn out that you and Gorgias do know.

71E   M: IT'S REALLY NOT that hard to say, Socrates. First, if you want the virtue of a man, it is easy to say that a man's virtue consists in being able to manage public affairs and thereby help his friends and harm his enemies — all the while being careful to come to no harm himself. If you want the virtue of a woman, it's not difficult to describe: she must manage the home well, keep the household together, and be submissive to her husband. The virtue of a child, whether boy or girl, is another thing altogether, and so is that of an elderly man — if
72A   you want that — or if you want that of a free man or a slave. There are lots of different virtues, as a result of which it is not at all hard to say what virtue is. There is virtue for every action and every stage in life, for every person and every capacity, Socrates. And the same goes for viciousness.

S: It must be my lucky day, Meno! Here I was, looking for just one virtue, and you happen by with a whole swarm! But, Meno, following up on this figurative swarm of mine, if I were to ask you 72B what is the true nature of the bee, and you said, there are all sorts of different sorts of bees, what would you say if I went on to ask: Do you mean that there are all these bees, of every sort, and that they differ from one another insofar as they are bees? Or that they don't differ from one another, insofar as they are bees, but they differ in other respects — in how beautiful they are, for example, or how big, and so on and so forth? Tell me, what would you answer if I asked you this?

M: I would say that one bee doesn't differ from another insofar as they are all bees.

S: What if I went on to say: Tell me this further thing, Meno. What 72C do you call that quality in respect to which they do not differ from one another, but are all alike? Doubtless you would have some answer for me?

M: I would.

S: The same goes for all the virtues. Even if they come in all sorts of different varieties, all of them have one and the same form that makes them virtues, and it's this form that a person should keep a close eye on when, in response to someone's question, he is giving a clear answer to the question of what virtue really is. Or do you 72D not understand what I'm saying?

M: I think I understand, but — then again — I don't have as good a handle on the question as I would like.

S: I am asking, Meno, whether you think it is only in the case of virtue that there is one for a man, another for a woman and so on, or whether the same goes for health and size and strength? Do you think that there is one health for a man and

another for a woman? Or, if it is health, does it have the same form
72E   everywhere, whether in man or in anything else whatever?

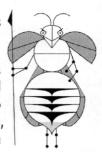

M: The health of a man seems to me the same as
that of a woman.

S: And the same goes for size and strength? If a
woman is strong, will her strength be the same and
have the same form? For by 'the same' I mean to
indicate that strength doesn't differ **as** strength,
whoever has it — man or woman. But maybe you
think there is a difference.

M: I don't think so.

73A   S: Virtue, then, will it differ **as** virtue — whether in a child or an old
person, a woman or a man?

M: I think, Socrates, that somehow this case is a bit different than
the others.

S: How so? Didn't you say the virtue of a man consists in being able
to manage the city well, whereas that of a woman consists in managing the household well?

M: I did.

S: Is it possible to manage a city well, or
a household, or anything for that matter, while not managing it **moderately**
and **justly**?

73B   M: Certainly not.

S: Then if they manage justly and moderately,
they must do so with justice and moderation?

M: Necessarily.

S: So both the man and the woman, if they are
to be good, need the same things: justice and
moderation.

M: So it seems.

S: What about your child and your old man? Surely they couldn't ever be good if they are ill-tempered and unjust?

M: Certainly not.

S: But if they are moderate and just?

M: Yes.

S: So all people are good in the same way, for they become good 73C when they acquire the same qualities.

M: It seems so.

S: And they would surely not be good in the same way if they did not have the same virtue.

M: They certainly wouldn't.

S: Therefore, since everyone's virtue is the same, try to tell me — and try to remember what you and Gorgias said — that same thing is.

M: WHAT ELSE BUT to be able to rule over men, if you 73D are seeking one description to fit them all.

S: That's just what I'm looking for. But Meno, is virtue the same for a child or a slave — namely, to be able to rule over a master? Do you think he who ruled would still be a slave?

M: I do not think so at all, Socrates.

S: It doesn't seem likely, my good man. Consider this further point. You say virtue is the capacity to rule. Don't you think we should add: justly and not unjustly?

JUSTICE = VIRTUE

M: I think so, Socrates, for justice is virtue.

S: Is it virtue, Meno, or is it **a** virtue? 73E

M: What do you mean?

S: What I would in any other case. Why not take roundness, for example, about which I would say that it is **a** shape, not that it **is** shape pure and simple. I wouldn't say it **is** shape, because there are other shapes as well.

M: What you say is quite true, since I also say that not only justice, but many other things as well, are virtues.

74A   S: What are they? Tell me, in the same way, if you asked me to, that I could name other shapes. So you go on and name other virtues.

M: I think courage is a virtue, and moderation, wisdom, and nobility, and very many others.

S: We are running into the same problem, Meno, but from a different angle. Once again we have found many virtues while looking for one. But as for that one, which unites all the others — we still can't find it.

74B   M: I still can't even figure out what you're looking for, Socrates, or lay hold of one virtue that covers all the others, as in the other cases.

S: It's no wonder. But I will make every effort, so far as I can, for us to make progress on this issue. For you **do** understand that it's going to be like this with everything. If someone asked you about what we were just discussing — what is shape, Meno? and you told him that it was roundness, and then he asked you what I just asked, namely, is roundness shape or **a** shape? — you would surely tell him it is **a** shape?

M: I certainly would.

74C   S: That would be because there are other shapes as well?

M: Yes.

S: And if he went on to ask what they were, you would tell him?

M: I would.

S: The same would go for color, if he asked you what it is, and you said it is white, and he interrupted by asking, is white color or **a** color? You would say it is **a** color, because there are other colors also?

M: I would.

S: And if he then asked you for a list of other colors, you would list   74D
others, all of which are colors just as much as white is?

M: Yes.

S: Then if he pursued the argument, as I did, and said: We keep on ending up back at the many. Stop answering me this way. Instead, since you call all these many things by one name, and since you say none of them is **not** a shape — even though none is the same shape as the others — tell me what **one** thing applies just as much to roundness as to straightness. Say what it is you call 'shape' — for   74E
example, when you say roundness is just as much shape as straightness is. You do say that, don't you?

M: I do.

S: And when you say that, do you say roundness is no more round than straight is, or that straightness is no more straight than round is?

M: Certainly not, Socrates.

S: All the same, you don't say roundness is more of a shape than straightness is — or vice versa?

M: That's true.

S: So what is this one thing to which the term shape generally applies? Try to tell me. For think what it would be like if you responded in the following way to the man who asked you all these questions about color and shape: I don't at all understand what it is you want,   75A
sir, and I don't know what you mean either. He would probably find this incredible and reply: You don't understand that I want to know what these cases have **in common**? Even hearing that, is it true you

would **still** have nothing to say, Meno, if someone asked: What is the **one** thing that applies to roundness and straightness and all the other things you call shapes, and which is the same in all of them? Try answering this question. It will be good practice for your answer to the question about virtue.

75B   M: No! You answer it for me, Socrates.

S: You want me to do this for you as a favor?

M: I certainly do.

S: Then you will be willing to tell me about virtue?

M: I will.

S: Let's forge on. The subject is worth it.

M: It surely is.

S: Now then, let me try to tell you what shape is. See whether you will accept the following account. Shape, let's say, is the one thing that invariably accompanies color. Does this satisfy you, or do you want to go about defining the term in some other way? For myself, I would be satisfied if you defined virtue in some such way as this.

75C   M: But this is a silly sort of definition, Socrates.

S: How so?

M: According to your definition shape is that which always accompanies color. All well and good, but if someone says he doesn't know what color is, and that he's just as much at a loss about color as he was about shape, what would you answer him then?

S: The truth, for my own part. And if my questioner turned out to be one of those clever debaters who turns everything into a com-
75D   petition I will say to him: I have given my answer. If it is wrong, it's up to you to take up the argument and refute it. On the other hand, if we are among friends — as you and I are — and if we want to have a discussion together, we must answer in some gentler way, one better suited to dialectic. By 'more dialectical' I mean something like

this: one must give answers which are not only true, but also make use of terms the questioner acknowledges that he knows. I will try to converse with you in this way. So tell me this. Is there something you refer to as 'the end'? In saying this I mean something like a limit   75E
or boundary — because all these terms are basically synonymous. Prodicus might want to split hairs at this point, but you surely call something 'finished' or 'completed'. That is all I am trying to get at, nothing fancy.

M: I do refer to such a thing, and I think I understand what you mean.

S: Additionally, you call a certain something a 'plane', and a certain something else a 'solid', as in geometry?

M: I do.

S: Then this is enough to tell you what I mean by 'shape'.   76A
For I say this of every shape: that which limits a solid, is a shape. In a word, a shape is the limit of a solid.

M: And what do you say color is, Socrates?

S: You are outrageous, Meno! You trouble an old man to answer questions, but you yourself are not willing to recollect and tell me   76B
what Gorgias says virtue is.

M: But after you have answered this, Socrates, **then** I will tell you.

S: Even someone who was blindfolded, Meno, could tell from your way of discussing things that you are handsome and still have lovers.

M: How is that?

S: Because you always order people around in arguments, as spoiled lover boys do. They behave like tyrants until one day when the bloom is off the rose. And you are not completely oblivious, I imag-   76C
ine, to my weakness for handsome men. So, I will do you the favor of answering.

M: By all means, indulge me.

S: Do you want me to answer **á la** Gorgias, this being the mode you would most easily follow?

S: Of course I want that.

S: Both of you subscribe to Empedocles' theory of effluences, am I right?

M: Certainly.

S: And so you believe there are channels into which and through which the effluences make their way?

M: Definitely.

76D S: And certain of them fit certain channels, while others are either too small or too big?

M: That is so.

S: And there is a thing you call 'sight'?

M: Yes.

S: From this, "comprehend what I state," as Pindar says: color is an effluence off of shapes that fits the organ of sight and is perceived.

M: You have answered the question most excellently, Socrates!

76E S: Perhaps it was delivered in the manner you're used to. And at the same time, I imagine, you could offer an analogous definition for what sound is, and smell, and many other such things.

M: Quite so.

S: This answer is theatrical, Meno. Thus it is more to your taste than the one about shape.

M: It is.

S: But it is **not** better, son of Alexidemus. In fact, I myself am convinced the other one is, and I think you would agree, if only you did

not have to go away before the Mysteries, as you told me yesterday that you must, but could stay instead and be initiated.

M: I **would** stay, Socrates, if you could tell me   77A
many things like these.

S: Then I won't spare any effort to tell you
these sorts of things, both for your sake and
for my own — though I may not be able to continue in
this vein for long. But come on, you too try to fulfill your
promise to me. Tell me the nature of virtue as a whole
and stop making many things out of one — as jokers
say to people who have shattered something. Please
allow virtue to remain sound and whole, and tell me what   77B
it is. You can use things I have said as examples.

M: I THINK, SOCRATES, that virtue is, as the poet says, "to find joy in beautiful things and have power." Therefore I say that virtue is to want the best things in life, and have the power to get them.

S: Do you mean that the man who desires the best things in life desires good things?

M: That's certainly right.

S: Do you take it for granted that there are people who desire bad things, and others who desire good things? Don't you think, my good man, that all men desire good things?   77C

M: I certainly don't.

S: You think some want bad things, then?

M: Yes.

S: Do you mean that they think the bad things are good, or that they know they are bad and nevertheless want them anyway?

M: I think there are both kinds.

S: Do you think, Meno, that anyone, knowing that bad things are bad, still wants them?

M: I certainly do.

S: Wants in what way? To have for himself?

77D M: Yes, to have them. What else?

S: Does he think the bad things benefit the one who has them, or does he perfectly well know they will harm whoever has them?

M: There are some who believe bad things benefit them, others who know that they harm them.

S: And do you think that those who believe that bad things benefit them **know** that they are bad?

M: No, that doesn't seem right at all.

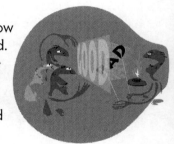

S: It's clear, then, that those who do not know things to be bad do not want what is bad. What they want are things they **think** are good, but which are in fact bad. It follows that those who have no knowledge about these things and believe them to be good clearly want good things. Isn't that right?

77E

M: In the case of these people, that's probably so.

S: Well then, those who you say want bad things, while believing that bad things harm the one who possesses them — do they actually know they will be harmed by them?

M: They must.

S: And don't they think those who are harmed are wretched to the extent that they are harmed?

M: That seems unavoidable.

78A S: And don't they think those who are wretched are miserable?

M: I think so.

S: Is there anyone who wants to be wretched and miserable?

M: I don't think so, Socrates.

S: Then no one wants what is bad, Meno — unless he wants to be in such a state. For what else is misery, if not wishing for bad things and having your wish come true?

M: What you are saying is probably true, Socrates. No one really 78B wants what is bad.

S: Weren't you saying just now that virtue is the desire for good things, and the power to acquire them?

M: Yes, I was.

S: It seems everyone satisfies the 'desire for' part of this definition, and no one is better than anyone else in this respect.

M: So it appears.

S: Clearly then, if any man is going to turn out better than the next, it is going to be due to superior talent at actually **getting** the things.

M: Quite so.

 S: So this is what virtue turns out to be, it seems, according to your argument: the power to 78C acquire good things.

M: I quite agree, Socrates. Now you have really hit the nail on the head.

S: Let's see whether what you have said is true in another respect — for you may well be right. You say that the capacity to get good things is virtue?

M: I do.

S: And by good things you mean, for example, health and wealth?

M: I also mean amassing plenty of gold and silver — and winning honors and public office.

S: So, by 'good things' you don't mean other sorts of things than these?

M: No, I mean all things of this kind.

78D S: Very well. According to Meno — hereditary guest friend of the Great King — virtue is getting your hands on the cash. Do you qualify this definition, Meno, with the words 'justly' and 'piously'? Or is it all the same to you — virtue either way — if you make your fortune unjustly?

M: Certainly not, Socrates.

S: You would call it viciousness, then?

M: That I would.

78E S: It seems, then, that the getting of gold must go along with justice or moderation or piety or some other element of virtue. If it does not, it won't be virtue, no matter what good things are obtained.

M: Yes. How could there be virtue if these elements were missing?

S: Then failing to acquire gold and silver, whether for oneself or for another, if these other elements were missing from the situation, would be a case of virtue?

M: So it seems.

79A S: It follows that getting hold of the goods will not be virtue any more so than failing to do so is. Apparently it's the case that whatever is done with justice will be virtue, and whatever is done in the absence of these good qualities will be vice.

M: I think it has to be as you say.

S: We said a little while ago that each of these things was a **part** of virtue — namely, justice and moderation and all such things?

M: Yes.

S: Then it seems you have been playing me for a fool, Meno.

M: How so, Socrates?

S: Because I begged you just now not to break apart or portion out virtue, and I gave examples of how you should formulate your answer. You paid no attention, going on to tell me that virtue is being able to get good things justly; and this, you say, is part of virtue.   79B

M: Yes, I do.

S: It follows then, from what you have agreed to, that doing whatever you do with **just one part** of virtue, is virtue. For you say that justice is a part of virtue, and that other, similar qualities are too. Why do I mention this? Because, although I begged you to tell me about virtue as a whole, you have fallen very far short of telling me what it is. Instead you say that every action **is** virtue if it is performed with **a part of** virtue, just as if you had already told me all about virtue as a whole and I must comprehend it instantly — even as you   79C
mince the thing to bits! I think we have to take it from the top, my dear Meno, and you must face the same old question again: what **is** virtue, if every action that is performed with a part of virtue is virtue? For that is what you are saying when you say every action performed justly is virtuous. Or maybe you don't think you should have to answer the same question all over again, because you think someone could know the nature of a part of virtue, while remaining ignorant of the whole?

M: I don't think so.

79D S: If you will recall, when I was answering you concerning shape, we rejected the sort of answer that tries to proceed in terms that might still be in need of investigation or haven't been agreed upon.

M: And we were right to reject them, Socrates.

S: Then surely, my good man, you must not think that while the nature of virtue as a whole is still under investigation you can make its nature clear to anyone by replying in terms of its parts, or by
79E saying anything else along these same lines. The same question will just be put to you all over again — namely, what **is** this virtue you keep going on about? But maybe you think I don't have a point?

M: I think what you say is right.

S: Then answer me again from the beginning: what do you and your friend say virtue is?

M: SOCRATES, EVEN BEFORE I met you, I
80A heard others talk about how you are always completely perplexed about everything, and how you drag everyone else down into the same pit of perplexity. And now here we are. I think you have been bewitching and enchanting me. You've cast some spell over me, so now I'm completely at a loss. In fact, if you don't mind my making a bit of a joke, I think you're very like a stingray — that strange flat fish that paralyzes anyone who approaches and touches it — and not just in that way. You look like one, too. Anyway, now you've done something like that to me, and paralyzed
80B me. Both my mind and my tongue are completely numb, and I really don't have any answer to give you. And yet I must have made a thousand speeches about virtue before now on many occasions — in front of large audiences, too, and at the time I thought I had made quite a good job of it. But now I cannot even say at all what virtue is. I think you are well advised not to sail away from Athens or go traveling, because if you behaved like this as a stranger in a strange land, you would probably be dragged off to prison as a wizard.

S: You are an unscrupulous rogue, Meno, and you nearly tricked me there.

M: How is that, Socrates?

S: I know why you likened me to a stingray. 80C

M: Why do you think?

S: So that I would liken **you** to something in return. I know that all handsome men delight in such comparisons, in which they invariably come off well — for things that can be likened to beautiful men must, I imagine, also be beautiful. But, all the same, I won't return your little favor. And as to this stingray — if it paralyzes itself, at the same time as it paralyzes everyone else, then I do indeed resemble it; otherwise, not. For it's not as though I myself have the answer when I reduce others to perplexity. Rather, I'm **more** perplexed 80D than anyone else, and I reduce others to the same state. So, as to the question of what virtue is, I don't know now, and **you**, though you might well have known in the past before you met me — well, now you at least **resemble** a person who has no idea. Nevertheless, I want to undertake a joint investigation, Meno, so that together we can figure out what this thing is.

M: How will you look for it, Socrates, when you don't have the slightest idea what it is? What sort of thing will you select as the object of your search from the class of things you don't know? Even if it's right in front of your nose, how will you know **that's** the thing you didn't know?

S: I understand, Meno, but don't you see what a fighter you've 80E hooked with this line? You are arguing that a man cannot inquire either about what he knows or about what he does not know. He cannot inquire about what he knows since he knows it; there isn't any need for inquiry. Nor can he inquire about what he does not know; for then he does not know what to look for.

M: Doesn't that strike you as a well-formed argument, Socrates? 81A

S: No, it doesn't.

M: Can you tell me why not?

S: I can. I have heard wise men and women talk about divine matters —

M: — What did they say?

S: Something true — so it seemed to me — and beautiful.

M: What was it, and who were the speakers?

S: The speakers were some of those priests and priestesses who take care to be able to give an account of their practices. Pindar says
81B the same as they did, I might add, and many of the other divinely inspired poets. What they say is this. See whether you think they speak truth. They say the human soul is immortal, and at one time it comes to an end — a thing called dying — and at another time it is reborn, but it is never utterly destroyed. Therefore one must live one's life as piously as possible:

> Persephone will accept requital for ancient sin from those
> Whose souls she will restore again to the sun above in the ninth year
> And from these seeds men will grow,
81C Noble kings, swift in strength, surpassing in wisdom,
> And for the rest of time men will call them sacred heroes.

As the soul is immortal, and has been reborn, time and again, and has seen both the things of this world and those of the underworld, and all matters — there is nothing it has not learned. So it is in no way surprising that it can recollect that which it knew before, both about virtue
81D and about other things. As everything in Nature is akin, and the soul has learned all, nothing prevents a man who has recalled one single thing — a process men call 'learning' — from dis-covering everything else; nothing, that is, if he is brave and does not weary of the search, for searching and learning are entirely recollection. We must, therefore, not

credit your debater's quibble. It would make us lazy, and is music
to the ears of spineless men, whereas my argument will make them
enthusiastic and keen searchers. I trust that this is true, and so I want
to inquire along with you into the nature of virtue.   81E

M: YES, SOCRATES, BUT what exactly do you mean when you say we
do not learn — that what we call learning is recollection? Can you
teach me that this is so?

S: As I said just now, Meno, you are unscrupulous. Here you are, asking if I can **teach** you that what we call 'learning' or 'being taught' is   82A
in fact recollection. You hope I will be caught contradicting myself
right away.

M: No, by Zeus, Socrates, I had no such intention. I just said it out
of habit. If you can somehow show me things are as you say, please
do so.

S: It's not so easy, but I am nevertheless willing to do my best for
your sake. Call one of these many servants of yours — whichever   82B
one you like — so that I can prove to you what I say is so.

M: Certainly. You there, step forward.

S: Is he a Greek? Does he speak Greek?

M: Oh certainly — born in my house.

S: Pay attention, then, and see whether you think he is recollecting
or learning from me.

M: I'll pay close attention.

S: Tell me this, boy. You know that a square figure is like this?

BOY: I do.

S: A square, then, is a figure all four of whose sides are equal?   82C

B: Yes, indeed.

S: And it also has equal lines, like so, through the middle?

B: Yes.

S: And a figure like this could be bigger or smaller?

B: Certainly.

S: If, say, this side were two feet, and this other side two feet, how many feet in area would the whole be? Think about it like this: if it were two feet this way, and only one foot that way, the figure would be one times two feet?

B: Yes.

82D S: But if it is two feet also that way, it would surely be twice two feet?

B: Yes.

S: How many feet is twice two feet? Work it out and tell me.

B: Four, Socrates.

S: Now let us have another figure with twice the area of this one, with the four sides equal like this one.

B: Yes.

S: How many feet will that area be?

B: Eight.

82E S: Come now, try to tell me how long each side of that figure will be. The side of this one is two feet. What about the side of the one that is double this one?

B: Obviously, Socrates, it will be twice the length.

S: You see, Meno, I am not **teaching** the boy anything. All I do is question him. And now he thinks he knows the length of the line on which an eight square foot figure is based. Don't you think so?

M: I do.

S: And does he know?

M: Absolutely not.

S: He thinks the line will be twice the length?

M: Yes.

S: Watch him now as he recollects things in order — the way one **must** recollect. Tell me, boy, do you say that a figure double the 83A area is based on a line double the length? I have in mind a figure like this one — not long on one side and short on the other, mind you — but equal in every direction like this one, only double the area — eight square feet. See whether you still believe it will be based on a line double the length.

B: I do.

S: Now the line becomes double the length if we add another of the same length, like so?

B: Yes indeed.

S: And the eight-foot area square will be based on it, if there are four lines of that length?

B: Yes.

S: Well, let us draw from it four equal lines. Surely that will be the 83B thing you say is the eight-foot area square?

B: Certainly.

S: And within this figure we now see four squares, each of which is equal to the four-foot area square?

B: Yes.

S: How big is it, then? Isn't it four times as big?

B: Of course.

S: Is this square, then, which is four times as big, twice as big?

B: No, by Zeus!

S: How many times bigger is it?

B: Four times.

83C S: Then, my boy, the figure based on a line twice the length is not double but four times the area?

B: What you say is true.

S: And four times four is sixteen, isn't it?

B: Yes.

S: On how long a line, then, should the eight-foot area square be based? This line yields a square four times the area of the original, doesn't it?

B: Yes.

S: Whereas this four-foot square is based on a line half the length?

B: Yes.

S: Very well, then. Is the eight-foot area square not double the area
83D of this one and half of that other?

B: Quite so.

S: Won't it be based on a line longer than this one, but shorter than that one?

B: I think so.

S: Excellent. You should say just what you think. So tell me, was this side not two feet long, and that one four feet?

B: Yes.

S: The line on which the eight-foot area square is based must then be longer than two feet, and shorter than four feet?

B: It has to be.

S: Try to tell me, then, how long a line you say it is.

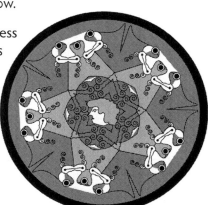

B: Three feet.

S: Then if it is three feet, let us add half of this one to itself, to make three feet? For this is two feet, and that is one foot. And here, likewise, we have two feet and one foot, and so that makes the figure you're talking about?

B: Yes.

S: Now if it is three feet this way and three feet that way, will the area of the whole figure be three times three feet?

B: So it seems.

S: How much is three times three feet?

B: Nine feet.

S: And how many feet did the area of the double square have to be?

B: Eight.

S: So the eight-foot area figure can't be based on the three-foot line?

B: Clearly not.

S: But on how long a line, then? Try to tell us exactly, and if you do not want to work it out, **show** me the line we want.

B: By Zeus, Socrates, I really don't know.

S: You realize now, Meno, the progress he has made in his recollection to this point. At first he did not know what the basic line of the eight-foot area square was — and he doesn't know even now — but he used to think then that he **did** know. He answered confidently, as if he knew, and he did not think he was perplexed. As it is now he **does** think he's at a loss, and so, although he doesn't know, neither does he **think** he knows.

M: That is true.

S: So he is better off now with regard to this matter that he doesn't understand?

M: It seems that way to me too.

S: Have we done him any harm by making him perplexed and paralyzed, like a couple of stingrays?

M: I don't think so.

S: At any rate, we have accomplished something useful, it would seem, with regard to his discovering how things really are. For now he will happily inquire into the matter, as one who doesn't know, whereas before he thought he could easily make many fine speeches to large audiences concerning the square of double area, and how it must have a base twice as long.

M: So it seems.

S: Do you think that before now he would have tried to find out or learn that which he **thought** he knew, but did not — before he descended into perplexity and realized he did not know but **wanted to know**?

M: I do not think so, Socrates.

S: The paralysis has benefited him, then?

M: I think so.

S: LOOK, THEN, AT HOW he will emerge from his perplexity and discover something by searching together with me. I'm only going to ask questions, not teach. You be on your guard against my teaching or explaining to him instead of asking for his opinion.

You, then, tell me: is this not a four-foot area figure? You understand what I mean?

B: I do.

S: We add to it this figure, which is equal in area?

B: Yes.

S: And we add this third figure, equal to each of the other two?

B: Yes.

S: Could we then fill in that space in the corner?

B: Certainly.

S: So we now have four equal figures?

B: Yes. 84E

S: Well then, how many times is the whole figure larger than this first one?

B: Four times.

S: But we were supposed to have one only twice as large, or don't you remember?

B: I certainly do.

S: Doesn't a line drawn from corner to corner cut each of these fig- 85A ures in two?

B: Yes.

S: So now we have four equal lines enclosing this new figure here?

B: They do.

S: Consider now: how large is this new figure?

B: I don't understand.

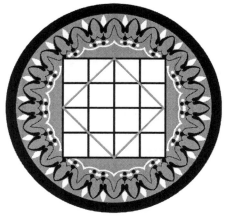

S: Each of these interior lines cuts off half of each of these four figures making it up, do they not?

B: Yes.

S: How many of this size are there in this figure?

B: Four.

S: And how many in this one?

B: Two.

S: What is the relation of four to two?

B: Double.

85B S: How many square feet are in this area?

B: Eight.

S: Based on what line?

B: **This** one.

S: That is, based on the line that stretches from corner to corner of the four-foot figure?

B: Yes.

S: Wise men call this the diagonal, so if 'diagonal' is its name, then according to you, Meno's slave, the double figure would be the one based on the diagonal?

B: Most certainly, Socrates.

S: What do you think, Meno? In giving his answers, has he expressed any opinion that was not his own?

85C M: No, they were all his own.

S: And yet, as we said a short time ago, he did not know?

M: That is true,

S: So these opinions were in him all along, were they not?

M: Yes.

S: So the man who is ignorant about some subjects — whatever these things may be — nonetheless has within himself true opinions about these things he does not know?

M: So it appears.

S: As of now these opinions have just been stirred up in the boy, as if in a dream, but if he were repeatedly asked these same questions in various ways, you know that in the end his knowledge about these things would be as perfect as anyone's. 85D

M: It is likely.

S: And he will know it all without having been taught, only questioned, by retrieving knowledge from within himself?

M: Yes.

S: And retrieving knowledge from within oneself — isn't that recollection?

M: Certainly.

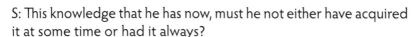

S: This knowledge that he has now, must he not either have acquired it at some time or had it always?

M: Yes.

S: If he always had it, he would always have known. But if he acquired it sometime, he couldn't have done so in his present life. Unless someone has been teaching him some geometry. For he will do just as well with all of geometry, and every other subject. Is there someone who has taught him all this? You really ought to know, especially as he has been born and brought up in your house. 85E

M: I know perfectly well that no one has taught him.

S: Yet he does have these opinions, doesn't he?

M: It seems undeniable, Socrates.

86A S: If he has not acquired them in his present life, isn't it clear that he had them and learned them at some other time?

M: It seems so.

S: Then that must have been the time before he was a human being?

M: Yes.

S: If, then, during both these times — when he was and was not a human being — he has had true opinions which only need to be awakened by questioning to become knowledge, won't it have to be the case that his soul **always** had in it all this knowledge? For it's clear that throughout all time he either was or was not a human being.

M: So it would seem.

86B S: And if the truth about reality is always in our soul, the soul must be immortal. And therefore you should take heart and seek out and recollect what you do not presently know — or rather, what you cannot presently remember.

M: I think that what you say is right, Socrates, but I don't know how.

S: I think so too, Meno. I wouldn't want to rely on my argument being correct down to the last detail, but I **would** fight to the last breath, both in word and deed, for this idea: we will be better men — braver and less helpless — if we will believe we **must** search for the things 86C we do not know, and reject the notion that there is no possibility of finding out what we do not know, nor any duty to search.

M: Here again, I think what you say is right, Socrates.

S: SINCE WE ARE of one mind about the duty to search for what one doesn't know, shall we try to find out together what virtue is?

M: Certainly. But Socrates, I would still really like to investigate what I originally asked you about, and hear what you have to say — whether we should proceed on the assumption that virtue is teachable, or is an innate gift, or something that accrues to men in some other way. 86D

S: If I could order you about, Meno — and not just myself — we would not have begun looking into whether virtue can or can't be taught before we figured out what it really was. But because you do not even bother to keep yourself in line — you are **so** fond of your freedom — you try to control **me**, and you do. I must yield to you. What else can I do? So it seems we must investigate a particu- 86E lar quality of a thing whose general nature is — we know not what! Well, the least you can do is loosen my collar just one notch, and consent to examine the question — whether virtue can be taught or has some other nature — by means of hypothesis. By 'hypothesis' I mean a method geometers often employ. For example, if someone were to ask them whether a certain area can be inscribed as a trian- 87A gle in a given circle, one of them might say, I don't yet know whether **this** area has **that** property, but I think I have a hypothesis that will move us forward with the problem: namely, if the area in question is such that when you apply it to the diameter of the circle, you find it falls short by an area equal to the applied figure, then I think you have **one** consequence, and if it is impossi- ble for it to fall short by this much, then some other consequence results. So I want to make a hypothesis before tell- ing you my conclusion about whether it is impossible to inscribe this area in the circle 87B or not. Let us do the same with virtue, since we know neither what it is, nor what prop- erties it has. Let us investigate whether it is teachable or not by means of a hypothesis, like so: of all the sorts of things existing in the soul, what sort would virtue have to be, in order to be teachable or not? First of all, if it is something like or unlike knowledge, can it be taught, or not — or rather, as we have been putting it, can it be recollected, or not? Let's not bother to disagree about which of the two names

87C   we employ. Here's the thing: can it be taught? Or isn't it completely obvious to everyone that the one and only thing a man can be taught is knowledge?

M: That would be my view.

S: Then if virtue **is** a kind of knowledge, it is clear that it could be taught.

M: Of course.

S: That question was quickly settled, then. If virtue is one sort of thing, it will be teachable, and if another, not.

M: Yes.

S: The next point to consider, it seems, will be whether virtue is knowledge, or something other than knowledge.

87D   M: That does seem to be the next question.

S: Well now, do we say virtue is anything other than good in itself? Does our hypothesis stand, that it is something good?

M: Of course.

S: If, then, there is anything else good that is different and separate from knowledge, virtue might well not be a kind of knowledge. On the other hand, if every good thing is to be found under the general heading of knowledge, we would be right to suspect that virtue is a kind of knowledge.

M: That is so.

S: Surely virtue makes us good?

M: Yes.

S: And if we are good, we are useful, for all that is good is useful.   87E
Isn't that so?

M: Yes.

S: So virtue, then, is a useful thing?

M: That's an inescapable conclusion of our argument.

S: Then let us consider, one by one, the sorts of things that are useful
to us: health, let's say, and strength, and beauty, and wealth. We say
that these things, and others of the same kind, are useful, don't we?

M: We do.

S: Yet we say that these same things also sometimes do us harm. Or   88A
maybe you would deny this?

M: No, it's as you say.

S: Look then, what deciding factor in each case makes them be useful to us at one time, and at another, harm us? Isn't it the case that
they are useful when they are used rightly, and harmful when not?

M: Certainly.

S: Let us now look at the qualities of the soul. There is a thing you
call moderation, and justice, courage, intelligence, memory, mag-
nanimity, and so on and so forth?

M: There is.   88B

S: Consider any and all items on this list you believe **not** to be knowledge but something else instead. Don't they all at times harm us, at
other times do us good? Courage, for example, when not based
on forethought, is mere recklessness. When a man is thoughtlessly
bold, he gets hurt; but when he is mindful of what he does, he benefits, doesn't he?

M: Yes.

S: The same is true of patience or mental quickness. Things that are learned and coordinated with sense are useful; those same things, when sense is lacking, are harmful.

88C   M: Very much so.

S: Therefore, in short, all that the soul does, and all that it endures, ends in happiness — if directed with good sense, but if that is lacking, things will go badly?

M: That is likely.

S: If, then, virtue is something in the soul, and necessarily useful, it must be a matter of mindfulness. For all the other qualities of soul

88D   are in themselves neither useful nor harmful. As accompanied by forethought or thoughtlessness, they become good or harmful. So, according to this argument, virtue, being useful in and of itself, must be a kind of mindfulness.

M: I agree.

S: Furthermore, those other items we were considering — wealth and the like — are sometimes good, sometimes harmful. Here again, isn't

88E   this the same as with the soul: with mindfulness as a guide, the soul's properties become beneficial, but when thoughtlessness leads, it causes them to be harmful. Isn't that so in these cases also: if the soul uses and directs material things rightly, they are made beneficial; if it directs wrongly, they become harmful?

M: Quite.

S: The mindful soul directs rightly, the thoughtless soul wrongly?

M: That is so.

S: Then we can say this is a general rule: every other thing in man depends upon the soul, and the things of the soul itself depend on mindfulness, if they are going to be good. According to this argu- 89A ment what is beneficial will be mindfulness, and we do say that virtue is beneficial?

M: Certainly.

S: Virtue then, as a whole or in part, is a matter of mindfulness?

M: I think that what you say, Socrates, is excellently put.

S: Then, if this is how it is, men can't be good by nature.

M: I think not.

S: For if they were, I suppose the results would have been this: if good men were so by nature, we would probably have people who recognized those among the young who were naturally good. We would take those they pointed out and guard them in the Acropolis. We would vault them up there far more carefully than gold, so that no one could corrupt them, and so that when they reached maturity they would be useful to their cities.

89B

M: Yes, probably so, Socrates.

S: Since the good are not good by nature, does learning make them 89C so?

M: I now think that must necessarily be so, Socrates. And clearly, on our hypothesis that virtue is knowledge, it must be teachable.

S: PERHAPS, BY ZEUS. But mightn't it turn out we were wrong to agree to this?

M: It seemed to be a correct statement just a minute ago.

S: We shouldn't only have thought it correct a minute ago. We should also think so now, and in the future, if it's going to be at all sound.

89D M: What is it? What point are you considering that is giving you trouble, and making you doubt now whether virtue is knowledge?

S: I will tell you, Meno. I am not retracting as incorrect the statement that virtue is teachable if it is knowledge, but see whether it isn't reasonable for me to have doubts. Tell me this: if any sort of thing is teachable — not just virtue — won't there necessarily be those who teach it and others who learn it?

89E M: I think so.

S: On the other hand, if the opposite were true, and there weren't teachers or students of a given subject, wouldn't we be right to assume the subject couldn't be taught?

M: Quite so, but do you think that there are no teachers of virtue?

S: I have often tried to find out whether there are any teachers of it, but in spite of my best efforts I cannot find any. This is so even though I have searched with the help of many people, and particularly those whom I believed to be best qualified for the job. But as it happens, Meno, Anytus is by great good fortune sitting here beside us now.

90A Let us include him in our search party. Doing so makes perfect sense, for Anytus is, in the first place, the son of Anthemion, a man both wealthy and wise — and who did not become rich by sitting on his hands, nor by being handed a gift like Ismenias the Theban, who recently became as rich as Polycrates. No, he rose up thanks to his own wisdom and hard work. What's more, he didn't make a name for himself

90B as an arrogant member of society, or get a swelled head and become annoying, but was regarded as a well-mannered and well-behaved man. Also, he raised our friend here well and gave him a good education — at least according to the majority of Athenians, for they are

electing him to the highest offices. It is right then to look for teachers of virtue — to see whether there are any and, if so, who — in
the company of such a man as this. Therefore, Anytus, please join
me and your guest-friend Meno here in our inquiry into the identi-
ties of teachers of virtue. Look at it in this way: if we wanted Meno
to become a good doctor, to what teachers would we send him?   90C
Wouldn't we send him to the doctors?

ANYTUS: Certainly.

S: And if we wanted him to be a good shoemaker, to shoemakers?

A: Yes.

S: And so with other professions?

A: Certainly.

S: Tell me a little more about this same point, as follows. We say that
we would be right to send him to the doctors if we want to make
a doctor of him. Whenever we say this sort of thing, we mean that   90D
it would be reasonable to send him to those who practice the discipline in question rather than to those who do not, and to those
who charge fees for this very discipline, and who have shown themselves to be teachers of those who wish to come to them and study.
Wouldn't this be our rationale in sending him off, and wouldn't we
be right?

A: Yes.

S: And the same goes for flute-playing and the other disciplines? It wouldn't make a lot of sense if those who
wanted to make someone a flute-player refused to   90E
send him to those who teach the instrument, and
make their living that way, and instead sent our
would-be flutist to pester with requests for
instruction those who neither teach the thing
in question, nor have a single pupil studying
it? Don't you think that would be a pretty idiotic way to go about it?

A: By Zeus, that's right — a stupid thing to do.

S: You're quite right. However, you can now enter into a little argument with me about our guest-friend Meno here. He has been telling me for some time, Anytus, that he longs to acquire the understanding and virtue that enables men to manage their households and their cities well — to care respectfully for their parents, to know how and when to welcome and send away citizens and strangers alike, as a worthy man should. Now consider, to whom should one properly send him to learn this virtue? Or maybe it is obvious, in light of what has just been said, that we should send him to those who profess to teach virtue, and have made themselves available to any Greek who wishes to learn — in return for a fixed fee?

A: Who exactly do you have in mind, Socrates?

S: I am sure you know perfectly well yourself. They are the men people call 'sophists'.

A: By Heracles, don't even say such things, Socrates! May no member of my household — may none of my friends, be they citizens or strangers — be so overcome with insanity that they willingly submit to be ruined by these people, who are manifestly a plague and source of corruption to all who follow them!

S: How do you mean, Anytus? Of all the people who set themselves up as professors of useful knowledge, are only this lot so different from the rest that they not only fail to improve, as the others do, the things they are given to work on, but on the contrary actually make them worse? And they have the gall to think they should be paid for it? I really can't quite believe you. For I know that one man, Protagoras, made more money off his wisdom than Pheidias, who crafted such remarkably fine works, or any other ten sculptors put together. Surely what you say is bizarre, given that no one who set up to repair old shoes, or old clothes, would be able to get away with returning all items in a more tattered state than when he received them. He would be out of business in a month. 91E Anyone who did business like that would starve to death, and yet you would have me believe all of Greece neglected to notice — for more than forty years! — that Protagoras was corrupting those who follow him, and sending them back out into the world in a worse condition than when he took them into his care. I think he was nearly seventy when he died, and he had plied his craft for forty years. During all that time, down to this very day, his reputation has remained consistently high. And it isn't just Protagoras. There are 92A lots of others, some born before him, some still alive today. Are we to understand from your charge that they cheat and harm the young knowingly, or that they themselves are blind to it? Should we think they're as crazy as all that, when some people say they're the wisest of men?

A: They are far from being crazy, Socrates. It is more a question of crazy young people being willing to pay their fees, and — even more so — relatives entrusting the young to such men. Most of all 92B it is a matter of cities allowing them in and not driving out any citizen or stranger who tries this kind of fraud.

S: Has some sophist done you wrong, Anytus? Otherwise, why would you be so hard on them?

A: No, by Zeus, I have never met a single one of them, and I wouldn't let any of my people do so either.

S: So you're totally unfamiliar with these people?

A: And I'm staying that way. 92C

S: How, my good sir, can you know whether there's any good in what they teach or not, if you haven't experienced it at all?

A: Easily. I've got **their** number, whether I've met them or not.

S: You must be psychic, Anytus, for how else could you know about these men, given what you say, I really can't imagine. However, let's set aside the question of where to send Meno to turn him rotten; let's grant, if you like, that it would be to the sophists. But tell us — and do your family friend here some good in the process — to whom in our great city a stranger should go to acquire, to a worthwhile degree, that virtue I was just talking about.

92 D

A: Why haven't you just told him yourself?

S: I did mention those whom I thought to be teachers of virtue, but you say I'm talking nonsense, and maybe you're right. So **you** tell him, now that it's your turn, which Athenian he should turn to. Tell him the name of anyone you want.

92 E

A: Why give him the name of any one man? Any Athenian gentlemen he runs across could make a better man out of him than any sophist, if he'll just follow their advice.

S: And have these gentlemen — noble men, and good — become virtuous automatically, without learning from anyone? Can they nevertheless instruct others in this thing they themselves never studied?

93 A

A: I believe these men have learned at the feet of the older generation, who were also fine gentlemen. Don't you think we have had many good men in this city of ours?

S: I certainly believe, Anytus, that there are many men here who are good at handling public affairs, and that there have been many more just like them in the past. But have they really been good **teachers** of this virtue of theirs? For **that** is the point we are discussing now, not whether or not there are good men here, nor whether there have been in the past. Instead, we have been investigating for some time whether virtue can be taught. Pursuing that investigation we ask this question: did the good men of today, and those of the past, know how to pass on their virtue — the thing that made

93 B

them good — to others; or is virtue not the sort of thing that can be transmitted or handed down from one man to another? This is what Meno and I have been investigating for some time. Look at it this way, from what you yourself have said. Would you not say that 93c Themistocles was a good man?

A: Yes. One of the very best.

S: He in particular would have been a good teacher of his virtue, if anyone was?

A: I think so, if he wanted to be.

S: But can you think he did **not** want other citizens to be noble men and good, especially his own son? Can you seriously think he begrudged this to his son, deliberately **not** passing on his own virtue? Haven't you heard that Themistocles taught his son, Cleophantus, 93d to be a good horseman? He could stand upright on horseback and shoot javelins from there and do many other remarkable things — all skills his father had taught to him, all requiring good teachers. Haven't you heard about this from your elders?

A: I have.

S: No one could say, then, that the son lacked natural aptitude altogether?

A: I should say **not**.   93e

S: But what about this: have you ever heard anyone, young or old, say that Cleophantus, the son of Themistocles, was good and skilled at the same pursuits as his father?

A: Never.

S: Are we supposed to believe he wanted to educate his son well, except when it came to that wisdom he himself possessed, in which his son was to be no better than his neighbors — still assuming that virtue can be taught?

A: Perhaps not, by Zeus.

94A S: In him you have a fine teacher of virtue, since even you agree that he was among the best men of the past. Let us consider another man, Aristides, son of Lysimachus. You will agree he was a good man?

A: I absolutely do, of course.

94B S: He too gave his own son, Lysimachus, the best Athenian education in all subjects that have teachers, but do you think he made him a better man than anyone else? You have been in his company and seen what kind of man he is. Or take the magnificent Pericles. You know that he brought up two sons, Paralus and Xanthippus?

A: I know.

94C S: You also know that he taught them to ride horses as well as any Athenian. He educated them in the arts, in gymnastics, and generally raised them up to be — in matters of skill — inferior to none. But didn't he want to make good men of them? I think he **wanted to**, but it was something that couldn't be taught. And so you won't think that only a few Athenians, the least significant ones, lacked this ability, I remind you that Thucydides too brought up two sons, Melesias and Stephanus, whom he educated well in all other things. They became the best wrestlers in Athens. He entrusted the one to Xanthias and the other to Eudorus, who were thought to be the best wrestlers of the time, don't you remember?

A: I remember I have heard that said.

94D S: It is surely clear that he wouldn't have had his boys taught these expensive subjects, but then fail to teach them what would make them good men — when that would have been free? Maybe Thucydides was a trifling person, who didn't have many friends among the Athenians and their allies? No, he belonged to a great house. He had great influence in the city and among the Greeks. So if virtue could be taught he would have found the man to make his sons good men, be that man a citizen or a foreigner — if he himself could not spare the time due to his public commitments. No, my friend Anytus, it looks as if virtue can't be taught. 94E

A: I think, Socrates, that you're too quick to speak ill of people. I would advise you — if you will take my advice — to be careful. Probably it works this way in other cities, but particularly in this one. It is easier to do people harm than good. But I think you knew that already. 95A

S: I THINK, MENO, that Anytus is angry, and I am not the least bit surprised. He thinks, first of all, that I am slandering these men; next, he thinks he is one of them. If it ever occurs to him what slander really is, his anger will evaporate, but the light hasn't dawned yet. So you tell me now, aren't there good men and true to be found among your people?

M: Certainly.

S: Well, then, do they make themselves available to the young as teachers? Do they agree that they are teachers, and that virtue can be taught? 95B

M: No, by Zeus, Socrates. Sometimes you can hear them say it can be taught; other times, that it cannot.

S: Should we say that they are teachers of this subject, when they do not even agree on this point?

M: I do not think so, Socrates.

S: Furthermore, do you think these sophists — who alone profess to be so crafty and wise — are teachers of virtue? 95C

M: This is what I admire most in Gorgias, Socrates — that you would never hear him promising such a thing. Indeed, he makes fun of others when he hears them making this claim. He says you should turn people into clever speakers.

S: You do not think, then, that the sophists are teachers of virtue?

M: I cannot say, Socrates. Like most people, at times I think they are, at other times I think they are not.

S: Are you aware that it isn't just you — and lots of other public figures — who think sometimes that virtue can be taught, sometimes that it can't be. The poet Theognis says the very same thing?

95 D

M: In which verses?

S: In his elegies, where he says:

And with those men eat, and drink, and with them
go about, and please those whose power is great.
For it is from the good that you will learn good. If you mingle
95 E   with wicked men you will lose even what wit you possess.

You see how here he speaks as if virtue can be taught?

M: So it seems.

S: Elsewhere, he changes his tune: "if this could be done," he says, "and wit implanted in a man," those who could do this, "would collect wages great and many." Furthermore:

Never would come from good father evil son,
96 A   for he would be persuaded by wise words. But by teaching
you will never make an evil man good.

You do see that the poet is contradicting himself concerning the subject at hand?

M: He does seem to be.

S: Can you think of any other subject concerning which those who set themselves up as teachers are not only unrecognized as teachers of others, but aren't even acknowledged to know about the subject themselves? Indeed, they are thought to be poor practitioners of the very thing they profess to profess, while those agreed to be excellent men sometimes say the thing can be taught, sometimes that it cannot? Would you say that people who are so confused about a subject can be effective teachers of it?

96 B

M: No, by Zeus, I would not.

S: If, then, neither the sophists nor the noble and good are teachers of this subject, clearly there would be no others?

M: I do not think there are.

S: Where there are no teachers, there are no learners?   96c

M: I think it's as you say.

S: We agreed that a subject boasting neither teachers nor learners is not teachable?

M: We have so agreed.

S: And there seem to be no teachers of virtue anywhere to be found?

M: That is so.

S: If there are no teachers, there are no learners?

M: That seems so.

S: Then virtue cannot be taught?   96d

M: Apparently not, if we have looked into this business correctly. I am led to wonder, Socrates, whether there are no good men either, or in what way good men come to be.

S: WE ARE PROBABLY poor specimens, you and I, Meno. Gorgias has not adequately cultured you, nor Prodicus me. We must then at all costs make our selves our own concern and find someone who will
96E   in some way make us better. I say this in view of our recent investigation, for it is ridiculous that we quite failed to notice that it is not only by the light of knowledge that men succeed in their affairs. That is perhaps why the understanding of how good men come to be eludes us.

M: How do you mean, Socrates?

S: I mean this: we were right to agree that good men must do good,
97A   and that things cannot be otherwise. Isn't that so?

M: Yes.

S: And that they will do good if they guide us correctly in conducting our affairs. We did well in agreeing to this?

M: Yes.

S: But that one cannot guide correctly without knowledge: our agreement to this proposition is likely to be incorrect.

M: How do you mean?

97B   S: I will tell you. A man who knew the way to Larissa, or anywhere else you like, who went there and guided others there would surely lead them well?

M: Certainly.

S: What if someone had a true opinion about which way was the right way, but he hadn't gone there himself and wasn't acquainted with the place? Wouldn't he also lead the way correctly?

M: Certainly.

S: As long as he has the right opinion concerning that which other people know, he will not be a worse guide than one who knows. For he has a true opinion, though not knowledge.

M: In no way worse.

S: So true opinion is in no way an inferior guide to action than knowledge. This is what we overlooked in our investigation of the nature of virtue, when we said only knowledge can culminate in proper action. For true opinion can do just as well. 97C

M: So it seems.

S: So correct opinion is no less useful than knowledge?

M: Yes, to an extent, Socrates. But the man with knowledge will always succeed, whereas he who has true opinion will only succeed at times.

S: How do you mean? Won't the one with the right opinion always be right, as long as his opinion is right?

M: That appears to be necessarily the case, and it makes me wonder, Socrates — this being the way of it — why knowledge is rated so much more highly than correct opinion, and what the difference is. 97D

S: Do you know what is puzzling you, or shall I tell you?

M: Go ahead, tell me.

S: It is because you have paid no attention to the statues of Daedalus — but perhaps you don't have any over in Thessaly.

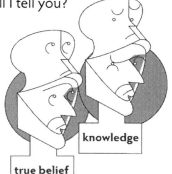

M: What are you driving at, Socrates?

S: That they too run away and escape if you forget to tie them down; but they stay put if properly tethered.

knowledge

true belief

M: So what? 97E

S: Acquiring an untied work of Daedalus is not worth much; it's like a runaway slave — for it won't stay put. A statue that is tied down, though, is very valuable, because the man's works are very beautiful. What am I driving at here? True opinions. True opinions, for as

98A long as they remain, are fine things and do nothing but good. But they don't hang around for long. They escape from a man's mind, so that they are not worth much until one tethers them with chains of reasons why. And these, Meno my friend, are threads of memory, as previously agreed. After opinions are tied down, in the first place they become knowledge; secondly, they remain in place. That is why knowledge is prized more highly than correct opinion. Knowledge differs from correct opinion in being tied down.

M: Yes, by Zeus, Socrates, it does seem to go something like that.

98B S: Indeed, I too speak now like a man offering guesswork in lieu of knowledge. However, I certainly do not think I am guessing when I say that true opinion is a different thing from knowledge. If I do claim to know anything else — and I would make that claim about few things — I would put this down on the list as one thing I do know.

M: Rightly so, Socrates.

S: Well then, isn't it the case that when true opinion guides the course of each action, it comes off no worse than knowledge?

M: I think you are right here too.

98C S: True opinion, then, is neither inferior to knowledge nor does less good in action, nor does the man who has true opinion in lieu of knowledge come off the worse.

M: That is so.

S: And we agreed that the good man does good.

M: Yes.

S: Since, then, it is not only through knowledge but also through true opinion that men are good, and do good to their cities; and since neither knowledge nor true opinion is innate in men, but both are acquired — unless you think either of these is naturally inborn? 98D

M: I don't think so.

S: Then if these things are not innate, men are not naturally good.

M: Surely not.

S: As goodness is not innate, we inquired next whether it could be taught.

M: Yes.

S: We thought it could be taught if it was knowledge?

M: Yes.

S: And that it was knowledge if it could be taught?

M: Quite so.

S: And that if there were teachers of it, it could be taught, but if there were not, not? 98E

M: That is so.

S: And then we agreed that there were no teachers of it?

M: We did.

S: So we agreed that it was neither teachable nor knowledge?

M: Quite so.

S: But we certainly agree that virtue is a good thing?

M: Yes.

S: And that which guides correctly is both useful and good?

M: Certainly.

99A S: And that only these two things, true belief and knowledge, guide correctly, and that if a man possesses these he gives correct guidance? The things that turn out right by some chance are not due to human guidance, but where there is correct human guidance it is due to two things, true belief or knowledge?

M: I think that is so.

S: Now because it cannot be taught, virtue no longer seems to be knowledge?

M: It seems not.

S: So one of the two good and useful things has been excluded, and knowledge is not the guide in public affairs.

M: I don't think it can be.

99B S: So it is not through some wisdom, or by being wise, that such men lead their cities — I mean the likes of Themistocles, and those others mentioned by Anytus just now? Here is the reason they cannot make others like themselves: it is not **knowledge** that makes them what they are.

M: You are probably right, Socrates.

S: Therefore, if it isn't through knowledge, the only alternative is
99C   that it is through **true opinion** that statesmen settle on the right course for their cities. As regards knowledge, they are no different from seers and prophets. They too say many true things when the divine inspiration strikes them, but they don't actually know what they are talking about.

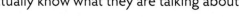

M: That is probably so.

S: Likewise, Meno, don't these other men deserve to be called 'divine': those who fail to comprehend the true import of what they say and do, yet say and do much that is truly important?

M: Certainly.

true belief

1st

false belief

2nd

GUIDANCE

knowledge

3st

S: So we would be right to say the seers and prophets just men- 99D
tioned are 'divine' and 'inspired' — likewise, everyone with a knack
for poetry. Likewise, politicians and public figures are nothing less
than divine and possessed when — under some god's inspiration
and influence — they give speeches that lead to success in important
matters, even though they have no idea what they are talking about.

M: Quite so.

S: Women are always calling good men 'god-like', and the Spartans
do the same when they deliver a eulogy. They say, 'this man is divine.'

M: And they seem to be, Socrates — though perhaps Anytus here   99E
will be annoyed with you for saying so.

S: I don't mind about that. We can hash it out with him some other
time. But for now, if we have been right in how we investigated
and what we said, virtue turns out to be neither innate nor earned.
It is something that comes to those who possess it as a free gift
from the gods — with understanding not included; unless, that is, 100A
you can point to some statesmen who could make another man a
statesman. If there were such a one, he could be said to rank among
the living as Homer said Teiresias ranked among the dead: namely,
"he alone kept his wits collected while the others flitted about like
shadows." In the same way such a man would, as far as virtue is concerned, stand forth as someone of substance — opposed, as it were,
to mere shadows.

M: I think that is an excellent way to put it, Socrates   100B

S: It follows from this whole line of reasoning, Meno, that virtue
appears present in those who have it only as a gift from the gods.
We will only really know about this, however, if and when we try to
investigate what virtue itself is — an investigation that must come
before that of how it comes to be in men. But the time has come
for me to go. Now you persuade your guest friend Anytus here of
all these things you have been persuaded to agree to, in order that 100C
he himself may become more agreeable. If you succeed, you will
also thereby confer a benefit upon the Athenians.

Chapter 9   Republic:
                                    Conflicts & Harmonies, Us & Them

1

OUR SELECTION is Book 1 of 10. But before we get to that, Plato's **Republic** has the wrong title.

The dialogue blueprints an ideal state, but what Plato has in mind isn't a republic in our sense — that is, a constitutional, representative form of government. James Madison: "If we advert to the nature of republican government, we shall find that the censorial power is in the people over the government, and not in the government over the people." That is a very republican, **un**-Platonic thing to think. In political philosophy, republicanism goes with anti-monarchism, yet Plato, we learn, is prepared to support so-called philosopher-kings. Republicans like Madison distrust kings because they love liberty and fear exclusive, hence arbitrary exercise of political power. Nor is this a peculiarly modern concern. Here is J.S. Mill, from the opening of his essay, **On Liberty** (1859), tracing it back:

The struggle between Liberty and Authority is the most conspicuous feature in the portions of history with which we are earliest familiar, particularly in that of Greece, Rome, and England. But in old times this contest was between subjects, or some classes of subjects, and the government. By liberty, was meant protection against the tyranny of the political rulers. The rulers were conceived (except in some of the popular governments of Greece) as in a necessarily antagonistic position to the people whom they ruled. They consisted of a governing One, or a governing tribe or caste, who derived their authority from inheritance or conquest; who, at all events, did not hold it at the pleasure of the governed, and whose supremacy men did not venture, perhaps did not desire, to contest, whatever precautions might be taken against its oppressive exercise. Their power was regarded as necessary, but also as highly dangerous; as a weapon which they would attempt to use against their subjects, no less than against external enemies. To prevent the weaker members of the community from being preyed upon by innumerable vultures, it was needful that there should be an animal of prey stronger than the rest, commissioned to keep them down. But as the king of the vultures would be no less bent upon preying upon the flock than any of the minor harpies, it was indispensable to be in a perpetual attitude of defence against his beak and claws. The aim, therefore, of patriots, was to set limits to the power which the ruler should be suffered to exercise over the community; and this limitation was what they meant by liberty.[1]

Plato worries about monsters, too, we'll see. But first, sticking with more standard forms of republicanism, you deal with the monster like so: tell that big, bad bird to stay in its box!

But how is **that** supposed to work?

It's complicated. Lots of strategies, no guarantees. Partly you work to humanize the beast. Make him put on a tie. Partly you rely on the fact that there's a little beast in all of us, even if we are all dressed like proper gentlemen. But if we're all just a bunch of vultures, behind the mask, doesn't that send us all back to savagery?

That's a worry! But maybe it can work. For starters, what stuff will make for a good vulture cage? We might try: **rights**. Traditional, republican construction material. We secure everyone's rights — the right of all citizens to speak in the ancient Athenian Assembly, for instance. This doesn't help women, children non-citizens or slaves, but it's a start.

But isn't that sort of ... flimsy? What **is** a right, when you get down to it? Just a metaphysical dream, right? Some transcendentally-notarized contract or receipt, allegedly shelved in some cosmic file?

Maybe, but republicans can be more down-to-earth than that. What we are doing, in securing rights, may be nothing pie-in-the-sky. We are engineering a balance of power in which it works out to be to everyone's advantage to keep talking, rather than brawling in the street.

Look at it this way. At first you have a more or less naked power struggle — not between individuals but between classes, groups, blocs; tribes and powerful families, most likely. (You didn't think the ancient Greeks suffered from **literal** giant bird attacks, did you?) Unless the fighting just goes on, the result is some sort of equilibrium. If we are both strong, we will eventually acknowledge

1   J.S. Mill's text is available in many editions. The passage is from paragraph 2 of Chapter 1.

VOTE FOR THE POOR!

VOTE FOR THE RICH!

THETES ARE NEAT

WHAT JOY! VOTE PENTACOSIOMED!

each other's strength, be motivated to come to some accommodation. If I am weak, you strong, or vice versa, someone ends up on top, someone ends up flat on his back. This, too, is equilibrium. Later constitutional developments and legal regimes of rights are, as it were, a refereed continuation of the fight, but by milder means. Arguing in the assembly is, if you like, fighting between roughly equal parties, only now we wear boxing gloves, consisting of norms and laws, procedures, so forth. You keep wearing the gloves because you want the other guy to keep wearing his gloves, too.

Where does Plato stand? He doesn't like tyrants; doesn't approve of arbitrary acts, by kings or anyone else. But it would not occur to him to combat these evils by constitutionally constraining rulers, mostly because of that crucial 'or anyone else' clause. Plato does not see the arbitrariness of **kings** as especially risky. Nothing is more arbitrary than a democratic jury of 500, putting Socrates to death. Politics, for Plato, needs to become reasonable — rational — not more popular and representative in the modern sense.

Plato's ideal political power players will not be constrained, externally, by checks and balances. They will be internally harmonized by rational dialectic. For Plato, healthy political order is, first and foremost, a function of correct **knowing**. You have to know what to want, ideally: harmony, not some second-best balance of power between antagonistic adversaries. This makes Plato much more utopian than your average republican; yet simultaneously more cynical. In the Mill passage, the danger tends to take on an Us vs. Them shape, with 'Them' assuming a monstrous aspect: Humans vs. Harpies!

For Plato, the threat to justice is that we have met the enemy, and he is … just Us.

A Fear Flock of Flap-and-Flay Buzzards Winging Out of the Skies From Beyond!

"THEM"

In Terrifying Xenovision!

We have met the enemy, and he is …

"US"

In Vibrant Self-Exam-O-Rama

2

Let's take a quick tour of Plato's ideal state, as blueprinted in **Republic**. Plato envisions a ruling class of Guardians, which he splits in two.

Mostly they will be 'auxiliaries', members of the military class, under the command of 'philosophers turned kings'.

Socrates decrees an improving Myth be told (415a-c): all citizens of the **polis** spring from the same soil. All are brothers; but with different of proportions of precious metal admixed in their natures: gold for (reason-loving) kings; silver for (honor-loving) auxiliaries; bronze or iron for the (appetitive) mass of ordinary citizens, the producers.

Note how this tribalist, tri-metalist fable apparently undermines my claim, in the previous section that Plato is above mere Us vs. Them antagonisms. Yes, but no. The common people, even the auxiliaries, may need some sense of Us vs. Them, to serve as a heuristic moral compass. But we philosophers, students of justice, know better. (Us vs. Them is for them, not us!)

Rulership is not strictly hereditary, nor single-handed, so 'king' is doubly misleading. But these 'kings' are not elected. They are raised out of the population in educationally and meritocratically rigorous fashion. Plato envisions a rational sifting — general testing of aptitudes — after which it is expected that heredity will tend to track merit, going forward, with exceptions. Plato is very concerned not to allow monarchy in the sense of family dynasticism. These rulers will not even **know** who their biological parents and children are.

No Euthyphro-type problems, if sons do not know fathers! Nor will the golds and silvers be permitted to own gold and silver, which would be another source of corruption. But the rulers of Plato's ideal polis are not its citizens' 'first servants', catering to the peoples' desires. They won't give the people what they ask for, whatever they ask for. Plato thinks the people won't know what's good for them. Of course, everyone wants what's good for them, in a sense. (See **Meno**.) Plato's rulers will provide **that**.

3

So: Plato's **Republic**. Why the misleading title? In Greek it's **Politeia**, which means, roughly, **political matters**. Alternately: **form of government, civic stuff**. There is a work by Aristotle whose title is translated **The Athenian Constitution**. That is, Athenian **politeia**. Aristotle describes an Athenian politician, Cleisthenes, "giving **politeia** to the masses." Sometimes that gets translated "handing over power," sometimes "expanding the franchise". He did the latter, resulting in the former, so slice it how you like, semantically. The word isn't sure which part of the process **it** wants to name. Thus, there is going to be a problem settling on an English title for Plato.

But **Republic**? It's an accident. A Roman author, Cicero, wrote a Socratic dialogue, **De re publica**, meaning **of public matters**, which got abbreviated **De republica** which isn't quite the same (but close enough for government work.) **De republica** is a fine Latin translation of Plato's title. But add in modern shifts in meaning, due to increased enthusiasm for elections, and you end up in a situation in which, if someone translates Greek into English, with a touch of Latin flair, Plato comes out sounding like he likes aspects of electoral politics he wasn't interested in; indeed, that he opposed.

At this late date we seem stuck with the name, so we may as well make the most of it. Above I quoted James Madison, sounding anti-Platonic. But I could have quoted Thomas Paine, even more eminent republican philosopher, sounding Platonic:

> The sovereignty in a republic is exercised to keep right and wrong in their proper and distinct places, and never suffer the one to usurp the place of the other. A republic, properly understood, is a sovereignty of justice, in contradistinction to a sovereignty of will.[2]

It seems an ideal republic might **not** be that thing I said republicans want: mere system for setting struggling citizens against each other, in the hopes some balance of power emerges from exhaustion of antagonisms. At any rate, as you read, do think about republicanism in the modern sense: the idea that good government depends on checks-and-balances, not because it's best, just the best we can do. Think about how a sense of the harsh, dynamic logic of conflict — monster logic: politics as power, power as corruption — filters through the conversations Socrates has with his three debating partners: Cephalus, Polemarchus, Thrasymachus.

2   P. S. Foner (ed.), The Complete Writings of Thomas Paine (Citadel, 1945), vol. 2, p. 375..

4

Having hardly started, let me spoil the ending. Book 1 concludes:

> S: Just as gluttons snatch at every dish that is handed along, and taste it
> before they have properly enjoyed the one before, so I, before actu-
> ally finding the first object of our investigation — what justice is — let
> that inquiry drop, and turned away to consider something about jus-
> tice, namely whether it is vice and ignorance or wisdom and virtue; and
> when the further question burst in on us, about whether injustice is more
> profitable than justice, I could not refrain from moving on to that. And
> the result of the discussion right now is that I know nothing at all. For if I
> don't know what justice is, I am hardly likely to know whether it is or is not
> a virtue, nor can I say whether the just man is happy or unhappy. (354b)

Reversing the metaphor, why are **we** biting off just this bit — one book
out of ten? Socrates himself seems to say Book 1 is not a well-balanced meal,
by itself. I will now compensate for that by providing a preview of how the
rest of **Republic** constitutes a long response to the concerns of Book 1.
The distractions he complains about manifest mostly during the heavy third
course, consisting of Thrasymachus' hard-to-stomach account of justice as
the advantage of the stronger. Whereas Cephalus, the old man, hopes for
harmony, or at least money; and Polemarchus, the son, draws up ideal battle-
lines, with an eye for honor; Thrasymachus has gotten in touch with his inner
vulture. What to make of this indigestible fowl?

Thrasymachus appears to offer two accounts of justice, not clearly consistent. The tenor of both is egoistic, hence immoralistic. Thrasymachus would
say he is realistic. His slogan (which may or may not be a definition) is 'justice
is the advantage of the stronger.' Pending fuller discussion, let me provide
a crib sheet. When the time comes, this may help you see
how Thrasymachus' two accounts may indeed be **one**,
presented in two ways.

The sophist got a wonderful, **awful** idea:

1. **Justice is non-explanatory.**
   (All preaching! no practice!)
2. **Injustice is explanatory.**
   (Everyone does it!)
3. **Justice is personally non-advantageous.**
4. **Injustice is personally advantageous.**
5. **Call injustice 'justice' and justice 'injustice'.**

The first time Thrasymachus pushes this cluster of claims, he makes the mistake of trying to apply 5 to 1-5 themselves. This makes 1-4 unclear and generates contradiction when 5 is applied, recursively, to itself. (Try it at home. Write down what 1-5 say, while doing what 5 says!)

When Socrates trips Thrasymachus up by exploiting how hard it is to lie and speak truth simultaneously (even if it's true you should lie!) Thrasymachus does not repent. He lets the mask of 5 slip, to display the beast of 1-4 to true, naked advantage. **This** is his philosophy: be the beast behind the human mask!

Thrasymachus' view has a commonsensical down-to-earthiness, despite its secretive airs. If he adds anything that hasn't already occurred to your neighborhood bully, it's a refusal to make excuses, and a pedestal of Grand Politics. "Temple robbers, kidnappers, burglars, con-men and thieves" (344c). Nothing unprofitable about small-time crime! But such petty stuff lacks a critical, Big Picture sense of how, once you are in, you ought to go all-in.

For most of us, doing wrong is tempting at the petty end of the scale, practically and conceptually. We will fail to contribute to the coffee fund, not murder a man. We'll rationalize wrong as right, in our private case, rather than reasoning wrong **is** right, in public cases. Thrasymachus' contribution is to argue 'go big or go home!' when it comes to committing and conceptualizing injustice. And clothing it!

Thrasymachus can help you in that department, too. It's your Soul. But also Men's Clothing, since clothes make the man. We need to take you to his specialty section for Big and Tall Men. The finest in this line are a tyrant's robes. Once you have seized power, anyone who points out, quite correctly, that you are unjust can be 'corrected', quite effectively. Soon everyone in the city will be praising your injustice — excuse me, Your Tyrantship, your 'justice'!

So Thrasymachus thinks of himself as dispensing self-help for the strong. But, even if you are weak, his philosophy has a few pointed things to say; maybe a few pointers for self-improvement.

If your personal best is only **perfect sheepishness, your** best bet is being a **sheep** in shepherd's clothing. Tell everyone 'Justice **is its** own reward.' Maybe this will pull **the** wool over someone's eyes, maybe not; but wool is the weapon you've got. (Socrates strikes Thrasymachus as an extremely woolly thinker.)

5

Thrasymachus does not do well defending injustice; neither in disguise, nor in naked, natural glory. Then, after he slinks off at the end of Book 1, tail between his legs, Book 2 begins with Glaucon and Adeimantus stepping forward to demand a rematch.

They do not approve of Thrasymachus' immoralism but are troubled by the thought that there is something to it. Glaucon offers a precise reformulation, in the hopes that Socrates can refute the most considered form of the thesis:

> They say to do wrong is naturally good, to be wronged is bad, but suf-fering injury so far exceeds in badness the good of inflicting it that when men have both done wrong and suffered it, have gotten a taste of both, those who are unable to avoid the latter and practice the former con-clude it is profitable to come to an agreement with each other neither to inflict injury nor suffer it. As a result they begin to make laws and settle-ments, and the law's command they call lawful and just. This, so they say, is the origin and essence of justice. (358e-9b)

Ah, 'they' say! So often, they = us! Think how harsh this is. Not that 'do wrong' might be for formula for profit, but that Wrong looks so Right! **That's** the one for me! You only quit because the game mechanics prove maddening. To win, you must sweep the table, getting Wrong just right! But how? Stumped for a strategy, it is rational to switch to an easier, coop-erative, second-best option: Justice.

This thought simultaneously spikes, yet shores up, Thrasymachus' basic stance. Spikes it, insofar as he prides himself on clear-eyed realism. He sees how things are, not how dreamers wish them to be! But seeing justice through eyes that cold and calculating should make justice seem relatively winning. In a social sense, justice is some sort of harmony. That's a deadly weapon!

A man is no match for a lion, but many men can bring down a lion. It takes trust and coordination, which justice provides! Justice is harmony, is **strength**. Anything wrong here? Granted, no primitive man ever drew up an 'I agree not to murder if …' contract, inaugurating civilization.

But that is not what worries Glaucon.

Rhetorically, it's a let down. If some epic poet sings to you the noble deeds of — oh, say, the Justice League! — you think: strong heroes! You don't think: what a bunch of weak, second-raters who didn't have what it takes to come out on top.

We need new entertainments, if we want true entertainments; if justice is truly second-best.

Conceptually, we've ceded key ground to Thrasymachus, on which he might rebuild, solidly. Justice is a powerful tool. He missed that. But is it necessarily always the best tool for me? We've granted wanting to play, and win, The Game of Wrong is rational. If The Game of Justice is chosen instead, strictly based on egoistic calculation that concedes the rightness of Wrong, what does that say about it, and us?

There is also a serious practical concern, even though the fable Glaucon goes on to narrate (359c), to make this vivid, doesn't sound especially realistic.

Once upon a time there was a shepherd, ancestor of a Lydian named Gyges.

There was a storm. The earth itself split open. The shepherd descended, discovering a cave. In the cave, a brass horse; in the horse, a dead giant with a golden ring. Ring of power, to turn the wearer invisible, so he becomes a superhero — The Invisible Shepherd! — guardian of the meek against all the wolves of the city!

'Taste **crook** — crooks!' No. Of course not!

Be realistic! Who wants to join some crummy Justice League? Do you know what happens in Aristophanes' play, **The Birds**? If you could fly, you could escape punishment for any crime, so you'd do what you liked. Which would be something bad, but (let's be honest) that wouldn't stop you. Likewise, if you could turn invisible you wouldn't fight crime, you'd commit it.

So this fairy tale has a realistic ending. Former shepherd seduces queen, murders king, sets himself up tidily as tyrant of Lydia.

Isn't this 'happier ever after', at least from the shepherd's point of view? Unjust, but what is justice? A tool. Why use it if you found a better tool in some weird tomb? Power corrupts. Absolute power corrupts absolutely. Why would that be true unless ethical corruption were, essentially, rational, enlightened self-interest?

But invisibility rings don't exist (you reasonably point out.) Can we dismiss the myth? No, it takes a real thing — **deception** — to illustrative extremes. Earthquakes happen, **too** (I'll leave the bronze horse and dead giant for you to puzzle out.) Had there been no earthquake, Gyges might have lived and died a shepherd, taking good **care** of the sheep. But when cracks open, all bets are off. That's important to remember. When social life is safe and steady, lots of people **act** just. But how deep does that go?

While we are at it, since I mentioned the Justice League, let's think what sorts of superpowers might make for a real one. Suppose the shepherd found, not an invisibility ring but a whole box of ... visibility rings, I guess you would call them. So long as you are wearing one, you have the superpower that everyone can see what you are up to. Gyges gets all his fellow shepherds to put them on. (It's impossible to take them off, let's add.) Crime is no longer a problem. Everyone does well and is very neighborly, as you can plainly see.

Call this harmonious pastoral scene: the Justice League! No heroes, no villains, but results as good as any comic book hero gets, punching villains.

Thinking about these extremes clarifies real situations, where things are in between. Injustice is typically too risky (no invisibility ring.) But sometimes you can get away with it (no visibility ring.) Then you would be **irrational** not to commit injustice, be it large or small. The lesson seems to be that Glaucon is right, so Thrasymachus was partly right. Glaucon polishes off the case for injustice by burnishing a pair of statues, as Socrates puts it (361d).

Behold the happy tyrant — perfectly unjust, yet praised for his 'justice'!

Or would you rather be **this** unhappy wretch: perfectly just but deprived of worldly goods, falsely accused of 'injustice', hence deprived even of the honor a reputation for justice brings?

What matters to us, as social beings: the truth about justice, or the label 'justice', true or not?

Wolf in shepherd's clothing? Or good shepherd with the extreme bad luck to get framed up in wolfskin?

You would rather be the happy tyrant, right? Conclusion: justice is not desirable in itself, only as a contingent means to selfish ends. Ergo, justice is only sometimes desirable; whereas, in a sense, injustice is always desirable (for you) insofar as you always want more than you can, justly, lay claim to. Right? The job of **Republic** is to argue: wrong.

6

Socrates' strategy for responding is as follows, starting in Book 2 (but really getting up to speed in Book 3.) You cannot understand what makes justice inherently advantageous until you understand what it **is**. First you should see the ideal city for what it might be. You can then see the validity of an analogy between City and Soul. It turns out, according to Socrates, that the three-level class-structure of the ideal city parallels proper order in the soul, which likewise has three parts — head, heart, and belly: a rational (philosophical) part; a spirited (honor-loving) part; an appetitive (desiring) part.

As usual, Socrates has a vivid image to illustrate. He asks us to imagine, "a sort of chimerical beast with many heads, a ring of them, taken from both tame and wild animals, able to change these and grow them out of itself" (588e). Those heads are your desires. You've got lots, pulling you in all directions. If you satisfy one (cut off a head) another grows to take its place.

Now, to go with this many-headed monster, another beast, a lion. It represents your 'spirit', your desire for honor and status. Beside the lion and the many-headed monster place a third figure: a man. He's your rational nature. Wrap them all up in one man-shaped package. You have: you! Socrates explains that anyone who claims injustice **benefits** a man is recommending a policy of feeding the beast, starving the man. The unjust man does not "accustom one part to the other or make them friendly," but dooms them to conflict, biting and fighting. If there is an argument that the possessor of the Ring of Gyges **must** degenerate into Gollum — wracked by wretched, insatiable desire — this is it. Instead of being snug in some Trojan Shepherd, wheeled in amongst an unsuspecting flock, the tyrant finds himself trapped inside **himself** with the worst monsters: namely, the worst parts of himself, let loose.

Conversely, the just man, even if he seems to have been thrown to the wolves, is safe within himself, so long as he maintains that inner harmony.

That's the theory.

I expect the reader has doubts; yet it does sound plausible that tyrants, rather than living happy, self-satisfied lives, are typically isolated, lonely, fearful, frustrated and angry.

But we have skipped a rather critical step. What **is** justice, either in City or Soul? Interpreters of **Republic** sometimes wonder whether 'justice' is an adequate translation for the main term under investigation — **diakiosunē**. The Greek has a different — broader — semantic coverage than English. If we want to understand Plato, we do well to say 'justice' while understanding it in a Greek way. But, be it noted, this doesn't mean it's necessarily a good idea to think in this Greek way, past the point of coming to understand Plato. Maybe our English sense of 'justice' will turn out to be, after all, more sensible.

7

Greek has three cognate terms — **dikaiosunē, dikē, dikaios.**

Dikaiosunē refers to a character trait, implying a more or less stable disposition to behave. The least awkward English rendition is 'just' — as in, 'he is a just man.' But we need something like 'justiness'. Let's say 'righteousness'.

Dikē is more a feature of systems than persons (but people are just little systems, aren't they? And systems are just large-scale dispositions of things to behave certain ways.) Dikē **is** a person, a goddess. You might say she's the goddess of systems administration. She is responsible for the smooth rotation of the seasons, for cosmic order and proportion — for due process, to use a legalistic phrase. What law courts provide, ideally, is **dikē**. She is, accordingly, the goddess of **mortal** justice. Here is a well-known parable from Hesiod, **Works and Days** (6th Century, BCE). The narrator lectures his brother, Perses.

> And now I will tell a fable for princes who themselves understand. Thus said the hawk to the nightingale with speckled neck, while he carried her high up among the clouds, gripped fast in his talons; and she, pierced by his crooked talons, cried pitifully. To her he spoke disdainfully: "Miserable thing, why do you cry out? One far stronger than you now holds you fast, and you must go wherever I take you, songstress as you are. And if I please I will make my meal of you, or let you go. He is a fool who tries to withstand the stronger, for he does not get the mastery and suffers pain besides his shame." So said the swiftly flying hawk, the long-winged bird.
>
> But you, Perses, listen to right and do not foster violence; for violence is bad for a poor man. Even the prosperous cannot easily bear its burden, but is weighed down under it when he has fallen into delusion. The better path is to go by on the other side towards justice; for Justice beats Outrage when she comes at length to the end of the race. But only when he has suffered does the fool learn this. For Oath keeps pace with wrong judgements. There is a noise when Justice [Dikē] is being dragged in the way where those who devour bribes and give sentence with crooked judgments, take her. And she, wrapped in mist, follows to the city and haunts of the people, weeping, and bringing mischief to men, even to such as have driven her forth in that they did not deal straightly with her. (l.ii.212-224)[3]

---

3   I like the antique style of this old translation, by Hugh G. Evelyn-White.

Hesiod is expressing the conventional moral notion that, in the long run, 'straight' pays. Anyway, incompetents like Perses should settle for a quiet, honest job where they can stay out of trouble. But suppose (just suppose!) the hawk is so strong he doesn't have to worry about Zeus striking him down?

Then, ideally, injustice is best? Hesiod would not **like** to be saying that. Still, isn't his hawk talking hard-headed, Thrasymachian/Glauconian sense?

Moving right along: **dikaios** (what Perses is being encouraged to exhibit) is to **dikaiosunē** as product to process. Actions are **dikaios**, as their doers are **dikaiosunē** (roughly). **Dikaios** is often linked to **hosiotes** (holiness), which facilitates expression of thoughts like, 'does right by men and gods alike.' This complementary yet contrastive construction encourages a sense of **dikaios** as something peculiarly mortal. But if it is good for me, won't it be good for gods? Obvious exceptions: sacrifices to the gods. Mortals should; gods needn't. (Think of Euthyphro's puzzles.) But, as a rule, being **dikaios** — through contrast with **hosiotes** — means doing the right thing, the **done** thing. In Greek **dikaios** denotes what your society expects of you.

In Book 1, Cephalus is a fine illustration. He is a 'just' man in part because he is presently conducting sacrifices in a dignified, orderly, appropriate, unstinting, non-excessive manner. He knows how he looks in the eyes of those around him: steady and proper. He **looks** just, hence **is** just.

Wanting things to have a steady evenness is a familiar preference, so it's not that we find Cephalus' attitude puzzling. But 'justice' is not the word **we** would choose. Think again of Gyges' earthquake. Due process of nature is the province of the goddess. So this tale starts with cosmic injustice, leading to human injustice (although storms are natural. I don't mean to tell the goddess her business.) It is only from odd angles that we are able to recover, in English, a sense of a conceptual linkage that seems stronger in Greek.

I have on my shelf a book about typography. It contains, as a bonus feature, an account of justice and its relationship to good and evil:

> JUSTIFIED
> The left and right edges are both even.
> When it is good: Justified text makes a clean, figural shape on the page. Its efficient use of space makes it the norm for newspapers and books of continuous text.
> When it is evil: Ugly gaps can occur as text is forced into lines of even measure.[4]

4   Ellen Lupton, **Thinking with Type: A Critical Guide for Designers, Writers, Editors, & Students**, 1st ed. (Princeton Architectural Press, 2004), p. 84.

You understand what she is talking about, right? On your word processor's tool bar is a button that looks something like that gentleman's shield: an icon for a setting allowing both sides to be equal.

Doesn't that look **just**, page-wise? Justice is: being justified, avoiding undue alignment with one side or the other, bias. When Confucius explains what it is to be righteous, saying 'if the mat is not straight, the master will not sit', he could be talking typography.

Crude attempts to force such even- ness (on the page, as in poli- tics) are often v e r y ugly. Someone is always pushing left, someone else right. How does **that** l o o k, overall? **Justified**? No!

A typographical sophist might add that the most sophisticated systems do not opt for this sort of perfect justice. Letting little things exceed the margins can make the margins appear neater. (Look at the comma ending the first line of the next paragraph. See how it **slightly** over-hangs? The whole page **looks** more even that way, even though it's uneven.)

So, per the terms of Glaucon's argument, it is indeed better to **appear**, not **be**, just. Negotiators, and judges know this, not just typographers.

'Justification' is mostly reserved for epistemological contexts in English. If someone tells you 'justify your claims', it won't cross your mind that you might press one word-processor button, tidying type, thereby fulfilling the letter of the requirement. Still, the semantic link is there Your conclusion is **justified** when it is proportional to your premises, does not exceed your evidence.

Failure to connect this tidying, visual balance 'mat is straight' sense of justice-as-evenness with the epistemology of justification makes it difficult to understand, among other things, Socrates' persistent use of craft analogies. He says a competent 'practitioner of justice' will not try to **exceed** another. He is preoccupied with excess — **pleonexia**. This does not seem intuitive.

First, we do not ordinarily speak of 'practicing justice' at all. Second, in cases where we do find it natural to talk about practicing a technical craft or skill, we find it natural to think of practitioners as in competition to be the best. But one typesetter would hardly try to make a **more** just margin than an already fully justified margin. 'My margin is even!' 'My margin is even **evener than even**!' Nonsense! Compare: one mathematician will not try to make a conclusion **more** proven, if it was fully justified to start with. These are the kinds of examples that will clue you in to how Plato is thinking when he says odd things about 'the craft of justice.'

8

Here is a positive declaration (finally!) of what justice comes to, from Book 2. Justice is **winning friends with yourself and influencing people-parts**:

> It looks like justice really turned out to be something like the following. It consists not in a man's external actions, but in the way he acts within himself, strictly concerned with himself and his inner parts. He does not allow any part of himself to perform the work of another, or the parts of his soul to interfere with one another. He puts in good order what are in the true sense of the word his own affairs. He is master of himself, puts things in order, is his own friend, harmonizes the three parts like the limiting notes of a musical scale, high, low, and middle, and any that may lie between. He binds them together, and from a plurality becomes a unity in himself. (443d)

Book 2 is still the start of the story, but this passage is a keynote. It helps you get what Plato is getting at. But, of course, making sense of what he is saying is not the same as thinking it makes sense. You may decide, on reflection, that the narrower, more English sense of 'justice' is more sensible. Plato's may not even look like an answer to 'what is justice?' Never mind a **good** one.

First, it's too personal. If justice is an order in the soul, you could have justice with only one person. We may think being a hermit in a cave is fine, if you are happy with that lifestyle choice, but we hardly call it 'justice'.

Second, it is supposed to be functional, yet is highly aestheticized. A person is not a page of type to be tidied. Left and right in politics (not that Plato knew about that, but he knew about partisanship) is not like left and right margins. Encouraging people to think you can eyeball justice as harmony — looks even to me! — is not merely not defining it. It looks like a potentially self-serving bait-and-switch. Plato is a keen detector of such bias in others. Cephalus knows money: credit and debit. So he hopes justice can be good business sense. His son can prevail when it comes to friend against enemy, so he hopes justice is an even fight. Maybe Plato's notion of 'harmony' is a substitution, to suit an aristocrat-philosopher's temperament and preferences? This brings us to a third concern.

Plato offers an incomplete scheme. Justice is some kind of harmony, or balance, or order. But when you have order, you may have injustice. Plato may be mistaking a necessary for a sufficient condition. Still, as I said, Book 2 is not the end of the story.

9

Food for thought! But let's not bite off too
much. Let's read from the start of Book 1.

Yesterday I went down to Piraeus ...

Piraeus is the port. But this is no easy stroll down to some
dock. Going down meant a 9 km hike, mostly between the
Long Walls (fortifications to ensure Athens' access to sea
and ships in time of war.) Piraeus is a rocky island with three
deep-water harbors — Kantharus, Munychia, Zea — affording
strategic access to sea routes.

... to offer up my prayers to the goddess and to see how they would
celebrate the festival (327a

The goddess is Thracian Bendis, whom the Athenians are
semi-identifying with Artemis, the huntress. The festival is taking
place because Bendis has won official, civic recognition. After
attending this public (daylight) event, Socrates is waylaid by a
friendly force of Polemarchus and friends. Socrates must stay
for the real fun, after the sun goes down! In the meantime, he
must come home to visit old Cephalus, who will be glad to
see him and talk with him! Eventually the full discussion circle
rounds out to include:

Glaucon, son of Ariston ... Polemarchus, son of Cephalus, ... Adeimantus, Glaucon's brother, Niceratus the
son of Nicias, and several others ... Lysias and Euthydemus ... Thrasymachus the Chalcedonian, Charmantides
the Paenian, and Cleitophon, son of Aristonymus.
Polemarchus' father, Cephalus, was there too. (328c)

A full cast! Few have significant speaking parts, but the social circle is
significant, so introductions all around are in order. Let's examine: setting,
event, characters.

The history of the port seems significant. Themistocles was the Athenian
leader who devised the city's anti-Persian naval strategy, thereby laying the
foundations for Golden Age glory. Development of Piraeus made Athenian
empire possible. Cephalus quotes Themistocles on this theme: the importance of knowing how to make use of what you've got (329e). Also, Piraeus
is a hotbed of democratic political activism.

The festival seems significant, per this remark by the geographer, Strabo:

> As in other things the Athenians always showed their admiration
> of foreign customs, so they displayed it in what respected
> the gods. They adopted many foreign sacred cer-
> emonies, particularly those of Thrace and
> Phrygia; for which they were ridiculed in com-
> edies. Plato mentions the Bendidean ... rites.[5]

But what's so bad about syncretism: fusion
of traditions, cultures, religions. Isn't diversity a
value? No doubt these comic writers were snobs
and/or nativist xenophobes, concerned to keep foreigners in their place with a bit of targeted laughter.

There is also a rationalistic concern. (Certainly there is
one for Plato!) Two groups — Thracian and Athenian — **sort
of** participating in one thing, **sort of** each 'doing its own thing.'
They don't even know quite **who** they are worshipping. One goddess or two?
Representations of Bendis are a muddle. Her tunic is Greek; that mantle is
Thracian. Socrates will argue that the 'democratic sort of man' is exactly like
this, hence his city as well. The democratic city:

> may, I said, be the most beautiful of cities — like a
> cloak that has been embroidered with designs of
> every flower, in every color. So it too may well
> appear the loveliest, as it is embellished with every
> sort of colorful character. And perhaps, I said, many
> would judge it to be the most beautiful, much as
> women and children do when they see things
> worked in bright colors. (557c-d)

Plato complains that in a democratic city there is 'equality between
equals and unequals alike.' This is respectful of the individual. But Plato
sees a lack of **proper** order. But again, is this just an aesthetic complaint?
Is Plato just substituting anti-democratic (and sexist) aristocratic aesthetic
sensibilities for rational argument?

Back to Bendis. Why **did** Athens 'naturalize' her? Athens will put Socrates
to death for worshipping gods other than those of the city. No doubt Plato
means for us to see terrible hypocrisy. Athens invites in gods other than
those of the city, throwing big parties for them, then executes Socrates on
false charges of doing that.

5   Strabo, **Geography** (10.3.18), trans. Hamilton, H.C. and W. Falconer.

Strabo notwithstanding, religious tolerance was not automatic in ancient Athens, with Socrates somehow the luckless exception. The ground shifted back and forth. In **Apology** Socrates argues he can hardly be corrupting the young by teaching that the sun is a stone, because anyone curious about that can buy the book in the market. He does not mention that its author, Anaxagoras, left town in a hurry after a stringent anti-atheism law passed. From the 5th Century on, Athens had atheistic intellectuals — sophists, speculators, dramatists in whose comedies the gods look downright silly. When tolerance snapped, there was often a trigger. In Anaxagoras' case, he was a friend of Pericles, whose enemies got at the great man by targeting those close to him.

In Bendis' case, the city faced a foreign policy challenge, which had a domestic angle. Good timber in Thrace for ship-building! The King of Thrace will be pleased to hear Bendis is at home in Athens. Also, Piraeus had a large foreign worker [**metic**] population. They are not, properly, participants in the political life of the city. (The Greek title of Plato's dialogue is, you recall, **Politeia**, which could be **citizenship**.) Athens has an interest in instilling in its non-citizen yet semi-permanent residents a spirit of semi-civic attachment. Recognition of Bendis was, quite likely, a politic fudge, to finesse a delicate Us vs. Them balance. Blur lines in Olympus, as in Athens. Throw enough parties, people start seeing double. (If mortals love it, it must be holy!)

Every new social, cultural, political, religious form comes out of some human mix. It's just that not all such forms get big coming-out parties, like Athenian Bendis. You could say this civic festival is **realpolitik** in action, but that's just another way of saying: it's an expression of what life is like. In her Thracian mantle, Athenian Bendis exemplifies humanism: inevitable pluralism.

The most prominent 20th Century advocate of pluralism, as a key philosophical concept, is Isaiah Berlin. He targets Plato as the arch-enemy of pluralism. Plato, like all Rationalists, thinks all genuine questions must have true answers; there must be a (rational) path to their discovery; they must all be consistent. Berlin thinks Plato makes the Good the enemy of lots of goods that just don't happen to fit together coherently. Plato does seem determined to insist things should make sense, be logical. On the other hand:

> I was delighted with the procession the inhabitants put on, but the Thracians' was just as beautiful, maybe more. (327b)

Is it plausible Plato is expressing pure disapproval by having his teacher call this foreign spectacle delightful? Perhaps Plato is drawing attention to his teacher's unfortunate tendency not to notice how dangerous his environment may be. Or maybe Plato is counting on reader to know the show isn't over.

There's going to be an all-night festival, which will be worth seeing.

Torch-race on horseback! The festival has two faces — light and dark. Polemarchus and co. are insisting Socrates stay past the day. They retire to Cephalus' house for a lot of talk — Plato's **Republic**, we call it — waiting for nightfall.

Don't spoil the fun by leaving. (328a)

10

Time to consider the company we keep.

The speakers are Cephalus, retired businessman; his son, Polemarchus; and Thrasymachus, the sophist; all three are **metics**, not Athenian citizens.

Glaucon and Adeimantus step forth from the background after Thrasymachus retreats, in Book 2. You may be interested to learn that their father, Ariston, had a third son, Plato. Why does our author have his older brothers team-up with his teacher to discover the nature of justice? Plato himself would have been just a boy at the time of this dialogue. But why stage it so he himself is conspicuously absent? A similar self-exclusion occurs in another dialogue, **Phaedo**, which narrates the death of Socrates in prison. Many friends and followers are present, but notice is taken of the fact that Plato is ill and absent. (Possibly he wasn't ill, just too busy pulling strings on all these puppets?)

Lysias and Euthydemus are two more sons of Cephalus. Lysias will become a famous speech writer, although he gets no lines here. Socrates critiques one of his speeches at the start of another dialogue, **Phaedrus**. There is a also a dialogue, **Euthydemus** — but that's a different Euthydemus. Nicias' father, Niceratus, was an Athenian general. Socrates debates him about courage in **Laches**.

Next comes Cleitophon. He has a dialogue named after him, which concerns the question of whether Socrates or Thrasymachus is the better speaker.

In the dialogue, and briefly in our reading, Cleitophon takes Thrasymachus' side. He seems to have been a politician. The last name is Charmantides. He says nothing; nothing is known of such a person.

These men are from the world of Athenian wealth and influence, which is at once impressively cosmopolitan and rather small. You wield influence by speaking well, which invests these verbal sparring matches with extra status anxiety. Relations are competitive but cordial — delicate friend/enemy dynamic.

One last, **little** thing.

This is not the world in which Plato is living and writing but that of half a century earlier. The festival of Bendis took place near the start of the Peloponnesian War (428 BCE.) or somewhat later (circa 413) while a peace between Athens and Sparta briefly held. Either way, Plato's audience is supposed to realize night is falling on this little group in more than one sense.[6]

In a few years (give or take) the war will be lost. Athens will be stripped of her empire and her democracy. Sparta will impose the oligarchy of the so-called Thirty Tyrants (including Plato's great-uncle, Critias, who also has his own Platonic dialogue. Like I said: small world.) Cephalus will be dead, his family fortune expropriated by the new regime. Polemarchus: executed on trumped-up charges; Lysias: narrowly escaped into exile. (We know all of this thanks to a later speech by him, accusing his family's killers and despoilers, who sound like perfect Thrasymachians.) Niceratus, too, will be executed. And, of course, Socrates will be executed — but by the democrats restored to power after the Thirty are overthrown in their turn.

So all this talk about justice may seem like just talk; but it is talk of serious things. Killing time before a time of killing. Friendly party will break into warring parties.

Circling back to our starting point, 'going down to Piraeus' — which could have been translated 'going under' — seems to foreshadow Plato's Myth of the Cave. The setting, the festive enthusiasm, the unreflective ritualism, the spectacle, this cast of characters, can all be seen as conducive to the cognitive limitations Cave-dwellers suffer.

The philosopher descends into this darkness, where treatment at the hands of the natives might get rough.

---

6   For a discussion of the dating dispute, see Christopher Planeaux, "The Date of Bendis' Entry into Attica" The Classical Journal 96.2 (2000).165-192.

11

In what follows, I give more pages to the old man and his son than to Thrasymachus. I begin and end with Cephalus. This seems not to accord with the dialogue, in which he makes an early exit; in which Thrasymachus takes up twice the space of father and son combined. Thrasymachus makes the bold moves that call forth the most energetic, Socratic refutations. Thrasymachus, unlike the father and son, is self-consciously theoretical. His is the position Glaucon and Adeimantus want reconsidered, occasioning whole book-length discussion of **Republic**.

In part, these very factors explain my approach. Thrasymachus! You can't miss him! It's obvious he's a provocative challenger of conventional notions. The father and son are another story. Their tag-team effort may look like a lackluster undercard fight, warming us up for the main event. But this under-sells Plato's rhetorical ingenuity as fight promoter. Worse, it risks misconstruing the subject matter of **Republic**.

Here we stand at the Gates of Utopia! **Republic** will blueprint an ideal city-state. Not a place you visit every day!

If **you** were standing at the gates of Heaven — or Hades (your mileage may vary); if you found yourself on the liminal verge of a new world, in an ethical sense, who or what would you expect to meet at the very threshold?

Probably some sort of guardian, right?

Angel with a flaming sword?

Dog with three-heads?

Here's my counter-offer. A retired businessman who tends to rattle on about the value of money.

How's that for casting against (justified?) type.

Think of it as an urbane variant on the traditional underworld guard dog of Greek myth, Cerberus, whose heads are said to stand for the past, present and future. **Republic,** Book 1, is a three-headed monster, barring passage into the other-world beyond: one head, that of a savage lion (Thrasymachus); next, the head of a hound (Polemarchus), friendly to those it knows, savage to strangers and enemies; first, but not least, the old man (Cephalus), a veritable Charon of preoccupation with accounts payable. (Every dead soul must pay a coin to cross over!)

Perhaps we can even identify these heads with past, present and future. Cephalus is old and passing. Polemarchus is in his prime. But he will be killed by tyrants practicing what Thrasymachus preaches.

But how does more myth-mongering (as if Plato needed it!) clarify **Republic**? How does Cephalus provide the keynote for what follows?

In Chapter 7, I mentioned that **Meno** (the dialogue) may confuse even philosophers, because Meno (the man) isn't interested in what academic ethicists tend to find interesting: normative moral theory. Maybe **Meno** belongs in the self-help section, alongside Dale Carnegie? In a similar spirit, **Republic** could perhaps do with creative reshelving into the economics section — if only economists weren't so infernally money-minded, like old Cephalus. He mistakes money for debt, debt for justice, justice for money.

Let me quote from a recent history, not of money (mind you!) but debt, by the anthropologist (anarchist/activist) David Graeber. He begins, as Plato does, with a personal conversation. Graeber was at a Westminster Abbey garden party (not quite a festival for a hybrid hunt goddess, but close enough.) He met, not a nice old businessman, but a nice lawyer, with whom, he had it on priestly authority, he could enjoy a pleasant conversation.

The subject was justice and financial crisis, but there came a hitch:

> "But," she objected, as if this were self-evident, "they'd borrowed the money! Surely one has to pay one's debts."
>
> It was at this point that I realized this was going to be a very different sort of conversation than I had originally anticipated.
>
> Where to start?[7]

Perhaps with the observation that unpaid debts are the soul of banking: no risk, no risk-management, no business model, no business.

Zeus forbid it should be impossible not to pay your debts!

7   David Graeber, **Debt: The First 5000 Years** (Melville, 2012), p. 2.

In a broader economic sense, debt-forgiveness is but one of a number of macroeconomic levers. But that does not ethically satisfy.

> For several days afterward, that phrase kept resonating in my head. "Surely one has to pay one's debts."
>
> The reason it's so powerful is that it's not actually an economic statement: it's a moral statement. After all, isn't paying one's debts what morality is supposed to be all about? Giving people what is due them. Accepting one's responsibilities. Fulfilling one's obligations to others, just as one would expect them to fulfill their obligations to you. What could be a more obvious example of shirking one's responsibilities than reneging on a promise, or refusing to pay a debt?
>
> It was that very apparent self-evidence, I realized, that made the statement so insidious. (3)

Graeber concludes:

> The very fact that we don't know what debt is, the very flexibility of the concept, is the basis of its power. If history shows anything, it is that there's no better way to justify relations founded on violence, to make such relations seem moral, than by reframing them in the language of debt—above all, because it immediately makes it seem that it's the victim who's doing something wrong. (5)

This could be a blurb for Plato's **Republic**; for Book 1, anyway.

On this view, Thrasymachus is not the problem. He's a symptom of Cephalus' problem. Cephalus-style money theory devolves into Thrasymachus-style violent practice. Graeber duly notes he is following in Plato's footsteps, without being inclined to dog Socrates' steps too far along **Republic**'s path:

> Socrates eventually gets around to offering some political proposals of his own, involving philosopher kings; the abolition of marriage, the family, and private property; selective human breeding boards. (Clearly, the book was meant to annoy its readers, and for more than two thousand years, it has succeeded brilliantly.) What I want to emphasize, though, is the degree to which what we consider our core tradition of moral and political theory today springs from this question: What does it mean to pay one's debts? (197)

Set this 'debt' frame, which places Cephalus first, beside the other, which puts Thrasymachus front and center. You needn't make any final choice between them.

12

Socrates' discussion with Cephalus begins with polite pleasantries. He respectfully inquires how old age is treating the old man, who takes a dignified stand, but there are darker hints. If Piraeus is the Cave, this resident is too old and creaky to get up and leave. Still, he seems content with slackening faculties. As he weakens, the beasts in him are getting lazy. He quotes the aged playwright Sophocles, concerning the joy of no-sex:

> "I'm glad to be done with all that. I'm like a slave who has escaped from a crazy, brutal master." I thought he was right then, and I still think so today. Because old age certainly does bring with it great tranquility and freedom. (329d)

No more parties or drinking! His old friends bemoan losses, but Cephalus is happy to be able to take it or leave it, hence leave it. Such stoical sentiments are common, conventional. The thought that you have desires you would like to discipline or eliminate is not mind-bending. But how can attempts to theorize this alleged state of affairs fail to be soul-splitting? You must have a true, better self, with **desired** desires; an untrue, worse self with **undesired** ones.

One of you is **really** you. So at least one of me is … Them? Which one(s)?

Plato, I said, will have a complex story to tell about tripartite division in the soul. Each of us is three selves in one: head, heart, belly. Cephalus is, literally, the head in this debate (English 'cephalic', from the Greek: of or pertaining to the head.) The son, Polemarchus, is spirited and honor-loving; Thrasymachus plays the greedy belly.

So, be it noted, with 'I'm like a slave', Cephalus is pre-subscribing to perhaps the most cognitively controversial aspect of Plato's picture of the Soul: 'mostly, I'm not me!' So this might be a preliminary advertisement. Divisions in the soul sounds kind of metaphysical, but even sturdy old respectable types believe something of the sort instinctively! On the other hand, this could be flipped into an argument against Plato. Is he just giving us rationalist repackaging of common cultural attitudes and stereotypes: women and wine the downfall of many a man. (Odysseus tied to the mast. Old, old story.)

Socrates responds to Cephalus' speech about the value of good character, of **his** good character, by provoking him. Is Cephalus' account of the source of his contentment credible? When Socrates flips it, this 'head' comes up … coins!

Most people wouldn't buy it, coming from you. They would say you bear your old age well not because of your character but because of your money. For, they say, it's easy being rich. (330d)

Cephalus denies it, yet concedes money may be necessary for the maintenance not just of his good life but of his good character. A poor old man can hardly be comfortable. More crucially, a rich man

need not deceive or defraud anyone, even unintentionally. Nor does he leave this world afraid that he owes sacrifices to the gods or debts to men. (331b)

We see here the blank obverse of the attitude Graeber grapples with in the garden. Not only must debts be paid; that is all you need. This is an issue in **Euthyphro**, recall. It is easy to talk about religion as if it were some sort of favorable balance of trade established between mortals and gods (14d). But can that make sense? How can religion be trade policy? How can ethics be a balance sheet of credits and debits? If right and wrong is, effectively, money, is it a unit of account, medium of exchange, or store of value? Is it easier to be a good man — just man — if you are rich? Poverty is a leading cause of crime. Ergo, wealth is a leading cause of **not**-crime? Can it be that ethical merit is heritable, not personally earned? My father passes on a pile of cash when he passes, perhaps. But can you set up a **moral** trust fund for your kids?

We are moving too quickly. The old man did not say all that. He's a businessman. As Socrates remarks in **Apology**, every tradesman thinks his trade affords insight. Ask a shoemaker about the meaning of life. He'll get a shrewd expression on his face: 'Life . . . is like a well-made pair of shoes.' Cephalus understands money so he tries to think through justice in terms he understands. Let's back up. We passed over what looks like a weakness in the old man's business-like exterior. Not quite a crack in the facade; more like structural subsidence — a sinking feeling.

All those stories about Hades he used to laugh at, about how the dead are made to pay for all the wrongs they committed in life. Now the stories torment him with the thought that maybe it's all true . . .

'He'? (He's like 'they', right? Them = Us = Me.)

Justice!
(card may be kept until needed or sold!)

The man who finds he has committed many unjust deeds in life both wakes from his sleep with a frightened start, as children do, and lives with despair by day. (330e-331a)

How would a placid old guy like Cephalus know a thing like that? The smooth surface of his character conceals dark depths.

Surprising? You don't get ahead in business by being everyone's best friend every day of your life, surely. To climb to the top of the Athenian arms industry, all the way from Syracuse, does not sound like an easy trip. Yes, it turns out Cephalus is an arms merchant, a beneficiary of Pericles' generous policy of encouraging foreign craftsmen to immigrate to Athens. Cephalus and sons own a profitable shield workshop in Piraeus. (We don't know this from the dialogue but from other sources.)

Here is a man who has spent his life making war material, but that you can feel **good** about, relatively. Weapons to **stop** harm. Cephalus like round metal objects — coins and shields — not sharp, edged ones. The great Athenian law-giver Solon deployed a mighty shield metaphor to describe the constitutional reforms he instituted to ward off open class warfare between rich and poor. I'll bet Cephalus likes this style of poetry.

I gave the common people as much privilege as was due
Neither taking honor from them nor overreaching for more
And to the powerful, splendid in their wealth
I arranged that they suffer nothing unseemly
And I stood up a strong shield, for each against each
So that neither could win an unjust victory. (frag. 5)

A good shield is a perfect symbol for ... **justice**! So why the bad dreams, old man?

Let's turn from anxiety to **philosophy**. Since he is not selling weapons of mass destruction to terrorists, it may be anachronistic to hint that Cephalus feels guilty about being an arms merchant. Still, Socrates raises the standard, modern concern about this profession. If you are willing to sell weapons to anyone with coin to pay, eventually you will end up selling to someone bad, some madman. You will have blood on your hands.

If you have a friend who leaves weapons with you, when
he is of sound mind, then asks for them back after he
goes mad, no one would say that you should give
them back, or that someone who did return them
was a just man; no more than you would say you
should always speak the truth to someone in such
a seriously disturbed frame of mind. (331c)

Addressed to Cephalus, this far-fetched scenario is just business as usual.
At some point some drunk hammered on the door, bellowing about needing
to pick up that shield he paid for. Cephalus had to decide whether to hand
over or tell the man to sleep it off. In a civic sense, Cephalus is aiding and
abetting his 'friend', Athens, who will presently lose everything, militarily,
with the 'help' of all his fine, well-balanced shields.

Quite apart from personal or civic relevance, the features of the case
carry us back to the issue of bad desire. The madman — 'not himself' — is an
intensification of the possibility that I may want bad things, or at least things
that are not good for me. Would you let someone do the wrong thing, just
because they want to, and can pay for the privilege? We also see Socrates
planting the thin-edge of a definitional wedge, by means of the madman case

But then, I said, speaking truth and returning what is owed is not a correct definition of justice. (331d)

As an objection this is plain unjust, since Socrates uncharacteristically did
not **ask** for a definition of justice. He asked the old man what money is good
for. There is no reason a true answer to **this** question, even if it turns out to
have something to do with justice, should automatically amount to a correct
definition of 'justice'. Still, if something's worth doing well, it's worth doing **at
all**. Cephalus thinks justice is important. But if you want to talk justice, you
should be prepared for hard thinking. Cephalus enjoys philosophy, yet his
interest is superficial. This is in character. One of the comforting features of
tending sacrifices for the goddess Bendis, of making sure your credits and
debits balance, is a sense of 'rightness', of security. Cephalus doesn't want
critical philosophy. He wants consolation from philosophy.

Let me give you some backstory for that Solon poem.

The historical record is thin, but Solon was a 6th Century (BCE)
Athenian politician (statesman/poet), famed for having saved
Athens in a constitutional crisis. No doubt there was more, but this
much seems clear. Athenian farmers were falling, more and more,
into debt-slavery. The Athenians didn't object to slavery. But it was

intolerable for there to be such evident, evil gaps opening between rich and poor citizens. In the crisis, Solon was granted extraordinary executive powers to wipe slate cleans, as it were; to re-inscribe the page of the polis 'evenly'. He wiped some slates, freed the debt-slaves, eliminating glaring inequalities, yet left the rich substantially secure in their possessions and traditional privileges.

What definition of 'justice' did Solon work from? He had a free hand, such as would-be tyrants and political philosophers mostly only exercise in dreams. He didn't have to defer to any 'but one **has** to pay one's debts!' knee-jerks, since stubborn insistence on that was the root cause of the crisis. He was no Cephalus, then. Or was he? In this moment of freedom to play Philosopher-King, Solon seems to have been prudent enough to play-act the mere moderate, lest he be denounced for playing tyrant. Solon relied on the ambiguities of 'equal' and 'balance' to muddle through, while stamping a proud, poetic face on the product, shielding it from doubt. He split differences, relying on customary notions of what is 'due', in the hopes of securing social stability. He projected an **appearance** of 'evenness' to Athenian eyes. Then, so the story goes, he left town so no one could raise objections. Just as Cephalus has enough sense to get up and leave, brushing Socrates off when he starts making uncomfortable trouble for an old man's superficial account of 'what is due'. Smart old man!

Solon is a fascinating figure for republicans like Madison (as I am sure he must have been for the author of **Republic**.) Why would, "a people, jealous as the Greeks [Athenians] were of their liberty … so far abandon the rules of caution as to place their destiny in the hands of a single citizen?" Should Solon be seen as a moral hazard; or an opportunity missed? "Solon … confessed that he had not given to his countrymen the government best suited to their happiness, but most tolerable to their prejudices."[8] Yet perhaps that was for the best — the second-best. Some constitution is better than none.

If Cephalus is only as wise as Solon, he's no weak head. So what's wrong with him? **Republic**, Book 1, deploys a rhetoric of decay. There is nothing to keep Cephalus' line from devolving into Polemarchus', then into Thrasymachus'; so the argument against the last scores against the first. Then again, maybe sometimes things run the other way? If Solon had been like Socrates, wouldn't that have led to civil war in the streets, likely as not?

8   James Madison, **Federalist** 38. For more on Solon, see John David Lewis, Solon the Thinker: Political Thought In Archaic Athens (Bloomsbury, 2006).

13

If Solon's metaphor of a shield is a symbol for old Cephalus' all-around ethical preference for customary norms and forms, the son is not far from the father. A shield is a **weapon**, as is every ready-to-hand implement, to the eye that sees the world in terms of conflict between Us and Them. A fable explains:

Once upon a time all the animals in the Zoo decided that they would disarm, and they arranged to have a conference to arrange the matter. So the Rhinoceros said when he opened the proceedings that the use of teeth was barbarous and horrible and ought to be strictly prohibited by general consent. Horns, which were mainly defensive weapons, would, of course, have to be allowed. The Buffalo, the Stag, the Porcupine, and even the little Hedgehog all said they would vote with the Rhino, but the Lion and the Tiger took a different view. They defended teeth and even claws, which they described as honourable weapons of immemorial antiquity … Then the Bear spoke. He proposed that both teeth and horns should be banned and never used again for fighting by any animal. It would be quite enough if animals were allowed to give each other a good hug when they quarreled …

The discussion got so hot and angry, and all those animals began thinking so much about horns and teeth and hugging when they argued about the peaceful intentions that had brought them together that they began to look at one another in a very nasty way. Luckily the keepers were able to calm them down and persuade them to go back quietly to their cages, and they began to feel quite friendly with one another again.[9]

The Solonic aim of a disarmament conference is to erect a shield 'for each against each', effecting escape from a Hobbesian State of Nature. But how to aim for an overall state of affairs in which no party enjoys an advantage, when each party is — who are we kidding? — angling for advantage?

9   Winston Churchill, speech at Aldersbrook, 24 October, 1928.

Everyone talks 'custom', 'defense', 'friend'. Everyone sees: enemies. It might seem Churchill is saying disarmament efforts are doomed to failure (barring divine interventions by Philosopher-Zookeepers.) In fact, his point was more moderate. At the conclusion of some actual negotiations he gave this speech, defending the wisdom of having kept details under wraps until a deal was done, lest popular antagonisms be inflamed.

What does this have to do with Polemarchus? Standard hoplite tactics: lock shields, crash through the enemy line. If justice is a shield, then, pushing this thought to its logical conclusion, justice is a weapon for pushing ... so long as you've got friends. Polemarchus:

> A friend ought to do good to a friend, never evil ... An enemy owes an enemy that which is due or proper to him — namely, something bad. (332c)

Churchill is glad to have men like Polemarchus on his side. But they aren't much use at the negotiating table. (Bunch of hot-heads!)

But wait, wasn't there a pile of money lying around here somewhere? Polemarchus is 'heir to' Cephalus' argument — as to his fortune — and Cephalus says justice is mostly 'paying debts'. Somehow money turned into a shield, now a sword? Polemarchus thinks he's defending dad's account, waving this sword? What's the connection? It is the **talion**. The term does not occur in Plato, but a scholarly account opens like so:

> The talion (the same Latin root supplies us with **retaliate**) indicates a repayment in kind. It is not a talon — not an eagle's claw — of which I must inform my students and even remind an occasional colleague. It is easy to excuse the misunderstanding. After all, the difference between talion and talon is but the difference of an i. And then one has to try hard not to imagine a bird of prey or carrion-eater swooping down ...[10]

Any chapter that begins with bird attacks, as this one did, can do with a similar, explicit warning against linguistic misunderstanding. No vultures, just the simple, intuitive logic of equal repayment in kind. **Lex talionis**, the law of retaliation: an eye for an eye, a tooth for a tooth, a dollar for a dollar, a favor for a favor.

10   William Ian Miller, **Eye For An Eye** (Cambridge 2005), ix-x.

I trust you are struck by the incongruity of the series.

Surely all 'repayment' is not morally equivalent. No one says double-entry bookkeeping is vengeful and bloody-minded. We do not feel finance is a form of feud. Why do we talk as if 'trading' punches is balancing accounts, to the point where we have one idiom that covers both cases: payback! Is banking the civilization of something that starts as a brawl? Is brawling a primitive urge to bank — to bring credits and debits into line? All this sounds weird. So, again, why does it feel right to **talk** as if banking and brawling have some common denominator: debt?

Plain old good neighborliness — favor for a favor — seems like yet a third thing. Is there some fourth thing — justice, maybe? — that all these reciprocal impulses aspire to express, each in its way? Is one of them already the true root of all?

The scholarly book cited above is substantially devoted to alleviating an erroneous sense that revenge cultures are savage, just because they sound quick to resort to dismemberment as a solution to life's problems. Often, on examination, **lex talionis** aspires to finely-graded measurement of man — that proverbial measure of all things! Any honor culture (revenge cultures always are!) will evolve a branch of accountancy nominally pegged to the common currency of the body. The goal is not mutually assured mutilation but stability, balance (equality), security. Payback is: harmony. But can a gouged eye be a symbol of harmony? It hardly looks neighborly!

Our thoughts about justice are spreading in puzzling ways: payback, loyalty, reciprocity, harmony? Yet we've been here before. The first thought that pops into Meno's head: "a man's virtue consists in being able to manage public affairs and thereby help his friends and harm his enemies" (71e). Euthyphro's first impulse is the opposite. It is absurd to say it would be just for him to side with dad **just** because he's dad (4b). But then, of course, he takes Zeus' side, just because he's Zeus. Can we crawl from this Cave of conventional notions, escape its close air of blood — pollution, miasma? Can we see the sun of the Good, limning the form of Justice? Speaking of which: what sort of good son and heir does Polemarchus shape up to be?

Cephalus emphasizes 'paying debts'. Polemarchus says this comes to 'giving back to each what is owed', per the wise words of the poet Simonides. Friends owe friends good, enemies ill. **That's** paying debts. Socrates glosses this as 'giving to each man what befits him'. Polemarchus agrees that sounds just fine (331d-2c).

14

It is fairly obvious how this will fall apart. Think again of Solon. If Polemarchus is to be believed, justice is fighting side-by-side with your 'friends' — fellow farmers, if you are a poor farmer; fellow land-owners, if you are a rich aristocrat; and setting up a shield between both, to give each 'what befits them', if you are lucky enough to be Solon. Not only is this an inconsistent result; it misses that the three parties here are playing different 'justice' games. The rich and the poor are fighting. Solon is straining to be above that. Polemarchus, because his instinct is to reach for a weapon that will afford him some advantage, misses the advantages of a shield wielded to no one's advantage. Hence we get Socrates' rather puzzling (to most readers) craft analogies.

> And what if someone were to ask him, "Simonides! What due or proper thing is provided by the craft of medicine, and to whom?" (332c)

Here Socrates picks up a thread he won't drop throughout Book 1. Justice is like medicine (like piloting a ship, like shepherding sheep.) It's a craft [**technē**]. English words (technical, technology) are suggestive of what he is getting at. But in a sense that's the problem. What is 'practicing the craft of justice'? That's an **odd** phrase. Socrates is playing it as a bit of a trick question.

> S: Then justice will be useless to men who aren't at war? (332e)

Polemarchus can hardly say yes, but his tendency to think in fighting terms means he has trouble articulating **how** justice could be of use **except** to take sides in some fight. Every craft means getting some advantage, doesn't it? Why bother mastering a craft unless there's an advantage to doing it right? But what is the advantage of justice? Proverbially, justice means: not taking advantage. But foregoing an advantage sounds plain imprudent — not crafty in the least. Polemarchus tries to wriggle out like so: justice is useful in making contracts. Practicing law indeed sounds like a promising candidate for technical 'practice of the craft of justice'. There is a problem, however. Departing from the text, for the sake of making Polemarchus' difficulty clearer: a lawyer is an **advocate** — hired gun in a legal battle. We're right back to fighting.

We might shift to consider the role of judge, like Solon. But even a judge is only useful in a fight — if only to settle it. Also, the judge's role tends to be constrained along a crucial axis. The Greek for just action, **dikaios**, carries the implication 'do the **right** thing', but also 'the **done** thing': follow precedent. In some traditions, follow the black letter. Even Solon, rewriting the constitution, is careful not to play the unprecedented utopian. He defers to a sense of each side's prejudices. That is not the same as justice, is it?

Let's try on a cruder costume for size. **Who is behind the** **mask of — the Justifier**! Was there an explosion involving an experimental typesetting system? Now **he has** the power of making margins even on both **sides**? Hardly! But since this is the Greek notion of justice, the **dikaiosunic duo** can include our hero's side-kick, Appropriateness Lad! (Neat fellow!)

Too cartoonish?

But Polemarchus is not sophisticated. He is not here because his way of thinking is **ratio-nally formidable**. He is here because his way of feeling is typical. He wants to **do good**. He thinks in terms of **fighting**. To see what is inadequate about this, we need a simple, sample **fighting do-gooder** as exhibit A.

What holds this picture together is not a rational argument but a wishful hope that strength and power, conventional manliness and justice shall not come apart.

Perhaps you have heard that 'with great power comes great responsibility.' That is a statement of how things **ought to be**. But, in popular literature, it can be more like a comforting **stipulation** of how things **are**. If your head is stuffed with epics tales of heroes, in which it is treated as a matter of course that power and virtue go naturally together — might makes right! Good guys win! Bad guys lose! — you keep revolving back to the same simple thought, over and over.

I still say justice is helping friends and harming enemies. (334c)

Why doesn't any member of the Justice League have the power of — oh, just for example: Justice? Why only powers for fighting? Strength, speed, flight. Why doesn't anyone tell stories about the ordinary man who was bitten by a radioactive philosopher and acquired a tingling 'justice sense'? This man acquired the ability to find genuine solutions to ethical prob-lems the ordinary man on the street regards as hopeless and insoluble! But how do you tell that as a human story? Perhaps people don't tell stories about a super-human justice sense because they can't conceive of **true** justice as some esoteric subject, which only a few super humans expertly grasp. Or maybe they just can't feed an appetite for honor on such abstract fare. No fight, no glory in victory. No glory? How can there be virtue? No virtue? How can there be justice? Good, without good guys and bad guys? What would that look like?

Why doesn't the fact that no one in the Justice League has justice powers, **per se**, strike us as an ironic omission, while we are reading the comic book? Probably because you can tell who the bad guy is just by looking at him. Who needs a 'justice sense' when the stories are all so simple and the characters are so luridly color-coded in the hero-villain department.

Which brings us back to Polemarchus. He's combative, not an utter fool. Obvious considerations allow Socrates to nudge him into modifying a definition that might work in a world of clear heroes and villains, but will predictably fail the politically complex context of real life.

> We should say instead that he is a friend who doesn't merely seem, but truly is, good. One who only seems good, but isn't, only seems a friend, but isn't. The same goes for enemies. (335a)

Obviously so! But his only highlights further problems. First, how to tell?

> Probably people become friends with those they think are good, and grow to hate the ones they judge evil. (334c)

This is interesting because it is so obviously upside down and backwards. By and large, in-group relations are inherited, not deliberately (let alone rationally) selected. You come to think people are 'good' because they are **your** people. Red ant fights black, not because any ant has a good argument about which sort of ant is truly good. We humans see to it that tribal life seems almost as simple as it is for those ants. A shield, for example, can serve not just for defense but to make things seem clear, which — if everyone just threw away their weapons — might be harder to make out.

Thus:

> Don't people often make mistakes about this, so that many of those they believe are good aren't, and vice versa? (334c)

Again, perfectly obvious. But this only makes a further problem more acute: if tribalism isn't a good heuristic, then we aren't refining Polemarchus' friend-enemy binary but bypassing it, trading it for something different and better? To recap:

Polemarchus inherits a money-based account, which he trades for **payback**.

This feeds into an intuitive, if underspecified tribalism:

Which gives way to an as-yet undeveloped moralism.

Which leads, ultimately, to doubts as to whether the consistently combative incidentals make sense, through these changes. No one wants what is bad, so bad people obviously need to be helped, not harmed (335b-e). We need a doctor, not a soldier.

So put down that spear and you've got it!

This is more or less the point at which Thrasymachus loses containment. But before we usher him onstage, let us consider more closely how things stand — or break — at this point.

15

"You and I are prepared to fight side by side against any who attributes such a saying [justice is helping friends and harming enemies] to Simonides or Bias or Pittacus, or any other wise man or prophet?" (335e). Polemarchus agrees, but Socrates is obviously ironizing about how he leaps at the prospect of any fight. (It's there in his name! **Polemos** means battle!) How likely is he to give up fighting, to be permanently argued out of his personal brand of ideal-ism — his image of the virtuous man as fighter — and also his sense of realism?

Consider a pair of poems by Tyrtaeus (5ᵗʰ Century BCE Spartan poet):

> It is noble for a good man to die, falling in the forefront
> Of battle, fighting for his fatherland.
> But there is nothing more wretched than leaving
> One's city and rich fields to beg,
> And wander with his dear mother, his old father,
> His little children and wedded wife …
> Let us die with no thought for our own lives.

There you have it! Idealism meets realism. Giving too many thoughts to your own life is going to be too **personally** costly in the long run. And again:

> This is the common good, for the polis and the whole demos
> When a man stands firm on the front ranks
> Without flinching and puts disgraceful flight completely from his mind
> Making his soul and spirit endure
> And with his words encourages the man stationed next to him.[11]

Fighting is the noblest way. Also, the only way.

Another poet, Archilochus, wrote about dropping his shield and run-ning — **what the hell, I can get a new one! At least I'm alive**! Reportedly, he was banned in Sparta. You want soldiers to think fighting is to their personal advantage. But, then again, you don't want them thinking too hard about payout matrices for fight-or-flight prisoner's dilemma-type situations. If every shield holds, everyone will probably be fine. If one man breaks, the formation collapses. Everyone is probably dead — with the exception of that one coward, who gets a healthy headstart for the hills.

11   Quoted in M. Gagarin and P. Woodruff (eds) **Early Greek Political Thought From Homer to the Sophists** (Cambridge UP 1995), 24-5.

If even **thinking** about dropping your
guard is too dangerous to be permitted, what
are the odds that Polemarchus will be able to
hold on to a dialectically innovative argument
to the denial of the proposition that "the just
man owes a debt of harm to his enemies and
one of aid to his friends" (335e)?

What is he going to sound like? — look like? — to his friends and his
enemies? Wise philosopher or idiot? There's a reason why this is the point
at which Thrasymachus, who prides himself on his realism and his capacity
for self-preservation, just can't take it any more.

16

But we will hold that beast at bay for one last section. Polemarchus, as I said,
is no theorist, just a tribalist. We are interested in him more for his heart than
his head. But suppose — just suppose! — he had a better head for tribalism?
What sorts of thoughts might he have thought through?

Aristotle famously declares, 'man is a political animal [**politikon zōon**]'.[12]
This thesis about the human zoo is more aspirational, less descriptively self-
evident, than we may take it to be. We tend to hear him saying, simply: humans
are social. Indeed, this is the core of Aristotle's case, but his conclusion is
narrower: man is suited by nature to live in a **polis**, a city-state in the Greek
sense. Man lives up to his potential only by living as a citizen, partaking of
public affairs — something that, obviously, very few human beings actually do.

A more realistic counter-conclusion, from the same premises about sociality, might then be this: mankind is tribal. The Greek for **tribe** is **ethnos**, corresponding to 'ethnocentric', an early 20th century coinage of the sociologist
William Graham Sumner:

> Ethnocentrism is the technical name for this view of things in which one's
> own group is the center of everything, and all others are scaled and
> rated with reference to it.

Unpacking 'group' more fully:

12 Aristotle, **Politics** (1253a). Even while arguing with reference to lines from
    Homer about 'clanless, lawless, homeless' men, i.e. utterly anti-social, 'fight-
    loving' specimens of our species, Aristotle makes clear he does not think
    bare sociality suffices for proper 'politics'. Our nature calls for civic com-
    munity [**hoi politai**], a concept that contrasts with, rather than encom-
    passing, mere allies [**hoi summakhoi**] who will have our back in a fight.

The relation of comradeship and peace in the we-group and that of hostility and war towards others-groups are correlative to each other. The exigencies of war with outsiders are what make peace inside, lest internal discord should weaken the we-group for war. These exigencies also make government and law in the in-group, in order to prevent quarrels and enforce discipline. Thus war and peace have reacted on each other and developed each other, one within the group, the other in the intergroup relation. The closer the neighbors, and the stronger they are, the intenser is the warfare, and then the intenser is the internal organization and discipline of each. Sentiments are produced to correspond. Loyalty to the group, sacrifice for it, hatred and contempt for outsiders, brotherhood within, warlikeness without, — all grow together, common products of the same situation. These relations and sentiments constitute a social philosophy[13]

But not a self-critical one, hence the ease with which Polemarchus is drawn into debate, then routed. But if Sumner is right that all humans are ethnocentric, that in itself is some sort of argument for tribalism. Can't ask people to go against nature. At any rate, we now have an answer to that puzzling question we started with: how can a fight be a symbol of harmony and balance? Obviously it can if peace is, as Sumner suggests, a condition generated by 'the exigencies of war'. Peace itself turns out to be a fighting stance!

Having introduced Polemarchus with a quote from one conservative statesman, Churchill, on the subject of disarmament, let me close with another, from US President Ronald Reagan, on the subject of private peace talks he had with Soviet General Secretary Michail Gorbachev:

When you stop to think that we're all God's children, wherever we may live in the world, I couldn't help but say to him, just think how easy his task and mine might be in these meetings that we held if suddenly there was a threat to this world from some other species, from another planet, outside in the universe. We'd forget all the little differences that we have between our countries, and we would find out once and for all that we really are all human beings here on this Earth together.

13   William Graham Sumner, **Folkways: A Study of mores, manners, customs, and morals** (Dover, 2002), 13, 12.

Well, I don't suppose we can wait for some alien race to come down and threaten us, but I think that between us we can bring about that realization.[14]

Note the irony: good things come from having friends, but having friends comes from having enemies. So having enemies is good? But the good of having enemies — so you can have friends — only alleviates problems that were caused by having enemies in the first place! Reagan **hopes** we can escape an absurd circle.

In **The Concept of the Political**, the 20th Century political philosopher Carl Schmitt argues that we cannot, unless we can escape from politics (understood now in a sense that stands Aristotle on his head.) "The specific political distinction to which political actions and motives can be reduced is that between friend and enemy." This antithesis is "relatively independent" of others: good and evil, beautiful and ugly (all the things Aristotle hopes we citizens can debate in a public way.) In **Euthyphro** (7d) Socrates suggests that if the gods fight, it must be because they have disputes about good and evil, beautiful and ugly. Schmitt would say: it's because they are **political**. Not so much when they squabble; rather, when a group or generation of gods wars with another. Right and wrong, beautiful and ugly, all the rest will get dragged in, but friend/enemy is the true root.

> The distinction of friend and enemy denotes the utmost degree of intensity of a union or separation, of an association or dissociation ... The political enemy need not be morally evil or aesthetically ugly; he need not appear as an economic competitor, and it may even be advantageous to engage with him in business transactions. But he is, nevertheless, the other, the stranger; and it is sufficient for his nature that he is, in a specially intense way, existentially something different and alien, so that in the extreme case conflicts with him are possible. These can neither be decided by a previously determined general norm nor by the judgment of a disinterested and therefore neutral party.

 Note the specific hint that no wise Solon can interpose a shield to give everyone 'their due'. It just isn't that **sort** of problem. Schmitt even makes Reagan's point about the aliens — up to a point.

14   Ronald Reagan, speech at Fallston, Maryland, 1985.

Humanity as such cannot wage war because it has no enemy, at least not on this planet. The concept of humanity excludes the concept of the enemy, because the enemy does not cease to be a human being.[15]

17

But do we need to be spiraling off into alien thoughts? Alien to the text of Plato's **Republic**, Book I, that is? Here's the point. Polemarchus is unlikely to convert permanently to the view Socrates is pushing. He will fall back into his old ways of thinking — but maybe more thoughtfully. He might get crafty about friend/enemy. But, once you have gotten to the point of thinking like Schmitt, you are working free of conventional moral notions. The arc of real politics is long but it bends towards injustice: disharmony!

Unleash the beast! Thrasymachus! His notorious definition of justice looks simple enough: 1) **justice is the advantage of the stronger** (338c). Later, however, he shifts to: 2) **justice is another's advantage** (343b). Do those come to the same? Let's sort it out.

First, I recommend the reader flip back to section 4; review my crib sheet for Thrasymachian lies. Why lie? Because he's cynical; also, a good speaker. Philosophers — simple creatures — couch claims in abstract, impersonal terms, even going so far as to peddle definitions. Sophists — shrewd beasts — tailor words to audiences. Thrasymachus will play the definition game, to show he can win it. But he keeps his eyes on the real prize. Present company in the house of Cephalus is all adult males, all rich and/or politically influential. 1) is thus an invitation. Go ahead! Take it all! (As Carnegie says, a speaker **sells** by giving an audience what it wants.) But then with 2) Thrasymachus speaks as if addressing the weak. There is a theoretical reason. He has defined 'strong' so strongly that present company is excepted. But he is also trying to denigrate Socrates as pathetic. No one likes a weakling.

In shifting between 1) and 2) Thrasymachus sometimes poses as a speaker of plain truth. Athenian justice is one thing; Spartan justice something else. No contradiction, just relative, local variability. But sometimes his craft of justice seems to be, as Socrates consistently suggests it should be, like medicine — well, like spin-doctoring. Rulers are unwise to speak the same language of 'justice' in public and private, even in the privacy of their heads. So hire Thrasymachus to run your PR! But does this mean his truth-telling was pure PR from the start? Anyway, do I need to spin doctor my soul? Now it gets tricky.

15   Carl Schmitt, **The Concept of the Political: Expanded Edition**, Expanded. (University Of Chicago Press, 2007), p. 27, 56.

In a well-known passage in **The Prince**, Machiavelli reads allegorical wisdom into an ancient myth concerning the education of Achilles and other Greek princelings by the centaur Chiron. A ruler must know the ways of beast and man alike. Justice **is** this crafty hybrid, Thrasymachus would add. And, just as a good ruler will betray his species, at need, Thrasymachus could turn traitor to his class. When he isn't advertising his services as advisor to insiders, he could be auditioning for the role of demagogue, drawing back the curtain of 'justice' from outside, exposing these sordid, self-serving schemes of the rich and powerful!

All in all, it makes quite a difference whether claims about 'justice' are relativistic, many-faceted truths or cynical, two-faced falsehoods. But Thrasymachus can keep up a good 'heads I win, tails you lose' game. This is how and why he comes off as a hard-headed, clear-eyed debunker of any ideal scheme (naive dream of proving what's Right everywhere, at all times.) Then, a moment later, there he goes, peddling his ideal portrait of a perfect Ruler, who has never existed outside Thrasymachus' wildest dreams.

He equivocates between **is** and **ought**; between realism and a kind of idealism. Does the study of justice properly entail studying how things are — existing order — or how they should be? Both, probably. A good philosopher will be careful; an effective speaker, opportunistic. When you are weak on **is**, shift to **ought,** and vice versa. Know the weak spots in your theory, not so you can repair them; so you can conceal them; so you can sell this stuff.

But what, then, do you believe, if you believe in the power of double-talk? One point on which Thrasymachus is quite consistent (until he starts sulking, saying 'yes, Socrates' to everything), is his **ethical egoism**. He is sure it is always rational, hence right, to pursue one's self-interest. But the subject under debate is justice, not egoism, and the relationship between the two is more strained than Thrasymachus sees, even if there is wisdom in egoism. But before we get to that complication, one last simple question.

What does Thrasymachus want from Socrates? To humiliate him? To teach him how to take over the **polis**? Is he competing with him for customers? Does he think the lure of strength will draw Socrates over to the Dark Side? What might the fantasy of total, philosophical victory look like, in the Cave of this sophist's head? He promises results, but the self-help ads might get a bit cartoonish.

JUSTICE as "DYNAMIC-TENSION"

How Soc's MIND brought him FAME instead of SHAME!

The argument that made a man out of "Soc"!

LET ME PROVE TO YOU
STRENGTH
IS WHAT MATTERS!
- THRASYMACHUS

"The strong do what they can.
The weak suffer what they must."
- Thucydides.

18

One of the frustrations of Plato, for many readers, is the incompetence of Socratic interlocutors. Cephalus and Polemarchus are cases in point. Earlier I said we may see them as undercards before the Big Fight. If so: what a pair of palookas! They throw one punch each, then fold. With Thrasymachus, we get a fighter who gets that advancing a general proposition means opening yourself up. So change up! Anticipate that counter-example counter-punch!

Then again, Thrasymachus doesn't have **a** theory of justice; at most a couple proto-theoretic combos that don't serve him as consistently as he expects. He starts precise; blocks a few shots, tries fancy footwork; takes hits, loses focus, starts swinging wildly. In the end, Socrates is playing his signature style of chin music once again. Glaucon's desire to see someone fight in the Thrasymachian style, but better, is thus understandable. So let me summarize that as an overlay of four distinct theories. The reader can judge for herself how best to synthesize these elements, locate them in specific passages, and/or evaluate their potential merit.

Conventionalism

Sometimes it is said that Thrasymachus is like an anthropologist, or student of comparative politics. No doubt he has read Herodotus' **Histories** (5th Century BCE), in which readers hear the tale of Gyges, and also learn lessons about how differently people do things in different places. Callatians (it is said) eat of the flesh of their dead and are horrified by the prospect of cremation. Greeks feel the opposite way. So honor has a socially conventional character. By saying 'we hereby honor the dead', we make it so; not as individuals, but collectively, in our tribes and cities.

Thrasymachus' opening gambit—justice one thing in a democracy, something else under monarchy, etc. (338e)—seems to fit in here. By declaring 'this is just', we make it so. Not naturally, but by convention, like 'pawns move this way' in chess. This makes all the more sense when we recall that **dikaiosunē** connotes regular order, the way it goes, the **done** thing. The goddess of justice is also a goddess of seasons, recall. If foreign justice is strange, that is no stranger than if winter is colder or summer hotter abroad. (Dress accordingly. What more can you say?) But there is a difference, and it has to do with the unsteady opposition between convention and nature. The sun doesn't shine, the rain doesn't fall, by convention.

It also has to do with the fact that Thrasymachus isn't hinting at the wisdom or correctness of any tolerant norm, based on recognition of the arbitrary character of conventional differences. Thrasymachus is a cosmopolitan character. For sophists, that's a professional prerequisite. 'When in Rome' and all that. But the fact that aristocratic laws favor aristocrats, whereas the **demos** — the people — say democracy is just, is not like that. These are not arbitrary points of etiquette. Thus one element we associate with ethical relativism — a characteristic 'who is to say?' gesture — is mostly absent.

Different strokes for different folks. This might become a perfectly particularized Protagoreanism: each man the measure of all things to do with him. (Women, too!) Or we might get a muddle of commonsense notions. Euthyphro's first thought is that there are many holy things. Meno's first impulse is to list all the things that make virtuous people different, rather than seeking one thing that makes them the same. Thrasymachus, too, starts with the many. But we are quickly moving in the opposite direction: towards a unified account; universal benchmark. One justice for all!

Remember Xenophanes? If cows had gods they would look like cows. That's because everyone is so self-regarding. Thrasymachus is just taking the next step: everyone is so self-interested. If cows had a sense of justice, count on that being good for cows. These are thoughts about what gets made true, by convention. But these thoughts are not themselves true by convention. The pattern is natural and necessary, not subject to change or reform, much less to 'make it so!' stipulative alteration. If everyone is self-interested; if 'justice' is conventional; then, naturally, the strong suit themselves. 'Justice' tracks the self-interest of the ruling class or power. Of course, this is not at all what most people think justice is. But that just goes to show that, far from being all true, by convention, all these substantially divergent, merely conventional local justices are all false … by nature.

Naturalism

But is this skeptical truth truly natural? If so, is it normative? Also, does justice turn out to be many or one?

Imagine that, instead of making trouble for Socrates, Thrasymachus finds work providing voiceover commentary for a nature documentary. Wouldn't that be more honest work, more scientific and educational to youth?

But I forgot to add: in this documentary the animals whose lives and deaths are recorded are human beings. Humans are animals, you may recall. See the great cat hunt the tiny deer! The mighty tyrant persecutes the democrats! 'If the coup is successful, the tyrant will eat well tonight! If not, he may slink off into the high grass of exile, living to overthrow another day.' As a scientific observer, you know better than to take sides. That would be sentimental foolishness. Neither predator or prey is right or wrong. Just eat or be eaten.

If there **is an ought**, it can only be that what there ought to be is: balance. If the regular turn of the seasons is justice, ecology is, too. Due process! The circle of life! Lions have their place in the food chain. **Pleonexia** — excess! — would be the opposite: preaching lions should lie with lambs. No biologist would recommend it.

I am getting mixed up, talking lions in one sentence, tyrants in the next. But does it matter? To repeat: humans are animals. Of course, one thing that makes humans unique, among animals, is that they think they know of a thing they call 'justice'. You never hear a deer cry 'injustice!' before a lion tears out its throat. But how does 'justice' operate, in the throat of a human?

I don't want to push Thrasymachus too far in a naturalist direction. (I predict he would endorse my documentary scheme, but if you want a more full-throated spokesman for 'nature', call Callicles, from Plato's **Gorgias**.) But let me take one last step on Thrasymachus' behalf. Teeth bite; claws rake; legs are for chasing and escaping. What is justice for, by nature? What advantage does the craft (adaptive trait, call it what you will) of crying 'justice!' confer in nature, red in tooth and claw? Thrasymachus does not pose the question in these terms, but I think he would understand, and have an eager, easy answer.

Justice is for fooling! It's a device, employed by predators and prey alike, to disorient and deceive. Weaklings may talk the strong out of preying on them. This is like an animal whose bright coloration mimics something poisonous. 'You'll pay for eating me!' A leader may hypnotize the masses into marching right into his greedy maw, sparing him the trouble of raising a paw. They don't call 'em 'charismatic megafauna' for nothing!

This explains why justice is one-yet-many, according to Thrasymachus. Illusions are like that. And surely we get what he is getting at. (Nothing you didn't learn from Churchill's field trip to the zoo, perhaps.)

People always seek some advantage. Still, this camoflage-and-dazzle conception of justice suffers from a glaring omission. If you ask an evolutionary psychologist what the use of a sense of justice is, in a moral animal, the answer won't be: to lie. Yes, humans **are** liars — and detectors of liars. Our capacity to concoct — and debunk — self-serving moral rationalizations goes with that. Still, our human sense of justice functions, first and foremost, to make us **harmonious**, i.e. willing to forego advantage. "Morality is a set of psychological adaptations that allow otherwise selfish individuals to reap the benefits of cooperation." Morality in what sense? "The essence of morality is altruism, unselfishness, a willingness to pay a personal cost to benefit others."[16]

That morality is, as it were, an amphibious adaptive trait, for creatures washing up from the seas of selfishness onto the shores of sociality, is hardly self-evident. (Plato won't admit justice is just a fish out of water, but he knows the feeling. He tells the Myth of Glaucus, per Chapter 7.) But this may be a more explanatory naturalism than Thrasymachus'. How long can horns grow before they are more tangled trouble than they're worth? How altruistic can we get, collectively, before all that collapses under the weight of our selfishness? Thrasymachus has not a wise word to say about any such functional trade-offs. So 'justice is the advantage of the stronger' doesn't just miss **justice** in a conventional sense. (Thrasymachus will wear that with pride.) It misses **advantage** and **stronger**, even in a natural sense.

Thrasymachus is bored by the idealistic tone of the debate; then irritated, in the end, by what must seem like pseudo-pragmatism. Socrates points out that a gang of thieves, who cannot trust each other, will hardly be strong (351e). Seriously? Is Socrates trying to provide a disproof of the possibility of criminal conspiracy? Preposterous! Naive! But that isn't his point. A theory that it is rational to exploit a system is not a rational theory of that system — of what functions it may have, actually and ideally. Thrasymachus has schemed how to work justice, but not explained how **it** works. **That's** Socrates' point.

<hr>

16 Joshua Greene, Moral Tribes: Emotion, Reason and the Gap Between Us and Them (Penguin, 2013), p. 23.

Egoism

Let turn back to Glaucon's point, per section 5. If justice is a second-best solution to a social coordination problem among egoists, Thrasymachus might be right about the egoism, even if he's wrong about justice.

Ethical egoism is the view that, for an action to be right, it must be self-interested. **Rational egoism** is the view that, for an action to be rational, it must be self-interested. Doing the just thing, in conventional terms, will often be neither rational nor right, on these views. Thrasymachus seems to think his collection of cynical observations about real politics amounts to an empirical proof of psychological egoism, from which the other two views follow. (**Psychological egoism** says that, in fact, everyone is self-interested.) But we seem to be skipping a few steps. Thrasymachus really just seems to find all three forms of egoism intuitive and obvious. So running them together feels right. He does not consistently distinguish them, although constructions like his 'ideal ruler' — we're getting to that! — show awareness that some such distinctions are needed.

Opponents like Glaucon share Thrasymachus' moderately undifferentiated egoistic outlook, if weakly. (Who among us isn't a bit self-centered?) The Glauconian theory that justice is a second-best stability point for the selfish is fatal to Thrasymachus' theory. Yet Glaucon's view is also fatal to Socrates' idealism. He wouldn't like justice-as-stable-side-effect-of-egoism any more than he likes the view that, if sea air makes you healthy, navigation is the craft of medicine (346b).

Let's go back to my earlier, simple question: what does Thrasymachus want? I hinted it's a bit unclear what his dream of victory looks like, here in the house of Cephalus. Does he want to save Socrates or destroy him? G.K. Chesterton: "To preach egoism is to practice altruism." Thrasymachus tries to force Socrates to pay to hear him teach (337d), not just because he likes money; also, because being seen giving away teaser samples is undignified. **Real** tyrants don't hand out freebies!

Still, it's not hard to get where Thrasymachus is coming from, intuitively. The value of knowing 'justice' is different in different places is so when you look around Athens, you don't mistake appearance for reality. All this could change! Sure, it looks stable, harmonious, natural, hence necessary. Surely the Athenian Empire shall endure! Just look at everyone speaking truth, paying debts, friends walking and talking, not a drawn sword in sight! Look at that old man, tending the sacrifices. Clearly, all is in order on earth, under Olympus. But the ground could shift, collapsing all that. If it comes to that, the worst thing I can do will be to cling to old 'justice' — now just some sorry, souvenir scrap. The best I can do will be to keep my mind open, my eyes clear. Maybe this sudden crack in the earth will open opportunities to take what I want, in the midst of chaos. Stranger things have happened.

Chance favors the prepared mind. Philosophy should prepare my mind, accustoming me always to penetrate polite veils. Politics is an armistice, like the peace temporarily holding in the long war between Athens and Sparta (if that theory of the dating of the dialogue's drama is correct.) Conflict is natural, hence (in one sense) ideal, i.e. typical, normal; harmony is the exception, hence (in a sense) non-ideal. Even if it turns out justice is an adaptation to allow cooperation, that's just another route to the same conclusion. No matter how you slice it, justice comes up a functional twist on a more fundamental theory of conflict: harmony as dynamic tension; dynamic tension as a method for building strength. Strength to serve self-interest.

Realism

Is there a theory of politics that goes with this way of seeing? Yes!

Early on, Socrates throws Thrasymachus off balance by pointing out that rulers sometimes miscalculate (339c). This raises an interpretive issue regarding 'justice is the advantage of the stronger' and 'it is just for subjects to do what rulers command.' Is justice, in such a case, what the ruler **does** command, or what he **should**, ideally? Thrasymachus opts for the latter, introducing the notion of a perfect ruler—one who never missteps in the rigorous pursuit of rational self-interest (340d).

This is flagrantly unreal. Feel admiration or horror, as you are inclined. No such Ruler will be found. He's unnatural!

Does this mean Thrasymachus answered wrongly, by his own lights? Not necessarily. He is abstracting and simplifying as physicists do when, for example, they model planets as perfect spheres, or surfaces as frictionless. Some models are elegant, simple and give answers that are approximately correct. Idealization is not make-believe. It does not preclude shrewd, albeit stylized contact with reality. Indeed, such 'ideal' theories may presume to penetrate, not merely approximate, the rough ground of phenomena—of power politics, for example.

Consider how Platonic the following passage sounds—how Thrasymachian. It is Hans Morgenthau, expounding what IR (international relations) theorists call 'realism'.

The difference between international politics as it actually is and a rational theory derived from it is like the difference between a photograph and a painted portrait. The photograph shows everything that can be seen by the naked eye; the painted portrait does not show everything that can be seen by the naked eye, but it shows, or at least seeks to show, one thing that the naked eye cannot see: the human essence of the person portrayed.

Political realism contains not only a theoretical but also a normative element. It knows that political reality is replete with contingencies and systemic irrationalities … Yet it shares with all social theory the need, for the sake of theoretical understanding, to stress the rational elements of political reality; for it is these rational elements that make reality intelligible for theory. Political realism presents the theoretical construct of a rational foreign policy which experience can never completely achieve.

At the same time political realism considers a rational foreign policy to be good foreign policy; for only a rational foreign policy minimizes risks and maximizes benefits and, hence, complies both with the moral precept of prudence and the political requirement of success. Political realism wants the photographic picture of the political world to resemble as much as possible its painted portrait. Aware of the inevitable gap between good — that is, rational — foreign policy and foreign policy as it actually is, political realism maintains not only that theory must focus upon the rational elements of political reality, but also that foreign policy ought to be rational in view of its own moral and practical purposes.[17]

This is as cogent a rationale for Thrasymachus' ideal Ruler model as one is likely to find. Morgenthau's realism-as-rationalism turns out to be, basically, egoism at the state level. ('Interest', understood as power. Not quite 'justice' as strength, but, once again, close enough for government work.)

I hope it is also apparent why I call this picture Platonic. The irrational world of experience around us is trying, semi-failing, to be like a simpler, more rational world, behind it. The judicious theorist therefore massages the data, **pour encourager les autres**.

But when is it reasonable to reason this way? Astrophysicists may model planets as spheres, but do not conclude, therefore, that these objects of study **ought** to be perfect spheres, so that data fudging is helpful nudging.

17   Hans Morgenthau, "Six Principles of Political Realism, in Morgenthau, Thompson, and Clinton, **Politics Among Nations** (McGraw-Hill, 1992), p. 10..

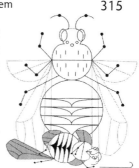

We don't think the universe suffers from what linguists call a competence/performance gap.[18] But speakers do. A theory of English syntax need not accommodate every mangled utterance by any native speaker. Or take an example from Chapter 7. If one biologist is puzzling over the function of a mysterious aspect of insect anatomy, and her colleague helpfully informs her it's not 'supposed to be' that way — leg's broken — this deletion of bad data from the set is sensible. Extending Morgenthau's metaphor: if you are commissioned to produce a scientific illustration of a type of insect, but the subject you can find to sit for its portrait suffers from a broken leg, feel free to repair the defect, imaginatively, for 'ideal' illustration purposes.

What if you are an economist, modeling agents as egoistic, rational actors, yet behavioral economists persist in informing you real subjects don't obey your model? When do you abandon your theory as falsified; when defend it weakly, as approximate; when defend it strongly, on the grounds that you have penetrated to a deeper, truer level? Morgenthau: "reality, being deficient in this respect, must be understood and evaluated as an approximation to an ideal system." How can you **know** a thing like that? Let's get back to the case at hand: justice. Gaze out over the polis. What do you see?

Bunch of moral animals.

Healthy specimens?

Nothing to write home to the Form of the Good about.

Second-best?

Most of them. If they are lucky.

But are they second-best first-best, or second-best second-best?

Come again?

I thought I had! Are they trying, but failing, to be optimal Glauconians? Or trying, but failing, to be perfect Thrasymachians? Or trying, but failing, to be perfect Platonists? Which target are they trying to hit, by nature, in theory, 'ideally', but missing, sadly, in real politics, in practice?

18   Ironically, this is close to Plato's actual view of astronomy and empirical science generally. Since the objects around us are imperfect copies of ideal Forms, we ought to treat empirical data points as 'trying' to be where the elegant math says they ought to be. (See **Republic**, 529b-530c).

'Trying' makes it sound like a psychological question, but the aspirational norm is more complicated.
Think about the broken leg case. It's easy to say a bug
leg is for walking. Mother Nature was 'trying' to build a
bug that could walk. That's informal shorthand for a long story about selective pressure and normal, biological function; one that doesn't involve attri-
butions of motive or deliberate design, strictly.

Even so, note how complicated such a case can get. Suppose these legs
are in process of evolving into wings (maybe we are studying fossils, so we
know this future.) Our pedestrian insect species is taking to the air! Suppose
you confront a broken, intermediate form, along this upward-bound path.
What do you call it, this battered, betwixt-and-between leg-wing? What is it
'for': earth or air? I'm drawing an analogy with the human moral sense which,
as noted, might be modeled as an amphibious affair: suspension between
selfishness and sociality. Think of Glaucus, half-fish, half-god. Think of Plato's
chariot team: winged and well-trained on one side; digging in asinine heels
on the other. Thrasymachus might prefer a different figure. Keen, obedient
steed, four strong feet on the ground; but, on the other side, foolish, dis-
obedient Pegasus, unbalancing things uselessly, in defiance of
gravity and common sense. Is morality 'for' raising ourselves, idealistically, or keeping us grounded, practically?
Do you train such a creature to 'be itself' by clipping its
wings or by growing them, so eventually it can wing somewhere better, even if it will be awkward for now?

19

Getting back to Thrasymachus, the following, Morgenthau-inspired argument is no good, hence no good for settling such issues:

P1: **A rational theory says people are ideally egoistic.**
P2: **I am a person.**
C: **It is ideal for me to be rationally egoistic.**

In P1, 'ideal' means **approximately**. By C, it means: **best**. We are equivo-
cating between good theories and good people, via erroneous hints that
the mark of the latter is to make for the former. (And should it turn out I am
more than one person in one … ?) If something like this simple argument still
sounds plausible — many find it so — consider whether you are crossing it
with a different class of shrewdness: if the other guy has a knife, get a knife.
Better: a gun. In soul terms, if everyone is a bit of a beast, grow your beast.

Nothing less would be safe. Prudence is rational. But it hardly follows being a beast is ideal, much less that things will go best if everyone is beastly; or that our measuring stick for rationality must be maximal beastliness. That it makes sense that beasts exist does not imply only beasts have made sense of existence.

It is a superficially curious fact that 'realism' is used as a term both for Platonism that credits the existence of abstract objects and for cynical, **realpolitik**-style theories of political dynamics. Then again, not so surprising. Reality is as reality does! Or might do. Plato is forever seeking an eternal, unchanging order of Being behind the superficial shadowplay of Becoming. Thrasymachus seeks to ground superficial patterns of disorder-masked-as-order in a deeper, permanent disorder-as-order. There are laws governing all the moving and shaking. Thrasymachus has a logical, theoretical mind; at least a limber, theoretical stance. He is prepared to revise or disregard received, conventional notions of justice, of right and wrong, to fit the pieces into a simpler, more explanatory pattern.

Two very different styles of drawing a sharp appearance/reality distinction, in a highly aspirational ethical spirit, make for an odd team, pulling the chariot of the Real in different directions. Pity the charioteer! Or maybe there's a crafty way to steer this team, after all?

By way of pulling thoughts together, one final theoretical complication is worth going over, concerning that puzzling and elusive, alleged **technē** of justice — the craft of 'practicing justice'. Whatever could it be?

Rather than tracing a tangled thread (which starts at 340d and really continues, with intermittent disappearances, until the end) let me tell another tale. This one is also from Herodotus' **Histories** (I.96-100). Once upon a time there was a Persian named Deioces, who coveted political power and set out to get it. He 'practiced justice' constantly and zealously, though the country was lawless, and though injustice is ever the enemy of justice.

Does that mean he wore a mask and jumped around on rooftops after dark?

Not in the least! He was a freelance judge and mediator.

Did he charge a lot?

No, he gave out freebies.

His fellow countrymen, seeing his justice was just, brought their cases to him. He, craving power, kept right on being honest and right. Thus he won praise, word spread and market-share increased. Men learned Deioces alone always gave fair judgment. Men appreciated the unprecedented level of customer service. Also, you can't argue with the price. More and more cases came to Deioces, since each turned out in accord with truth and fairness.

Finally, having completely cornered the market for justice by this innovative strategy of just plain being just, Deioces jacked up prices. He would judge no more — it was not to his advantage to neglect his private interests in such a fashion. The crime rate shot up. Persians gathered, conferred and a proposal was made (here one suspects a strategic scattering of Deioces' friends in the audience, amplifying the chorus): "We can't go on living this way. Let's set up a king! The land will then be justly governed and we can tend to our private affairs without being eaten up by injustice!"

And **that's** how King Deioces won his crown. How do you suppose he ruled? Happily ever after? Justly ever after. Justly ever happily? How to you suppose his son turns out? The fable is provocative in that it lends support to Socrates **and** Thrasymachus. So it can also be read as a challenge to both.

The fact that we can even make sense of the story shows we believe there is such a thing as justice, apart from any advantage the zealous and constant practice of this 'craft' may or may not bring its 'practitioner'. There is such a thing as giving fair judgment, whether it is to your advantage or not. Just as there is such a thing as being a good doctor, or a competent musician, whether or not you get paid for your services. Conceding even this much is a fatal blow to Thrasymachus' theory. If there is such a thing as fair judgment, in the abstract, it is simply false that justice is the advantage of the stronger, as Socrates forces him to concede.

All the same, there is not much comfort for Socrates if the engine will only run on the fuel of egoistic desire for power by any means necessary. And if justice itself is, at best, a by-product. This mix seems explosive, unstable.

We seem threatened, not with the worst of all worlds, exactly, but perhaps with being stuck in the worse of two possible worlds. It is possible to imagine a harmonious, just order. We **could** live well there. Still, we may not be able to realize the ideal, people being the beasts they are. Can't get there from here, maybe. (We can only visit on utopian holiday, in our minds.)

20

Let me conclude this chapter in a way that may pull all three dialogues in this book together. It is appropriate that Thrasymachus comes last. He is, in a sense, the embodiment of everything Plato hates. He's a standing temptation. Yet Thrasymachus is not so personally attractive. (I don't deny he's fun to watch!)

What does he lack? He's no Romantic. By which I mean: he may be 'mad, bad and dangerous to know,' but he doesn't put that on a business card he hands you, with a Byronic flourish. There no whiff of brimstone coming off him. No Faustian thrill of forbidden knowledge, for which he sold his soul. Thrasymachus isn't Nietzsche, sailing out of sight of moral land, beyond good and evil, seeking new spiritual shores. He isn't one of those fascinating, Hollywood-style psychos, with all the extra twists. He wants to 'stand tall' (338b). He wants **stuff**: money, sex, fast chariots, one presumes. For someone with the vision to penetrate the conventional veil of morality, he isn't all that visionary about values. When push comes to shove, it's pushing and shoving all the way down. He's a greedy bully.

Even the mafia has got family values. Which brings me to another thing Thrasymachus isn't: an apologist for egoism on the grounds that it's a disguised form of family values, or altruism. 'Greed is good,' announces the capitalist. Adam Smith's invisible hand means me, looking out for #1, helps everyone. Practicing egoism is, on this theory, more altruistic than preaching altruism (which never gets results.) Good argument or not, Thrasymachus doesn't bother. Here are some things he might say, except he doesn't care. Destruction stimulates the economy and provides a pleasing spectacle to the gods. When I'm tyrant, there will be good jobs in the palace for people to say I'm 'just'. (You want the youth of today to have good jobs in tomorrow's disinformation economy, don't you, Socrates?) A tyrant with the know-how to seize power knows how to run the place. I'll keep the other harpies away.

No one **wants** to be bad. (Remember that argument from **Meno**?) Your basic bully, he has some self-serving story to tell, however ridiculous, about how he's the true champ of the little guy! Thrasymachus, lacking any such impulse to excuse himself, seems more like a personified person-part than a complete moral personality. Cephalus, on the other hand! **He** seems like a real guy, waiting to die.

21

I've said a lot about Cephalus, I know, but I think there's a tendency not to say enough. Here are two typical enough views of the old man. Basically, he's a hollow shell of conventionality. Crack him; there's no **there** there. Julia Annas writes:

> What is wrong with this view [Cephalus'] … First, it leads to complacency … justice is not perceived as something diffi-cult, which might involve effort, and which you might not be sure you had achieved. Secondly, precisely because justice is not thought of as needing much effort, no need is felt to think about it much, and so people like this are very quickly reduced to silence by Socrates; their beliefs have no intellectual backing. Once complacency is shaken, it leaves a void. And thirdly, that void is all too plausibly filled by skepticism … Once your confidence is shaken that justice is sticking to a few simple rules, there is nothing to put in its place except the skeptical view that justice is nothing but a racket.[19]

Nickolas Pappas puts the same point, even more harshly:

> [Cephalus] has absorbed his society's rules of good behavior to such an extent that he genuinely seems to feel happiest when acting rightly, but without being able to explain why … When we hear him speak of following religious customs as if he were buying insurance, and quote Sophocles, Themistocles, and Pindar rather than think for himself, we yearn for something more substantial. No reader misses Cephalus after he goes off to make his sacrifice; and he would not miss the discussion that follows, since it could only confuse him … In modern parlance, he is a bourgeois philistine.[20]

I don't wholly disagree, but I like to think there's more going on.

Is it really plausible that Cephalus could emigrate from his home city, live as a non-citizen in a complex, sophisticated foreign society for decades, negotiating all the political, cultural and economic difficulties in time of major war, without it occurring to him that 'just do the customary thing' might, in some circumstances, be a less than utterly satisfactory rule for living?

That would be naive. He **can't** be so empty after all these years, can he?

19   Julia Annas, **An Introduction to Plato's Republic** (Oxford University Press, USA, 1981), p. 21.
20   Nickolas Pappas, **Routledge Philosophy GuideBook to Plato and the Republic**, 2nd ed. (Routledge, 2003), p. 31.

22

At the risk of spiraling loose from **Republic** again, let me venture a speculative, extended comparison with Alfred Nobel — of Nobel Prize fame. He invented dynamite, among other, often explosive devices. ('Dynamite' from the Greek for power, but the full, original trademark adds '**safety** powder'. Power plus stability: elusive, beguiling synthetic compound!) Cephalus is a **metic**; that is, a non-citizen in Athens. Nobel, too, was a **metic** in the arms industry. You go abroad to supply weapons to foreigners. (It pays the bills.)

Like Cephalus, whose says his father wasted away much of the family fortune before Cephalus managed to earn it back, Nobel knew what the turning wheel of fortune feels like. His father got rich and went bankrupt. Twice. His nephew would lose an oil fortune after the Russian Revolution and have to sneak into exile, literally in disguise (as Cephalus' son, Lysias, would do after Athenian democracy falls and Polemarchus is put to death.) Like Cephalus, Nobel was scrupulous — to the point of obsession — about debt payment. When asked to write a short autobiography, he listed his greatest virtue as "keeping my nails clean, never being a burden;" his greatest sin, "not worshipping mammon." His biographer writes:

> The writer Robert Musil once declared that some wealthy people experience their fortune as an extension of themselves. Nothing could have been more foreign to Alfred. Each new million contributed not one inch to his mental and spiritual growth. Clichéd though it might sound, what he was seeking could not be bought for money. The letters he wrote late in life bear the imprint of a severely — even clinically — depressed human being. In his solitude he counted how many real friends he had. Every year, their number declined in his calculations. He felt nothing but loneliness was waiting for him at the end of the road.[21]

Socrates notes that Cephalus, too, does not seem to be one of those rich people who regard their wealth as noble extensions of their own persons. He compliments him on this, apparently un-ironically. Nobel said his one request was "not to be buried alive." Important events in his life: "none." He was afraid no would miss him when he went away and, like Cephalus, was subject to uncomfortable glimpses of the afterlife. He didn't much care for the looks of the place and set out to shore up his character by buying as much justice as he could find for sale on the open market.

21 Kenne Fant, **Alfred Nobel: A Biography** (Arcade Publishing, 1993), p. 157.

Cephalus is not sure whether an old man's other-worldly nightmares are due to bodily weakness, but, in Nobel's case, the cause was shoddy journalism. His brother died; a French newspaper wrote an obituary for Alfred, by mistake. He got to read in the paper about the death of the "merchant of death," who spent his life discovering new ways "to mutilate and kill." He had read this sort of thing before and been stung. He was a man of conscience and peace; his inventions had civilian and defensive uses (which was true.) But this time "the spirits of Niflheim" [Norse land of the dead] would not be appeased. He rewrote his will in secret, leaving little to his family. The rest endowed the prizes that bear his name — for Peace, Literature, Physics, Chemistry and Medicine.

Cephalus says he likes philosophy, but doesn't have much to say, does he? What sort of philosophy did Nobel espouse? The Nobel Foundation has a selection of his aphorisms on their official site. You might expect these to be culled with an eye for the cloudy but heavily silver-lined — hope, truth, justice, idealism, solid foundations. You would be **half** right. Here are some:

> Hope is nature's veil for hiding truth's nakedness.
>
> Lying is the greatest of all sins.
>
> The truthful man is usually defeated by the liar.
>
> We build upon the sand, and the older we become, the more unstable this foundation becomes.
>
> Justice is to be found only in the imagination.
>
> The best excuse for the fallen ones [prostitutes] is that Justice herself is one of them.
>
> It is not sufficient to be worthy of respect in order to be respected.
>
> Self-respect without the respect of others is like a jewel which will not stand the daylight.
>
> Worry is the stomach's worst poison.
>
> Contentment is the only real wealth.[22]

It's pessimistic, verging on nihilistic, but tempered with business-like nods to the importance of effective public relations and not worrying too much. Why would a man who believes this sort of thing think it worthwhile to endow an intellectually idealistic foundation? There is a notorious clause in Nobel's will. The prize for literature goes to "an outstanding work of literature in an

22   http://www.nobelprize.org/alfred_nobel/biographical/aphorisms.html

ideal direction." You can imagine what headache that has caused. (What a phrase to be the hinge of a legal instrument. Yet what other phrase could express the desire that the money be spent to figure out what the ideal thing **is**, ideally?) Nobel seems to have been aware of the tensions: "I am a misanthrope and yet utterly benevolent, have more than one screw loose yet am a super-idealist who digests philosophy more efficiently than food"(2). In public what people got out of him was: "pay me the money you owe when it is due, sir." But rattling around, under cover of this philistine exterior we find not just an ambitious Polemarchus, cynical Meno, corrosively skeptical Thrasymachus, and prudent Carnegie, but an implausibly idealistic Plato. (If you read his biography there is plenty about religion, too.) It is speculation to lay Alfred Nobel's temperament as a template over Cephalus, just because he too is a rich old arms manufacturer who says philosophy is the only appetite he has left; who has bad dreams, emphasizes the values of truth, is punctilious about debts, and seems to think the best use for money is to buy justice. But I think it is important not to assume outwardly conventional morality is indicative of psychological dullness or intel-lectual simplicity. There are obvious reasons why Cephalus **looks** simple. He wants to win friends and avoid worries. The Athenians disapprove of resident foreigners expressing loud opinions about politics. He is not a citizen — not a partaker in **politeia**. If speaking the truth, by his lights, might make Athenians dislike him, he is likely to keep his thoughts to himself. That doesn't mean he has none.

23

Alfred Nobel is exceptional on account of what he did with his money. But thoughts like his — alternating, violent flashes of cynicism and idealism, pad-ded out with prudence and common sense — are perfectly normal. That the day-tight compartments of conven-tional morality contain such a volatile mix is remarkable, noteworthy.

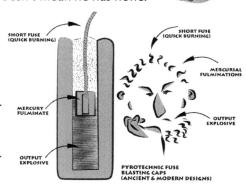

It doesn't seem **safe**. And when you put so many volatile day-tight com-partments together ...? I quoted C. Wright Mills, near the end of Chapter 7, emphasizing Plato's 'sociological imagination'. Let me quote Mills at the end again. He is, it seems to me, a fine foil for Plato because he sees it will never do, while seeing as well why something of the sort might have to do.

Our problem, he begins, begins in private life, and that, in a sense **is** the problem:

> Nowadays men often feel that their private lives are a series of traps. They sense that within their everyday worlds, they cannot overcome their troubles, and in this feeling, they are often quite correct: what ordinary men are directly aware of and what they try to do are bounded by the private orbits in which they live. [23]

He moves on to consider conflict, how the self-interested, merely personal angles on conflict are real, but insufficient:

> Consider war. The personal problem of war, when it occurs, may be how to survive it or how to die in it with honour: how to make money out of it; how to climb into the higher safety of the military apparatus ... But the structural issues of war have to do with its causes; with what types of men it throws up into command; with its effects upon economic and political, family and religious institutions, with the unorganized irresponsibility of a world of nation-states. (16)

And the city — the **polis**. "Consider the metropolis — the horrible, beautiful, ugly, magnificent sprawl of the great city." (Very like a soul, is the city.) Rich people may deal with the problem by walling themselves off, tending private gardens and conducting private rituals.

> But all this, however splendid, does not solve the public issues that the structural fact of the city poses. What should be done with this wonderful monstrosity? Break it all up into scattered units, combining residence and work? Refurbish it as it stands? Or, after evacuation, dynamite it and build new cities according to new plans in new places? What should those plans be? And who is to decide and to accomplish whatever choice is made? (16)

You see, I just wanted to get that last charge of dynamite laid, for better and worse, potentially.

At least I **hope** you see.

23   C. Wright Mills, **The Sociological Imagination** (Oxford University Press, USA, 2000), p. 1.

Chapter 10
REPUBLIC BOOK I

Summary of Sections

Prologue:
Seeing Things

[3 2 7 A-3 2 8 B]

After attending a festival in honor of Bendis, Socrates, Glaucon and Adeimantus are obliged to go home with Polemarchus and friends, where they meet his father, Cephalus.

Cephalus:
Telling Truth & Paying Debts

[3 2 8 B-3 3 1 B]

Cephalus speaks of old age and the value of money. Being old needn't be a bad thing, so long as you have good character. The main benefit of wealth is to allow you to speak truth and pay what you owe to gods and men. But is this a good definition of justice? Speak truth and pay debts? If your friend has gone mad, and wants weapons back that he left with you, should you give them back? Cephalus' account cannot be right. Cephalus withdraws, leaving the argument to Polemarchus.

Polemarchus I:
A Friend Does Good to a Friend,
Evil to an Eenemy

[3 3 1 E-3 3 4 B]

Polemarchus takes up where Cephalus leaves off. Justice is giving to each what is owed. A friend will do good to a friend, evil to an enemy. So: justice must be the craft of doing good to friends, evil to enemies. But what use will justice then be, except in time of war? It will be useful in partnerships, and when things are held in trust. An awkward consequence: always justice is useful when the things concerned are useless, useless when they are useful. Also, it turns out the just man must be a sort of thief. Polemarchus denies this was what he had in mind.

Polemarchus II:
Do Good to our Friends When They Are Good ...
The Just Man Harms No One

[3 3 4 B-3 3 6 A]

Polemarchus reaffirms his Simonides-inspired thesis that justice is helping friends and harming enemies. Does 'friend' cover only real friends or also apparent friends? The former. But soon another modification is needed. It is argued that the just man will harm no one. Polemarchus agrees.

Thrasymachus I:
Justice Is the Advantage of the Stronger

[3 3 6 B-3 4 0 C]

Thrasymachus explodes in irritation. He demands that Socrates not just ask but answer. He will not accept definitions like 'justice is the right'. But what if one of the forbidden answers is the right one? Thrasymachus says he has a better answer. Justice is the advantage of the stronger. But what does this mean? It is a theory of politics. Different governments establish different laws, but always for their own advantage. These laws are called 'justice'. But are the rulers infallible? No. So sometimes justice is both the advantage and the disadvantage of the stronger, according to the terms of the definition.

Thrasymachus II:
Measuring With a Precise 'Ruler' ...
Craft Analogies

[3 4 0 C-3 4 3 A]

An attempt at repair. Did Thrasymachus mean: what the stronger thought to be to his advantage? He instead defines 'ruler' narrowly, to exclude anyone who mistakes his advantage. A new tack: what is the point of a craft like medicine or piloting a ship? To heal the sick and keep the passengers safe. Do crafts like these seek their own advantage or that of those they serve? That of those they serve. The arts are rulers and overseers of their subjects? Yes. But no craft commands the disadvantage of what it serves; rather, its advantage. By implication, this will apply to justice.

Thrasymachus III:
The Advantages of Injustice

[343A-347E]

T: Your nanny never taught you the difference between shepherds and sheep. Rulers, like shepherds, tend their flocks for their own advantage. Thrasymachus delivers his great speech in favor of perfect injustice. S: you do not seem to be discussing the art of shepherding — and ruling — according to the accepted strict sense. In general, the art of getting paid must be distinct from the various other arts.

Thrasymachus IV:
Does the Just Man
Try to Gain Advantage Over the Just?

[347E-350C]

But is Thrasymachus at least right that the life of the unjust is more advantageous than that of the just? S: do you admit that justice is virtue and injustice vice? Skilled musicians and physicians do not try to better others who also know what to do; they only seek to better than those who do not know. Therefore, the just are like skilled craftsmen, the unjust unlike them. The just are likely to be good and wise, the unjust the opposite.

Socrates: The Virtue of the Soul is Justice ...
Yet We Don't Know What It Is

[350D-354C]

Does injustice have strength? It seems not. But can a state perhaps wield power without justice? An argument: injustice impairs coordination; therefore, it is incompatible with strength. But are the just happier than the unjust? Everything is said to have its function and corresponding virtue, which allows it to perform its function. The function of the soul is to live and regulate life. Its virtue is justice. So the soul of the good man must live well; that of the bad man badly. He who lives well is happy; he who lives badly is miserable. Since misery is unprofitable, injustice can never be profitable. And yet: all this is cast in doubt by the fact that we do not know yet what justice is.

YESTERDAY I WENT DOWN to Piraeus   327
with Glaucon, son of Ariston, to
offer up my prayers to the goddess and to see how they would
celebrate the festival, which was a
new thing. I was delighted with the
procession the inhabitants put on, but
the Thracians' was just as beautiful, maybe
more. When we had finished our prayers and watched the show   B
we headed back into the city. Just then Polemarchus, son of Cephalus,
happened to catch sight of us from a distance as we were starting
home and told his servant to run ahead and bid us wait. The servant grabbed me from behind by the cloak, and said, Polemarchus
says to wait.

I turned around and asked where his master was.

There he is, coming after you, so wait for him, said the boy.

Of course we will, said Glaucon. After a little while, Polemarchus   C
caught up. With him were Adeimantus, Glaucon's brother, Niceratus
the son of Nicias, and several others who had been at the procession.

Polemarchus said to me: Socrates, it looks like you and our friend
here are already headed back to the city.

You've guessed right, I said.

But don't you see how many of us there are, he replied?

Of course.

You'll have to be stronger than all of us, or you'll have to stay where
you are.

Isn't there another way, I said: namely, we could persuade you to let us go?

But can you persuade us if we won't listen? he said.

Certainly not, replied Glaucon.

Then we aren't going to listen, you can count on it.

328 Adeimantus added: Don't you know about the horseback torch-race in honor of the goddess? It's going to be this evening.

Horses! I replied. That's something new. You mean the riders will carry torches and pass them, like batons, during the race?

Yes, said Polemarchus. Not only that but there's going to be an all-night festival, which will be worth seeing. Let's get up after dinner and go see it. We'll get together with lots of young men there and
B   talk. So stay. Don't spoil the fun by leaving.

Glaucon said: It looks like we have to stay.

Then that's the way it has to be, I replied.

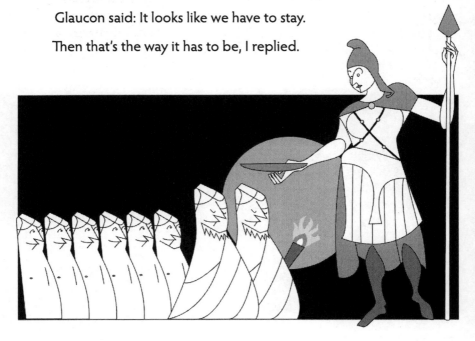

So we went with Polemarchus to his house; and there we found his brothers Lysias and Euthydemus, and with them Thrasymachus the Chalcedonian, Charmantides the Paenian, and Cleitophon, son of Aristonymus. Polemarchus' father, Cephalus, was there too. I had   c
not seen him for a long time and thought he looked very old. He was sitting on kind of a cushioned chair, with a garland on his head, since he had just finished making sacrifice in the courtyard. There were other chairs arranged in a circle, and we sat down by him.

He greeted me eagerly, and then said: You don't visit me as often as you should, Socrates. If I were still able to visit you, I wouldn't   d
have to ask you to come here. But as I can't, you should come down to the Piraeus more often. For I have to tell you that the more the pleasures of the body fade, the more the pleasure and charm of conversation increase. Don't say no, then. Keep company with these young men, come visit us and make our house your home.

I replied: I like nothing better than talking with my elders, Cephalus. I think of them as travelers who have taken a journey I may have to   e
make myself, so I ought to find out from them whether the road is rugged and difficult, or smooth and easy. So this is the question I would particularly like to ask you, who have arrived at that stage in life the poets call the "threshold of old age" — Is life harder towards the end? What can you tell us about it all?

I will tell you, by Zeus, he said, that my own feeling is this, Socrates. Men my age flock together. We are birds of a feather, as the proverb   329
says. At our meetings most of my friends weep and moan — they long for the pleasures of youth, and reminisce about sex and drinking and feasting and everything else like that. They feel annoyed, as if they have been robbed of something great, and say life used to be good, now it's not worth living. Some complain about old people being disrespected in their own households. They sing a sad   b

song blaming age for being the cause of all their woes. But to me, Socrates, they put the blame in the wrong place. If old age really caused all these evils, I — and every single other old man, for that matter — would feel the way they do. But I don't, and neither do others. I particularly remember what the poet Sophocles said, when he was old and someone asked, How's your sex life, Sophocles — can you still make love to a woman? Be quiet, he replied, I'm glad to be done with all that. I'm like a slave who has escaped from a crazy, brutal master. I thought he was right then, and I still think so today. Because old age certainly does bring with it great tranquility and freedom. When the fierce passions relax their grip on us, then, just as Sophocles says, we escape the clutches not just of one crazy master but a whole gang of them. The truth is, Socrates, all these complaints, all those about family as well, are due to one cause — not old age, but a man's character. If a man is calm and happy, he won't mind the weight of old age on his shoulders. If he isn't, Socrates, both age and youth alike will be unbearable.

C

D

I admired him for saying all this, and — wanting to hear more — I tried to get a rise out of him.

E   Yes, Cephalus, I said. But I think most people wouldn't buy it, coming from you. They would say you bear your old age well not because of your character but because of your money. For, they say, it's easy being rich.

You're right, he replied. They wouldn't buy it, and there's something to that, but not as much as you might think. I could answer back the same way Themistocles answered that Seriphian who insulted 330 him, saying he wasn't famous on his own account but because he

was Athenian. To that he said: It's true. I couldn't have been a famous Seriphian, but you'd be a nobody Athenian. The same applies to those who are poor and miserable in old age. A man of good sense won't find it easy being both old and poor. But being rich won't make you happy if you lack good sense.

Can I ask you, Cephalus, whether you made your fortune or inherited it?

Made it! Socrates, do you want to know how much I'm a self-made man? When it comes to money matters, I'm halfway between my father and grandfather. My grandfather, after whom I'm named, doubled and tripled what he inherited, which was about as much as I have. My father Lysanias ended up with less. So I'll be happy to leave to my sons no less — in fact, a bit more — than I started out with myself.

That's why I asked, I replied, because you don't seem to obsess about money. Men who don't inherit often do. Those who make money love it twice as much as other people. For just as poets love their own poems, and fathers their sons, so the self-made men love what they make, their money, as their own creations — also, money comes in handy, as everyone knows. So rich men are hard to get along with. They don't talk about anything but money.

That's true, he said.

Very much so. But may I ask another question? What do you consider to be the greatest benefit you have derived from your great wealth?

Most people probably wouldn't believe me if I told them. But let me tell you. You should really know, Socrates, that when a man thinks he is near death, he starts to care about things, be afraid of things — things he never gave a thought to before. All those stories about Hades he used to laugh at, about how the dead are made

to pay for all the wrongs they committed in life. Now the stories torment him with the thought that maybe it's all true. Furthermore, the man himself, either due to the weakness of old age, or because he is getting closer and closer to the things beyond, sees them a bit more clearly. He is overcome by doubts and fears, and he begins to reckon things up and consider whether he has ever done wrong to anyone. The man who finds he has committed many unjust deeds in life both wakes from his sleep with a frightened start, as children do, and lives with despair by day. But the man who finds he has a clean conscience, sweet good hope is constantly beside him — a good nurse in his old age, as Pindar says. For he put this thought very charmingly, Socrates, that whoever lives his life justly and righteously,

> Sweet hope
> Who above all guides the wandering purpose of mortals
> Gladdens his heart, walks by his side,
> And comforts his old age.

These are wonderfully fine words! Thus I lay it down that this is the chief value of acquiring wealth, not to every man but to a man of good sense. Namely, he need not deceive or defraud anyone, even unintentionally. Nor does he leave this world afraid that he owes sacrifices to the gods or debts to men. Having money is more than a little help in this regard. And of course it has many other uses. But on balance — setting one thing against another — I, for one, affirm that this is the most profitable use of wealth, for an intelligent man.

Well put, Cephalus, I replied. But concerning this thing you have been talking about — namely, justice — shall we say, without qualification, that it is this? To speak the truth and give back whatever you may owe anyone? Isn't doing these very things sometimes just and sometimes unjust? I mean something like this. If you have a friend who leaves weapons with you, when he is of sound mind, then asks for them back after he goes mad, no one would say that you should give them back, or that someone who did return them was a just man; no more than you would say you should always speak the truth to someone in such a seriously disturbed frame of mind. D

You're absolutely right, he replied.

But then, I said, speaking truth and returning what is owed is not a correct definition of justice.

To the contrary, Socrates — interrupted Polemarchus — this is the exactly correct definition, if Simonides is to be believed.

Very well, said Cephalus. I bequeath the argument to you all. I have to look after the sacrifices.

Polemarchus is your heir anyway, isn't he? I said.

Yes, indeed, he answered laughing, and went away to the sacrifices.

TELL ME THEN, O NOBLE HEIR to the argument: what it is that Simonides had to say about justice that you feel is correct? E

He said that to give back what is owed to each person is just. I think in saying that he spoke well.

It's not easy to doubt the word of a wise and inspired man like Simonides, but his meaning — though maybe it's clear to you — is far from clear to me. To go back to what we were just saying, of course he doesn't mean that I should return weapons to anyone if he asks for them back when mad. And yet a thing held in trust is a 332 sort of debt owed, isn't it?

True.

The weapons shouldn't be given back to anyone whatsoever, if he should ask for them sometime when he is mad?

Certainly not.

When Simonides said justice was the repayment of what is owed,
he meant something different from this sort of case?

Something very different, by Zeus, for he thinks that a friend ought
to do good to a friend, never evil.

I see. You mean, then, that to return a thing owed to another — for
example, to give back gold that someone has deposited with you — if
some harm would come about due to the return, and if both parties are friends, is not the repayment of what is owed. That is what
you would think he would say?

Exactly.

And are enemies also to receive what we owe them?

Certainly, he said, they are to
receive what we owe them.
An enemy, I take it, owes an
enemy what is due or proper
to him — namely, something
bad.

Simonides apparently spoke of the nature of justice in that way poets
speak — very obscurely, for he really meant that justice is giving to
each man what befits him. This he termed 'what is due.'

That must have been what he meant, he said.

By Olympus! I replied. And what if someone were to ask him,
Simonides! What due or proper thing is provided by the craft of
medicine, and to whom? What answer do you think that he would
give?

He would of course reply that medicine provides drugs and meat and drink to human bodies.

And what good thing is provided by the cook's art, and to what?

Flavor to food.   D

And what is it that justice gives, and to whom?

Assuming, Socrates, that we are to proceed on the basis of the analogy, then justice is that craft which provides good to friends and evil to enemies.

Then he means that justice is doing good to your friends and evil to your enemies?

I think so.

And who is best able to do good to his friends and evil to his enemies with regard to sickness and health?

The physician.

Or when they are on a voyage, amidst the perils of the sea?   E

The ship's pilot.

And with regard to what actions, and with a view to what end, is the just man best able to harm his enemies, while doing good to friends?

In warring against the one, and siding with the other.

But isn't a doctor useless to those who aren't sick, Polemarchus?

That's true.

And a ship's pilot is likewise useless to those who don't sail?

Yes.

Then justice will be useless to men who aren't at war?

I can hardly agree with that.

You think justice may also be of use in peace?

333   Yes.

Like farming for getting grain?

Yes.

Or shoemaking for getting shoes — that is what you mean?

Yes.

So what similar use or profitable power does justice have in time of peace?

When it comes to making contracts, Socrates, justice is of use.

And by contracts do you mean partnerships, or something else?

Partnerships.

B   But is the just man or the skillful player a more useful partner at a game of, say, checkers?

The skillful player.

And when it comes to laying stones or bricks is the just man a more useful partner than the mason?

The opposite is the case.

Then in what sort of partnership is the just man a better partner than the mason, or than the harp-player — in just the way that the harp-player is the better partner when it comes to plucking the right notes?

In partnerships concerned with money, I think.

Yes, Polemarchus, but surely not in the use of money when you want to buy something in common. For you don't want a just man to go

in with you when it is time to buy or sell a horse. A man who knows   c
horses would be altogether better, no?

Certainly.

And when you want to buy a ship, you go in with a shipwright or
pilot?

True.

Then in what joint venture of gold or silver is the just man to be
preferred?

When you want the money to be kept safely in trust.

You mean when money is not wanted, but put away somewhere
for the time being?

Precisely.

That is to say, justice is useful while the money is useless?

That is the inference.   D

In the same way, when you want to keep a pruning knife safe, justice is useful to the individual and to the state; but when you want
to use it, better call a gardener?

So it seems.

And when you want to keep a shield or lyre safe, not use them, you
would say justice is useful; but when you want to use them, a
soldier or musician is the man for you?

Necessarily.

And so on and so forth in all other such things.
Always justice is useful when the things concerned are useless, useless when they are
useful?

It would follow.

E   Justice surely doesn't turn out to be worth much if it's only useful in connection with useless things. But let us consider a further point: isn't it true that the man who is the best at landing punches — in a boxing match or in any kind of fighting — is also best at blocking punches?

Certainly.

He who is best at preventing or curing disease is also best at inducing it?

I think so.

334   He who is best at securing an army camp is also best at stealing a march on the enemy, regarding all their stratagems and affairs?

Certainly.

Then he who is a good holder of anything is also a good thief of it?

That, I suppose, would follow.

Then if the just man is good at holding money, he is good at stealing it.

According to our argument, so it would seem.

Then, at the end of it all, the just man has turned out to be a sort of thief. This is a lesson you likely learned from Homer. He had a soft
B   spot for Autolycus, the maternal grandfather of Odysseus, about whom he said:

He exceeded all men in theft and lies.

So you, Homer and Simonides all agree that justice is an art of theft, practiced to help friends and harm foes — that was what you were saying?

No, certainly not — though now I don't know what I did mean.

NONETHELESS, I STILL SAY JUSTICE is helping friends and harming enemies.

By 'friends' do we mean those who appear to each man to be worthy, or rather those who actually are, even if they don't seem to be? And I would ask the same concerning enemies.

C

Probably people become friends with those they think are good, and grow to hate the ones they judge evil.

Yes, but don't people often make mistakes about this, so that many of those they believe are good aren't, and vice versa?

People do make mistakes.

Then in their eyes those who are good will be enemies and those who are evil will be friends?

Certainly.

In that case these people will be right to do good to evil people and evil to good ones?

D

It would seem so.

But the good are just, and the sort who would not do wrong?

True.

Then according to your argument it is right to harm those who do no wrong?

No, Socrates, this result is wrong.

Then I suppose we are right to harm the unjust, and aid the just?

I think it comes out better that way.

But note what follows, Polemarchus. For all those who are mistaken in their judgments about men it will be right to harm their friends, for

E

they are wicked, and aid their enemies, who are actually good. But in affirming this we say the opposite of what we said Simonides meant.

That certainly is the result, he said. Let's make a correction. We probably haven't defined the words 'friend' and 'enemy' properly.

How did we define them, Polemarchus? I asked.

We said that someone who seems good is a friend.

How are we going to fix the problem?

3 3 5   We should say instead that he is a friend who doesn't merely seem, but truly is, good. One who only seems good, but isn't, only seems a friend, but isn't. The same goes for enemies.

You would argue that the good are our friends, the bad our enemies?

Yes.

So you suggest that we add something to our previous definition of the good man. Just now we said that it is just to do good to our friends and evil to our enemies. Now we should add this: it is just to do good to our friends when they are good and evil to our enemies when they are evil?

B   Yes indeed, he said, that seems very well put.

Then again, should the just man really injure anyone at all?

Certainly he should. He should injure those who are both wicked and his enemies.

When horses are injured, are they thereby improved or made worse?

They become worse.

Worse, that is, with respect to those virtues that make horses into good horses — not, say, with respect to those virtues that make dogs into good dogs.

The horses are made worse as horses.

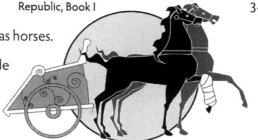

And injured dogs are made worse with respect to their canine virtue, not their equine virtue?

Of course.

And about men, my dear friend, won't we have to say that when C injured they are made worse with respect to their distinctly human excellence or virtue?

Certainly.

But justice — isn't that the special virtue of humans?

That too must be granted.

Then men who are harmed, my dear friend, must we not grant that they are necessarily made unjust?

It seems likely.

But can the musician, by performing music, make men unmusical?

Impossible.

Or the rider by riding make bad riders?

Not at all.

Then can the just by justice make men unjust? In general, can good D men make evil ones by means of virtue?

Assuredly not.

For I don't think it's the characteristic function of heat to make things cold; rather, the opposite of heat has that function.

Yes.

Nor does dryness, but rather its opposite, make things wet.

That's quite right.

Nor then is it the characteristic function of the good to do harm, but that of its opposite?

It seems so.

And the just man is a good man?

Certainly.

Then to injure someone, whether a friend or anyone else at all, is not the act of a just man, Polemarchus, but an unjust man — his very opposite?

I think what you've said is the absolute truth, Socrates.

E   Then if someone says justice consists in paying debts, and means by that, that the just man owes a debt of harm to his enemies and one of aid to his friends, then he was no truly wise man who said it. For it cannot be true, if, as has been shown, it is never right to harm anyone.

I concede it, said Polemarchus.

In which case you and I are prepared to fight side by side against any who attributes such a saying to Simonides or Bias or Pittacus, or any other wise man or prophet?

I am quite ready to fight by your side, he said.

336   Shall I tell you who I think came up with this saying that justice is to aid one's friends and harm one's enemies?

Who?

I believe it was Periander or Perdiccas or Xerxes or Ismenias the Theban, or some other rich and mighty man, who was pleased to regard himself as having great power.

What you say is very true, he said.

Yes, I said. But if this definition of justice also breaks down, what other can be offered?

MANY TIMES IN the course of this discussion Thrasymachus had tried to jump in and interrupt the argument but had been prevented by the rest of those present, who wanted to hear things out. Now, when I had just said this and Polemarchus and I had paused, he could contain himself no longer. Gathering himself up, he hurled himself upon us like a wild beast bent on tearing and devouring us. Polemarchus and I were quite panic-stricken at the sight of him.

B

He roared out to the whole lot of us: What utter nonsense have you been spouting, Socrates? And why do the both of you prize idiots give way to what the other says? If you really want to know what justice is, Socrates, you should not **only** ask questions, and then win the competition by refuting what anyone answers. After all, you know it's easier to win when you ask than when you answer. Now **you** answer the question yourself, and say what **you** think justice is. And I won't have any of this justice is what ought to be, or the beneficial, or the profitable, or the advantageous, but express clearly and precisely whatever you say, for I'm not going to accept anything of that sort from you.

C

D

I was near panic at hearing this outburst, and I could hardly look at him. In fact, I think that if I had not just then looked at him before he looked at me, I would have been struck dumb. But as it was, when he began to be exasperated by the argument, I looked at him first, so that I was able to reply.

E

Thrasymachus, I said, with just a slight hitch in my voice, don't be so critical of us. Polemarchus and I may be guilty of making mistakes in our argument, but you should know we weren't doing it on purpose.

If we were looking for a piece of gold, you wouldn't say that we were giving way to each other, and thereby destroying our chances of finding it. Why, then, when we are seeking justice — a thing more precious than much gold — do you assert that we are stupidly giving in to each other and not doing our utmost to get at the truth? You know it isn't so, my good friend; it's just that we aren't capable. And since that is the way of it, people like you — who are so terribly clever — should pity us instead of being angry.

How like you, Socrates! he replied, with a bitter laugh. Hercules knows there's no mistaking your usual irony! I knew it — didn't I just say it? — that whatever he was asked he would refuse to answer. He falls back on irony. And he'll do anything rather than answer a straight question put to him.

You are a sophist, Thrasymachus, I replied, so I think you can appreciate how, if someone asks a man to say what numbers make up twelve, and while he asks adds, Don't, my good man, say that twelve is twice six, or three times four, or six times two, or four times three, for I won't accept any nonsense like that from you — I think it must be clear to you that no one could answer the question when put that way. But what if he said to you: Thrasymachus, what do you mean? Am I not supposed to give any of those answers you forbid? What if one of them is the right answer, you uncanny man? Am I supposed to lie and say something other than the truth? Is this what you want? — How would you answer?

The way you talk, you would think the two cases had something in common.

Nothing prevents it, I replied. But even if they don't, but it appears to the one being questioned that they do, shouldn't he speak his mind whether we forbid him or not?

I expect then, he said, that you are going to make one of the forbidden answers?

I wouldn't be too astonished if I did — if upon reflection I think any of them is any good.

But what if I give you an answer about justice, he said — one differ- D ent from and better than any of these? What penalty should you have to pay then?

What else, I said, than the penalty ignorant people always pay to the wise? The proper penalty is learning the answer from one who knows it, and this is what I think I deserve to suffer.

You are so naive, he said. In addition to the penalty of learning, you'll have to pay money.

I will pay when I have some money, I replied.

It's all right, Socrates, said Glaucon. If it is money you are worried about, Thrasymachus, we will all chip in to pay for Socrates' schooling.

Oh yes of course, he replied, and then Socrates will do as he always E does — he'll refuse to answer, and when someone else answers, he'll shred his argument.

But, my good friend, I said, how can anyone answer a question who doesn't know the answer, and says he doesn't know the answer; who, even if he knew a little something by way of answer, has in any case been all but forbidden to say what he thinks by a rather formidable man? No, you should talk instead, as you say you know the answer, 338 and have something to say. So don't think of doing anything else, but be gracious enough to answer me, and don't selfishly keep silent, but speak up for the edification of Glaucon here, and everyone else.

As I was saying this, Glaucon and the rest of the company joined in my request and Thrasymachus, as anyone could see, was really eager to speak, because he thought he had an excellent answer, and would soon be standing tall in our eyes. For a while longer he held out, pretending to insist on my answering, but in the end he agreed to begin. Behold, he said, the wisdom of Socrates. He refuses B to teach, and goes about learning from others, to whom he never pays so much as a thank you.

That I learn from others, I replied, is quite true, Thrasymachus, but that I am ungrateful, I deny. I have no money, and therefore pay in praise, which is all I have to give. You will soon find out how ready I am to praise a good speaker, for I expect you will answer well.

C

Listen up, then, he said. I declare that justice is nothing but the advantage of the stronger. And now why don't you all praise me? Oh, but wait. Of course you won't.

Let me first make sure I understand, I replied, for now I don't at all. Justice, you say, is the advantage of the stronger. But what, Thrasymachus, is this supposed to mean? You cannot mean to say that because Polydamas the wrestler is stronger than we are, and because eating beef makes his body strong, that this diet is therefore both suitable and just for all of us who are weaker than he?

D

You are disgusting, Socrates, you take my meaning that way, so that you can do my argument the most harm.

Not at all, my good sir, I said, but try to express yourself more clearly.

Well, he said, perhaps you have heard about how forms of government differ from place to place: there are tyrannies, and democracies, and aristocracies?

Yes, of course.

And isn't this the thing that has power in each state: the ruling party?

Certainly.

E

And each government establishes laws with an eye to its own advantage — the democracy making democratic laws and the tyranny tyrannical ones, and so forth. And these laws, which are made by them for their advantage, are the justice that they hand down to their subjects. And whoever breaks these laws is punished as an unjust lawbreaker. And that, my good man, is what I mean when I say that in all states there is the same principle of justice: namely, the advantage of the established government. And as the government must be supposed to have power, the only reasonable conclusion to be drawn is that everywhere you go there is but one principle of justice: namely, the advantage of the stronger.

339

Now I understand you, I said. Whether you are right or not I will try to discover. But first let me say that you, Thrasymachus, say that justice is the advantageous, which is something you forbade me to answer. It is true, however, that in your definition the words 'of the stronger' were added.

A little something added, maybe, he said.

It is not yet clear that it is a big something, either. What is clear is that we must first investigate whether what you have said is true. Now, we both agree that justice is advantage of some sort, but you go on to say 'of the stronger.' I'm not sure about this, and must therefore consider further.

JUSTICE

B

Consider away, he said.

So I will, I said. First tell me, do you admit that it is just for subjects to obey their rulers?

I do.

C

But are the rulers of each of these states absolutely infallible, or do they sometimes make mistakes?

Obviously, he replied, they sometimes make mistakes.

Then in making their laws they may sometimes make them the right way, sometimes the wrong way?

I agree.

When they make them rightly, they make them to their own advantage; when they make a mistake, the laws are not made to their advantage. Do you agree?

Yes.

Anyway, the laws which are made must be obeyed by the subjects — and that is what you call justice?

No doubt about it.

D   Then justice, by your argument, is not only obedience to the advantage of the stronger, but also the reverse, what is not to his advantage?

What are you talking about? he asked.

I am only repeating what you said, I think. Here, let's consider: haven't we admitted that the rulers can mistakenly betray their own advantage by making the commands they do, and also that for those who are ruled to obey these commands is justice? Didn't you say as much?

Yes.

E   Then you have to think that it is just to do what is to the disadvantage of those who rule and are stronger, whenever the rulers unintention-ally command things which are bad for them. For if, as you say, it is just to perform those very things which the rulers command, in that case — O, wisest of men — is there any escape from the conclusion that it is just to do the opposite of what you say? For the weaker

340 are commanded to do what is to the disadvantage of the stronger?

Yes, by Zeus, this is clear as day, Socrates! said Polemarchus.

Yes, said Cleitophon, breaking in, if anyone asked **you** to be a witness.

Who needs a witness? said Polemarchus. Thrasymachus plainly admitted rulers may sometimes make commands not to their advantage, and that for subjects to obey these commands is justice.

But, Polemarchus, Thrasymachus said that for subjects to do what was commanded of them by their rulers is just.

Yes, Cleitophon, but he also said justice is the interest of the stronger; and, while holding both these positions, he admitted as well   B
that the stronger may command the weaker, who are his subjects, to do things that are not to his advantage. It follows that justice is just as much the injury as the interest of the stronger.

But, said Cleitophon, when he said 'the advantage of the stronger', he meant what the stronger thought to be his advantage — this was what the weaker had to do. His position is that this is justice.

That isn't what he said, Polemarchus retorted.   C

Never mind that, Polemarchus, I replied. If he now says this is how it is, let us accept his statement.

TELL ME, THRASYMACHUS, is this what you meant to say justice was? What the stronger thought to be his advantage, whether it really is or not? Shall we say this is what you mean?

Absolutely not, he said. Do you think I would call someone who makes a mistake 'the stronger' at just the moment when he makes some mistake?

Yes, I said, my distinct impression was that this was exactly what you did when you admitted that the ruler was not infallible but might   D
sometimes make mistakes.

You argue like a slanderous witness in court, Socrates. For example, do you call someone who is mistaken about the sick 'a doctor' just in virtue of the fact that he is mistaken? Or do you say that he who makes mistakes in math is a mathematician when he is making the mistake, and precisely because he is mistaken? We do say 'the doctor has made a mistake' or 'the mathematician has made a

E   mistake' or 'the grammarian has made a mistake', but this is just a loose way of talking. For I think none of them, insofar as he is what we call him, ever makes a mistake. So, to be perfectly strict about it — since you are such a stickler for strictness — no skilled craftsman ever makes a mistake. It is when his knowledge fails him that he goes astray, and in that moment of failure he is not really a skilled craftsman. And so, no craftsman, wise man, or ruler makes a mistake while he is a ruler in the strict sense, though people do commonly say, 'the doctor has made a mistake' or 'the ruler has made a mistake'. It is in this common way of speaking, then, that you must take the answer I gave you just now. To be perfectly precise we should say

341   that the ruler, insofar as he is a ruler, does not make mistakes, and does not mistake his own advantage when he lays down commands, and this the subject must do. Therefore — as I said in the first place, and now I say it again — justice is the advantage of the stronger.

STRICT RULER

All right then, Thrasymachus. But do I really seem to you to argue like someone committing perjury in court?

That's for sure, he replied.

So you must think I put these questions to you with the intent of personally libeling you in the argument?

B   I don't think it, I know it. But it's not going to get you anywhere: you can't harm me by stealth, and you will never beat me by sheer force of argument.

I wouldn't dream of trying, my dear man! But in order to prevent this sort of thing from happening again, please define in what sense you speak of 'the ruler' and 'stronger'. Do you mean the so-called ruler or the ruler in the precise sense, whom you were just telling us about? For whose advantage, as being the stronger, will it be just for the inferior to act?

I mean the ruler in the strictest of all senses, he said. And now, go ahead, smear my argument, make your false accusations! I'm not asking you to play nice. You're just not up to the job!

Do you think, I said, that I am crazy enough to shave a lion in his den, or spread libels about Thrasymachus?

Why, he said, you tried it just now, you feeble fellow.

Enough of these pleasantries, I said. Just tell me this: what does the physician do, in the strict sense you articulated just now? Does he heal the sick, or does he make money? And remember, I am now speaking of the true physician.

He heals the sick, he replied.

And the ship's pilot — I mean, the true pilot — is he a captain of sailors or a mere sailor?

A captain of sailors.

I don't think we have to take into account the fact that he sails about in a ship, nor the fact that he is called a sailor. He's not called a pilot because of his sailing, but because of his craft and his authority over the sailors.

That's exactly right, he said.

Now, I said, for each of these cases, isn't there something that is advantageous?

Certainly.

Towards which the craft, I said, is directed; it seeks to secure and furnish this advantage to them?

Yes, that's the point.

And is there any advantage for each of the crafts aside from its becoming as perfect as possible?

E   What are you talking about?

It's like this, I said. Suppose you were to ask me whether the body is self-sufficient, or whether it has needs. I would reply: The body has all kinds of needs. This is why the art of medicine was invented, because the body can fall ill and lacks the capacity to heal itself. The art was constructed to this end, to provide these advantages to the body. Do you think I would be right in saying this, I asked, or not?

342   Quite right, he replied.

But how about this? Does the art of medicine get sick itself? Or can any other art be in need of some virtue or quality — as the eye can need sight, and the ear hearing, so that they require some art to seek out and provide this advantage to them? Can there be any fault in the art itself, so that each art requires some further art to seek out what is advantageous to it, and another art must be found for the second one, and so on to infinity? Or does each art

B   look out for its own advantage? Or does each art in fact need neither itself nor another art to seek out a remedy for any defect? For no art has either any defect or error in itself, nor is it the business of any art to seek what is advantageous to anything other than the art's subject. For isn't every true art pure and faultless, so long as it is precisely and entirely itself? Consider that we are speaking in your precise sense. Is it so, or not?

It appears to be so, he said.

Then medicine does not serve the interests of medicine, but the   c
interests of the body?

True, he said.

And the point of the art of caring for horses is not to care for itself,
just to care for horses, nor does any other art look after itself — since
it doesn't need anything — but rather that thing of which it is the art?

So it seems he said.

But surely, Thrasymachus, the arts are the rulers of, and stronger
than, their subjects?

He conceded this point with great reluctance.

Then, I said, no craft considers or commands the advantage of the
ruler or superior, only that of the subject it rules and the inferior?   D

He eventually was brought to admit this too, though he tried to
contest it.

Once he had agreed I continued, saying: Then no physician either,
insofar as he is a physician, considers his own good in what he
prescribes. He considers rather what is good for the patient.
For you agreed that the physician in the strict sense is a
ruler having the human body as his subject. He is no mere
money maker. You granted this much?

He agreed.

The same goes for the ship's pilot, in the strict
sense of the term; he is a ruler of sailors and
not a mere sailor?   E

That was admitted.

And such a pilot and ruler will consider
situations and issue commands, not
for his own private advantage, but
rather the advantage of the sailor
under his command?

He gave a reluctant yes.

So then, Thrasymachus, there is no one in any ruling position, insofar as he is a true ruler, who seeks out and gives commands for things that are to his own advantage. He always commands what is in the best interest of those he rules, or the subject-matter of his art. He looks to that, and on what is advantageous and suitable to that alone, in all that he says and does.

343 When we had gotten to this point in the argument, and everyone saw that the definition of justice had been completely upset, Thrasymachus, instead of replying, asked: Tell me, Socrates, have you got a nanny?

WHAT DO YOU MEAN? I said. You really ought to be answering my questions, not posing new ones.

Because she lets you go around sniveling and never wipes your snotty nose. She has not even taught you to tell the difference between the shepherd and the sheep.

What makes you say that? I replied.

B Because you imagine that the shepherds or cowherds are considering the good of the sheep and cattle, and that when they fatten and tend them they are looking out for anything other than their own self-interest or that of their masters. And in particular you imagine that the rulers of states, I mean those who truly rule, think any differently about their subjects than a man about his flock, and that they are looking out for anything but their own interests,
C day and night. Oh, no, and you are **so** far off the mark in your ideas of the just and unjust that you don't even realize that justice and the just are literally this: another's advantage — the advantage of the ruler and the stronger, and a source of harm for the subject or servant. And injustice is the opposite. Injustice lords it over those

who are both simple, in every sense of the word, and just. They, being subjects, do what is to the advantage of the stronger man. They serve him D and minister to his pleasure, which is very far from being their own. You must look at the matter, my extraordinarily simple-minded friend, in the following way: the just man is always a loser compared to the unjust man. First, he loses when it comes to private contracts: when a just man has an unjust partner, and the partnership is at an end, you will find that the unjust man walks away with more and the just man gets less. Second, in dealings with the state: when it's time to pay taxes, the just man pays more and the unjust man less on estates of equal value. Likewise, when there is anything to be gotten the one gains nothing, E the other much. Look also at what happens when it comes to serving in public office: apart from any other loss, the just man can count on his personal affairs suffering from his neglect, while he, because of his justice, makes no profit from the state. To make matters still worse, he is hated by his friends and associates because he refuses to help them bend and break the law. But the tables are turned in the case of the unjust man. I am speaking, as I have been from the very start, of the man with the power to commit 344 excesses on a massive scale. Consider such a man, then, if you wish to judge for yourself how much more he personally prof-its by being unjust, rather than just. You'll see what I mean most easily if we turn to that highest form of injustice —

the case in which the criminal is the happiest man
on earth, and his victims, and those who refuse
to commit crimes are the most miserable. In a
word, I speak of tyranny, when, by force or fraud,
property is stolen from its owners not little by
little but wholesale. Everything goes into one
bag: sacred things as well as profane — private

B   and public. Were someone to commit these acts on a petty scale
and fail to get away with it, he would be severely punished and
regarded with the worst kind of contempt. Those who commit such
partial forms of injustice are called temple robbers, kidnappers,
burglars, con-men and thieves. But if men will go to the additional
trouble of relieving their victims of their freedom as well as their
property — enslaving the citizens — why, then, far from being called
these insulting names they are deemed happy and blessed, not only

C   by their fellow-citizens, but by all who hear that they have ascended
to the very pinnacle of perfect injustice. For it is not the fear of
doing wrong, but of **being a victim** of it, that calls forth people's
denunciations of injustice. Thus, Socrates, injustice, committed on
a grand scale, is a stronger, freer, more masterful thing than justice,
and — as I declared from the very start — justice is the advantage
of the stronger, whereas injustice is a man's own profit and interest.

D   Thrasymachus, when he was done pouring out this veritable bathtub
of words down the drains of our ears, obviously had a mind to get
up and leave. But the whole lot of us would not let him. We insisted
he should remain and defend his position. And I asked him with
particular urgency: Thrasymachus, I said to him, you excellent man;
after hurling such a suggestive argument at us, you can't intend to
run off without staying either to teach us properly or learn yourself
whether it is true or not. Do you think that what you are trying to

E   define is such a trifling matter: the whole life path that would make
life most worth living for each of us?

You think I don't see the importance of this question?

You appear not to, I replied, or else you do not care for any of us,
Thrasymachus. It's the same to you whether we live better or worse,
on account of not knowing what you say you know. So please, friend,

do not hide the light of your wisdom under a bushel. It will not be   345
a bad investment for you to do so many of us a good turn. For my
own part, I openly declare that I am not convinced, and that I do
not believe injustice to be more profitable than justice, even if we
allow it free play and do not hamper its desires. Let us assume then,
my good man, there is an unjust man, let him be capable of committing injustice by fraud or force. All the same I am not convinced
injustice is advantageous. There may be another among us who   B
feels the same way, so that I am not the only one. Persuade us then,
you excellent gentleman, really persuade us that we are wrong in
preferring justice to injustice.

And how am I to persuade you, he said, if you are not already
convinced by what I have just said. What more can I do for you?
Would you have me cram the proof down your throat, right into
your very souls?

Zeus forbid! I said. Don't do that. But first, stand by your original
arguments, or, if you change your mind, change it openly, and don't
try to deceive us. As it is now, Thrasymachus, if you will only recall   C
what was previously said, you must see that although you began by
defining the true physician in an exact sense, you did not observe
similar exactness when speaking of the shepherd. Instead, you think
that the shepherd, insofar as he is a shepherd, tends the sheep, not
with a view to the good of the sheep, but like a diner or gourmet,
with a view to the pleasures of eating mutton; or, again, with a view
to selling in the market, like a trader, not a shepherd. Yet surely the   D
art of the shepherd is concerned only with how to provide the best
for those sheep over which he is set, since the perfection of his art
is already ensured whenever all the requirements of it are
satisfied. It's just as I thought we found it necessary to agree
a little while ago about every form of rule: when it is rule
in the precise sense — whether public or private — it   E
doesn't consider anything other than the advantage of the subjects or the ones cared for. You, on
the other hand, seem to think that the rulers of
states — that is to say, the true rulers — actually like being in positions of authority.

I don't think it, by Zeus. I know it!

What about this, Thrasymachus, I said. Don't you know men never volunteer for other offices, but instead ask for pay? This implies the benefits of ruling are not going to go to them, but to the ones they 346   rule? Let me ask you a question: Don't we say that each of the various arts is distinct from the others in virtue of some distinct power or function? And, my dear exalted friend, do say what you really think, that we may make a little progress.

Yes, that's what makes them distinct, he replied.

And each art gives us a particular good and not merely a general one — medicine, for example, gives us health; navigation, safety at sea, and so on with the other arts?

Yes, he said.

B   And doesn't the art of getting paid have the special function of making us money? Would you say that the art of medicine and that of navigation are the same? Or, if you want to define things with your usual precision, if the navigator becomes healthy because sailing on the sea is good for him, would you call his craft medicine rather than navigation on that account?

Certainly not.

You won't say either that, just because a man happens to be in good health on payday, that therefore getting paid is medicine?

I should say not.

C   Nor would you say that medicine is the art of getting paid, just because a man takes fees when he heals someone?

Certainly not.

And we have admitted, I said, that each art aims at some particular benefit peculiar to it?

Granted.

Then whatever common benefit all craftsmen enjoy must clearly result from their joint practice of some one thing common to them?

Probably, he replied.

And when the craftsman is benefited by making money this is due to some application of the fine art of getting paid?

He agreed reluctantly to this.

Then the benefit of getting paid money doesn't come to the various craftsmen by the practice of their various crafts. If we consider it with precision, we'll see that while the art of medicine produces health, it's the art of getting paid that produces the doctor's wages. And while the art of building produces buildings, it's again the accompanying art of getting paid that brings in the fees, and likewise with all the other arts. And so the various crafts are doing their particular work, benefiting the subjects over which they rule. But would the craftsman himself receive any benefit from his art if money weren't added into the mix?

It doesn't seem like it, he said.

Doesn't he even provide a benefit when he works for nothing?

I think he does.

Then, Thrasymachus, it's clear now that no craft or form of rule provides what is beneficial to itself. It is all just as we said earlier: they prepare and command what is in the interests of their subjects, and the strong rulers attend to the good of these weaker ones, not their own good. And this is why, my dear Thrasymachus — as I was just now saying — no one volunteers to govern, because no one likes to take up the weary task of straightening out other people's problems. Instead he asks to be paid for it, because the man who is going to practice his craft well, never does or orders what is best for himself, when he issues orders in accordance with his art, but always what is best for his subjects. For this reason, it seems, potential rulers must be paid in one of three sorts of coinage: money, or honor, or punishment for refusing.

What are you saying, Socrates? said Glaucon. I understand the first two modes of payment, but what the punishment is I don't quite see, or how a punishment can even be a payment.

B   You mean that you don't understand the nature of this payment for the sake of which the best men take up the reins of power, when they consent to do so? Of course you know that ambition and greed are held to be, and indeed are, disgraceful?

I do, he said.

This, I said, is why good men are not willing to rule for the sake of money or honor. They don't wish to be seen openly demanding payment for service in government, as that would earn them the name of hired hand; nor do they wish to earn the name of thief, by

C   dipping their hand in the public till. Not being ambitious, they do not care about honor. As a result of all this, a yoke of compulsion and penalty must be laid upon their necks, if they are to consent to rule. And this, I imagine, is the reason why willingly seeking office, when one might have waited to be compelled, has been deemed dishonorable. But the essence of the punishment is that he who refuses to rule is liable to end up being ruled by one worse than himself. The way I look at it, fear of this bad result makes the good take office, whenever they do, and then they approach it, not as something good or in the expectation of enjoying themselves, but as a necessary evil since they are unable to foist off the chore of rul-

D   ing on anyone as good or better than themselves. Indeed, if there were a city entirely peopled by good men, we might well find men would contend as eagerly to avoid public office as they do here to obtain it. In that place it would become quite clear that the nature of the true ruler is not to look after his own interests, but rather those of his subjects. And everyone who knew this would choose rather to receive a benefit from another, instead of being put to

E   the trouble of conferring them all around. So I am about as far as it is possible to be from agreeing with Thrasymachus that justice is the interest of the stronger.

BUT LET'S TAKE THIS MATTER UP again later. This fresh claim appears to me to be a far more serious one, when Thrasymachus says that the life of the unjust man is more advantageous than that of the just man. And which one, Glaucon, do you prefer? Which statement seems truer to you?

For my part, I certainly think the life of the just man is more advantageous, he answered.

You did hear, though, all those wonderful things the unjust man has,   348 as Thrasymachus set out for us just now?

Yes, I heard, he replied, but he hasn't persuaded me.

Then shall we try to persuade him, if we can find a way, that what he says isn't true?

We certainly ought to try, he replied.

If, I said, we set against his speech a speech of our own, enumerating in turn the advantages of being just, and then he responds, and we respond to that, in the end we would have to count up and measure the goods in each of our speeches, and for that we would need   B judges to make the distinctions. On the other hand, if we do as we have been doing, and simply agree with one another when a good point has been made, we can be both judges and advocates ourselves.

That's certainly right, he said.

Which method do you prefer? I asked.

The one you propose.

Well, then, Thrasymachus, I said, suppose we begin at the beginning and you answer me. You say perfect injustice is more profitable than perfect justice?

C   Yes, I say it, and I have given you my reasons.

And what is your view about these two items in question? Would you call one of them virtue and the other vice?

Certainly.

I suppose that you would call justice 'virtue' and injustice 'vice'?

That's **ever so likely**, you perfect innocent, seeing that I affirm injustice to be profitable and justice unprofitable.

What else then would you say instead?

The very opposite, he replied.

What! You call justice vice?

Department of Lofty Naivete

No, I think I would call it lofty naivete.

Then would you call injustice malignity?

D   No, I think it would be better to label it prudent counsel.

And do unjust men appear to you to be wise and good?

Yes, he said, at least those who have the power to be overwhelmingly unjust, and therefore have the power to bring whole city-states and tribes of men to their knees, because **you** probably think I've been advocating a line-up of pickpockets. It is true that even this sort of thing has its profitable side, as long as you don't get caught,

E   but petty thievery isn't worth discussion in comparison to what I just talked about.

I don't think I actually have missed your point, Thrasymachus, I replied, but still I am quite amazed at the thought that you class injustice with wisdom and virtue, and justice with the opposite.

Certainly I do class them in this way.

Now that's a more difficult assertion, my good friend, I said. At any rate, it's hard to know what to say. For if you were to claim that injustice is more profitable, while granting that it is a shameful vice, a position some others do take, an answer might be given to you on the basis of conventional moral notions. But by now I can see perfectly well that you will just go on to say that injustice is strong and honorable; to the unjust you will attribute all the qualities that we used to attribute to the just, since you don't hesitate to place injustice with wisdom and virtue.

349

You have foreseen most infallibly, he replied.

Well, I said, I shouldn't flinch from following the argument to its conclusion, as long as I believe that you are actually speaking your mind. For I don't think, Thrasymachus, that you are having us on, but rather you are telling us your real opinions concerning the truth.

I may be serious or not, but what difference does it make to you? Why don't you refute the argument?

No difference at all, I said, but will you be so extremely good as to answer just one more question? Does the just man try to overreach or gain any advantage over the just?

B

Far from it. If he did that he would not be the simple, unassuming creature he is.

And would he try to overreach or outdo justice?

He would not.

How would he regard any attempt to gain an advantage over the unjust man? Would he consider that just or would it be unjust?

He would think it just, he said, but he wouldn't be able to overreach him in this way.

That's not what I asked you, I said. My question is whether the just man, while refusing to have more than another just man, would wish and claim to have more than the unjust has?

C

Yes, that's how it is, he replied.

And what of the unjust — does he claim to overreach and outdo the just man and the practice of justice?

Of course, he said, since he wants to get the most for himself out of every situation.

Therefore, won't the unjust man also overreach and outdo another unjust man and the practice of injustice, since he strives to have more than everyone?

True.

D

We may put the matter this way, I said. The just man does not seek to get the better of those like himself, but does seek to get the better of those unlike him, whereas the unjust man wants to get the better of those both like and unlike himself?

You've got it, he said.

But the unjust man is wise and good, and the just man is neither of these?

Right again, he said.

And isn't it also true that the unjust man is like the wise and good and the just man unlike them?

Of course, he said. He who is of a certain nature is like others who are also of that nature; he who is not, is not.

Excellent. Then each of them, I said, is like his like?

What else do you think? he replied.

E

Very good, Thrasymachus, I said. Now you would admit that one man is a musician and another not?

Yes, I would.

And who is wise and who foolish, when it comes to music?

Clearly the musician is wise and the unmusical one is foolish.

And he is good with respect to the things he knows well, and bad with respect to things of which he is ignorant?

Yes.

And you would say the same sort of thing of the physician?

The same.

And do you think, my excellent friend, that a musician tuning his lyre would want or claim to exceed or go beyond a fellow musician, when it comes to tightening and loosening the strings just so?

I do not think that he would.

But he would claim to exceed the non-musician?

Necessarily.

And what would you say of the physician? In prescribing food and 350 drink would he wish to go beyond another physician or beyond the practice of medicine?

He would not.

But he would wish to outdo the non-physician?

Yes.

What about knowledge and ignorance in general? See whether you think any man who has knowledge would wish to choose to say or do something other than or more than another man who has knowledge. Would he not rather do the same as his like in the same case?

I suppose it must be so, he said, in such cases.

But what of the ignorant man? Wouldn't
he want to outdo both the wise man
and his fellow fool alike?

Maybe so.

And he who knows is wise?

I say yes.

And he who is wise is good?

I'll agree.

Then the wise and good man will not desire to get the better of his
like, but of his unlike and opposite?

I suppose so.

Whereas the bad and ignorant will desire to get the better of both?

Yes.

But we said, didn't we, Thrasymachus, that the unjust man tries to
get the better of both his like and unlike? Didn't you say this?

Yes, I did, he replied.

But the just man will not want to get the better of his like but only
his unlike?

Yes.

Then the just man is like the wise and good, and the unjust man like
the evil and ignorant?

That seems to follow.

And each of them is like his like, and is of the same sort as that which
he resembles?

Yes, we agreed to that.

Then the just man has turned out to be wise and good and the unjust man evil and ignorant.

THRASYMACHUS MADE ALL THESE ADMISSIONS, not readily, as I repeat   D
them, but with foot-dragging and reluctance, and he was sweating like mad, since it was summertime. Then I saw something I had never seen before: Thrasymachus blushing. But when we agreed that justice was virtue and wisdom, and injustice vice and ignorance, I said: Good. Let's take this as an established point. But we were also saying that injustice is something strong, don't you remember, Thrasymachus?

Yes, I remember, he said, but I am not at all satisfied with what you are saying, and I've got plenty to say about it. If, however, I were   E
to answer, I know perfectly well that you'd accuse me of ranting. Therefore either let me have my say, or if you would rather ask the questions, do so, and I will answer 'very good,' and nod yes and no, just as one does when old wives are telling their interminable tales.

I don't at all want you to go against your own beliefs.

Very well—just to please you—since you will not let me speak. What else would you have me do?

Nothing, by Zeus, I said, and if you are so disposed, I will now ask and you shall answer.

Ask away, then.

Then I will repeat the question I asked before, in order that our   351
examination of the respective natures of justice and injustice may be advanced in a rigorous manner. The claim was made, I think, that injustice is stronger and more powerful than justice. But now, if justice is wisdom and virtue, it will easily, I imagine, be shown to be stronger than injustice, since injustice is ignorance. No one could fail to recognize that now. But I want to examine the matter, Thrasymachus, in a different way, one which is not so simple: you would not deny that a state may be unjust and may be unjustly attempting to enslave other states, or may have already enslaved   B
them, and may be holding many of them in subjection?

Certainly, he replied. I would add only that this is what the best state will particularly do, the state which has gone the furthest towards perfect injustice.

I know, I said, that this was your position. But I am considering this further point: will the state which has gotten the better of another state in this way have or exercise this power without justice, or will it necessarily combine the power with justice?

c   If, he said, what you were saying just now is right, and justice is wisdom, then only with justice; but if I am right, then with injustice.

I am delighted, Thrasymachus, to see you not only nodding yes and no, but making answers which are quite excellent.

I am trying to please you, he replied.

You are too kind, I said. Would you have the good grace also to inform me whether you think that a state, or an army, or a band of robbers and thieves, or any other gang of criminal conspirators could accomplish anything if they wronged one another?

D   No indeed, he said, they could not.

But if they didn't wrong one another, wouldn't they be more likely to?

Certainly.

And this is because factions, Thrasymachus, are the results of injustice and hatred and infighting, whereas justice gives rise to harmony and friendship. Isn't that so?

Let it be so, he said, so that I won't disagree with you.

How good of you, my noble friend! I said. But tell me this: if it is the nature of injustice to arouse hatred wherever it is, whether it springs up among slaves or among free men, will it not make them

hate one another and set them at odds and make them incapable
of coordinated action?   E

It certainly will.

What about this: if injustice is found in two people only, won't they
quarrel and fight, and be enemies to one another and to just men?

They will, he said.

And suppose, you uncanny fellow, that injustice lurks in the heart of
a single person. Will it lose its power to cause animosity, or retain it?

Let us assume the power would remain.

Then isn't the power which injustice exercises of such a nature that
wherever it takes up residence, whether in a city, a family, an army,
or any other group at all, that thing is first rendered incapable of   352
coordinated action because it is torn apart by factions and disagreements. In the second place, doesn't it become its own enemy, as
well as an enemy of its polar opposite, the just? Isn't that how it is?

Yes, certainly.

Then won't injustice be up to these same old tricks
when it takes root in a single individual? In the first
place, it will render him incapable of action because he
is torn by warring desires and is not of one mind about
anything. In the second place it will make him his own
worst enemy, and an enemy of the just. Isn't that so?

Yes.

But, my friend, I said, surely the gods too are just?   B

Have it that they are.

But if so, the unjust will be the enemies of the gods, Thrasymachus,
and the just will be their friends?

Enjoy this rich banquet of words, I certainly won't stop you from gorging yourself. I wouldn't want to upset your fans here by objecting.

Well then, keep answering as you have been, and heap up my plate with the full menu. For we have already shown that the just are clearly wiser and better and abler than the unjust, and that the unjust are incapable of common action. But in addition to this, if we ever say that men who are unjust have accomplished some common undertaking, our statement won't be altogether true. If they had been perfectly evil, they could not have restrained themselves from attacking one another. Clearly there must have been some remnant of justice in them that prevented them from attacking one another at the same time as their victims, and it was in virtue of this that they accomplished whatever they did. They were only half-bad in the way they went about their evil venture, I expect, for those who are utter villains, and overwhelmingly unjust, can't do a thing. That, I believe, is the plain truth of the matter, not what you said before. But now we have to consider whether the just have a better life than the unjust and are happier, which was the further question we proposed to examine. They already appear to, I think, given what we've said so far. But all the same we must analyze the question better. For this is no ordinary topic we are discussing: the right way to live.

Proceed with our inquiry, he said.

So I will. Tell me, wouldn't you say that a horse has a specific function?

I should.

And would you define the use or function of a horse — or of anything — as that which could not be done, or not as well, by means of any other thing?

I don't follow you.

It's like this: can you see with anything other than your eyes?

Certainly not.

Or hear, except with your ears?

Not at all.

These then may truly be said to be the functions of these organs?

They may.

But you can cut off a vine-branch with a dagger or with a carving-knife — with any number of tools, in fact? 353

Of course.

And yet nothing works quite as well as a pruning-hook made for this purpose, am I right?

True.

So we must assume, then, that this is the function of a pruning-hook?

We must.

Now then, I imagine, you will understand the meaning of my earlier question better — whether the function of anything would be that which either it alone can do, or that which it does better than anything else?

I see what you mean, he said, and I agree that this is what something's function is. B

Good. And don't you think that each thing to which a function has been assigned also has some virtue? Let's take it from the top. We say that eyes have a function?

Yes

And isn't there some virtue in eyes?

Yes.

And the ear, too, has its function and its virtue?

Yes, a virtue also.

And what about all the other things, isn't it the same for them?

The same.

c   Pay attention now. Could the eyes possibly perform their function if they were lacking in the virtue that is peculiar to eyes — if they had some defect instead?

How could they? he asked. For I assume you mean blindness instead of sight.

Whatever their virtue may be. But you are getting a bit ahead of the game. I am only asking whether the things perform their functions well by means of their peculiar virtues, and fail to do so through some defect?

I'll grant you this much is true.

Then the ears, too, cannot perform their function when deprived of their peculiar virtue?

Certainly.

D   And the same argument will apply to all the other things?

I agree.

Well, then consider this next: doesn't the soul have a function nothing else can perform? For example, to oversee and command and deliberate and the like? Aren't these the proper functions of the soul, and can they rightly be assigned to any other thing?

To no other thing.

And what about life? Shall we say that's a function of the soul too?

Most assuredly, he said.

And don't we also say that the soul has a virtue?

We do say so. E

And can the soul, Thrasymachus, perform its particular function well if deprived of its peculiar virtue, or is this impossible?

It is impossible.

Then a bad soul must necessarily govern and manage things badly, and the good soul will do all these sorts of things well?

Yes, necessarily.

And we have admitted that justice is the virtue of the soul, and injustice its defect?

We did admit that.

Then the just soul and the just man will live well, and the unjust man will live badly?

So it appears, he said, according to **your** argument.

But he who lives well is blessed and happy, and he who lives badly 354 is the opposite of happy?

Absolutely.

Then the just is happy, and the unjust wretched?

So be it.

But surely it doesn't pay to be miserable, but to be happy.

Of course not.

Then, my blessed Thrasymachus, injustice can never be more profitable than justice.

Let this, Socrates, he said, be your feast at the festival of Bendis.

A feast for which I have you to thank, Thrasymachus, now that you have grown mild-mannered and stopped being so hard on me. All the same, I have not been wined and dined to my satisfaction; but that was my fault, not yours. Just as gluttons snatch at every dish that is handed along, and taste it before they have properly enjoyed the one before, so I, before actually finding the first object of our investigation — what justice **is** — let that inquiry drop, and turned away to consider something **about** justice, namely whether it is vice and ignorance or wisdom and virtue. And when the further question burst in on us, about whether injustice is more profitable than justice, I could not refrain from moving on to that. And the result of the discussion right now is that I know nothing at all.

For if I don't know what justice is, I am hardly likely to know whether it is or is not a virtue, nor can I say whether the just man is happy or unhappy.

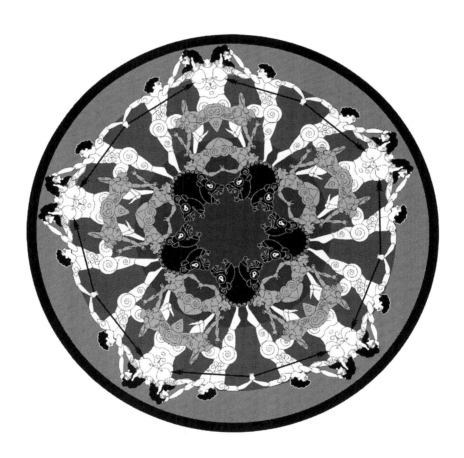

Made in the USA
San Bernardino, CA
21 September 2016